THE MEMOIRS
OF PRINCESS DASHKOVA

S. A. Mad.^{me} la Princesse de Daschkaw,
née Comtesse de Worontzow Dame d'honeur de Sa Majesté
l'Imperatrice de toutes les Russies Chevalier de l'Ordre de
Ste Catherine, Directeur de l'Academie Imp.^{le} de Sciences President de l'Acad.^{ie} Imp.^{le} Russe. Membre de l'Acad.^{ie} Royales de
Stokholm de celles de Berlin et d'Erlange de la Société Oeconomique
de St Petersbourg et de la Société Philosophique de Philadelphie.

The Memoirs

of Princess Dashkova

TRANSLATED AND EDITED BY KYRIL FITZLYON

FROM "BROOKE" COPY (p 285)

INTRODUCTION BY JEHANNE M GHEITH

AFTERWORD BY A. WORONZOFF-DASHKOFF

DUKE UNIVERSITY PRESS

Durham and London 1995

First published in 1958 by John Calder (Publishers) LTD.

Copyright © John Calder (Publishers) LTD.

Reprinted by permission of Calder Publications,

London/Riverrun Press, New York.

This edition copyright © 1995 Duke University Press.

All rights reserved

Printed in the United States of America on acid-free paper ∞

Typeset in Perpetua by Tseng Information Systems, Inc.

Library of Congress Cataloging-in-Publication Data

appear on the last printed page of this book.

CONTENTS

ILLUSTRATIONS

PREFACE

W hen I sat down to write the introduction to Dashkova's *Memoirs,*
I had a moment of crisis: Why, I wondered, had I decided that it would
be a good idea to reissue the memoirs of an eighteenth-century Russian
princess? Who would be interested in her and what relevance could she
possibly have for readers of English in the late twentieth century? Dashkova's times and her reminiscences, which I had found so compelling
when I initiated the project, suddenly seemed very far removed from the
lives of late twentieth-century readers, partly, I now realize, because it
had been almost a year since I had read the *Memoirs.*

As I reread the work, I found myself once again totally absorbed by
the figure of Dashkova, a strong, outspoken, extremely intelligent, sometimes annoyingly self-righteous, courageous woman. At least that's "my"
Dashkova; the image I get when I read her *Memoirs.* I wish I could know
what your image is of her after reading the *Memoirs;* I am very curious
about how people react to Dashkova's writing.

Students in my classes have had very strong responses to Dashkova's
Memoirs: some have been fascinated, many have found her self-righteous,
others have found her interesting for what she reveals about the lives of
women in eighteenth-century Russia. These students influenced my views
on Dashkova a great deal and many of my comments are responses to
questions they raised in class about the princess and the role of women in
eighteenth-century Russia. For your insightful comments and thoughtful
and thought-provoking reading and responses, my thanks go to: Ashley
Barfield, Sara Seten Berghausen, Sandy Bostian, Chelsea Chesen, Julie
Fishman, Jay Forrest, Julie Freeman, Kate Horst, Laura Krech, Jeff John-
son, Kay Sinnema, Mee Ae Song, Laura Weatherly, and Laura White.

Many others have also contributed to this project. I especially want to thank: Ken Wissoker of Duke University Press for much wise advice delivered with a sense of humor; Kathleen Hannan for expert editing and lively discussion, and Sally Kux, Barbara Norton, Stephanie Sandler, Banu Subramaniam, and Alexander Woronzoff-Dashkoff for insightful readings, comments, and questions.

Jehanne M Gheith

INTRODUCTION
Jehanne M Gheith

༄༅

For my part I think she [Dashkova] would be most in her element at the Helm of the State, or Generalissimo of the Army, or Farmer General of the Empire. In fact she was born for business on a large scale which is not irreconcilable with the Life of a Woman who at 18 headed a Revolution & who for 12 years afterwards govern'd an Academy of Arts and Sciences. —CATHERINE WILMOT, *The Russian Journals of Martha and Catherine Wilmot, 1803–1808*

The Princess Dashkova, as Catherine Wilmot's statement implies, was a forceful and intelligent woman.[1] She was also unconventional and courageous: While visiting Danzig (present-day Gdansk), at an inn frequented by "Russians and all really distinguished travellers" (118),[2] Dashkova was dismayed to see two pictures depicting battles in which the Russians were defeated and the Prussians victorious. Dashkova took exception to this representation of events and decided to change it. She first tried to go through official channels, but discovered that even two prominent and powerful Russian citizens, Rähbinder, the Chargé d'Affaires, and the sometime military commander Aleksei Orlov, were convinced that there was no way to remove the paintings. Dashkova, changing her strategy, took matters into her own hands. She ordered paints bought, locked the door to the main room of the inn where the paintings hung, and with two (male) allies, spent most of the night repainting the uniforms to show the Prussians defeated and the Russians victorious. And she left Danzig within two days.

Dashkova's action demonstrates the possibilities open to those outside official structures of state. By this I do not mean to suggest that Dashkova was powerless; she was a privileged member of the Russian aristocracy.

But, as a woman, she could not be Chargé d'Affaires or a military commander,[3] and so her relationship to official structures was different from those of Rähbinder who, because he was committed to working through official channels, could do nothing about the paintings (118). Dashkova (who seemingly was not traveling in any official capacity) was not bound by conventional solutions as she indicated in her first question to Rähbinder: why, she wanted to know, didn't the wealthy Orlov simply buy the paintings and burn them (118)?[4] She did not have the money to put this solution into practice; but, relying on her wits and will, she effected a change that those in (officially) powerful positions declined to bring about.

This repainting reveals a great deal about Dashkova's faith in the power of representation (an important fact to keep in mind as one reads her self-representation). All autobiographical writing is to some extent interpretation, and Dashkova's, as this episode suggests, is constructed with an eye to showing Russia (and herself) in a favorable light. This incident also illustrates Dashkova's belief that the representation of "reality" has tremendous power to influence others: it does not matter who actually won or lost, what matters is the representation. Revising, repainting history, unhesitatingly inscribing her version of "reality" into the paintings, Dashkova displays a breathtaking self-confidence.

There is also a rebellious, playful side to Dashkova's repainting. The princess, usually described as serious, intelligent, respected, sometimes as humorless,[5] locked herself into a room with two gentlemen,[6] and painted late into the night; this is one of the most memorable images in the *Memoirs*. Dashkova thoroughly enjoyed changing the representation of reality and making events come out the way that she wanted them to. She states: "I was as happy and as nervous of not being allowed to finish my boyish prank as a naughty child in dread of his parents' return" (119).

Finally, this episode indicates Dashkova's devotion to Russia, something she emphasizes throughout her narrative. Very little is known about women's relation to the Russian state since women (in most cases) did not hold government posts and did not serve in the military, the two traditional venues for expressing love of country. How did women conceive of and express their relationship to the state and how did that relationship differ from that of men such as Derzhavin and Bolotov, two male memoirists of the eighteenth century? Dashkova's memoirs are one important source of information about the relations of women to the Russian state, both in her description of her own activity and in her commentary on other women's involvement at the Russian court and abroad.

Ekaterina Romanovna Dashkova (1743–1810) née Vorontsova, was one of the first women to hold public office in Europe; she was Director of the Petersburg Academy of Sciences and founder and President of the Russian Academy (1783–94).[7] She was the author of numerous plays, articles, and one of the first Russians to edit a journal, *Sobesednik liubitelei rossiiskogo slova* (*The Companion of Lovers of the Russian Word*), 1783–84. Dashkova was internationally known: she was a member of the American Philosophical Society (Benjamin Franklin nominated Dashkova for membership).[8] As a girl of nineteen, she played an important role in the coup that brought Catherine II to the throne, an event that continued to matter deeply to Dashkova for the rest of her life.

Despite her remarkable achievements, Dashkova died in isolation, forgotten by all but a few, and she has continued to be largely forgotten today. There is no entry for her in such major reference sources as Victor Terras's *Handbook of Russian Literature* (1985). Students, undergraduate and graduate, are rarely required or encouraged to read her *Memoirs,* and relatively little scholarly research has been done on Dashkova, although this situation has begun to change in recent years.[9] The fact that Dashkova continues to be overlooked, even in studies of women's history, indicates both the extent to which historians of Russia have neglected women and the extent to which even feminist revision of history is too often shaped by historiographical models that concentrate on the figure of the ruler rather than moving to a broader, more inclusive notion of what constitutes "history."[10]

My discussion locates Dashkova's *Memoirs* in several different contexts: the network of relationships between Russian aristocratic women in the eighteenth century (a topic that has been very little studied); women's negotiation of "public" and "private" in Russia (and how this encourages rethinking these terms); the political, emotional, intellectual, and perhaps erotic relationship between the female subject (Dashkova) and the female ruler (Catherine II); and, finally, how Dashkova's memoirs fit into the tradition of autobiographical writings by Russian women and enable us to make broad cross-cultural comparisons with women's autobiographical writings in other traditions.[11]

Other important questions include: What do these memoirs and their later reception reveal about constructions of femininity in Russia and about specific Russian understandings of gender and of the individual? What have Russians considered important in telling a life, and, more specifically, telling a woman's life?

On one level, Dashkova's multi-layered memoirs represent an attempt to balance "public" and "private," [12] revealing the difficulties encountered by a highly intelligent woman struggling to be both prominent in the "public" realm and "feminine" as that was defined by her culture (which included being active in the "private" realm of home and family). Dashkova presents the dilemma of a woman who wanted a "public" life at a time when women rarely participated in state service. As Catherine Wilmot noted (see epigraph), Dashkova was well suited to hold an official post (even to be a leader of state) [13] yet, given the conventions of femininity in Russia, she could not directly express a desire for such a role, perhaps not even to herself. [14]

Dashkova begins her memoir by situating herself in both "public" and "private" domains: within the realm of the court and within a network of female relationship. The first event she describes is her baptism; she notes that the Empress Elizaveta (usually called Elizabeth in English) and the Grand Duke (the future Peter III) were her godparents. Traditionally, the godmother holds the infant girl at the baptismal font and Dashkova [15] calls attention to this fact, saying that the Empress, "held me at the baptismal font, while the Grand Duke . . . was my godfather" (31). In beginning her *Memoirs* with this image of being held by Elizaveta, Dashkova stresses her connection, physical and spiritual, with the female ruler. Much of the rest of Dashkova's "life" is narrated from the perspective of her relationship with Catherine II, so that these first sentences are a particularly appropriate beginning to her narrative.

Dashkova further emphasizes the nexus of female relationship by noting that the honor of having Elizaveta as godmother was granted not because the princess's uncle was related by marriage to the Empress but because of Elizaveta's friendship with Dashkova's mother. Dashkova describes her mother as one "who with the greatest tact, zeal and, I may say, generosity, supplied the Empress—then still a Princess living in straitened circumstances at the Court of the Empress Anna—with whatever was necessary for her household and her dresses of which she was very fond" (31).

This first paragraph and the subtexts embedded in it provide a key for understanding the dilemma of an aristocratic woman in eighteenth-century Russia who attempted to be involved in the "public" sphere. Dashkova's aforementioned uncle, Mikhail Vorontsov, aided Elizaveta in the coup that brought her to the throne in 1740. For this he was rewarded by high court appointments, eventually becoming Grand Chancellor; he was also granted military rank and estates. Dashkova, too, participated in a coup which brought a female ruler to power; and Dashkova, like her uncle, was eventually rewarded with estates and government posts, but she never attained (or was never granted) as politically influential a position as that held by her uncle. Nor did she develop the kind of friendship with Catherine II that she describes her own mother as having with Elizaveta. Perhaps because Dashkova wanted both the political influence traditionally associated with males in Russia and the close friendship associated with females, she was frequently disappointed in both the lack of a "private" friendship with the Empress and by her own "public" role.

In directing the two academies, Dashkova entered the realm of government service in a way unprecedented for a woman. She initially refused the post of Director of the Academy of Sciences in a letter to Catherine II (the letter remained unsent), citing her gender as the reason: "God himself, by creating me a woman . . . exempted me from accepting the employment of a Director of an Academy of Sciences" (201). It was so unusual for a woman to be appointed Director of the Academy of Sciences that officials did not know what the proper procedures were: Prince Viazemskii, the Minister of Justice, asked the Empress Catherine whether Dashkova should be sworn in as were all employees of the state. Catherine's answer ensures that Dashkova will begin her duties on the same basis as other (male) employees: "Unquestionably [she should be sworn in] . . . for I have never made a secret of Princess Dashkova's appointment to the Directorship of the Academy; true enough, I have no need for fresh assurances of her loyalty to me and the country, but the ceremony would give me pleasure because her appointment would thereby gain in sanction and publicity" (206).[16]

Despite Dashkova's protest that her gender made her unfit to head the Academy of Sciences, she took on the post and proved herself eminently capable of fulfilling her duties—more capable, in fact, than the previous director had been. Dashkova secured the Academy of Sciences' financial position, oversaw the compilation of and contributed to the Academy's first Russian dictionary, had academy buildings put up, and instituted a series of lectures for less privileged nobles, which she herself occasionally attended—perhaps the first example of a Russian woman who received a form of higher education.[17]

The discrepancies between Dashkova's competent actions and modest words are part of a larger pattern: throughout her *Memoirs* she describes her achievements in a language of self-effacement. The constant tension between confident self-presentation of her own actions and words— which are often bold and brilliant—and the modest disclaimers with which she follows or anticipates these descriptions may seem confusing at times. My students have often labeled this tension self-righteous or hypocritical, for Dashkova seems to present herself as "great" and then say how little she deserves such a representation.[18]

But this vacillation served Dashkova well: while she may have believed her own self-effacing words, she also used these and other conventions common among women aristocrats of her time [19] (perhaps unconsciously) as a way to attain her own goals. For example, knowing that the members of the Academy would be at best ambivalent about having a woman in a position of authority over them, Dashkova, when taking the oath of loyalty to the Crown, gently deflected possible resistance by bringing up the issue of her femaleness directly: "You are . . . surely as surprised as I am myself at seeing me come here [the Chamber of the Senate] to swear an oath of loyalty to Her Majesty whose very name has for long been engraved on my heart. But one must obey, and not believe oneself exempt from a duty prescribed for all. To this is due this unusual event—the appearance of a woman in your august sanctuary" (207).

Couching her directorship in the deferential language of obedience of a loyal subject, Dashkova both defuses potential hostility and constructs a relationship between herself and members of the Academy as loyal subjects of Catherine II. This, under autocratic rule, was a nearly unassailable position: how could anyone grumble against Dashkova if she were merely fulfilling the sovereign's will? While such statements may have been an honest expression of her own ambivalent thoughts and feelings, they could also work brilliantly to facilitate her work with the Academy. With this approach, Dashkova lessens any suspicion that she might be "unfeminine" and establishes herself as an imperially sanctioned, and yet unthreatening, leader. By directly and publicly addressing the issue of her femininity, by reassuring Academy members that they would maintain a measure of control—it is still *their* "august sanctuary"—by proclaiming her "ignorance" to her audience (206), and focusing directly on the unusual nature of her role, Dashkova opens a space within which to work effectively. This is but one example of her negotiation of the feminine conventions of her time and class or estate (*soslovie*).[20] Her memoirs are full of such examples and, in fact, this movement between a rhetoric of self-effacement and describing accomplishments unusual for a woman in this period is a central feature of Dashkova's text.[21]

Aristocratic women were expected to be modest in the eighteenth century,[22] and Dashkova had internalized this attitude: When speaking of Mrs. Damer, a talented sculptress, Dashkova notes approvingly Damer's inclination "to hide her natural superiority" (173). (This refers, apparently, to the artist's reticence about her intellectual abilities—Dashkova is delighted that she discovers only by accident that Damer reads Greek [175]). Such a formulation poses difficulties for an intelligent woman writing about her life: Dashkova values intellect, education, and modesty (hiding talents). The latter makes depicting her own abilities extraordinarily complicated: how does one both represent and hide one's intellect?

One of Dashkova's solutions is to present her own importance as reflected in others' responses to her. Instead of direct statements, she shows how famous others—figures like Diderot, Voltaire, King Frederick II (the Great)—insisted on meeting her and how impressed they were, usually by her intellect.

Far from being awed by the acknowledged great minds of the day, Dashkova, in most cases, reports not so much what these figures said but rather her own words,[23] thereby emphasizing her effect on her interlocutors rather than theirs on her. For example, she describes how she changed Diderot's views on serfdom (124–25) and argued with the Austrian diplomat Prince Kaunitz about Peter I. After describing such interchanges in great detail, however, Dashkova often makes disclaimers. In the case of her conversations with Kaunitz, she reports her reaction on learning that he had been impressed by their conversation: "I had never had a sufficiently high opinion of myself to imagine that my conversation could interest a Minister with so distinguished a mind as Kaunitz. . . . If I had sharply criticized the Prince's ideas it was because I loved truth and my country in equal measure" (182).

Many of my students have found this vacillation confusing and I also find it frustrating; rather than being a strong woman and proud of it, Dashkova diminishes her own accomplishments. But both these reactions reflect a late twentieth-century perspective. In fact, Dashkova's double self-presentation is part of what enabled her to attain so much within the conventions of her society: by giving the words about her own intelligence to authoritative others while she herself makes disclaimers, she is able to present herself as brilliant in a way that would not threaten either her own or others' conceptions of what it meant to be a "good" woman. It is impossible to know to what extent Dashkova had internalized her disclaimers or to what extent she used them consciously to facilitate her role as a powerful leader. It is clear though, that this was an effective way to present herself (would any other form of presentation have been acceptable or convincing to her hearers, and later, her intended readers?).

DASHKOVA AND CATHERINE II

Russia was ruled by women for approximately two-thirds of the eighteenth century,[24] yet there is very little scholarship about the implications of this for women and for men.[25] Dashkova is one example (perhaps the most prominent) of someone for whom it was very important that Russia was governed by a woman; it is not a coincidence that the first woman to hold such important government posts was appointed by a woman. Dashkova's achievements are inextricably linked with Catherine II, not only because of her own strong feeling for the Empress but also because Dashkova could not have had the influence at court that she did had the ruler been male.

There is some debate as to whether gender was a factor in eighteenth-century evaluations of female rulers, but, as David Griffiths and Barbara Norton each demonstrate, women were usually thought less suited to rule than men (both in and after the eighteenth century).[26] Female rule changed Russian society, affecting both the structures of the family and court life. Robin Bisha argues that, in the eighteenth century, due to the combination of female rule and greater contact with the "West,"[27] daughters' needs began to be taken into account in Russia for the first time and that this radically changed expectations about marriage and family.[28] She also shows that throughout the eighteenth century women had unprecedented access to female rulers and that this was reflected in the court and beyond.[29] Norton's and Bisha's arguments are supported by the fact that shortly after coming to the throne Pavel (Paul) I (re)established a rule of male primogeniture,[30] so that women could no longer lead Russia.

Dashkova's relationship with Catherine II is an example of how women's having informal access to the ruler could have far-ranging effects. The princess notes that the Empress frequently invited Dashkova "to her Jewel Chamber . . . where we used to sit and talk alone and quite freely while her hair was being combed and dressed" (239–40). Under male rule, it is men who have access to the ruler in such moments, and it is in these informal encounters that much of the business of state is contracted. The Russian Academy, for example, was born out of one such casual conversation (between Dashkova and Catherine, 213). Thus under female rulers, women had easier access to the ruler and, presumably, more influence on the "public" sphere.

There is another equally important, though less easily described and analyzed, side to the relationship between Dashkova and Catherine: their emotional and intellectual relationship. Dashkova invested a great deal of energy in Catherine; she also identified with the Empress (e.g., 77–78). Friendships between women have been variously described as supportive, rare, and/or competitive (or some combination of these):[31] the relationship between Dashkova and Catherine II was all of these.

Dashkova describes her relationship with Catherine II as one of mutual intellectual attraction. They met when Dashkova (then Vorontsova) was only fifteen and the Grand Duchess (the future Empress) nearly twice that age. Dashkova was a particularly welcome ally for the Grand Duchess: Dashkova's elder sister, Elizaveta, was the mistress of the Grand Duke—Catherine's husband, the future Peter III—a fact that the powerful Vorontsov family was trying to use to increase their own influence. Thus, the relationship with Dashkova meant that Catherine had a friend in the "enemy camp." The Grand Duchess captivated the young Dashkova by her conversation, her intellect, and her charm. According to Dashkova, Catherine had already heard about the younger woman's intellectual abilities, and Dashkova presents intellect as the magnetic force of their relationship: "I could argue, perhaps, that as there were no other two women at the time, apart from the Grand Duchess and myself, who did any serious reading, we were mutually drawn toward each other" (36). While Dashkova certainly exaggerates here (there were other well-read women in eighteenth-century Russia),[32] the intellectual attraction and bond between the two was powerful and long-lasting. From the extant letters of Catherine II it is clear that their intellectual exchange was intensely exciting—they commented on one another's manuscripts, discussed their reading, and recommended books to one another not only in the 1760s but even in the 1780s when their relationship was more distant and often strained.[33] It is no accident that when Catherine appointed Dashkova to a government post it was as head of the two academies; their intellectual relationship was consistently lively and the realm of intellect was where Catherine trusted Dashkova the most.[34]

After Catherine became Empress, her relationship with Dashkova became more distant, and at various points deteriorated seriously, especially in 1793 after Dashkova allowed the publication of Iakov Kniazhnin's play *Vadim of Novgorod*. In light of recent events in France, where the Revolution of 1789 had toppled the monarchy and raised the specter of republicanism across Europe, Catherine interpreted this play, in which Vadim speaks for the Novgorodian *veche* (a kind of popular assembly), as antimonarchical and became extremely angry with Dashkova.[35] In 1794, Dashkova left Petersburg; after this she did not see Catherine before the latter's death in 1796, but remained devoted to the Empress for the rest of her life. Catherine Wilmot writes:

> She [Dashkova] has promised to shew me the Empress Catherine's letters. . . . Indeed, it is necessary to qualify oneself with the knowledge of public things and characters during the time of Catherine the Second, for to these the princess perpetually alludes; and her mind wanders so naturally back to the court, and study, and toilet, and boudoir of that empress, that I am beginning to fancy myself a party concerned in the revolution. . . . the principal salon here is ornamented with a colossal picture of Catherine on horseback in uniform; besides this, there are portraits of her in every room.[36]

One can read this relationship as either obsession or deep devotion; in either case, Catherine's importance for Dashkova is clear. I see the intensity of this relationship as a tribute by Dashkova not only to Catherine personally but also to the Empress as representative of Russia, for Dashkova believed that Catherine's reign was crucial for her country's well-being.[37]

Dashkova had one other relationship that was of equal or nearly equal significance to her relationship with Catherine: her marriage. Empress and husband are inextricably connected in Dashkova's *Memoirs*. For all her protestations of love for her husband, Dashkova's depiction of her relationship with Catherine is far more compelling than her portrayal of her marriage. This, I think, is partly because her husband died when she was only twenty and partly because of her own desire to work in the "public" sphere; Catherine could link "public" and "private" in a way Dashkova's husband could not. The erotic also may play a role in Dashkova's relationship to Catherine, and I explore this facet of their friendship later in this essay.

Especially while her husband was still alive, Dashkova frequently juxtaposed husband and Empress. After meeting the future Catherine II, Dashkova noted: "She [the Grand Duchess] had a powerful rival for the affections of my heart, in the person of Prince Dashkov to whom I was already betrothed. But soon he came to share my opinion of her, and all rivalry ceased" (36). This implies that the Grand Duchess had the first claim on her affection and loyalty; it is Prince Dashkov who is the interloper on an already established relationship (even though Dashkova was betrothed to him). And the conflict is resolved not by a lessening of Dashkova's feeling for either, nor by a change in the Grand Duchess; rather it is Prince Dashkov who had to change. (One wonders what would have happened had the Prince not come to respect Catherine II?) Later in life, too, Dashkova continued to equate her relationships with her husband and the Empress: "I know of only two things which could have stirred up the small portion of bile which nature had mingled in my composition; the infidelity of my husband . . . and whatever could tarnish the fame of my sovereign, Catherine the Second.[38]

There are also some important parallels between husband and empress in the first of the two bedroom scenes between Dashkova and Catherine.[39] Dashkova, on learning that the Empress Elizaveta is dying, goes to the Grand Duchess to offer her support and allegiance to Catherine's cause. Even though Dashkova herself was sick, and it was late at night and cold (it was December in St. Petersburg), she did not hesitate. Further, the entrances to the palace were guarded, and Dashkova did not know exactly where the Grand Duchess's rooms were located; she could easily have ended up, as she notes, in the Grand Duke's rooms rather than the Grand Duchess's (48). But Dashkova found her way to Catherine, who, though she was already in bed, received the princess, and insisted that she warm up in bed before talking. Catherine expressed worry for Dashkova's health: "What brings you here, my dear princess, at this hour and at such risk to your health, which you know to be precious to your husband and to me?" (49).

Prince Dashkov echoes this concern for the princess's health: when Dashkova returns home after visiting Catherine, the prince praises her for her action, but his praise was "qualified . . . by his fear that my nocturnal escapade might have been detrimental to my delicate state of health" (50). Dashkova's visit to Catherine recalls a similar visit to Prince Dashkov when he was sick (41–42), at a time when Dashkova herself was in labor. (Given the difficulty of giving birth, this act establishes Dashkova as a determined woman and loving wife, if a little careless of her maternal obligations.)

Dashkova equates her relationships with Catherine and Prince Dashkov throughout the *Memoirs;* she is intensely emotionally involved with each of them (as she later becomes with Martha Wilmot, the Anglo-Irish woman to whom Dashkova's memoir is dedicated). The support of her female friends (usually non-Russian) was very important for Dashkova, who seems to have had a capacity for deep relationship, expressed mainly for women friends. It is too early to say to what extent this depth of friendship was typical for Russian women in the eighteenth and nineteenth centuries,[40] but it does suggest that, for Dashkova, Catherine was friend, model (as a powerful woman), and ruler of Russia, about which Dashkova cared deeply. Catherine both empowered Dashkova, by giving her a role in the polity, and was destructive for her, by withdrawing her friendship for reasons Dashkova did not fully understand. The friendship between the two both complicated the relationship of subject and ruler and was complicated by it. It is easy to imagine that the relations between two competent, intelligent women, who were both involved in the "public" sphere at a time when that was unusual for women, would be both threatening and reassuring, supportive and competitive.

A question that frequently comes up in my classes is whether and to what extent the relationship between Dashkova and Catherine can accurately be described as erotic. This question is in some senses anachronistic (for understandings of sexuality in eighteenth-century Russia were different from twentieth-century and "Western" assumptions and perceptions). Yet it is an important question. There is (and was then) a fine line between intensity of intellectual and emotional exchange and erotic intensity, and it is difficult, perhaps impossible, to finally distinguish between these areas.[41] At least on Dashkova's side, the intensity of her attachment to Catherine borders on the erotic, although by that I do not mean to suggest an explicitly sexual (physical) relationship. But being close to Catherine meant being close to a forceful intellect, a female model, and power (the ruler of Russia); these factors all combine to create a relationship which we would now probably define as erotic, though it might not have been thought of in that way at the time.[42]

Dashkova played a major role in the coup of 1762 that brought Catherine II to the throne. Although, as many scholars have indicated, Dashkova exaggerated her own importance,[43] she did help place Catherine in power through her decisiveness, quick mind, and her influence over key figures like Nikita Panin. Dashkova describes these days as some of the most exciting of her life. Of her meeting with Catherine II, just after the latter had been declared Sovereign of all the Russias, Dashkova notes: "No happiness could ever have exceeded mine at that moment. It had reached its summit" (78). This is a rare instance of Dashkova expressing happiness, and it does not seem coincidental that this is a moment in which "public" and "private" are joined.

Throughout the period preceding the coup, Dashkova was able to use her intellect and influence to effect meaningful change; she was publicly recognized by the soldiers and privately by Catherine (who had just been proclaimed Empress, 77–78). When the two women then express their affection for one another, Dashkova describes a deep sense of connection with Catherine II. Listening to the Empress tell of her escape from Peterhof, Dashkova says, "I relived in my own emotions all the hopes and fears she must have felt" (77). Such moments of connection are rare in this narrative, which is largely about Dashkova's sense of isolation. In the scenes around the time of the coup, however, something like her full power could be expressed and appreciated: what could Dashkova have accomplished if she had regularly had an outlet for her affection, talents, and energies and a forum of those who would respect her?

Shortly after this scene, Catherine and Dashkova review the troops; they are dressed in the uniforms of the Preobrazhenskii[44] Regiment (an important symbol and one appreciated by the troops, for Peter III had abolished these uniforms and instituted unpopular "Prussian-type" uniforms). This image of two women reviewing troops strikes me as both powerful and exhilarating: how often does one see women as military commanders? To be two women, friends, joined in such a moment must have been thrilling for Dashkova. This very public moment is closely followed by the second bedroom scene, which takes place shortly after Catherine has been proclaimed Sovereign of all the Russias. On a march with the troops, they halt for three hours. Catherine and Dashkova lie together on the only bed in the house, and talk about the manifestos Catherine plans to propose, and their fears and hopes (79). In this scene, Dashkova and Catherine are intellectual equals in a way that would have been impossible (or at least extremely unlikely) if the ruler had been a man.

This image of two women talking in bed is a lovely moment of closeness, powerfully evoked. In these intimate moments with her ruler and friend, public and private meet again, and this fusion seems to be what Dashkova longed for most of all.

DASHKOVA'S LATER YEARS

Dashkova, as Barbara Heldt points out, experienced the extremes of isolation and fame.[45] Prominent in her youth and again in the 1780s, in the latter years of her life, Dashkova lived alone, distant both from the capitals, and, for the most part, from her relations. When Pavel I came to the throne in 1796, he punished those who had worked against Peter III, including Dashkova, who was exiled to a distant estate on the upper Volga. Later she was allowed to come back to her beloved Troitskoe, the estate where she had planted or supervised the planting of "every tree and every shrub" (218). She lived away from the capital and on her estate for the rest of her days; her last "public" act, as A. Woronzoff-Dashkoff points out, was to write her memoirs.[46]

Dashkova's last years on her estate are a good example of why it is impossible to distinguish sharply between "public" and "private." She remained extremely active in her later years, as Catherine Wilmot attests:

> (. . . she helps . . . the masons to build walls, she assists with her own hands in making the roads, she feeds the cows, she composes music, she sings & plays, she writes for the press, she shells the corn, she talks out loud in Church and corrects the Priest if he is not devout, she talks out loud in her little Theatre and puts in the Performers when they are out in their parts, she is a Doctor, an Apothecary, a Surgeon, a Farrier, a Carpenter, a Magistrate, a Lawyer; . . . and yet appears as if she had her time a burthen on her hands).[47]

In running her estate, Dashkova fulfilled many roles that would now be considered part of the "public" rather than the "private" realm. But, although active and productive, she was also extremely isolated. The last years of her life were difficult partly due to her strained relations with her children. Although Dashkova lived in close physical proximity to her son and daughter, she rarely saw either of them. Dashkova's relationship with her daughter, Anastasiia, had long been complicated. She did not pay as much attention to her daughter's education as she did to her son's and she also married her daughter off early to A. E. Shcherbinin, an officer in the Russian army. The marriage was unhappy and to complicate matters further, Anastasiia fell into debt. Dashkova, though disapproving (she had struggled hard to keep herself free of debt) paid her daughter's debts on several occasions. But, after Anastasiia acted disrespectfully to Dashkova's friend and surrogate daughter Martha Wilmot, Dashkova gave up on Anastasiia and, citing her daughter's "disrespect" and "low morals," cut Anastasiia out of her will except for a small sum paid annually.[48] Dashkova's son, Pavel, also disappointed her greatly. She put a lot of energy into his development and ensured that he received a thorough education (he received an M.A. from Edinburgh University); he later became a Lieutenant-General under Pavel I and also served briefly as military governor of Kiev. As she notes in the *Memoirs,* Dashkova was deeply hurt when, in 1785, her son married a woman of a lower class without telling his mother beforehand. Her son's death in 1807 was a terrible blow to Dashkova and it was only after his death that she achieved a partial reconciliation with her daughter-in-law, Anna.

Dashkova died in 1810. This woman, who had been a prominent figure in the coup of 1762 and directed two academies, died nearly completely forgotten; only a small group including friends, perhaps some relatives, the village priest, and serfs attended her burial.

In the last decade of Dashkova's life she developed a friendship that proved to be not only a source of the emotional and intellectual support that her relationships with her children did not provide but also the inspiration for writing her memoirs:[49] Martha Wilmot, cousin of Dashkova's "dearest and best friend" (280) Mrs. Hamilton, arrived in 1803— and stayed for five years.[50] Dashkova claimed that, though her relatives had wanted her to write her memoirs, she had always refused, and that it was only her affection for Martha Wilmot that prompted her to write them. Heldt points out that it was "almost obligatory" for a woman to apologize for writing an autobiography.[51] But even if Dashkova's explanation for writing the *Memoirs* is part of her rhetoric of self-effacement, it is still significant that she claims that female friendship is what impelled her to inscribe her life.

It was also Martha and Catherine Wilmot, these Anglo-Irish sisters, who translated and copied the memoirs and Martha Wilmot, who, despite opposition from Dashkova's brother Simon Vorontsov, made sure they were published. So Dashkova's initial forays into the "public" realm were inspired and facilitated by one woman, Catherine II, and her last (the writing and posthumous publication of her memoirs) were expedited by two other women. Dashkova was inspired first by the older Catherine and then by the younger Wilmot sisters, for whom, in turn, she was a figure of inspiration. This is a nicely balanced image of female friendship and support: the Wilmots saw Dashkova's story as important, as history, and insisted that it not be lost; it is, in turn, largely because of Dashkova that we know anything about the Wilmot sisters.[52]

CONSTRUCTING AUTOBIOGRAPHICAL IDENTITY

The genesis and publishing of Dashkova's memoirs indicates the extent to which Russian "selves" were constituted in relation to other nationalities:

Dashkova, a Russian woman, wrote her memoirs (*Mon histoire*) in French at the inspiration of the Anglo-Irish Martha Wilmot. The memoirs were first published in English in 1840,[53] and did not come out in Russian until 1859 (a translation of the 1840 English edition). All of this suggests a complex network of international relationships, making it difficult to define these memoirs as belonging to a single nationality.[54]

I am particularly interested in the fact that Dashkova's memoirs were composed in French. While this is partly because, for all practical purposes, French was the only language Dashkova and the Wilmot sisters shared, many other issues are raised by Dashkova's use of French to write her "history." Many theorists have argued that human identities are formed linguistically, by and in relation to the languages we learn.[55] Given that Dashkova spoke very little Russian until she was married, to what extent is she "Russian"? One answer to this is that throughout the eighteenth century and well into the nineteenth, French was the language of the Russian aristocracy; and so, to speak French as one's first tongue did not make one any the less Russian. But it is not so simple, for two of the most famous examples of autobiographical writing by women in the eighteenth century were written in Russian as were many other works by both women and men (for instance, Labzina, Dolgorukaia, Bolotov, Derzhavin).[56] And Aleksandr Herzen, an astute commentator on Russian society, said of his father, who was educated in the late eighteenth century: "When he was being educated, European civilization was still so new in Russia that to be educated meant being so much the less Russian. To the end of his days he wrote more fluently and correctly in French than in Russian." [57]

All of this suggests that identities in Russia were shaped in relation to Western Europe; Russian identities were being formed by and in relation to non-Russian languages and traditions. But Russians also constituted themselves in relation to their "Eastern" neighbors, particularly those in the Caucasus; in fact, the Russian aristocracy's emphasis on Western European traditions was, in part, a way to differentiate itself from the "barbaric East." Thus, the very concept of a Russian (or, in this case, a Russian woman) is complicated in ways that Western European or North American identities are not.[58]

WOMEN'S AUTOBIOGRAPHICAL TRADITIONS

As Heldt demonstrates in *Terrible Perfection,* there is a rich tradition of autobiographical writings by women in Russia, a tradition which has remained largely unexplored. Despite Heldt's identification of autobiography, together with the lyric, as the central mode for women authors in Russia,[59] very few studies have been done of Russian women's autobiographical writings. Further, the major collections of theoretical writings on autobiography by women do not include analyses of Russian women's autobiography (with two exceptions).[60] Given these factors, it seems reasonable to ask: how might autobiographical writings of Russian women (including Dashkova's memoirs) disturb and illuminate current theories of women's autobiography?[61]

Russian aristocratic society modeled itself on France, yet was inevitably based on, permeated with, Russian and "Eastern" traditions (the latter from the Caucasus, Crimea, and Central Asia): Russia is a sometimes uneasy combination of "East" and "West," and so is a provocative site for comparison and exploration of theories that have been created in and for numerous groups and phenomena in "East" and "West."

Various theories and models have been proposed in the "West" for the life writing of women in the "East" and the "West"; usually "Western" women are seen as paradigmatic and "Eastern" women as interesting in the ways they diverge from "Western" patterns. Many "Western" theorists of autobiographical writings of women have claimed that women's autobiography (in contrast to men's) tends to be more personal, more relational, and more focused on the family.[62] Estelle Jelinek, for example, claims that unlike men's autobiographies, "women's autobiographies rarely mirror the establishment history of their times."[63] These are problematic assumptions, but they underlie many explications of women's autobiographical writings in the "West." Of course, those memoirs (by both men and women) that do focus on the domestic reflect their cultures as much as any memoir that concentrates on affairs of state; they simply depict different aspects of the culture, those that have traditionally been devalued but which are no less important than more public histories.

Many theories about "third world" and Latin American autobiographies by women focus on the autobiographer as spokesperson for her people: scholars argue that, unlike in the so-called "first world," where women, like men, speak for/as individuals, in the "third world," autobiographers speak for others as well as themselves, as a member of a community. Doris Sommer, for example, in discussing the *testimonio,* details some of the ways that conceptions about individuality differ in the "first world" (Western Europe and North America) and in Latin America.[64] She argues that the *testimonio* comes from and participates in a culture that "does not equate identity with individuality,"[65] a statement that could also apply to

Russia. Sommer's argument suggests that there are fascinating points of comparison between Latin American and Russian autobiographies, for, while the relationship between community and individual may be similar, the cultures are very different in other ways.

Studies of women's autobiography have generally been defined by the study of "Western" women, and although some scholarly works have focused on cross-cultural comparison (for example, Brodzki and Schenck, ed., *Life/Lines;* Lionnet's *Autobiographical Voices;* and Smith and Watson, ed., *De/Colonizing the Subject*), the field is still, to my mind, too much defined by the Anglo-French-American heritage with too little emphasis on cross-cultural comparison. Much of the comparative work I have read challenges ethnocentric assumptions about how identity is constructed, but at the same time it risks a certain ethnocentrism, which is, perhaps, inevitable, at least given the ways identity, nationality, and criticism are currently constructed. Yet I wonder if scholarship of autobiography is particularly susceptible to this; if, because many of us read autobiography as if it were truer than fiction, critics identify with the life stories of those they write about. And if this is true, then does this unconscious identification make it easier to be ethnocentric, harder to see and acknowledge one's own cultural assumptions?[66] The study of autobiographical writings by Russian women can be particularly useful in challenging such assumptions for they (including Dashkova's *Memoirs*) break down the dichotomy of "East" and "West," describing different concepts of both individuality and community, and, perhaps, of what it means to speak.

There are many kinds of women's autobiography, both in the "West" and elsewhere, as much recent theory of autobiography has shown;[67] there are multiple ways of constituting a self, multiple understandings of identity and gender depending on factors such as culture, historical period, class, race, religion, and sexuality. Although a strict typology of Russian women's autobiographical forms would be out of place here, delineating several broad, sometimes overlapping categories may be useful. These autobiographical writings range from the memoirs of the ruler or public leader[68] to childhood memoirs;[69] from pseudo-autobiographies[70] to the autobiographical writings of women literati[71] (including pieces like Tsvetaeva's innovative prose fragments);[72] from writings that concentrate on an unusual event or series of events[73] to prison memoirs.[74] There is another important subgenre of Russian women's autobiographical writings: those that ostensibly focus on famous (usually male) others, often a husband.[75] As Beth Holmgren has shown in the case of Lidiia Chukovskaia and Nadezhda Mandelstam, however, writing about another can be a way to author oneself and comment on one's times.[76] Because Russian women's autobiographical writings have been so little studied, it is too early to say definitely how Dashkova's memoirs participate in these traditions. But her memoirs do fit into several of the categories listed above: she discusses her activities and achievements in both "public" and "private" spheres; she was an author; she defines herself in relation to a famous other (Catherine II); and, though she was never in prison, she describes an experience of exile.

And just as Dashkova's memoirs balance individual achievement and connection with others, many later autobiographies do the same: negotiating how to represent achievements in the "public" and "private" spheres is a prominent facet of the autobiographical writings of many Russian women, though they depict these struggles in very different ways (as one would expect, given different time periods, positions in society, personalities). Dashkova's memoirs indicate that women's representations of talent or achievement, and of their relationships to family, friends, and state have a long and rich history in Russia.

Cross-cultural comparisons of women's self-representations are vital for understanding how gender is constructed in various times and places, and for deconstructing various ideas about femininity as monolithic. Many have discussed the multiplicity of gender (noting that women of different classes, races, times, etc., have very different experiences), but much scholarship also reveals underlying assumptions that women everywhere and of every time are similar in some fundamental ways.[77] It seems much more likely to me that we often think of women as similar because it is easier than exploring the subtleties of cultural and social constructions of gender or examining our own assumptions about what it means to be a woman (or man). Comparing women in different cultures makes it much more difficult to retain uncomplicated essentialist assumptions.[78]

Dashkova's memoirs raise many complex issues around the construction of Russian female identity in the eighteenth century and beyond. Study of her work (and that of other Russian women authors) and engaging women's work, worlds, and identities can lead to reconceptualizing Russian literary and historical traditions that have generally omitted writings by women; further, examining Dashkova's work in cross-cultural perspective encourages asking new questions and developing new approaches to and understandings of gender, identity, nationality, and self-representation.

NOTE ON TRANSLITERATION

The problem of how to transliterate Russian names is always a thorny one, with no perfect solution. I have updated the transliteration of proper names to accord with a modified Library of Congress system (with the exception of reference materials, I have not included the symbol to indicate where a soft sign appears in the original Russian). There are several exceptions: because I hope that Dashkova's *Memoirs* will have a readership of both Slavists and non-Slavists, I have throughout the text, retained the familiar English spellings of most place names as well as some proper names (e.g., I have kept "Catherine," "Peter," and "Maria") rather than changing them to "Ekaterina," "Petr," and "Mariia." In addition, I have retained Fitzlyon's spelling of last names such as "Leontiev," for the sake of consistency between the text and the index.

Notes

Full references to all cited works are found in the bibliography.

1   Herzen agreed with Wilmot's statement. A. I. Herzen (Gertsen), *Polnoe sobranie sochinenii*, 12: 361.

2   All references to Dashkova's *Memoirs* are to the present edition.

3   While Russian women, notably Nadezhda Durova (who served in male disguise), have occasionally participated in the military, they have not held official positions of power as Aleksei Orlov did during the Russo-Turkish war of 1770; similarly, it was extremely rare for women to participate officially in the civil service. Durova and Dashkova are exceptions to a general rule.

4   In this statement, Dashkova suggests that Orlov lacks either imagination or courage. Given the longstanding rivalry between Orlov and Dashkova, this entire episode can also be read as Dashkova's asserting her superiority over Orlov: he may have the money and the power, but she, through her intelligence, proves herself more capable of defending Russia than he.

5   Catherine Wilmot in Bradford, II: 356–57.

6   These are Volchkov, the Secretary of the Russian Legation and the Counsellor of the Russian Embassy, Stählin, who was also an artist.

7   Officially, Dashkova held the posts until Catherine II's death in 1796, but she requested and received a two-year leave from her duties in 1794.

8   When Dashkova was elected to the Society, it was called the Philadelphia Philosophical Society.

9   See the bibliography for recent scholarship on Dashkova including works by David Griffiths, Cynthia Whittaker, and A. Woronzoff-Dashkoff.

10   Dashkova is not mentioned in such works as *A History of Their Own* (Anderson and Zinsser, eds.) where Catherine II figures prominently.

11   It is difficult to know exactly what terms to use in discussing autobiographical writings, as scholars debate the meanings of the various terms, "memoir," "journal,"

"autobiography," "diary," etc. "Memoir" is generally used to refer to a work that focuses more on the historical time period than on the development of individual personality. Because I believe this to be a false (and misleading) dichotomy, I use the terms interchangeably throughout this essay. For scholarly discussions of these terms, see, for example, Gunn, *Autobiography: Towards A Poetics of Experience;* Olney, ed., *Autobiography: Essays Theoretical and Critical.*

12   Barbara Heldt also discusses Dashkova's memoirs in terms of "public" and "private," focusing on the separation between these two spheres and how Dashkova, over time, maintained a balance between them (*Terrible Perfection,* 68–76); I concentrate more on moments when "public" and "private" meet in Dashkova's text. As much scholarship (mainly of "Western" contexts) has shown, "public" and "private" are complicated terms; here I use "public" to mean widely acknowledged or official participation in the realm of court or state and "private" to refer to other kinds of activities, including running estates and family duties. In the Russian context of this period, these terms are troublesome, for court and state politics were family-based, as Robin Bisha points out in "The Promise of Patriarchy: Marriage in Eighteenth-Century Russia," 18. But, while there was no clear delineation of these realms, Dashkova does alternate her descriptions of court and estate/family; I have continued to use the terms in order to show this alternation, and attempt throughout, but especially toward the end of my argument, to show how these areas of "public" and "private" intersect. For discussions of "public" and "private," see Helly and Reverby, ed., *Gendered Domains: Rethinking Public and Private in Women's History* and Offen, Roach, and Rendall, ed., *Writing Women's History: International Perspectives;* in the latter, see especially Gisela Bock's essay, "Challenging Dichotomies: Perspectives on Women's History," 1–23.

13   Catherine Wilmot in Wilmot, 211.

14   For discussions of what it meant to be a woman in Russia in the eighteenth century, see Bisha and Vowles. See also the memoirs of Dolgorukaia, Labzina, and Catherine II, and the Wilmot sisters' accounts of their time in Russia (in Wilmot and Bradford).

15   I will refer to the princess as Dashkova throughout the essay. Technically, she should be called Vorontsova or Ekaterina (Catherine) before the marriage, but such usage is confusing, especially given that Catherine II and Dashkova had the same first name.

16   From a late twentieth-century perspective, it is tempting to see Catherine's answer as a statement about the importance of women being recognized publicly for their work. I am not at all sure that this was the Empress's view, however; given their relationship, Catherine's answer could just as easily indicate that she knew that this recognition would be important to Dashkova. Thus, her answer may simply have been a diplomatic move to encourage the new director.

17   Women were not allowed to attend institutions of higher learning in Russia until the middle of the nineteenth century. On women's education in Russia, see, for example, Dudgeon, "Women and Higher Education in Russia, 1855–1905"; Johanson, *Women's Struggle for Higher Education in Russia, 1855–1900;* Likhacheva, *Materialy dlia istorii zhenskogo obrazovaniia v Rossii 1086–1901;* Stites, *The Women's Liberation Movement in Russia.*

18   This is partly due to the linguistic norms operative in the eighteenth century; for ex-

ample, Catherine II, Dolgorukaia, and Labzina employ a rhetoric of self-justification similar to that used by Dashkova. See the bibliography for full references to these memoirs.

19   The expectations and roles of peasant women, merchant women, and others were often very different from those of aristocratic women. For research on Russian women of classes other than the aristocracy, see, for example, Farnsworth and Viola, ed., *Russian Peasant Women;* Glickman, *Russian Factory Women;* Meehan, *Holy Women of Russia.*

20   The system of division along socioeconomic lines is very different in Russia than in the "West"; in describing the Russian case, I follow the common practice and use the term "estate."

21   Perhaps this is part of Dashkova's "masquerade." For an excellent discussion of Dashkova's various disguises, see A. Woronzoff-Dashkoff, "Disguise and Gender in Princess Dashkova's *Memoirs.* "

22   For information on expectations of women in eighteenth-century Russia, see Bisha, "The Promise of Patriarchy."

23   Heldt points this out in the case of Diderot. See Heldt, 73.

24   Catherine I (1725–1727); Anna (1730–1740); Elizaveta (1741–1761); Catherine II (1762–1796).

25   Exceptions include: Bisha, "The Promise of Patriarchy"; Griffiths, "Catherine II and the Problem of Female Sovereignty"; Meehan-Waters, "Catherine the Great and the Problem of Female Rule"; Madariaga, *Russia in the Age of Catherine the Great;* and Norton, "Historical Assessments of Russia's Eighteenth-Century Female Monarchs."

26   In separate works, David Griffiths and Barbara T. Norton convincingly refute Brenda Meehan-Waters's arguments that the issue of gender was not, in fact, significant in the eighteenth century. See Griffiths, Norton.

27   I have put "East" and "West" in quotation marks throughout this essay for two reasons: both as a reminder that these terms are dependent on one's location and one's point of view (Asia is not East if one is in Asia) and because these terms carry a range of associations for many people; they are culturally marked and mean much more than geographical location.

28   Bisha, 1.

29   Bisha, 36.

30   Although there is a lively debate among historians about the intentions and implications of Peter I's having his second wife, Catherine I, crowned in 1725 and his declaration that the ruler could name any successor, it appears that by so doing he made it possible for women to rule.

31   See Todd, *Women's Friendship in Literature,* especially the introduction, conclusion, and chapter 7; Faderman, *Odd Girls and Twilight Lovers;* Heilbrun, "Vera Brittain's *Testament of Experience* " and "Winifred Holtby" in *Hamlet's Mother and Other Essays* and her *Writing a Woman's Life;* Woolf, *A Room of One's Own,* 86–89.

32   Bisha, 52.

33   See, for example, the selection of Catherine II's letters translated into English in Bradford, II: 63–112.

34   As Madariaga suggests, Catherine may have had other reasons for appointing Dash-

kova Director of the Academy of Sciences. In a letter to Grimm (29 April 1783), Catherine indicates that she appointed Dashkova to head the Academy of Sciences hoping that this would keep Dashkova too busy to get involved with other areas of court life. Cited in Madariaga, 535, 648. I do not think this detracts from my argument, for, in addition to the evidence of mutual respect seen in their correspondence, if Catherine had not valued Dashkova's intellect, it is unlikely that she would have entrusted the leadership of both Academies to her.

35 See Wachtel, *An Obsession with History* for a perceptive discussion of Kniazhnin's play and Catherine's reaction to its publication (19–36). Wachtel argues convincingly that Catherine's exaggerated response was due more to literary jealousy than to fear of political insurrection.

36 Bradford, II: 343.

37 Fitzlyon, 288; Bradford, II: 143–47; 148–49; Wilmot, 159.

38 Bradford, II: 155–56 (letter to Mrs. Hamilton, undated).

39 Dashkova also briefly mentions a third time when the two women shared a bed: "We broke our journey at Prince Kurakin's country house, which had only one bed and again we had to share it."

40 On female friendship, see note 31 above. On homoeroticism and female friendship, see Faderman, *Surpassing the Love of Men;* or Castle, *The Apparitional Lesbian.* Very little research has been done on either female friendship or homoeroticism in the Russian context, especially concerning the eighteenth century. For lesbian relationships in and after the Silver Age, see Burgin's works and Forrester, "Wooing the Other Woman."

41 By "erotic," I mean intense emotion with a potentially sexual or sensual expression. Faderman's comments about English- and Frenchwomen in the eighteenth century are suggestive for the Russian context. She notes that given societal norms about female sexuality, "it probably occurred to few of them [upper- and middle-class women] that the intense emotion they felt for each other could be expressed in sexual terms—but that emotion had all the manifestations of Eros without a genital component" (*Surpassing,* 90). It is, of course, finally impossible to know whether one person's feelings for another were erotic unless there is direct evidence, but both Faderman (*Surpassing*) and Castle make convincing cases (along very different lines) for why it is important to consider Eros as a component of same-sex relationships in earlier periods.

42 Judith Vowles argues that as early as the eighteenth century, visitors from the "West" tended to sexualize Russian behavior not considered sexual by Russians at the time. See Vowles, "Marriage à la russe."

43 See, for example, Fitzlyon's introduction to *The Memoirs of Princess Dashkova,* 12; Heldt, 69; Hyde, *The Empress Catherine and Princess Dashkov,* 60.

44 Although this is probably coincidental, it is curious that the Russian word means "transfiguration," as in the New Testament event, and the root of the word means "transformation." This seems peculiarly appropriate for two women, dressed not only in men's clothes, but in military uniform, thus reversing traditional male/female roles, something they each go on to do in more substantial ways.

45 Heldt, 69.

46   See A. Woronzoff-Dashkoff, "Disguise and Gender in Princess Dashkova's *Memoirs*," 74.

47   Wilmot, 201.

48   Ogarkov, 78.

49   See pp. 280–281 and Martha Wilmot's "Personal Narrative of the Editor" (to Lord Glenbervie) in Bradford, II: 239–40.

50   Martha's sister, Catherine, also stayed with Dashkova; she arrived in 1805 and left in 1807.

51   Heldt, 66–67.

52   The Wilmot sisters' description of their time in Russia is fascinating for what it reveals about differences in the position of Russian and British women and in the customs of the two cultures. See Wilmot and Bradford. Judith Vowles also discusses these (and other) documents in "Marriage à la russe."

53   This version of the *Memoirs* was highly edited. For information on specific omissions and rearranging of material, see the Afterword to the present edition and A. Woronzoff-Dashkoff, "Additions and Notes in Princess Dashkova's *Mon histoire.*"

54   For insightful perspectives on how Russians have defined themselves against both "East" and "West" see Hokanson, "Empire of the Imagination: Orientalism and the Construction of Russian National Identity in Pushkin, Marlinskii, Lermontov, and Tolstoi" and her "Pushkin's Invention of the Caucasus." On a related topic, see also Edward Said, *Orientalism;* although Said refers to Russia only in passing, his discussion of the "Western" construction of the "Orient" is suggestive for the Russian case.

55   See, for example, Michel Foucault, *The Archeology of Knowledge and the Discourse of Language* (especially 50–55); Paul de Man, *Allegories of Reading.*

56   Labzina may have written her memoirs in Russian, rather than in French, because she occupied a lower social position than Dashkova or Dolgorukaia and / or because she grew up in Siberia, and so, far away from St. Petersburg or Moscow, where western, and particularly French, influence was greater than in the outlying districts. But the Princess Dolgorukaia, who, like Labzina, wrote in Russian, resembled Dashkova in that she was of the upper aristocracy, and grew up in a major city (Dolgorukaia probably grew up in Moscow; Dashkova in Petersburg). See *The Memoirs of Princess Natal'ja Borisovna Dolgorukaja,* a bilingual edition (Russian and English) edited and translated by Charles Townsend; and Labzina, *Vospominaniia.*

57   Herzen, *My Past and Thoughts,* 67.

58   I do not mean to suggest that "Western" identity is less complicated than "non-Western"—simply that the complications are different.

59   In *Terrible Perfection,* Heldt contends that autobiography and lyric poetry are the two main ways that women participated in the Russian literary tradition. While I think that women's prose had much more influence and interest than Heldt implies, it is true that autobiographical writings and/including lyric poetry occupy a prominent position in the writings of Russian women.

60   The exceptions are Jane Marcus, "Invisible Mediocrity" in Benstock, ed., *The Private Self* and Mary Zirin's translation of Nadezhda Durova's "My Childhood Years" (plus brief introductory article) which appears in *The Female Autograph,* edited by

Domna C. Stanton. Among the other studies I have in mind are Smith, *A Poetics of Woman's Autobiography;* Brodzki and Schenck, ed., *Life/Lines;* Lionnet, *Autobiographical Voices;* Smith and Watson, ed., *De/Colonizing the Subject.*

61 Beth Holmgren makes related points in "For the Good of the Cause: Russian Women's Autobiography in the Twentieth Century." Unfortunately, her arguments could not be incorporated here as her essay was published after mine had gone to press.

62 See, for example, Jelinek, ed., *Women's Autobiography,* especially Jelinek's introduction; Mason, "The Other Voice: Autobiographies of Women Writers," in Olney, ed., *Autobiography;* Smith, *A Poetics of Woman's Autobiography.* Heilbrun's *Writing a Woman's Life* also concentrates mainly on North American and Western European traditions.

63 Jelinek, 7.

64 See Sommer in Brodzki and Schenck; Gunn in Smith and Watson. Again, these arguments are specific to certain classes and time periods: Huda Shuraawi, an Egyptian feminist (1879–1947), for example, does not speak for her people in the way Gunn describes late twentieth-century Palestinian activist Leila Khaled as doing. I do not mean here to blur national distinctions between Palestinians and Egyptians, but rather to point to the differences between women who live in the "Third World."

65 Sommer, 111.

66 I am grateful to Stephanie Sandler for raising these issues and for helping me to formulate and clarify my thinking about female identity and autobiographical writings across cultures.

67 In a recent essay, Linda Peterson, in discussing autobiographical writings of English women similarly argues that these do not comprise a single distinct tradition. See Peterson, "Institutionalizing Women's Autobiography: Nineteenth-Century Editors and the Shaping of an Autobiographical Tradition."

68 See, for example, Catherine II's memoirs. The English edition is *The Memoirs of Catherine the Great,* Dominique Maroger, ed.

69 Examples include Sofiia Kovalevskaia's *Vospominaniia* (translated into English as *A Russian Childhood*) and Lidiia Chukovskaia's *Pamiati detstva* (English title: *To the Memory of Childhood*).

70 Andrew Wachtel defines the pseudo-autobiography as "a first-person retrospective narrative based on autobiographical material in which the author and the protagonist are not the same person" (Wachtel, *The Battle for Childhood,* 3). Wachtel's model focuses on boyhoods rather than girlhoods, and there are significant differences in the pseudo-autobiographies of girls and boys in nineteenth-century Russia (cf. Panaeva's *Semeistvo Tal'nikovykh* [*The Tal'nykov Family*] and Tur's *Semeistvo Shalonskikh* [*The Shalonskii Family*]). See also Mary Zirin's discussion of girlhoods, "Butterflies with Broken Wings?—Early Autobiographical Depictions of Girlhood in Russia," in Liljeström, Mäntysaari, Rosenholm, ed., *Gender Restructuring in Russian Studies,* 255–66.

71 See, for example, A. Ia. Panaeva, *Vospominaniia* and N. S. Sokhanskaia, *Avtobiografiia.*

72 Marina Tsvetaeva, "Otets i ego muzei" ("Father and His Museum"); "Dom u starogo Pimena," ("The House at Old Pimen's"); "Mat' i muzyka" ("Mother and Music"); "Chert" ("The Devil") in J. Marin King's translations of these works, *Marina Tsvetaeva, A Captive Spirit: Selected Prose.*

73   See, for example, the memoirs of Labzina, Dolgorukaia, Durova.

74   See, for example, Evgeniia Ginzburg, *Journey into the Whirlwind* and *Within the Whirlwind* and Irina Ratushinskaia's *Grey is the Colour of Hope.*

75   The writings of Anna Dostoevskaia, Nadezhda Mandelstam, and Anna Larina ostensibly focus on their famous husbands (the husbands of the first two were writers, the latter was married to Nikolai Bukharin, the Bolshevik leader and theoretician who was arrested and shot in 1938 after a show trial).

76   Holmgren, *Women's Works in Stalin's Time.*

77   For recent illuminating discussions of essentialism, see Diana Fuss, *Essentially Speaking: Feminism, Nature and Difference* and Judith Grant, *Fundamental Feminism: Contesting the Core Concepts of Feminist Theory.*

78   Amy Kaminsky discusses some of the perils and possibilities of cross-cultural feminist scholarship in "Issues for an International Literary Criticism."

THE VORONTSOV FAMILY

Illarion (1674–1750)=Anna Maslova (168?–1740)

Roman (1707–83)
=Marfa Surmina
(1718–45)

Praskovia
=Sergei Tatishchev
and issue

Daria (1713–65)
=Petr Khrushchev

Mikhail (1714–67)
(Grand Chancellor)
=Anna Skavronskaia
(1723–75)

Ivan (1719–89)
=Mariia Volynskaia
(1725–93)

Pelageia (1721–57)
=Aleksandr
Narbekov

Mariia
(1737–17??)
=Petr Aleks-
androvich
Buturlin
(1734–87)
and issue

Elizaveta
(1739–92)
=Aleksandr
Polianskii

Aleksandr
(1741–1805)
(Imperial
Chancellor)

Ekaterina
(1743–1810)
=Mikhail
Dashkov
(1736–64)

Simon
(1744–1832)
=Ekaterina
Seniavina
(d. 1784)

Anna
(1743–69)
=Aleksandr
Stroganov
(1734–1811)
no issue

Artem
(1748–89)
=Praskovia
Kvashnina-
Samarina
and issue
(daughters)

Anna
(1750–1807)
=Vasilii
Naryshkin
(1740–1800)
and issue

Illarion
(1760–91)
=Irina
Ismailova
(1768–1848)

Anna
=Baron
d'Hoggier

Anastasiia
(1760–1831)
=Brig.
Shcherbinin
no issue

Mikhail
(1761–62)

Pavel
(1763–1807)
=Anna
Alferova
(1773–1810)
no issue

Mikhail
(1782–1856)

Ekaterina
(1783–1856)
=George
11th Earl of Pembroke
(1759–1827)
and issue

Aleksandr

Ivan Vorontsov-
Dashkov
(1790–1854)
=Aleksandra
Naryshkina
(1817–56)
and issue

THE DASHKOVS, PANINS, KURAKINS, AND REPNINS

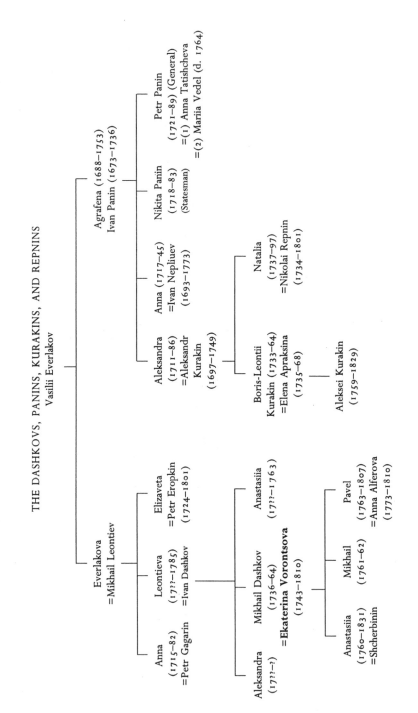

THE MEMOIRS
PART I

CHAPTER I

❧❀❧

I was born in St. Petersburg in the year 1744.[1] The Empress Elizaveta had just returned from Moscow where she had been for her coronation. She held me at the baptismal font, while the Grand Duke, known afterward under the name of Emperor Peter III, was my godfather. This honor was not granted by the Empress because of her family connection with my uncle the Grand Chancellor,[2] who was married to Her Majesty's first cousin,[3] rather it was due to her friendship with my mother[4] who with the greatest tact, zeal, and, I may say, generosity, supplied the Empress—then still a Princess living in straitened circumstances at the Court of the Empress Anna—with whatever was necessary for her household and her dresses of which she was very fond.[5] I had the misfortune to lose my mother when only two years old, and it was entirely through friends and people who still admired her and were grateful to her that I later learned to know her fine qualities, her generosity, and her kindness.

At the time of that sad event I was living with my grandmother (my mother's mother) on one of her beautiful estates, and it was only when I was four years of age that she could be prevailed upon to take me back to St. Petersburg and let me have a rather different upbringing.

A few months later, the Grand Chancellor, who was my father's eldest brother, removed me from my grandmother's loving care and made me share in the education of his only daughter, who afterward became Count-

---

[1] This must be a slip of the pen. Princess Dashkova was born in 1743.—K. F.

[2] See Index under Vorontsov, Mikhail.—K. F.

[3] See Index under Vorontsova, Anna.—K. F.

[4] See Index under Vorontsova, Marfa.—K. F.

[5] So fond, indeed, that she left 15,000 dresses at the time of her death.—K. F.

ess Stroganova.[6] The same room, the same masters, even dresses cut from the same cloth, all, in fact, should have made us into two perfectly similar individuals; and yet never have two people been so different at all the various periods of their lives. (Those who claim to know all about education, please note; also those who want to impose their ideas and their theories in connection with a subject so precious and so decisive for human happiness, and yet so little known, because a single brain cannot comprehend it in its entirety with all its numerous ramifications.)

I shall not speak of my family. Its ancient lineage and the many brilliant services of my ancestors have made the name of the Counts Vorontsov as famous as anyone more attached than I am to importance of birth could possibly desire. My father, Count Roman, the Chancellor's second brother, was young and liked to enjoy life. He, therefore, paid scant attention to his children, and was delighted when my uncle, in grateful memory of my late mother as much as out of friendship for him, assumed the responsibility for my upbringing. My two sisters—Countess Maria, later Countess Buturlina, and Countess Elizaveta, later Madame Polianskaia—were taken care of by the Empress and lived at the Court, having been appointed maids-of-honor while they were still children. My elder brother, Count Aleksandr, was the only one of us to have made his home with my father, and the only one I knew from childhood. I often saw him, and my fondness for him ripened into a friendship and trust which he never betrayed. My younger brother[7] lived with my grandfather in the country, but even when he came to live in town I saw him as rarely as I saw my sisters. I mention this circumstance because it later had some influence on my character.

My uncle spared nothing to give us the best masters, and according to the ideas of the time we received the very best education; for we had a perfect knowledge of four languages, particularly French; we danced well and drew a little; a state councilor taught us Italian and Mr. Bekhteev gave us Russian lessons whenever we felt like it; we were attractive to look at and our manners were ladylike. Everyone had to agree that our education left nothing to be desired.

And yet, what was done for the improvement of our hearts and minds? Nothing at all. My uncle had no time, and my aunt had neither the ability

---

[6] Princess Dashkova went to live with her uncle in 1750 when she was seven years old, not four.—K. F.

[7] See Index under Vorontsov, Simon.—K. F.

nor the inclination. I had a proud nature, allied in some way to a sensitive and inordinately affectionate character. Ever since I was a child I craved for affection, I wanted the sympathy of those I loved, and when at the age of thirteen I began to suspect that I was receiving neither, I was overcome by a feeling of loneliness. It was then I had an attack of measles, and that together with my peculiar character completed my education and made me what I am.

An order-in-council forbade all communication with the Court to families in whose houses there were cases of skin diseases such as small-pox or measles, for fear of infecting the Grand Duke (later Emperor) Pavel. At the first symptoms of measles I was, therefore, taken to the country, ten miles from Petersburg, accompanied by a German lady and by a major's wife, as well as by my maids; but this was not enough for my sensitive nature and for my loving heart (for I did not like those two ladies). Neither could it satisfy my ideas of happiness, which demanded the presence round me of affectionate friends and relations.

Measles principally affected my eyes; I was not able to do any reading, of which I was, I may say, passionately fond. I sat in deep dejection all day and brooded over myself and my family. And thus, from being lively, gay, mischievous even, I became serious-minded and studious, spoke little and then only when sure of my facts.

As soon as my illness was over I threw myself into reading. Bayle, Montesquieu, Voltaire, and Boileau were my favourite authors; I succeeded in proving to myself that time never drags even if one is alone and I tried to acquire all the resources that are bestowed by courage, firmness, and inner repose. My brother Aleksandr had gone to Paris and I thus had no one on whose affection I could rely to salve the wounds inflicted by the indifference that I perceived all around me. Reading soothed me and made me happy, music I enjoyed and it moved me, but once outside my own room I became listless. The sleepless nights caused by reading and my general mood gave me an appearance of ill-health which worried my worthy uncle and even the Empress Elizaveta. She ordered her doctor Boerhaave to give me treatment, which he did with unfailing zeal. After thoroughly studying and examining me for what I was thought to have, namely, a general decline, he declared that physically I was as well as anyone could wish, and that it was probably something weighing on my mind that reacted on my physical well-being. Thereupon I was subjected to innumerable questions. Most of them, however, were dictated neither by feeling nor by any interest for me and thus could not draw a sincere confession from me, a confession which, in any case, would have presented nothing but an incoherent portrayal of my pride, of my wounded sensibility, of my resolve to became all I could be by my own efforts, and of my presumptuous attempt to be self-sufficient. It could even be that anything I said would be interpreted as a reproach. I therefore decided to say nothing of what absorbed me in my heart of hearts; nerves and headaches were the only reason I gave for the sickly looks everyone tried to see in me. And in the meantime my mind was developing and gradually attaining maturity. The following year, on rereading Helvetius's book *On the Understanding* I was struck with the thought that unless it were followed by a second volume better adapted to the understanding of most men, enumerating a theory more applicable to the circumstances of the time and generally accepted notions, its principles would merely serve to destroy the harmony and break the link uniting the several parts which both promote and constitute civilized society. I cite this reflection of mine because it gave me later much real satisfaction.

Politics have always interested me, ever since my earliest years. When still a child, I obtained my uncle's permission to rummage among the papers which were in his safekeeping as Chancellor, in search of treaties, negotiations, etc., with other Courts. I found curious and interesting things among them. I remember two, made to strike the imagination of a child and give food for thought even to more mature minds. One was a letter from a Shah of Persia, addressed to Catherine I, wife of Peter I, on the occasion of her accession to the throne. After a few compliments, he wrote more or less as follows: "I hope, my well-beloved sister, that God has not given you a love for strong drink. I, the writer of this letter, have eyes like rubies, a nose like a carbuncle and cheeks like flaming fire, and am compelled by this unfortunate propensity to pass my days as well as my nights groaning on a bed of pain." The Empress's fairly well known taste for vodka lends even more point to this letter.

And here is another story. An embassy was sent to China—I forget under whose reign—to offer congratulations to an Emperor on his accession to the Chinese throne. The Russian ambassadors were not received any too well and came back ill-pleased with their mission. The Government, however, deeming it bad policy to take note of the contempt of the Chinese monarch, sent other persons with letters thanking his Chinese Majesty for the flattering reception of its ambassadors and making proposals for a trade agreement. His Chinese Majesty's answer was this: "You are very absurd to take pride in our reception of your ambassadors.

Do you not know that when we ride on horseback in our streets there is not a *beggar* but has the right to look at us?"

Mr. Shuvalov, the favorite of the Empress Elizaveta, had pretensions to being a Maecenas and ordered for himself all books that appeared in France. He learned from persons whom he flattered in order to rise in popular esteem that I was passionately fond of reading, and when some of my judgments and remarks were repeated to him he offered to act as my book agent and to obtain for me all the literary novelties which might appear. I was delighted, particularly the following year when after my marriage we left for Moscow, where at that time bookshops had nothing but well-known works, the best of which I already had in my own little library of nine hundred volumes. That year I acquired the *Encyclopaedia* and Morelli's dictionary and never would the finest piece of jewelry have given me as much pleasure. Thus it was that all my pocket money was spent on the purchase of books.

All the strangers, artists, and men of letters, as well as the Ministers of foreign Courts residing in Petersburg who visited my uncle almost daily, were tormented by my relentless curiosity. I questioned them on their respective countries, their forms of government, and the comparisons which I made to my own country often made me ardently desire to travel. I did not think that I might one day have enough courage to do so. I believed, on the contrary, that my sensibility and weak nerves would ruin my life by making it impossible for me to bear the pain of disappointment and wounded pride. I imagined that I already was all that I should ever be, and if I could have been told then all that I would have to suffer I would have prayed for my life to end, for I was beginning to have the foreboding that I would not be happy in this world.

My fondness for my brother Count Aleksandr made a very regular correspondent out of me. I wrote to him twice a month and I gave him town, Court, and my personal news. I wanted to arouse his interest and give him pleasure, and whether my later style of writing has been good or bad I owe it to the kind of journals I wrote for a beloved brother.

The same winter, 1759, the Grand Duke, known afterward under the name of Peter III, and the Grand Duchess, later called—and with truth—Catherine the Great, came to have supper and spend the evening with us. The rather prejudiced description which strangers had given her of me and her conviction that I spent almost all my time studying and reading, earned me her esteem, which subsequently had great effect on the whole of my life, and put me on a pedestal on which I never thought I should find myself. I could argue, perhaps, that as there were no other two women at the time, apart from the Grand Duchess and myself, who did any serious reading, we were mutually drawn toward each other; and the charm, which she knew how to exert whenever she wanted to win over anyone, was too powerful for an artless little girl like myself, who was not even fifteen, to refuse her the gift of my heart for evermore. And yet she had a powerful rival for the affections of my heart, in the person of Prince Dashkov to whom I was already betrothed. But soon he came to share my opinion of her, and all rivalry ceased.

The Grand Duchess was exceedingly kind to him, and I found her conversation delightful. She was high-minded in her ideas and, I perceived, well informed on a variety of subjects. To me she appeared the favored child of nature, and she forthwith captured my heart and mind and inspired me with enthusiastic devotion. She spoke to almost no one but me during the whole of that long evening; but it did not seem long to me, and it was the initial cause of a number of events of which I shall speak later.

However, I must now return to my narrative where I left it, in the July and August that preceded that evening. My uncle as well as my aunt and my cousin were in Peterhof and Tsarskoe Selo together with the Empress. An indisposition, as well as my taste for study and a quiet life, kept me back in town. I went out occasionally to the Italian Opera and visited precisely two houses—that of Princess Golitsyna, who was very fond of me, as was her husband, a very intelligent old man of sixty-five; and that of Madame Samarina, whose husband was attached to my uncle's house and visited us literally every day. It so happened that Madame Samarina was ill one day, and I went to have supper and spend the evening with her. On arrival in her house I dismissed my carriage and gave orders for it to be back at eleven o'clock together with my maid to fetch me. It was a beautiful night, and after supper Madame Samarina's sister suggested that as their street was little frequented I should send my carriage forward to wait for me at the end of it, while she would walk up with me. I agreed, as I felt I had to have some exercise. We had hardly taken a couple of steps before I saw a man—who appeared to me a giant—approaching us from a side street. I was startled, and he was quite close to us when I asked who he was. She named Prince Dashkov, whom I had never seen before. As the Samarins knew him, he entered into conversation with her and accompanied us in our walk. He only occasionally addressed himself to me, and when he did so it was with a shy politeness which appealed to me. I have often been inclined since to attribute this meeting and the favourable impression we could not help creating on each other to a special and unavoidable dispensation of Providence. For had Prince Dashkov's name been mentioned at home, where he was not received, I would have heard unfavourable comments about him, and details of a certain intrigue would have come to my knowledge which would have destroyed all thought of uniting our two lives. I do not know what he had heard about me before he met me, but it is certain that an intrigue he had had with a very near relative of mine whose name I cannot divulge, and the wrongs both apparent and real of which he was guilty toward her, convinced him that he must not entertain either thought, desire, or even hope of ever making me his own. Never, it seemed, could our union occur; but heaven willed otherwise, and nothing was able to prevent our hearts from irrevocably giving themselves to each other. My family made no objection, and the Princess, his mother, who ardently wished to see him settle down as a family man, and was for ever imploring him to do so, was delighted when she knew that he was about to marry, even though he had rejected her choice of a wife. She heartily approved of his own choice and was pleased with the connection he was forming with our family. As soon as the Prince felt that nothing but our union could make him happy, and had obtained my permission to speak to my family, he requested Prince Golitsyn next time he went to Peterhof, to plead his cause with my uncle and my father, asking them, at the same time, to keep it secret until he had had time to make the journey to Moscow to obtain his mother's consent and blessing for our marriage.

One day, shortly before the Prince's departure, Her Majesty paid a visit to the Italian Opera where she sat in her box—protected by a grille—next to ours. She was accompanied only by my uncle and Mr. Shuvalov. As she proposed to have supper after the opera at my uncle's house, I stayed at home in order to receive her. The Prince was with me. When the Empress arrived she treated us both with great kindness, and like a true godmother she called us into another room and told us that she was aware of our secret. She praised the Prince for the consideration and dutiful respect he showed his mother, wished us all possible happiness, assured both of us of her abiding interest in our fate, and finally informed the Prince that she would command Field-Marshal Count Buturlin to grant him leave of absence for his journey to Moscow.

The tender, indeed bewitching, kindness that Her Majesty was pleased to show us affected me to such a degree that I could not conceal my emotion. The Empress tapped me gently on the shoulder, kissed my cheek and said:

"Compose yourself, my child, otherwise they might think I have been scolding you."

Never, never could I forget that scene which attached me still more to such a kind-hearted sovereign.

On his return from Moscow the Prince was introduced to all my family, and it was only the very grave and very dangerous illness of my aunt, the wife of the Grand Chancellor, that deferred our marriage until the month of February. Then a relapse of her fever compelled my aunt to keep to her bed, so that we had a very quiet wedding, and it was only in May, when my aunt's health gave us no more cause for alarm, that we could leave for Moscow.

Here a new world opened for me, and a new way of life which intimidated me all the more as I could find in it nothing in common with anything to which I was accustomed. I spoke Russian badly and my mother-in-law spoke no other language, which added to my embarrassment. My husband's family consisted mostly of elderly people, and though they showed me great indulgence on account of their love for him—for they had wanted him to marry because he was the last Prince Dashkov—I could see I appeared a stranger to them and they all wished I were more of a Muscovite. I therefore resolved to apply myself to the study of my native tongue, and soon my progress won the approbation of those worthy people. Throughout their lives I had for them the highest regard and affection, which they repaid with true and sincere friendship even after my husband's death, when the ties that bound us to each other could by any other girl of twenty have been considered as dissolved.

CHAPTER II

⚜

My daughter was born on 21 February the year following our marriage, and in May we accompanied my mother-in-law to Troitskoe. My
harpsichord and library made time fly as if on wings. In July my husband
and I made an excursion to his estate in Orel; I was again pregnant, but
the Prince took so many precautions during the journey that I did not
suffer the least inconvenience. We came back to Moscow toward the end
of his leave, and I wrote to my father in Petersburg asking him to exert
his influence to have it extended.

The Empress Elizaveta was weak and ailing, all her courtiers were beginning to turn their attention to her successor, and it was this, I think,
that gave the Grand Duke a more effective command of the Preobrazhenskii Guards whose Colonel-in-Chief he was. My husband was a junior
captain in that regiment, and his application for another five months'
extension of leave (to cover the time of my confinement) had to be made
to the Grand Duke. The latter thought, perhaps, that in refusing this request unless Prince Dashkov came to Petersburg for a fortnight, he was
being particularly gracious. My father judged it to be a friendly gesture,
and insisted on my husband making the journey. I was disconsolate, and
the idea of our separation distressed me so much that I could no longer
enjoy my happiness while I still had my husband with me. I anticipated
the sorrow of his absence and the pain of our farewells, and I think my
health suffered in consequence. At last, on 8 June, my husband left, and I
was so overwhelmed with grief that I succumbed to fever and delirium.
But I think this was due to nerves and mental agitation rather than to
an organic disease, and I probably owe much to my obstinate refusal to
take any of the doctors' prescriptions. At the end of a few days, illness

was succeeded by depression. I wept, and my tears were a relief to heart
and nerves. But they made me too weak to hold a pen and write to my
husband as I should have liked to do all day and all night. My youngest
sister-in-law looked after me tenderly, but this, too, made it difficult for
me to write. I was only seventeen and I loved my husband passionately;
this explains my emotions at the time.

Their Imperial Highnesses were most kind to my husband and made
him participate in sledge parties they had in Oranienbaum. Unfortunately
he caught a bad chill as a result, and fell ill of the quinsy, but knowing
how alarmed his mother and wife would be if he did not arrive on the
day appointed, he paid no regard to his sickness and left Petersburg with
an inflammation of the throat. Throughout the journey he never left the
coach except to sip some tea, but when he finally reached the gates of
Moscow he found his voice was gone and he was unable to utter a word.
He knew the terrible impression his appearance in that state of health
would make on both mother and wife, as both of us were apt to lose
our heads at the slightest mishap that might befall him. He therefore explained to his valet, in sign language, that he wanted to be driven round
to his aunt, Madame Novosiltseva, his mother's sister, where he would
gargle so as to be able to say a few words on arrival home. His aunt,
however, seeing what state he was in, made him go to bed, and sent for a
doctor. To avoid arousing our suspicions the post-horses were retained in
order to drive him up to our house the following morning, so as to give
the impression that he had not stopped anywhere else on the way. For on
finding that the Prince was beginning to sweat, the doctor ordered him
to stay in bed till the following morning. It was 1 February, and the frost
was moderate, but it was advisable not to expose the patient to more
cold.

In the meantime, events were taking place in our house which could
have had very serious consequences. My maid, who was my age and
infinitely thoughtless, knew that I had started my labor pains. My mother-
in-law and her sister, Princess Gagarina, who had been present at my first
confinement, were sitting in my room together with the midwife. I went
into the privy next door for a moment, and my maid took advantage of
this to tell me that the Prince had arrived. I uttered a cry which fortunately was not heard by my mother-in-law. The maid implored me to say
nothing, because the Prince did not want us to be told that he had arrived
in Moscow, but was staying at his aunt's instead of coming home. To form
any conception of the effect that my maid's rash confidence produced on

me it must be remembered that I was a hot-headed and impetuous girl of
seventeen, desperately in love, and with no idea of happiness apart from
loving and being loved, regarding riches and pomp as burdens of no use
for a quiet enjoyment of felicity.

I forced myself to appear as calm and composed as I possibly could as
I went back to the Princess and told her that I was no longer in pain, and
that apparently what I had taken to be the beginning of labor was merely
colic. I added that I should probably be in labor for over twenty hours,
as I had been the first time, and that I therefore begged her and my dear
aunt to go and rest in their own rooms. I promised that should the right
symptoms return I should take the liberty of letting them know and of
soliciting their presence.

As soon as they had left I asked the midwife to follow me. Convinced
that I was going to give birth in a few hours' time, she stared at me in
wide-eyed amazement as if I had gone off my head, and said in her Silesian
dialect that she would never encourage such folly or answer before God
for the death of an innocent girl. Her refusal threw me into despair; I was
embarrassed and my voice shook as I replied that I only wanted to go a
very short distance to see my husband who must be lying ill or wounded
since he had not come back to his own house, and that if she did not wish
to accompany me I was determined to go by myself.

"And we shall have to go on foot," I added.

"Good heavens!" she cried. "That is even worse!"

"It is the only way to do it," I said. "My mother-in-law's windows
give out on to the courtyard, and she would hear the sound of the horse
and sledge. She would probably die of fright on seeing me go out, and
quite apart from having no desire to kill her, I am afraid she might try to
stop me."

At last the midwife took pity on me and agreed to accompany me. We
took with us an old servant employed to read prayers in my mother-in-
law's house, and together they supported me under the arms as we started
to go down the stairs. But I had hardly descended a few steps before the
pains started once more. The midwife then tried to drag me up again,
while I resisted and leant on her as heavily as I could in order to slide
down. In the end we reached the bottom of the stairs with a few halts on
the way; we crossed the street, but my pains began and subsided at least
five times before we reached Madame Novosiltseva's house. I cannot now
understand how I was able to negotiate the fairly long staircase of her
house. Heaven must have been on my side, for I succeeded in reaching

the room where my husband was lying. But when I saw how pale he was I fainted away, and it was thus that I was carried out of the house, put on a bed which had been placed on an ordinary sledge and then, on arrival back at our house, carried upstairs to my room by the midwife, the good old man and three of Madame Novosiltseva's servants, so that my mother-in-law never heard anything. The violence of my labor pains brought me back to life and I sent for my mother-in-law who had given orders to be woken up in such an emergency.

It was eleven o'clock at night when she and her sister came, and in less than an hour I gave birth to a son who afterward received the name of Mikhail. My mother-in-law left my bedside for a moment, and I took advantage of this to tell my maid to despatch the good old man to my husband with the news of my happy delivery of a son.

The Prince often made me shudder with horror at his account of my appearance at his bedside together with the midwife and the old man. He had been flattering himself that no one in our house knew about his arrival, and when he saw me faint, the fright he had in discovering that I was in labor made him furious that his secret had not been kept. He told me how he had rushed out of bed in order to follow me, how his aunt had run about the room wringing her hands, how it was only after she had told him that his mother was sleeping and knew nothing of his arrival that he had given up his intention, and how when he saw the old man, for no reason at all he had jumped out of bed. Soon his joy was as unbounded as had been his despair, he threw his arms around the old servant and kissed him, he gave him his purse, he danced, he cried, and did not want to go back to bed. He asked for a priest to come and take a thanksgiving service for my successful delivery. And his aunt and all her household were in an uproar of joy all night thanks to my escapade.

At six o'clock in the morning, which was the time at which his mother went to church for early Mass, the post-horses were harnessed back to his carriage and in this way he returned home. On seeing his carriage being driven into the courtyard my mother-in-law came out to meet him. She was at the top of the stairs when she noticed his pallor and his muffled throat and threw herself down the steps. Another tragedy would have occurred if my husband had not had the agility and strength to catch her in his arms. In fact, his mother's and his wife's exaggerated love caused him a great deal of unpleasantness that day.

He carried his mother into our room instead of hers, and was thus able to be with me. Our joy was restrained by our fears for each other's health, but at the same time it gave us strength.

As it is customary for friends and relatives to visit a young mother and child, my mother-in-law, for appearance's sake, had the Prince's bed made up in his dressing-room. It was next to my bedroom, and we suffered the tortures of Tantalus, for we could neither see nor speak to each other. I realized perfectly well that my husband was much more comfortable where he was, and as I did not have sufficient strength in me to get up and steal into his room for a moment, tears were my only solace. But we soon devised another. My mother-in-law had given me a kind old servant to look after me. We made her our Mercury, and no sooner would my mother-in-law leave my husband to go and have a rest than we would start writing the tenderest of notes to each other, and make the old servant take them 'round. At night, while my husband was sleeping, I would write to him again, so that our kind Mercury could let him have a note from me whenever he awoke.

Such behavior was prompted by our inordinate love for each other, though persons more coldly wise (whom, personally, I should suspect of being devoid of heart and feeling) might call it childish. For the continual tears and the writing in the evening strained my eyes. However, looking back now on the forty sorrowful years that have passed since I had lost my adored husband, I can honestly say that I would do it again whatever the penalty.

After three days of this, my Mercury betrayed me—for my eyes' sake, it seems—to my mother-in-law who, fearing for my health, severely lectured me. She even threatened, though in a softened tone, to take away my pens and paper. Fortunately for all of us, the abscess my husband had in the throat burst, his fever left him, and he was allowed to visit me.

My own recovery was slow to get under way, but I was only seventeen, and as soon as I regained a little strength my health improved by leaps and bounds.

CHAPTER III
꧁✦꧂

We were due shortly to return to Petersburg and therefore did not go to the country. I was pleased at the prospect of staying in town again, seeing my own family and being no longer disconcerted, as I frequently was, by habits and customs which I sometimes encountered in certain houses and which so little resembled those I had been used to from childhood. Everything was so different to life in my uncle's house (which was furnished in the best and latest European style and could truly be called princely) that often I felt bewildered.[1]

10 June was finally fixed as the date for our departure from Moscow, but there were endless delays for various reasons, as when the Prince yielded to his mother's entreaties to postpone our journey by several days. All this took so much time that we did not arrive in Petersburg till 28 June. The same date twelve months later marked one of the most memorable and most glorious days in the history of my country.

But that year, it was merely delightful and happy, and I gazed with lively curiosity out of the carriage window. Petersburg appeared to me so beautiful, and I expected at every moment to see someone of my family; I was nearly in a fever by the time I reached the house the Prince had rented for us.

[1] The furniture in Vorontsov's house had belonged to Madame de Pompadour, who had grown tired of it and sold it to Louis XV. The King presented it to the Chancellor in the hope of encouraging his pro-French sympathies. The most magnificent of Vorontsov's residences was built in 1759 by the Italian architect Rastrelli in the style of so-called Russian classicism. Under Pavel I it became the headquarters of the Russian branch of the Maltese Order, and still later—from 1802 to the Revolution of 1917—it was used as a military school, known as His Imperial Majesty's Corps of Pages. It is now a museum.— K. F.

As soon as I had installed my daughter in a room next to mine, I went to visit my father and my uncle, but neither of them was in town. The following day my father told me that by the Empress's command all officers of the Preobrazhenskii Guards who had been invited by Their Imperial Highnesses to Oranienbaum should proceed there, together with their wives, and that we were among those the Grand Duke had named. The news saddened me, for I regarded with distaste the restraints of Court life and had no desire to leave my daughter. However, my father was kind enough to let us have his house between Petersburg and Oranienbaum and all my worries faded away.

We soon took possession of it and the following day went to pay our court to Their Imperial Highnesses. The Grand Duke said to me:

"Since you do not want to live here, you must come here every day and I expect you to spend more time with me than with the Grand Duchess!"

I said nothing, but resolved to take advantage of every pretext not to go to Oranienbaum every day, and whenever I had to go there to remain as much as possible in the company of the Grand Duchess, who gave me far greater proofs of her friendship and esteem than to any other ladies in Oranienbaum. The Grand Duke was quick to notice the friendship his wife bore me and the pleasure I had in being with her. Taking me aside one day, he made the following extraordinary remark to me, revealing both the simplicity of his mind and the goodness of his heart:

"My daughter," he said, addressing me thus because he was my godfather, "remember it is safer to live and deal with simpletons like us than with those great minds who squeeze all the juice out of a lemon and then throw it away."

I have often thought of this little speech afterward and discovered by pure chance the source which gave rise to it and put it into my godfather's head. But at the time I replied that I did not understand the meaning of those words and that His Imperial Highness should recollect that his august aunt, the Empress, had commanded that we should pay our court equally to the Grand Duchess and to him.

Here I must add, in justification to my sister, that she never claimed that I should pass more of my time with her and she never made any difficulties for me.[2] But the Grand Duke decided, from that moment on, as I had occasion to notice, that I was nothing but a little fool.

However, I was not always able to avoid going to the Grand Duke's entertainments. Sometimes they took place in camp where His Imperial

[2] Dashkova's sister, Elizaveta Vorontsova, was Peter III's mistress.—J. G.

Highness passed the time smoking with his generals; the smoke drifted out of his tent and thus inconvenienced us less than it would have in a closed room. I may add that those Holstein generals were either ex-Prussian warrant officers or sons of German shoemakers who had escaped from their families. Never, I think, was there anyone less fitted to hold that rank, except the Gatchina generals of Pavel I.[3]

The festivities always ended with a ball and a supper in the Grüne Salle, that is the Green Hall, the walls of which were decorated with pine and fir tree branches. In camp and at the Grand Duke's other festivities German was spoken in preference to other languages, and those who did not know German had at least to know the names and expressions in common use if they did not want to become objects of ridicule.

At other times the Grand Duke entertained his guests on one of his estates which had a house of modest dimensions, almost like a middle-class home. It did not have room for everyone and the company, which was, therefore, less numerous, whiled away the time after tea and punch playing campis, a silly game, but one of which His Imperial Highness was very fond.

What a difference I found in the way in which time was spent with the Grand Duchess! There wit, good taste, decorum, were the order of the day, and if Her Imperial Highness's friendship for me seemed to grow stronger every day, my husband and I, too, became increasingly attached to that remarkable woman—remarkable alike for her mind, her wide knowledge, and the boldness and originality of her ideas. She was permitted to visit Peterhof, where the Empress was residing, once a week to see her son, the Grand Duke Pavel. Her husband, who treated him with complete indifference, never bothered to come. Whenever she knew I was not at Oranienbaum, on her way back she used to stop her carriage opposite our house and send a message asking me to join her and pass the rest of the evening with her. If ever she did not come to Oranienbaum she wrote to me, and thus there were established between Her Imperial Highness and myself a correspondence and a mutual confidence which were the happiness of my life, for such was my devotion to her that apart from my husband and my children I would have sacrificed everything for her sake.

But our return to town brought with it a change in our established

[3] Officers of the "model army" trained by Pavel at his residence of Gatchina near St. Petersburg.—K. F.

habits. I no longer saw the Grand Duchess, and we had to rely entirely on little messages which we exchanged fairly frequently.

One day at a dinner for eighty persons given in the palace the Grand Duke spoke of a Mr. Chelishchev, ensign in the Horse Guards, who was carrying on an amorous intrigue with a Countess Gendrikova, cousin of the Empress Elizaveta. The Grand Duke, who had been drinking wine and who anyway had the mind of a drill-sergeant, remarked that Chelishchev deserved to have his head cut off as a lesson to other officers who might presume to make love to maids-of-honor and relatives of the Sovereign.

The sycophantic Holsteinians murmured and nodded in approval of the Grand Duke's words, but I said to him:

"Never, Your Imperial Highness, have I heard of mutual love being punished in so tyrannic a fashion or so terrible a fate being visited on a lover who is loved in return."

"You are a child," he replied, "and you do not understand that failure to inflict the death penalty whenever necessary is a weakness which produces insubordination and all kinds of disorders."

"But, Your Imperial Highness," I said, "you are speaking in front of people in whose hearts this subject must strike inexpressible terror, since no man has suffered the death penalty in this country within the lifetime of practically any of your guests, except that of your venerable generals."[4]

"That means nothing, I must insist," replied the Grand Duke amid total silence, as everyone was following our conversation; "in fact, that is precisely why disorder has grown and why there is no discipline and no subordination. I tell you," he added, "you are a child who cannot understand these things."

"I readily admit, Your Imperial Highness, that I do not understand all this, but what I know and feel is that Your Imperial Highness has forgotten that your aunt the Empress is still alive."

All eyes were turned on me. But for reply the Grand Duke merely put his tongue out at me, which was something he did even at priests in church. I was pleased, in a way, because this proved that he was not angry with me and it did not provoke me to further answers.

As among those present there were many officers of the Guards and of the Cadet Corps, ostensibly commanded by the Grand Duke, this conver-

---

[4] The death penalty was abolished in Russia by the Empress Elizaveta. The practical effect of this measure, however, was slighter than Princess Dashkova seems to suppose: police methods of questioning prisoners and the punishments to which criminals were subjected effectively took the place of an official death sentence.—K. F.

sation soon became known throughout Petersburg and earned trust and praise for me beyond my merits. The Grand Duchess herself mentioned it to me the following day, in a manner which was highly flattering. Personally, I attached no importance to it, for in my ignorance of the world in general and of Court life in particular, I did not know how dangerous it was, especially at Court, to do what I thought, was the duty of every honest soul: always to speak the truth. I did not know that even though the monarch may forgive you, the courtiers never can. However, it was due to this little occurrence and to a few others like it that several of my husband's fellow officers were quick to give me their confidence and that I gained the reputation of being sincere, firm, and patriotic.

The health of the Empress Elizaveta was declining day by day. I shared with all my heart the profound grief of my whole family and particularly my uncle, the Grand Chancellor, both because I was fond of the Empress who was also my godmother, and because my stay at Oranienbaum had opened my eyes to all that my country could expect from a Prince who was ignorant, narrow-minded, ill-disposed toward his people and priding himself on being always at the orders of the King of Prussia, to whom he referred, even when alone among his intimates, as "the King my master."

In the middle of December I fell ill and even stayed in bed for several days, but on learning on 20 December that the Empress had but a few more days to live, I put on my boots, wrapped myself up in furs and drove in my carriage to the wooden palace which the Empress and the Imperial family were then occupying on the Moika. I stopped the carriage at some distance from the palace and, ill as I was, went on foot to find the back stairs used by the servants of their Imperial Highnesses. I never knew before where those stairs were, but I wanted to use them that time in order to reach the Grand Duchess's apartments without being seen at such a late hour—it was midnight by then. Fortunately, the Grand Duchess's principal personal maid—Katerina Ivanovna—happened to be in the little entrance lobby and saved me from any fatal misadventures, for I did not know the place at all and might just as well have entered the rooms occupied by Peter III's valets as his wife's boudoir.

I made myself known to Katerina Ivanovna and said that I wanted to speak to the Grand Duchess.

"She is in bed," replied the maid.

"It does not matter," I said. "I must speak to her."

Thereupon, as I had already gained her friendship and confidence, she ushered me into a room while she went to announce my presence to Her Imperial Highness. The Grand Duchess was extremely surprised and could hardly believe Katerina Ivanovna, for she knew me to be ill and never expected me to come on such a bitterly cold night when all the exits and entrances of the palace were guarded or watched.

"Let her come up, for God's sake," she cried.

I went in and found the Grand Duchess in bed. She made me get into it and sit up while I warmed my feet, before she allowed me to speak. As soon as I came to a little and no longer felt so cold, she asked me:

"What brings you here, my dear Princess, at this hour and at such risk to your health, which you know to be precious to your husband and to me?"

"I can no longer," I replied, "endure the uncertainty of the dark clouds which are gathering 'round your head. For Heaven's sake, have confidence in me; I deserve it now and I hope to deserve it even more in the future. Tell me what your plan is; what do you intend doing to ensure your safety? The Empress has but a few days, perhaps only a few hours more to live— can you make use of me? I am yours to command—tell me what to do."

The Grand Duchess could not refrain from tears. She took my hand, pressed it to her heart and said:

"I am more grateful to you, my dear Princess, than I could possibly express, and it is with perfect truth and every confidence in you that I say to you now: I have formed no plan. I can undertake nothing and I must and shall meet bravely whatever may befall me. God is my only hope and I put my trust in Him."

"Well, then, Ma'am," I said, "your friends must act for you. For my part, I shall yield to none in zeal and in the sacrifices I am ready to make for you."

"For Heaven's sake, Princess, do not expose yourself to any dangers for my sake. Do not bring upon your head misfortunes which I shall always regret. Besides, what can one do?"

"All I can tell you now, Ma'am," I answered, "is that I shall do nothing to compromise you. I alone shall suffer if suffer I must. My devotion will never be a cause of pain or misfortune to you personally and you will have no reason to regret it."

The Grand Duchess would have continued, would have warned me against the zeal and enthusiasm and perhaps against the rashness and in-experience natural at the age of seventeen, but I interrupted her and said, as I kissed her hand:

"I cannot remain with you any longer without it being dangerous to both of us."

She threw herself into my arms and for several minutes we remained locked in close embrace. Then I jumped out of her bed, leaving her disturbed and upset, and had to muster all the courage I had to regain my carriage.

My husband's surprise when, on returning home, he failed to find his sick wife, can well be imagined. His worry, however, did not last long for I came back very soon after him. When I told him about my little adventure and explained my motives and my firm resolve to serve my country and save the Grand Duchess, I received his full approval as well as more praise than I deserved, qualified only by his fear that my nocturnal escapade might have been detrimental to my delicate state of health.

All my tiredness and my worries and all the risks I had run appeared to me worthwhile when my husband, who had spent the evening with my father, told me of the conversation he had had with him. For it left me with no doubt in my mind that even if my father did not say so in so many words, he to a very large extent shared our views on the consequences— alarming to every true patriot—which were likely to follow the change of master after the death of the Empress Elizaveta.

CHAPTER IV

On 25 December, Christmas Day, we had the misfortune of losing the Empress Elizaveta. It has been maintained by certain writers of memoirs on Russia that the Guards regiments marching to the palace to swear the oath of allegiance to their new sovereign did so with every sign of joy. However, nine out of every ten inhabitants of Petersburg would testify to the contrary. I can myself assert as a fact I saw with my own eyes that the Guards regiments (including the Semenovskii and the Izmailovskii, which passed under my own windows) looked gloomy and dejected. The men all spoke at once but in a low voice, and the confused, stifled murmur which arose from the ranks sounded so menacing and alarming, so desperate even, that I could not help wishing myself a hundred miles away so as not to hear it. My husband was at the other end of town with his Preobrazhenskii regiment and no news reached me, but the behavior of the two regiments I have described made it clear enough that Elizaveta had breathed her last.

That day, which our Church celebrates as one of its greatest festivals and which is as a rule the occasion for popular rejoicing, wore an almost sinister aspect, with grief painted on every face. I was ill and saw no one of my family. The Grand Chancellor was also ill. When, three days after his accession, the Emperor paid him a visit and sent up a page to ask me to pass the evening with him, I excused myself on grounds of ill health, but the next day the invitation was repeated. A week later my sister wrote to tell me that the Emperor was displeased with me for not coming, and did not really believe in my indisposition. That evening, therefore, in order to avoid all unpleasantness between the Emperor and my husband, I presented myself at Court, but not before I had seen both my father and my uncle. The Empress was not present. She never left her room except to sit by the lifeless body of the Sovereign and to see to it that all that was customary on such occasions was being done. She was bathed in tears all the time, and the only news I received of her came from one of her footmen.

Peter III's first words to me as I came in concerned my sister, and were so extraordinary that I did not know how to reply to them. What he said fully indicated his intention to be rid of the Empress Catherine so as to be able to marry the Countess Elizaveta. Whenever he spoke on this subject he always did so in a low voice, referring to the Empress as "*she*" and to the Countess as *Romanovna*.[1] "I advise you," he said, "my little friend, to pay a little more attention to us; the time may perhaps come when you will have reason to repent of any negligence shown to your sister. It is in your own interest to win her affection and influence her mind—that is the way in which you can become of any consequence in the world."

On this occasion I pretended not to understand what the Emperor had said, and hastened to take part in a game of *campis*. I found the game a little expensive, as the minimum stake was ten imperials (100 roubles) a time and the Emperor always won, because he never took counters but simply pulled an imperial out of his pocket every time he lost, and paid it into the pool; as he probably had more than ten imperials in his pocket he always remained the winner and carried off the pool. The pool was exhausted pretty quickly and His Majesty proposed a second, but I begged to be excused from taking part in it. The Emperor insisted that I should play again and even ended by offering to go halves with me, but I replied with the air of a foolish child that I was not rich enough to let myself be cheated in this way, and that if His Majesty put down his money on the table like the rest of us we should have some sort of a chance, but as His Majesty kept his money in his pocket while he played, so that we could not see how much he had left, he always remained last in the game and took over all our stakes in the pool.

I must admit it was rather bold of me, but then it must be borne in mind that I was disgusted with my Sovereign's contemptible action; besides, my husband's obedience to his mother and his fondness for her made him (in spite of his debts) be satisfied with whatever she was good enough to send him for our expenses—a modest amount, although the

---

[1] Elizaveta Vorontsova's patronymic, her father's Christian name being Roman.—K. F.

whole property, having belonged to his father, was now owned by the Prince and not by his mother. Hence, the very idea of increasing my husband's difficulties frightened me, and this may serve as an excuse for my remark. The Emperor did not take offense at it, and being convinced I was a child (because he imagined it was only recently he had held me at the font), obstinate and perhaps foolish, he gave some fatuously jocular answer and granted me permission not to play.

The party that evening and almost all the following evenings consisted of the two brothers Naryshkin and their wives, Mr. Izmailov and his wife, the Countess Elizaveta, Mr. Melgunov, Gudovich, Ungern (the Emperor's General A.D.C.), the Countess Bruce, and two or three other persons whose names I cannot remember. All of them looked at me with wide-eyed astonishment and I soon heard them say: "She is a proud woman," just as in Oranienbaum I myself heard the same thing said in German by the Holstein generals who thought I did not understand that language.

The rest of the company was in the next room where, as I passed, I had the impression of witnessing a masquerade. Everyone had changed his dress. Not a man but was laced into his uniform, booted and spurred— even old Prince Trubetskoi. That ancient courtier who had never been a soldier, now that he was seventy wanted to look like one. On the day of the Empress's death he was lying in bed with his legs swollen so that they were as fat as his body; and yet that same evening he was running about giving orders to the officers of the Izmailovskii Regiment, of which he had, some time previously, been appointed lieutenant-colonel. This Guards regiment had a high standing at Court and constituted in a sense a ramification of it, and never took part in war. As he already held some civilian office, Prince Trubetskoi did not command the regiment. I was assured that he possessed the secret of all beggars, such as the ability to induce swellings whenever he wanted, and so on.

All ladies of the Court and all ladies of quality, according to their husbands' ranks, had received the order to be in attendance by turns in the room where the catafalque was placed. The walls were draped in black and candles were burning in innumerable candelabra all round the catafalque; and as the rites of our Church require priests to read the Gospel in the same room for a period of six weeks, the place looked even more gloomy, august, and imposing. (The Gospel is read for crowned heads and bishops; for others, the Psalms.)

The Empress visited the room every day and bathed in tears the precious remains of her aunt and benefactress.[2] Her grief won the sympathy of all onlookers. Peter III, on the other hand, came but rarely, and when he did come it was to laugh with the ladies on duty, ridicule the clergy that happened to be there, or scold the Duty Officers and N.C.O.'s for their curls or cravats or uniforms.

The British Minister (Keith) was second only to the Prussian Minister in the esteem of the Emperor. That worthy old man loved me like a daughter. Princess Golitsyna (whom I have already mentioned), my husband, and I dined with him every week, and as his Christian name was Robert of which Roman—my father's name—is the Russian equivalent, he used to call me his daughter when there were no strangers present. He saw with regret (and said so when there was no one about but our little set) that the Emperor seemed to make it his aim to be criticized and perhaps finally despised. As to the other Ministers, His Majesty treated them very badly and they could hardly have been attracted by his manners.

One morning the Emperor sent a message to my uncle, the Grand Chancellor, to say that he would visit him for supper. My uncle wanted to stay in bed all that day and the prospect of the supper could hardly have given him any pleasure. He sent a message to my sister, the Countess Buturlina, to my husband, and me to come to his house. The Emperor came at seven o'clock and remained in the sick man's room till supper was served. He excused my uncle from being present at it, and we (that is, Countess Stroganova, Countess Buturlina, and I) took advantage of my uncle's absence to behave as we pleased and to wander among the guests on the pretext of doing the honors of the house. As a matter of fact this sort of thing rather suited His Majesty's taste, for he hated all ceremony or etiquette. I was standing behind his chair when he turned to the Austrian Ambassador, Count Mercy, and to the Prussian Minister and told them how when he was still in Kiel in Holstein, his father (who was alive at the time) had ordered him to chase Bohemians out of the town. He took a squadron of light cavalry and a company of foot and dislodged them in a trice. I saw Count Mercy turn pale and then red as a beetroot because he did not know whether the Emperor meant Bohemians in the sense of wandering, fortune-telling gypsies or Bohemians in the sense of subjects of the Empress, Queen of Hungary and Bohemia. The Ambassador was in agonies, all the more so as he knew by then that the order to disengage

[2] Catherine II was related to Elizaveta I by marriage. Charles Peter of Holstein-Gottorp (Peter III) was Elizaveta's nephew.—J. G.

themselves from the Austrian army had already been despatched to our troops.

Happening, as I have said, to be at that moment behind His Majesty's chair, I bent down and whispered to him in Russian that he ought not to tell such stories to foreign representatives, and that if there had been gypsy rogues and beggars in Kiel the police force, and not he, would have been sent to chase them out, for he had been a mere child then. (It should be remembered that I always spoke to His Majesty in the tone of a stubborn child myself and called him Papa.)[3]

"You are a little fool," he said, "and you always argue with me."

He was well in his cups, and I was sure he would not remember this conversation on the following day. I left his chair as if nothing had happened.

I remember one evening at the Palace the amazement with which all of us present saw His Majesty, after talking for a long time on the subject of the King of Prussia, turn to Mr. Volkov and remind him of how during the late reign they had many a time laughed at the failure of the resolutions and secret orders sent by the Supreme Council to the Russian armies in Prussia; the failure, said His Majesty, was due to his and Mr. Volkov's habit of communicating the contents of these orders to the King. Mr. Volkov, who had at that time been first and only Secretary to the Council, blushed and turned pale and blushed again. Quite unconscious of his friend's discomfiture, however, Peter III continued to boast of his services to the King of Prussia in connection with the warnings he and Mr. Volkov gave him of Russian intentions.[4]

The Emperor never came to the Court chapel until just as Mass was about to finish. There he made faces, acted the buffoon, and imitated poor old ladies whom he had ordered to curtsey in the French style instead of inclining their heads as is the Russian custom. These poor old ladies were hard put to it not to stumble when they had to bend the knee, and I remember seeing Countess Buturlina, my eldest sister's mother-in-law,

---

[3] Peter, in fact, would have been aged six or seven at the time of the alleged episode, as his wife was the first to point out many years before Princess Dashkova. However, says Catherine II in her memoirs, this did not deter him from repeating his favorite story of his to all and sundry on innumerable occasions.—K. F.

[4] This story was later hotly denied by Volkov in a letter to Grigorii Orlov written about three weeks after Catherine's accession to the throne. He was, it is true, imprisoned for a short time after the coup d'état, but was very soon let out again and eventually made a brilliant career for himself in the new reign. See Index for further details.—K. F.

ready to fall as she was making this forced curtsey. Fortunately, people round her held her up.

Peter III showed nothing but the greatest indifference to the Grand Duke Pavel—he never saw him. The young Prince, however, saw his mother every day. He had as tutor the elder of the Panin brothers, who had been recalled by the late Empress in order to take up that office. When Prince George of Holstein-Gottorp, uncle of the Emperor as well as of the Empress (being the brother of her mother, the Princess of Anhalt-Zerbst), arrived in Petersburg, Mr. Panin acting through Mr. Saldern—who later played an important role and became Russian ambassador in Poland, but who then acted as a kind of mentor to Prince George—obtained that the Prince of Holstein-Gottorp and the Prince of Holstein (also, though more distantly, related to their Majesties) should prevail on the Emperor to be present when the Grand Duke was being examined for progress in his studies. It was only after repeated entreaties on their part that the Emperor agreed. "What for?" he said. "I shall not understand anything."

As he was leaving after the examination, the Emperor remarked aloud to his uncles:

"By God, that scamp knows more than we do!"

He wanted to reward him on the spot with the rank of warrant officer in the Guards, and it was only with difficulty that Mr. Panin was able to have that honor deferred on the pretext that this would make the Grand Duke conceited, that he would imagine himself to be a grown-up man, and that it would distract him. Peter III swallowed all these reasons without further ado, and without so much as a suspicion that the tutor was making a fool of him. He also believed that he would be amply rewarding Mr. Panin by making him a general in the infantry, and had Mr. Melgunov announce it the following day.

To grasp fully how much this must have dumbfounded Mr. Panin it must be remembered that he was a man of forty-eight, sickly, and fond of a quiet life, most of which he had passed at the Russian or (as minister) at foreign courts. He wore a wig with three ties hanging down his back, was studied in his dress, always the perfect courtier—a somewhat old-fashioned one, truth to tell, like a picture-book idea of those at the court of Louis XIV—and with a loathing for all drill-sergeantry and barrack-room manners.

He said to Mr. Melgunov that he could hardly believe it was His Majesty's intention to bestow this honor upon him of all people, that it did not fit him at all and that he was prepared to desert to Sweden rather than accept it. The Emperor could not understand how anyone could refuse the rank of an infantry general, and remarked:

"I have always been told he is an intelligent man. How shall I ever be able to believe it again?"

His Majesty had to be content with giving him a civilian rank of equivalent distinction.

This is the right moment for me to speak of the nature of the relationship which existed between my husband and the Panins. The latter were first-cousins of my mother-in-law, through their respective mothers, the Misses Everlakov, one of whom had married a Mr. Leontiev and the other a Mr. Panin. The two brothers—sons of Mr. Panin—were thus my husband's cousins once removed. The younger brother was an army general serving in Prussia which we had defeated. The elder had been despatched on some foreign mission as Envoy Extraordinary when I was still an infant, and I saw him for the first time on our return from Oranienbaum in September. Since then I saw him but rarely until the reign of Peter III when the Conspiracy began to gain in substance. He had a great feeling of friendship for my husband, and cherished grateful memories of his father's—Prince Dashkov's—kindness for him when they were both young. But when, as a result of the Revolution, I became an object of envy, neither these very natural relationships nor my passionate love for my husband were proof against slanderous insinuations which credited this respectable old cousin with being either my lover or my father—on the supposition that he had been my mother's lover. Had he not been of real service to my husband and helped my children, I should have hated him as the unwitting instrument of those who were trying to besmirch my reputation. I can truly say that I had greater respect for his younger brother, the General, because of his soldierly frankness and firmness of character which squared far more with my own, and while his first wife, whom I loved and esteemed from the bottom of my heart, was still alive, I visited those two more frequently than I did the Minister. But enough on a subject which is painful to me even now.

CHAPTER V

Ogxo

One morning, in the second week of January 1762, as the regiment on duty was marching toward the palace for the changing of the guard, the Emperor fancied that the company commanded by Prince Dashkov had not deployed in the correct manner. He ran up to my husband, like a true corporal, and told him that he had not deployed his troops as he should. The Prince denied the charge firmly but calmly. However, when His Majesty began to insist, my husband, who was very touchy whenever he believed his honor to be in the slightest impugned, replied with some heat and so much vigor that the Emperor, whose attitude to duels was apparently that of a Prussian officer, thought himself in danger and promptly retreated, leaving the Prince with as much haste as he had previously approached him.

When my family and I heard about that scene we came to the conclusion that the Emperor would not always yield and retreat before my husband's quick reactions, and that people might be found to explain to him that it was *his* business to make the Prince yield and retreat rather than the other way about. We agreed that the safest thing would be to separate them for a time. I was particularly in favor of this course because, as if by intuition, I never doubted that the Emperor would be dethroned, and being firmly resolved to take part in the action, I was eager for my husband to be in a foreign country, so that if any catastrophe should befall me he should not have to share it. As envoys had not yet been appointed to all the foreign missions to announce His Majesty's accession to the throne, I implored my husband to accept such an appointment, and when he agreed I entreated the Grand Chancellor to obtain a mission for him. My uncle promised me this, and the following day the Prince was informed that he was to be sent to the only mission still vacant, which was Constantinople.

In the ordinary way, this would not have been my choice, but as one must always choose the lesser of two evils, I preferred the idea of his being in Constantinople to seeing him in Petersburg endangering his life by his quickness to take offense, or by the failure of the plans into which I had thrown myself heart and soul and which robbed me of sleep, undermined my health, and made me lose weight.

The Prince was allowed to select his own colleagues. All of them were given their traveling expenses and paid their salaries six months in advance, in Petersburg. At last, in the month of February, the Prince left. I remained behind, feeling ill and sad and with nothing to cheer me up except for the different plans which I kept forming and rejecting and which distracted me sufficiently to soothe somewhat the grief of separation from a beloved and esteemed husband.

My husband proceeded slowly on his journey. He stayed for a long time in Moscow and then accompanied his mother to Troitskoe, her estate on the way to Kiev, where he remained till the beginning of July.

I had an unpleasant experience two days after the Prince's departure. Some sailors working at the Admiralty in Petersburg, taking advantage of the fact that I had kept only a few servants with me, smashed a window and broke into the room where a maid of mine kept my linen, my clothes, and even my money (for I entrusted everything to her). They took all the linen there was, as well as all the money and a fur coat lined with silver damask. It was the fur coat that helped to trace the burglars, but in the meantime I remained without money and without even personal linen except for what happened to be in the wash. My sister, Countess Elizaveta, sent me some fine holland; I told her that what I needed most was a shift or two while mine were being laundered, and she sent these immediately. I have recounted this little misfortune because it was my first lesson in poverty and want, but not the last I experienced in my life. Besides, it distressed me to have to borrow money and add to the Prince's debts.

The Emperor continued to behave in his usual way. When peace was concluded with the King of Prussia his joy and boasting knew no bounds. He wanted to celebrate it by giving a grand official banquet to which he invited foreign Ministers and the nobility of the first three classes. The Empress was sitting at her usual place at the center of the table, but Peter III sat down in an opposite corner close to the Prussian Minister. He proposed three toasts to be drunk in goblets to the sound of the fortress cannon: "To the health of the Imperial family," "To that of His Majesty the King of Prussia," and "To the happy continuance of the present peace."

The Empress began by the toast to the Imperial family. When she had drunk it, Peter III sent his General A. D. C. Gudovich, who was standing behind his chair, to ask her why she had not risen from her seat when drinking to the health of the Imperial family. The Empress replied that as the Imperial family consisted only of His Majesty, her son and herself, she did not conceive it possible that the Emperor should require her to do so. When Gudovich came back with this reply, the Emperor ordered him to tell her that she was a fool (*dura*—a much stronger word in Russian) and ought to have known that the Imperial family included also his two uncles, the princes of Holstein. Fearing, apparently, that Gudovich would not use the same expression, he repeated it loudly enough to be heard by the whole table. The Empress immediately burst into floods of tears, but in an attempt to regain her composure by diverting attention to something different, she asked my cousin Count Stroganov, who was in attendance behind her chair, to entertain her with some of the amusing little stories he knew so well how to tell. He did his best to restrain his own grief at this deplorable scene, for he was greatly attached to the Empress and highly disliked by the other side, all the more so as his wife, who was very friendly with both my sister and Peter III, could not bear the sight of him. He prattled on, saying anything that came into his head which might amuse the Empress and make her laugh, but no sooner was the dinner over than he received the command to retire to his country house near Kamennyi Ostrov and to stay there till further orders.

The events of the day made a great sensation in town. The Empress gained increasing sympathy, while contempt for the Emperor grew in proportion. Thus, every day he smoothed out for us the difficulties in the way of his own overthrow—a lesson to the great of this world teaching them that contempt for the ruler is as likely to cause his fall as will his own tyranny. For this of necessity brings in its wake chaos in administration and distrust of the judiciary, and unites everyone in one desire—*the desire for a change.* Limited monarchy, headed by a master who could be a father to his people and who knows himself respected and even loved by his subjects, and yet feared by the wicked, must be the goal of every thinking person. For power, lodged with the masses, whose opinions are lightly held and forever changing, is unstable; it is exercised either too slowly or with undue precipitancy; the great variety of views and convictions deprives it of harmony.

One day the Emperor came to see my uncle, the Grand Chancellor, together with the two Princes of Holstein and his usual suite. The Empress never joined in these parties, and always went out in her carriage to take the air. My health was none too good at the time, and whenever possible I begged to be excused from taking part in these festivities, which, truth to tell, did not amuse me in the slightest. My surprise was great the following day when I heard that the Emperor and Prince George, after a dispute during which each held firmly to his own opinion, had, in true Prussian-officer style, drawn their swords and made ready to kill each other. At that precise moment old Baron Korf (my aunt's brother-in-law) threw himself on his knees between them crying like an old woman, and told them that if they wanted to fight they would have to do it over his dead body. Korf—a nice man, for that matter—was liked both by His Majesty and by the Prince of Holstein-Gottorp, and he put a stop to this ridiculous scene, which must have alarmed my uncle although, as he was still ill in bed, he had not witnessed it personally. I was very worried for him when I heard that my aunt, leaving the room just as the two combatants were about to begin their fight, had run in fright to my uncle and could tell him nothing but the worst. At last, however, other people were able to inform him that Baron Korf had smoothed down all the difficulties and effected a reconciliation between uncle and nephew.

This ridiculous scene was not the last. There were several others of similar intensity but of a different kind, until His Majesty finally left for Oranienbaum and went thence to Kronstadt to inspect the fleet before starting a war against the King of Denmark. This war completely captured his imagination in spite of all remonstrances and in spite even of the advice given to him by Frederick the Great who, in one of his letters to the Emperor, used all his eloquence in the attempt to dissuade him from his intentions.

In the meantime I spared no effort to foster or encourage the right principles in my husband's friends, among them such men as Mr. Passek and Mr. Bredikhin, both of them captains in the Preobrazhenskii Guards. The latter was related to us through his wife, a Princess Golitsyna. There were also the brothers Roslavlev, one a major and the other a captain, in the Izmailovskii Guards. These two I saw but rarely and only when chance brought us together, until the month of April when I found it essential to ascertain the sentiments both of the troops and of the public in Petersburg. But I continued to frequent as usual the houses of my relations as well as Mr. Keith and, in fact, tried to behave outwardly as I had always done and to be seen in places where I had always been seen. And it was only when I was by myself that I showed any signs of being worried by plans and projects which could reasonably be regarded as far beyond my strength.

Among the foreigners who had come to seek their fortune in Russia there was one, a Piedmontese by origin, of the name of Odart, enjoying the patronage of my uncle, the Grand Chancellor, who had obtained for him the place of Under-Secretary at the Ministry of Trade. I met him and found him to be well-informed, a man with a receptive mind, crafty and lively, but weak in health and no longer young. He soon found he was unfit to hold his post, because he knew neither our language, nor the produce of our land, nor the system of our river communications nor any of the other things necessary in his position. He therefore asked me to obtain for him employment in the service of the Empress. I spoke to Her Majesty, thinking that she might make him one of her secretaries. But she answered that as her only correspondence was with her own family, she had no need for a secretary and that she would only give rise to suspicions and occasion offense by giving this post to a foreigner. Besides, she had never seen him and did not know him. However, I prevailed upon her to attach him to her service in the capacity of adviser on land improvement and in order to establish manufactories on the paltry little estate recently given to her by Peter III.

The statement may be found in certain of Her Majesty's letters that I was entirely responsible for introducing Odart to her and that when Count Stroganov was banished to his country place I advised Odart to follow him, for his health's sake. In fact, however, he was far from being in my confidence or in the position to direct my actions, and I never saw much of him. During the time when the last dispositions were being made for the revolution, especially during the last three weeks preceding that fortunate turn of events, I did not see him a single time. All I wanted was to obtain for him a means of livelihood and a pleasant post, but I never asked him his advice, and never would he have dared suggest that I should give myself to my cousin, Count Panin, as the libelous pamphleteers have allowed themselves to say with no reason or truth.[1] But many Frenchmen have dipped their pens in gall to write about Catherine the Great and thought they could not blacken her enough without disfiguring Catherine the Little, for we both bore the same Christian name.

But to return from this digression. The officer commanding the Izmai-

[1] Among "the libelous pamphleteers" was Rulhière, whom Princess Dashkova met in St. Petersburg and was to meet again later in Paris, as described in the present *Memoirs.* — K. F.

lovskii Guards was Field-Marshal Razumovskii, a gay and thoughtless creature of whom His Majesty was very fond. Nevertheless he saw how unfit the Emperor was to govern the Empire and how great the disaster for which the country was heading. Count Razumovskii loved his native land as much as his apathy and his indolence allowed him, and he was popular with his regiment—it was important, therefore, to have him on our side. But how could he be won over? This was something which I believe nobody thought possible. Extremely rich, holder of the highest ranks and decorations, and loathing all activity, he would have shuddered if faced with a conspiracy in which he would have had to play the part of a ringleader in order to bring about a revolution. All these considerations did not make me abandon my intention of having him on our side.

The two brothers Roslavlev and Captain Lasunskii had great influence with the Count; they saw him every day and were on intimate terms with him, but did not flatter themselves that they could stir him into the activity we desired. I advised them to speak to him every day, vaguely at first and then gradually more explicitly, on the subject of the rumors that were being spread, of a great conspiracy, of a revolution which was going to take place. As he would certainly not denounce them and report on their conversations, they could, as soon as our plot was ripe, reveal to him their true intentions and make him feel that he too was *one of us,* that he could no longer draw back, for they had informed the other conspirators of the conversations they had had with him, which he had neither censured nor opposed, and finally that his position was quite as dangerous as theirs and that he would lessen the risk he was running by remaining at the head of his regiment while cooperating with us.

All went off according to my instructions and was a complete success.

I continued to visit as always the British Minister, Mr. Keith. One day in the course of conversation he told me it was being rumored in town that the Guards were on the point of mutiny and that the war with Denmark was the main cause of it. I asked him whether anyone mentioned the names of the ringleaders.

"No," he replied, "and I don't believe any ringleaders exist. For the generals and other officers could not object to a war where they could win distinction. That is why," he added, "these rumors, these indiscreet remarks will lead to nothing but a few people being punished, a few sent to Siberia, and a few soldiers being flogged."

I could not help feeling worried because these rumors were so widespread, but there was no help for it other than precipitating the crisis.

In the meantime, I led a life that could not fail to affect my health. I continued to visit my family as frequently as ever and, during post-days, was fully occupied writing voluminous letters to my husband, crying the while at the thought of his absence; during the rest of the week I spent the entire time, except the few hours needed for sleep, working out my plans and reading everything that had ever been written on the subject of revolutions wherever they happened to occur. As I was not very strong I lost my bright complexion and was rapidly losing weight as well. A cold I caught while out in marshy country very nearly finished me off completely.

It came about in this way. A few miles out of Petersburg, on the way to Krasnyi Kabak, was a stretch of land covered with marshes and thick forests, which it was suggested to Peter III might be distributed among individual owners. Most of the richer gentry had their lands drained and made into charming properties. But one such allotment was given to a Holstenian from Oranienbaum. Now, these Holstenians were for the most part worker apprentices who had escaped from their masters, while some of them were soldiers or warrant officers who had deserted from the armies of various German princelings. They were well received at Oranienbaum, were drafted into the troops of Peter III (then still Grand Duke), received rapid promotion and quickly rose in rank. The particular Holstenian who had been allotted this piece of marshy land, had one look at it, was frightened by the investment of capital and labor it entailed, and gave it back to the government to be re-allotted to anyone willing to accept it.

My father was very keen that I should have that little piece of ground, and it was in vain I protested my inability to deal adequately with it for lack of any funds even to make a start. He insisted that I should have it and promised to build a little timber house for me. In the end I yielded to my father's pressure, but remained fully resolved not to incur any expense which might inconvenience my husband, limiting myself to whatever was necessary for a frugal table for myself, my little daughter, and my servants. I imposed the strictest economy on myself, wore nothing but the oldest clothes and remains of my trousseau, and even restricted my *penchant* for books, etc., as much as possible.

There happened to be in Petersburg at the time about a hundred peasants belonging to my husband. They came to town every year and made a great deal of money by undertaking all kinds of work. As a mark of their esteem and gratitude for the prosperity they enjoyed, they offered to dig canals, first for four days at a stretch and then to take turns at it during holy days which would otherwise have been their days of leisure. By their exertions they were soon able to raise the level of the ground, drain it and make it fit to have a house, offices and courtyard built on it. It occurred to me not to give a name for the time being to this first piece of land I ever possessed as my own, but to wait for the successful outcome of the revolution and then call it in honor of the Saint on whose day the revolution had taken place.[2]

I went out riding there with my cousin, Count Stroganov, one day, and on seeing what I thought was a dry meadow decided to take a walk through it. But no sooner did I attempt it than I sank up to my knees in the bog and caught a severe chill with a very high temperature in consequence. As soon as the Empress was informed, she wrote a very friendly letter to me saying how worried she was about my health and how angry with my *cavaliere servente* Count Stroganov—the *monkey,* as she generally and very deservedly called him in her letters to me, for his ugliness and his pranks—because he had not taken sufficient care of me and had failed to prevent the accident.

I received this letter when my fever was at its highest, and my answer must have reflected the incoherence of my mind. All I could remember later was that I wrote partly in Russian and partly in French, half in verse and half in prose. When I had recovered, the Empress asked me, in one of her little notes, since when I had begun to dabble in prophecies; she could perfectly well understand, she said, the Russian verses with which my fondness for her had inspired me, but apart from these expressions of warm and tender friendship, she could make nothing of my letter, and was particularly puzzled by my reference to a certain day which had to come, and when it did it would give a name to my first estate.

All my family came to see me, including Count Panin who came as often as his duties as tutor to the Grand Duke Pavel allowed. As it was essential for us to have a man of his calibre on our side, I ventured on several occasions to speak to him of the possibility of Peter III's fall. I asked him what the consequences were likely to be, how we should be governed and who would govern us. My cousin fondly imagined that his ward might govern according to the laws and the Constitution of the Swedish Monarchy.

[2] The revolution occurred on 28 June, which happened to be the day of St. Cyrus and St. John (*Kir* and *Ian* in Russian); the estate—formerly Krasnyi Kabak—therefore received the name of Kirianovo.—K. F.

In the meantime a circumstance occurred which I have omitted to relate and which gained for me Mr. Panin's confidence, because Prince Repnin, a favorite nephew of his, for whose character he had a great regard, showed in a most impressive way that he both esteemed and trusted me.

I often met Prince Repnin at Princess Kurakina's, for Repnin's wife, who was sister to Prince Kurakin and hence my husband's cousin, lived with the Kurakins. In fact, Prince Repnin knew me very well and was aware that my high principles combined with a lively feeling of patriotism would not allow me to be guided by motives of personal interest or family aggrandisement.

The day on which peace with the King of Prussia was celebrated, Peter III gave a dinner in honor of it, as I have already mentioned. This, however, did not satisfy him and he ordered a supper at the Summer Palace to give vent to his joy in his own way without ceremony and in the company of his friends, a few ladies of the town, his favorite generals and officers, and the Prussian Minister. He was carried away from the table at four o'clock in the morning, put into his carriage, and driven back to the Palace, which he was too drunk to enter by his own unaided efforts. But before leaving the Summer Palace he conferred on my sister Elizaveta the Order of St. Catherine, the constitution of which allowed it to be conferred only on members of the Imperial family and on princesses of foreign ruling houses. An exception was made for ladies who, though not of Royal rank, had saved the life of their Sovereign, or rendered some spectacular service to their country. In practice, however, none had received it during the preceding reigns.

At the same time the Emperor told Prince Repnin that he would send him as Minister Resident to Berlin where he would have to obey the will and orders of His Prussian Majesty.

On leaving the Summer Palace at about five o'clock in the morning, Prince Repnin went straight to my house. I was not up yet, but he insisted that I should be told of his arrival. I was startled out of my sleep by a servant knocking at the door of my powder room next to my bedroom. I, in turn, woke up my personal maid, an excellent old woman who always slept by my bedside, and made her get up. She went off in a vile temper to see for herself, and came back to inform me it was my cousin, Prince Repnin. I hastily put on a dress, wondering at the early hour, and was amazed at the Prince's news as well as at the great agitation of his manner, for without further ado he simply blurted out:

"All is lost, my dear cousin; your sister has received the Order of St. Catherine and I am being sent as Minister and, in effect, Adjutant to the King of Prussia."

Astounded as I was at these words, I did not want to prolong the Prince's visit. I told him, therefore, that it would be as useless trying to foresee logical consequences flowing from a brain such as Peter III's, as it would be to fear any coherence in his actions. I strongly advised him first to go and have a rest and afterward warn his uncle, Mr. Panin, of all that had occurred that evening.

When Prince Repnin had gone, I did not go back to bed, but turned over in my mind the various tentative schemes which I had heard discussed by our conspirators, sketches of projects, as it were, to bring the Revolution to a successful conclusion. They were nothing but conjectures and vague designs without any fixed plan; there was no agreement on any single course of action, except the decision to strike as soon as His Majesty should leave for Denmark with his troops.[3]

I decided to unburden myself with no reservations to Mr. Panin the very first time I saw him. He, as always, insisted that formalities be observed and the cooperation of the Senate obtained.

"That would be splendid," I said, "if only we were granted the time. I agree with you that the Empress has no claim to the throne, and that by rights it is her son who should be proclaimed Sovereign with the Empress as Regent until he comes of age, but you forget that not one in a hundred would regard the removal of the Sovereign as anything but an act of violence."

I then named to him the main conspirators, such as the brothers Roslavlev, Lasunskii, Passek, Bredikhin, Baskakov, Prince Bariatinskii, Khitrovo, etc., etc., as well as the Orlovs whom they had asked to join the movement. My cousin was both surprised and alarmed to learn how far I had committed myself, and this without saying anything to the Empress for fear of compromising her. However, I saw that what he lacked was determination rather than courage, and to cut short useless discussion I managed to convince him of the importance of having on our side a man like Teplov, who had just been released from the fortress where he had

[3] As Duke of Holstein-Gottorp, Peter III had pretensions to Schleswig, then under Danish sovereignty, and was determined to seize it by force. However, the plan was frustrated by Peter's overthrow. By the Treaty of 1773, Catherine II ceded Holstein-Gottorp to Denmark in exchange for Oldenburg and Delmenhorst.—K. F.

been imprisoned by Peter III. He had a facile and eloquent pen, and I thought of making him the Empress's secretary, a capacity in which he would be particularly useful in the very beginning when manifestos, decrees, etc., etc., would have to be quickly prepared and proclaimed. I told Mr. Panin that I hardly ever saw Teplov and that he (Panin) was the only man I knew who could bring Teplov over to our side. This, I said, was all the more necessary as Teplov exercised considerable influence over Count Razumovskii. Besides, I made my cousin promise not to speak to any of the conspirators about his scheme for proclaiming the Grand Duke, as this would serve no purpose whatever apart from making his motives suspect as coming from a tutor in favor of his charge. I assured him that I, on the other hand, could make this proposal to the conspirators with some hope of success, as they all knew me to be the most sincere friend the Empress had in the world. In fact, I did suggest it, but Fate intervened to frustrate what seemed the most reasonable of our plans: we were unwittingly betrayed by a soldier who, thinking that Captain Izmailov was also a conspirator, told him what he had just heard from Captain Passek. The latter was arrested in consequence, and as the conspiracy was discovered I forced the issue by making the Empress come to town.

The Archbishop of Novgorod, a prelate of great learning, was generally respected and idolized by the whole clergy. His distinguished mind and wide knowledge enabled him to see all the more clearly how much the authority of the Church would suffer under a sovereign such as Peter III. He did not conceal his grief on that account, and was ready to second our efforts up to the limit imposed by his Pastoral office. This was a great deal, for he combined with his many other qualities a moving and manly eloquence that carried away his audience.

For about ten days there was no change—events hung fire. In the meantime, the conspirators increased in number without being able to form any reasonable or definite plan. I had the satisfaction of hearing from Prince Volkonskii, an uncle of my husband's who had just returned from the army and had come to see me en tête-à-tête, that the soldiers found it most unnatural to turn their arms against Maria Theresa and in favor of the King of Prussia against whom they had fought for many years.[4] There

[4] The Russian army fought on the side of the Empress Maria Theresa against Frederick the Great of Prussia in the Seven Years War. On his accession to the throne, Peter III, an ardent admirer of Frederick, immediately suspended all military operations and saved Frederick from utter defeat. He did not, however, as Princess Dashkova seems to suggest, then proceed to attack Austria: he merely left her to carry on the war alone.—K. F.

Prince Mikhail Dashkov, husband of Princess Dashkova.
(From a miniature by an unknown artist)

was general discontent among them, he said; and I saw that the Prince was on our side rather than against us. I informed Count Panin of this, and we found no difficulty in inducing him to act or at least to appear at the critical moment.

Every other day I went to my little place in the country (or my little piece of marshland, rather) in order to be alone and to put down on paper those of my ideas that I was not yet quite clear about in my own mind. By these frequent visits to the country I gave the impression of being absorbed exclusively in improving and beautifying my estate. The Empress wrote to me fairly often. She was in good health and did not seem at all worried, as, indeed, she could not have been, for she knew as little as we did that the day of decision was so near.

In the meantime, Peter III's behavior occasioned growing disgust, while in his capacity of legislator he aroused an increasing and ever more general contempt. In the preceding reign certain representatives of the Serbian people, and of those who had taken refuge in the dominions of the House of Austria, as well as Hungarians and others of the Greek faith, had come

Prince Grigorii Orlov.
(From a portrait by Torelli)

to ask the Empress Elizaveta to grant them land in her domains where their people could settle to escape the persecution of Maria Theresa's all-powerful Catholic clergy. Although Her Majesty had the highest regard for the Empress of Germany she had let herself be swayed by her religious convictions, which demanded that due protection be extended to peoples of the Greek Rite persecuted for their faith. The representatives were well received, were granted some fine lands in the southern parts of Russia, and lent money to help them defray their emigration expenses as well as to enable them to form a few regiments of Hussars. One of these representatives, a certain Horvat, a man with ingratiating manners and an intriguer by nature, worked his way into the confidence of influential people and of those responsible for organizing the despatch of the Serbians to their new home. The money was therefore entrusted to him, but when several thousand Serbs arrived at their place of destination, which was given the name of New Serbia, Horvat took to treating them as slaves and kept back the money.

These wretched people successfully complained to the Empress, who sent out Prince Meshcherskii to investigate and redress their grievances. But Elizaveta's illness and subsequent death, as well as other important matters, prevented the Senate from making a final decision on the subject. As soon as the Empress was dead, Horvat appeared in Petersburg and made a present of two thousand ducats each to the three noblemen whom he considered to be the most powerful. These were Lev Naryshkin, who owed his favor to his buffoonery, General Melgunov, and the Procurator-General Glebov. The two latter immediately informed Peter III who said to them, "Well done," praised them for not concealing their bribe from him, went equal shares with them, and promised to go to the Senate himself in order to obtain a decision in Horvat's favor. He did this the very following day, and Russia lost thereby a hundred thousand inhabitants who were quite ready to go to Russia provided they knew that their countrymen enjoyed the protection which they had been promised. When the Emperor learned that Lev Naryshkin had received an equal sum, but had not told him about it, His Majesty took away from him all the money he had received from Horvat without even leaving him half as he had done in the case of the other two, and teased him for several days afterward, asking him what he had done with his bribe. A transaction of this kind, which immediately became the talk of the town, would have demeaned a private individual; in the case of the Sovereign it served to increase the contempt in which he was in any case held. And among those who laughed at Peter III there was nothing but scorn for him and his ridiculous buffoon Lev Naryshkin.

A short time afterward the Emperor made the entire Izmailovskii Regiment witness a farce which was hardly credible. Field-Marshal Count Razumovskii, who was its Colonel-in-Chief, though not himself a soldier, was obliged, like all the other commanders, to deploy the whole of his regiment and make it execute certain maneuvers in the presence of the Emperor, who was pleased with the appearance of the troops. Everyone was in a gay mood and the dinner promised to pass off in the best humor imaginable, when Peter III caught sight of his negro, whose name, I believe, was Narcissus, some distance away engaged in a great fight and using his fists in the process. This amused him. But when he was told that the negro was fighting with the regimental scavenger, Peter III was seized with obvious dismay, and exclaimed:

"Narcissus is lost for us."

No one understood what he meant by that, and Count Razumovskii asked him why he had said it.

"Come now," said the Emperor, "don't you feel that no real soldier can ever again associate with him, since he has sullied his honor by coming in contact with a scavenger?"

Count Razumovskii, affecting to share the Emperor's prejudice, suggested that the negro be covered with the regimental banner. On that, Peter III threw his arms around the Count and thanked him for having given him the idea. All his good humor came back, and he had the negro summoned to his presence.

"Do you know," he said to him, "that the disgrace of having been touched by a scavenger has lost you to our society?"

Narcissus did not understand a word of all this drivel and maintained, on the contrary, that he had defended himself bravely and had given a sound thrashing to the rascal who had struck him. He became even less amenable when he saw that he was to be passed three times under the banner by way of purification, and he had to be held down by four men before the purification ceremony could be successfully accomplished.

But this was not enough for the Emperor, who wanted a few drops of the negro's blood to be drawn with the point of the banner in order to purify and rehabilitate him to the full. Narcissus shrieked and swore at the Emperor, causing all the officers to suffer torments in trying to suppress their desire to laugh, while the Emperor looked upon the scene as a solemn act. It can easily be imagined in what esteem he was held after exhibitions of this kind.

My father was not highly regarded at Court, and although the Emperor showed occasionally a certain respect for my uncle, the Grand Chancellor, he never let himself be guided either by his advice or by the requirements of a sound policy for which he had no understanding whatever. To be general and drill sergeant on parade in the morning, to have an excellent dinner with a good bottle of burgundy, to spend the evening with his buffoons and a few women, and to do whatever he was ordered by the King of Prussia—this was Peter III's idea of bliss. And this was, during the seven months of his reign, the pattern of his daily life, which certainly inspired no respect.

Eager to reconquer from the King of Denmark a handful of land which he considered belonged to him, he did not want to put off the war till after his coronation.

CHAPTER VI

The departure of the Court for Peterhof and Oranienbaum left me with more leisure at my disposal. I no longer spent my evenings at the Emperor's parties, and I thought myself very fortunate to be able to stay in Petersburg. Complete calm seemed to reign in that city, except that certain soldiers in the Guards, fearing that they might at any moment be taken off to fight the King of Denmark, were anxious to act at once. They invented and circulated disturbing rumors concerning the Empress, and those members of our conspiracy who were officers and were responsible for their conduct had the greatest difficulty in restraining them. I authorized one of the officers to tell the soldiers that I was in daily communication with Her Majesty, and that I would warn them through their officers the moment the time had come to act.

And so there the matter rested till 27 June (new style), a day forever memorable for Russia; a day of terror and of happiness for the conspirators, a day that gave final shape to their dreams and ended by realizing them, while only a few hours earlier not one of us knew how and when to broach our schemes; a day that cut the Gordian knot tied by ignorance, and discord, and disagreement about the great event; a day that summoned Providence to lend a helping, if invisible, hand in accomplishing a disjointed plan dreamt about rather than studied by a group of ill-assorted individuals with little sympathy or understanding for each other, and yet united by a desire that they knew to be general, even though they dared not refer to it by the name of *Revolution*.

If all ringleaders of conspiracies admitted how much chance and opportunity had contributed to the success of their various enterprises, they would have to come down from their own lofty pinnacle. Personally I am quite ready to own that though I had been perhaps the first to grasp the possibility of ousting an incompetent monarch, and though I had considered the subject and pondered on it as much as any mind can at the age of eighteen, Passek's arrest produced a greater effect on me than any of my reading or my cogitations or my pondering.

And so it was in the afternoon of 27 June that Grigorii Orlov came to tell me that Captain Passek had been placed under arrest. The latter had been to see me the previous day together with Bredikhin and warned me of the impatience with which the Grenadiers, more than any other regiment, were waiting for their chance to overthrow Peter III; it would suffice, they claimed, to lead them to Oranienbaum against the Holstein troops for everything to be over at once. They added that current rumors filled the troops with apprehension for the Empress's safety and drove them out of their barracks; it would be difficult to hold them back for any length of time, and the turmoil would cause our whole plan to miscarry and would expose us to terrible dangers. I saw that these gentlemen were thoroughly alarmed, and wanting to show them that I was not afraid of sharing their dangers I allowed both of them to tell their troops that I had just heard from the Empress who was living quite calmly at Peterhof, and that they must keep calm too, because we should not let slip the proper time for action. Mr. Passek and Mr. Bredikhin spoke to the soldiers in that sense that very same day with nearly fatal consequences to all of us, for Major Voeikov of the Preobrazhenskii Guards immediately placed Captain Passek under arrest.

I must mention here that after my conversation of the previous day with Mr. Passek and Mr. Bredikhin on the subject of the soldiers' impatience, which I have just described, I felt unable to place much reliance on the officers' power to restrain their soldiers. I therefore wrote to Madame Shkurina, wife of the Empress's personal valet, asking her to send her carriage and four post-horses immediately to her husband in Peterhof with a request from me to keep it always in readiness for the Empress's use should she need it urgently to go to town. For in such a case she would not be able to ask for one of the Court carriages. Mr. Panin, who regarded such an eventuality as remote and uncertain, dubbed this little piece of foresight on my part a *useless act,* and yet God alone knows if without that carriage we should ever have attained the fulfilment of our desires. For Mr. Izmailov, who as Comptroller of the Household was responsible for issuing all orders at Peterhof, could not have been less devoted to the Empress's cause and would therefore have prevented her flight if she had asked him for a carriage.

When Orlov came to inform me of Passek's arrest—an unpleasant piece of news of which he knew neither the cause nor any of the details—my cousin, Mr. Panin, happened to be with me. Whether it was that his cool and phlegmatic temperament did not allow him to view the whole thing in as tragic a light as I did, or whether he wanted to conceal from me the full extent of the danger, he assured me with his usual composure that Passek's arrest could well be a punishment for some minor breach of service discipline. But I saw immediately both that there was no time to lose and that much of it would have to be wasted in trying to convince Mr. Panin of the necessity for quick and decisive action. I agreed with him that Orlov should go to the regimental barracks and try to obtain particulars concerning Passek's detention, that is—whether he had been arrested as an officer or as a criminal. Orlov had to report to me and if rapid action was indicated one of his brothers had to inform Mr. Panin as well.

As soon as Orlov was gone, I pretended to have great need of a rest and begged my cousin to forgive me for asking him to leave. My cousin left at once, and I lost no time in donning a man's greatcoat and setting out on foot to the Roslavlevs' house.

I had not gone very far when I saw a man on horseback riding full gallop. How shall I say—was it the inspiration of the moment or some other cause that made me guess him to be one of the Orlovs? For I had never seen or known any of them except Grigorii. Unable to stop his impetuous course otherwise than by calling out his surname, and being convinced, God knows why, that he was a member of that family, I shouted: "Orlov!" He halted and asked:

"Who is calling me?"

I came up to him, gave my name, and asked him where he was going and whether he had any intelligence for me.

"I was going to you, Madam, to inform you that Passek is kept under arrest as a State criminal and that there are not only four soldiers at his door, but also two posted at every window. My brother is gone to inform Count Panin and I have just been to Roslavlev."

"Did he appear to you dismayed at the events?" I asked.

"He did, slightly," he replied. "But why do you remain out in the street, Princess? Allow me to accompany you home."

"There is no one in the street," I said, "and it might be even less desirable that you should be seen by my servants. Besides, I have this only to say to you: go and tell Roslavlev, Lasunskii, Chertkov, and Bredikhin to go without a moment's delay to the barracks of their regiments, the Izmailovskii Guards, and to remain there to receive the Empress, for it is the first regimental barracks on her route. Then you or one of your brothers must fly like lightning to Peterhof and tell Her Majesty on my behalf that she should take the post carriage which will be waiting for her, and drive off at once to the Izmailovskii Regiment where she will immediately be proclaimed Sovereign, that she should then repair to the next regimental barracks on her way, and that the matter is of such urgency and the loss of a single minute can be so dangerous that I would not delay you by writing to her. Tell her that I spoke to you in the street and implored you to hasten the moment of her arrival. She will understand how essential it is for her to come here as quickly as possible. Good-bye. I may go and meet her myself tonight."

I returned home in such agitation of mind and spirits that all inclination to sleep was banished. To my great disappointment I learned from my maid that the tailor had not yet brought my suit of man's clothes, but I wanted to allay any suspicions my servants might have and therefore retired to bed.

An hour had scarcely passed when I heard someone knocking at the front door. I jumped out of bed and went into the next room where I found my visitor waiting for me. He turned out to be a young man with whom I was not acquainted—the fourth of the Orlov brothers. He came to ask me whether it was not too early to bring the Empress to town and perhaps frighten her to no avail. At these words, anger and anxiety overwhelmed me and I expressed myself in no uncertain terms about the presumptuousness of these brothers who had been so slow in carrying out the orders I had given to Aleksei Orlov.

"This," I said to him, "is no time for trying to spare Her Majesty some moments of anxiety. I would sooner she were brought here in a dead faint than left in Peterhof either to spend a life of unhappiness or to share the scaffold with us. Tell your brother to go at once as fast as his horse can carry him, and bring us the Empress, before Peter III takes sensible advice and either sends someone to town or turns up himself and upsets once and for all what Providence, even more than us, seems to have contrived in order to save Russia and the Empress."

He was impressed by my arguments and would, he assured me as he left, personally see to it that his brother carried out my instructions to the letter.

When he was gone, I was assailed by thoughts and images, all of them melancholy rather than otherwise. And so the night dragged on. I could do nothing, and in default of male clothes I could not even follow my natural impulse to go and meet the Empress. The night seemed to last a lifetime, and imagination never failed to add a semblance of reality to the pictures it evoked by filling them, as in actual life, with moments of happiness and centuries of gloom. Sometimes I would have bewitching visions of the Empress's triumph and of my country's happiness. But in an instant they would all be gone and their place taken by others of quite a different kind. The slightest noise made me jump and in my mind's eye I saw the Empress—that idol of my heart and soul—pale, disfigured, dying, the victim more perhaps of our love for her than of our rashness. I drew a mental picture of the fate that would await me, and my only consolation was that I should suffer death like all those whom I had involved in my own ruin. But then again hope revived.

Happiness came at last when I learnt that Her Majesty had arrived at the barracks of the Izmailovskii Regiment and had been unanimously proclaimed Sovereign, that she had proceeded thence to the Kazan Cathedral where there was a great concourse of people all eager to swear allegiance to her, and that the other regiments, both Guards and of the line, had done so too.

It was six o'clock in the morning when I ordered my maid to make ready the dress I wore on State occasions, and later hastened to the Winter Palace where I knew she had to appear. I shall never be able to describe how I reached her. All the troops that happened to be in Petersburg had joined the Guards Regiments and now surrounded the Palace, filling the great square and sealing off all avenues of approach.

I therefore left my carriage and was about to cross the square on foot when I was recognized by some officers and soldiers. Suddenly I felt myself borne aloft over the heads of all sorts and conditions of men and heard myself called by the most flattering names. Blessings and wishes of prosperity accompanied me till finally I was carried into Her Majesty's ante-chamber with one sleeve lost, dishevelled, and in the greatest possible disarray. But in my state of excitement I imagined all this to represent a sort of Triumph. Besides, I neither could, nor had the time to, put it right and therefore presented myself to the Empress just as I was.

We threw ourselves into each other's arms. "Thank God," "Thank Heaven" was all either of us was able to utter.

Her Majesty then told me the story of how she had stolen away from Peterhof. My heart beat faster as I listened to her, and I relived in my own emotions all the hopes and fears she must have felt in those critical moments. I too confided in her how anxious I had been during those hours of distress and pain which were decisive for her fate and for the happiness or unhappiness of the Empire. I told her the annoying mishap which had prevented my going out to meet her. Again we threw ourselves in each other's arms. No happiness could ever have exceeded mine at that moment. It had reached its summit.

Suddenly I noticed that she was still wearing the Order of St. Catherine and had not yet put on the blue ribbon of the Cross of St. Andrei. (The blue ribbon was not worn by the wife of the Emperor; she was entitled only to the Order of St. Catherine which had been founded by Peter I for his own wife. The Emperor Pavel was the first to grant the blue ribbon to his wife and the Emperor Aleksandr followed his example in this respect.) I ran to Mr. Panin to borrow his blue ribbon, which I put on the Empress's shoulder. Thereupon she took off her own insignia of the Order of St. Catherine and asked me to put them in my pocket.

After a light dinner we proposed to go with the troops to Peterhof. The Empress and I decided to wear the uniform of one of the Guards regiments; she therefore borrowed Captain Talyzin's uniform for the purpose and I that of Lieutenant Pushkin, as these two officers were roughly similar to us in height. These uniforms, by the way, were those the Preobrazhenskii Regiment formerly wore from the time of Peter the Great down to the reign of Peter III, who abolished them in favor of Prussian-type uniforms. And it is a peculiar thing that no sooner did the Empress arrive in Petersburg than the soldiers threw off their new Prussian uniforms and donned their old ones, which they somehow managed to find.

I went quickly home to change so as to be more useful to the Empress in case of need. When I came back to the Palace, Her Majesty, together with those senators that happened to be in town, was holding a kind of council regarding the manifestoes that should be immediately published, etc., etc. Teplov acted as secretary.

It was more than likely that Peter III had by now been informed of the Empress's flight from Peterhof and of the excitement in town. It therefore occurred to me that he could well have been advised by someone in his entourage to act with courage and determination and to come to Petersburg, if necessary in disguise. This thought struck me so forcibly that I did not want to wait till the sitting of the Council was over. I had no right to force my way into that august assembly, but the two junior officers posted at the door either thought the order they had received not to let anyone in did not apply to me or else it never occurred to them that I should not go in. In any case they opened the door for me. I went quickly

up to Her Majesty's chair and whispered into her ear what my apprehensions were, adding that if she wanted to take preventive measures she
had better take them now without loss of time. Thereupon Her Majesty
summoned Mr. Teplov to write out an order and relevant instructions in
two copies, to be given to two men who were to be posted at the mouth
of the two rivers which formed the only possible approaches to the city.

The Empress, who foresaw the embarrassment that my appearance
might cause, explained to those venerable old statesmen, who failed to
recognize me, who I was and said that my friendship for her, always on
the alert to help, had suggested something she had forgotten.

I looked like a boy of fifteen in my uniform, and the appearance of a
young and totally unknown Guards officer in the midst of their sanctuary speaking in Her Majesty's ear must have been strange indeed. But no
sooner did she mention my name than they all rose from their seats and
gravely bowed to me in solemn welcome. I really did behave rather like a
small boy and at this mark of respect I blushed and was overcome with
confusion.

Soon after the sitting was over and the Empress had given orders to
ensure the safety of the city, we mounted our horses and reviewed the
troops, who numbered twelve thousand without counting the volunteers
who were increasing every moment.

The troops had been on foot for the past twelve hours and therefore
as soon as we reached Krasnyi Kabak, just over six miles away from the
city, we made a three-hour halt. We too were badly in need of rest. I had
scarcely slept at all for a whole fortnight, and although I could not have
fallen asleep at that actual moment, it was the greatest possible bliss to be
able to stretch myself out on a bed and rest my tired limbs. There was only
one bed in that house, which was nothing but a wretched tavern, and Her
Majesty decided that we should both of us lie on it without undressing.
The bed was filthy, and I covered it with a large cloak which I obtained
from Colonel Karr; but scarcely did we lie down than I noticed a small
door by the Empress's pillow, leading I knew not where. This worried
me, and I asked her permission to get up and explore the passage. On
opening the door I saw that it led into a dark cubby-hole and thence into
the yard outside. I had two sentries of the Horse Guards Regiment posted
there with strict orders not to move without my permission and not to
let anyone near that door. After this, I went back to bed, and as we could
not sleep, Her Majesty read out to me the various manifestoes that she
intended to publish on our return to town. We told each other our fears,
but henceforth they were overshadowed by our hopes.

CHAPTER VII

In the meantime Peter III could come to no decision, and failed even to listen to the advice of Field-Marshal Münnich who happened to be with him at the time. He came to Peterhof, went back to Oranienbaum, and finally yielded to pressure from his friends who urged him to go to Kronstadt and make himself master of the place and of the fleet. But he arrived too late. Admiral Talyzin, who had been despatched by the Empress, was already in command and refused Peter III permission to land. He was therefore forced to return to Oranienbaum, whence he sent General Izmailov with overtures couched in the most submissive terms and with offers of abdication.

Izmailov reached us when we were already on our way to Peterhof. His language was very different to that of my uncle the Grand Chancellor, who came at the moment we were leaving the city and remonstrated with the Empress. Seeing that his arguments got him nowhere, he retired to his own house and refused to swear the oath of allegiance to her. He assured Her Majesty that he would undertake nothing against her by word or deed, but at the same time would not betray the oath he had sworn to Peter III so long as the Emperor was alive. He begged the Empress to appoint an officer who would be attached to his person and see everything that took place in his house, and then withdrew with quiet dignity. I admired my uncle's dignified behavior all the more since I knew in what low esteem he held the Emperor, and how much the true patriot in him was grieved at the sight of the Sovereign's total incapacity to govern and the dire consequences that were likely to follow.

The Empress sent General Izmailov back to the Emperor beseeching him to persuade His Majesty to give himself up and thus avoid all the incalculable mischief which could not otherwise be prevented; she would then undertake to render his existence as pleasant as possible in any residence he might choose some distance away from Petersburg, and would do her utmost to provide for all his desires.

We were approaching Trinity Convent when the Vice-Chancellor Prince Golitsyn arrived with a letter from the Emperor, while the number of followers in our wake was swelled every instant by all those who were leaving him of their own accord.

As Oranienbaum is only about six miles away from Peterhof, Peter III arrived very shortly after us, accompanied by General Izmailov and his A. D. C. General Gudovich. He was conducted, unseen by any but a very few, to a remote apartment where dinner was served. Afterward he left for Ropsha, which had belonged to him when he was Grand Duke and which he now chose in preference to any other residence. The Emperor was accompanied by Aleksei Orlov, who had under him Captain Passek, Prince Fedor Bariatinskii, and Lieutenant Baskakov of the Preobrazhenskii Guards, to whom the Empress had entrusted the custody of his person. I did not see him, though I could have, but I was assured that he was little affected by his situation, enjoyed a good appetite, drank his favorite wine—burgundy—and wrote two or three letters to his august wife. I shall quote only one of them in which his abdication was well and clearly stated; after naming a few persons (including his favorite negro Narcissus) whom he desired to have with him with the Empress's permission, he mentioned also the provisions he would like to have, which were: burgundy wine, a few pipes, and tobacco.

But enough on the subject of a prince, unfortunate because placed on a pedestal high above his natural level. He was not wicked, but his incompetence and lack of education, as well as inclination and natural bent, all combined to make of him a good Prussian corporal and not the Sovereign of a great Empire.

Ever since the previous day I had had no rest, but so subordinate are my physical needs to my spiritual and mental preoccupations that I only felt tired whenever I sat down. I had continually to rush from one end of the Palace to the other as well as to make occasional visits to the sentries downstairs posted at the various entrances. On one occasion after speaking to the Empress's cousin, the Princess of Holstein, I went back to ask Her Majesty whether she would consent to see her for a moment. What was my surprise at finding Grigorii Orlov, on the pretext of having hurt his leg, stretched out on a sofa in one of the rooms, opening large bundles of papers which I recognized to be communications from the Supreme Council, such as I had seen in my uncle's care during the reign of the Empress Elizaveta. I asked him what he was doing, and he replied:

"The Empress has ordered me to open them."

"I doubt it," I said, "since no action need be taken on them for a few more days till the Empress appoints people who will officially deal with them. But neither you nor I are qualified for that work."

On this I left him to go and argue with the soldiers, who, thirsty and tired, had broken into a cellar and were drinking gallons of Hungary wine straight out of their hats, thinking it to be a kind of light mead. I succeeded better than I hoped. The soldiers emptied on the ground all the wine in their hats, rolled the barrels back into the cellar, and sent instead for water from a spring. I was all the more surprised by this proof of their esteem and confidence as they had not obeyed their officers who had spoken to them before me. I gave them whatever money I had left, then turned my pockets inside out to show I had no more to give, and promised that on our arrival in town all the taverns would be open to them and they would be able to drink at the expense of the Crown. My arguments were appreciated and had the desired effect.

I should mention here that this was all my own money. I had never asked the Empress for money, nor received any from her, nor for that matter, had I ever accepted any from the French Ambassador as some writers have claimed. It is true that offers of loans—and immense loans at that—had been made to me, but my answer had always been that with my knowlege or consent no foreign money would ever be employed to bring about the Revolution in Russia.

When I came back to the Palace I saw in the room in which Grigorii Orlov was lying on a sofa a table laid for three. I pretended not to notice. Presently Her Majesty was told that her dinner was served. She invited me to share it, and to my great annoyance I saw it being served by the side of Orlov's sofa. Apparently my face betrayed my emotions, which were those of anger, tempered by sadness, for I sincerely loved the Empress. She asked me what the matter was.

"Nothing," I said, "except that I have had no sleep for the past fortnight and am terribly tired."

She then begged me to lend her my support against Orlov, who wanted to leave the service.

"Just think," she added, "how ungrateful I should appear if I allowed him to retire."

My reply was the opposite of what she wanted it to be. I told her that now she was Sovereign she was in the position to reward him in a manner which would make his fame resound far and wide, without compelling him to stay in the service. It was then I realized with a pang that Orlov was her lover, and that never would she be able to keep it a secret.

After our meal and Peter III's departure, we left Peterhof. We broke our journey at Prince Kurakin's country house, which had only one bed and again we had to share it. Our next stopping place was Katerinhof where there was a vast concourse of people, and the populace was coming over to our side in droves, ready to defend us in case of a pitched battle between our troops and the Holstenians who were generally hated.

Our entry into the city beggared all description. Countless people thronged the streets shouting and screaming, invoking blessings upon us and giving vent to their joy in a thousand ways, while the old and the sick were held up at open windows by their children to enable them to see with their own eyes the triumph that shone on everyone's face. The music of the regimental bands, the peal of church bells, the holy altars aflame with lights and shining through the open doors of churches from the darkness within, revealing groups of priests in sacred vestments with their crosses held high aloft as if to consecrate the universal joy-—such was the general picture which presented itself to my eyes, but which I can but very imperfectly describe, as, overwhelmed by my own emotions and almost oblivious of reality, I rode by the side of the Empress. I rode reflecting on the blessings of a bloodless Revolution, and contemplating in this gift of Heaven both a beneficent Sovereign and an adored friend whom my own efforts had helped to rescue from a perilous situation, even, perhaps, from a horrible fate, and to place on the throne of my beloved country.

I was so overwhelmed by a host of different sentiments and by the desire to see my father, my uncle, and my daughter, that we no sooner arrived at the Summer Palace than, without leaving the Empress time to enter it, I asked her for permission to take the carriage that had followed us on the way in order to visit them. Her Majesty immediately granted me the permission I asked for and kindly besought me to return as quickly as possible.

My uncle's house happened to be the nearest, and so I went to him first. I found him in fairly good spirits and as cool and collected as ever. He spoke to me of Peter III's overthrow as of something he had expected, and then gave me a few words of warning on the subject of the friendship of princes, which, he said, was neither very stable nor very sincere. He had had proof of this in the reign of a Princess who had avowedly been friendly to him and to whom he had been devoted from the time of his youth, yet all the purity of his actions and intentions had not saved him from the poison of intrigue and envy.

From him I went to my father, who was not quite his usual self. His annoyance was due to the behavior of Mr. Kakovinskii, the officer detailed to look after him and see that he was not disturbed by a chance brawl among drunken soldiers, which might easily have occurred as there were two Guards regiments stationed next to his house. On the pretext that the house possessed a great many servants, Mr. Kakovinskii retained a considerable number of soldiers who were in need of rest, while we had only just enough soldiers left in town to relieve the troops guarding the various palaces, including that of the Grand Duke Pavel, who had remained in Petersburg with his tutor. (It became evident soon afterward that Mr. Kakovinskii was a man of unsound mind. During our stay in Moscow he publicly abjured the Greek faith and became a Catholic.)

On arriving at the courtyard of my father's house I recognized a junior officer, adjutant to Lieutenant-Colonel Vadkovskii who had remained in command of all the Guards in town during our absence. The adjutant had just asked for thirty soldiers who were, in effect, useless in my father's house, but were badly needed to relieve those who had remained at their post for double the usual time.

I told Mr. Kakovinskii that he must immediately carry out Mr. Vadkovskii's wishes, and added that I myself saw no necessity for having a hundred soldiers in my father's house. And when I saw a soldier posted at the door of every room I told him he had misunderstood Her Majesty's wishes and instructions. He was there, I said, to guarantee the safety of the house and not to create the impression that my father was fomenting sedition. I told the soldiers they had been needlessly ill-treated, and that only ten or twelve of them should stay and await new orders.

My father received me without a trace of anger, but said he was sorry to have been kept for the past twenty-four hours as a prisoner of State. He complained, too, of my sister Countess Elizaveta's presence in the house. I assured him that his first grievance sprang from the foolish behavior of Kakovinskii and that I was certain he would not have a soldier in the house before nightfall. As to the second of his complaints, I implored him to have some sympathy for my sister's position and to remember that his house was the only respectable and, indeed, natural shelter left to her;

later, means could be found in all decency to give effect to their mutural desire not to live under the same roof.

My father did not want to let me go, but I pointed out to him that I had to go and see my sister, then go home, see my daughter and change into something other than my military uniform, and that the Empress had asked me to come back to her as soon as possible.

It was only with difficulty that he allowed me to visit my sister. He had never had much affection for her, and the low esteem in which she held him when, after the first few weeks of Peter III's reign, he had lost all influence and prestige and become a nonentity, did little to improve matters.

Immediately I entered my sister's room she began complaining bitterly about what had happened. I assured her of my affection and my readiness to serve her, and told her I had not spoken about her to the Empress, being convinced that Her Majesty was kindly disposed toward her and prepared to treat her with generosity. She should have no fear, I said, but that everything possible would be done for her. And indeed, the Empress merely expressed the wish that she should not be present at the Coronation festivities. Apart from that she sent her several messages to assure her of her protection.

My sister left some time before us for an estate of my father's in the neighborhood of Moscow. Later, after the Court's departure, she lived in Moscow till her marriage to Mr. Polianskii, after which she frequently stayed in Petersburg where her husband had a house and land. Her Majesty became godmother to her son, and on my return from abroad I even prevailed on Her Majesty to make her daughter a maid-of-honor.

On leaving my sister, I went home to kiss my little Anastasiia. These three visits had taken a long time, and by then it was very late. I therefore had no time to change and tidy myself, and I was in a hurry to go to the Palace. My maid told me that she had felt a weight in the pocket of my dressing-gown and found it to be the Order of St. Catherine in diamonds. It was the Empress's. I took it. As I entered the room next to that of the Empress, I saw Grigorii Orlov and Kakovinskii coming out of it, and when I went up to the Empress I could no longer doubt that Orlov was my enemy. For no one else could have introduced Kakovinskii to the Empress. Besides, Her Majesty immediately reproached me for having spoken to that officer in French in front of soldiers, thus arousing the suspicion that I wanted him to dismiss them.

I answered curtly and my face wore the expression of the most perfect disdain. "It is too early, Ma'am," I said. "You have not been on the throne for more than a few hours and your troops, who have shown every sign of trusting me implicitly, could hardly have worried about what I might say in whatever language it might be." And I handed her back the Order of St. Catherine so as to cut short this conversation.

"Come, now," she said, "you will admit, though, that you ought not to have dismissed the soldiers."

"True enough, Ma'am," I said, "in spite of Mr. Vadkovskii's entreaties I should not have interfered with that fool Kakovinskii, and should have left you with no guard to relieve those who were looking after your safety and the safety of your Palace."

"Now, now," she said, "let's leave it at that. So much for your quick temper, and this"—making a move to pin on my shoulder the Order which I had returned to her—"is for your services."

Far from kneeling to receive the decoration, I said to her: "Forgive me, Your Majesty, for what I am going to say to you. You are approaching the moment when, for all you may wish to the contrary, truth will be banished from your ears; I implore you not to confer this Order on me, because if it is meant as an ornament you know that I set no store by such things; if it is for my services, then, however mediocre they may appear to some people, in my own eyes they cannot be repaid because I am not to be bought, nor ever shall be, at any price."

Her Majesty embraced me, with the words: "At least let friendship enjoy its rights."

I kissed her hand—and there I was in an officer's uniform, with a ribbon (but no star) across the shoulder, only one spur, and looking for all the world like a little boy of fourteen.

Her Majesty then told me that she had already despatched a Guards lieutenant to my husband, with a note to make him turn back on his tracks and join us as quickly as possible. This news gave me so much pleasure that I immediately forgot all the very justifiable anger I felt toward her.

I stayed for about another hour with the Empress. She told me she would have an apartment ready for me in this same Palace the very next day; I requested that she should leave me at my own house till the arrival of my husband, and that we should then move in together.

The Hetman Count Razumovskii and Mr. Panin left the Empress's apartments at the same time as I. I repeated to them what I had seen at Peterhof and the conversation she had had with me during dinner, and told them I was sure Orlov was Her Majesty's lover, to which Mr. Panin replied: "It's lack of sleep for a fortnight at a stretch and your eighteen years of age that have excited your imagination."

"Very well," I said to him, "I agree, but as soon as you satisfy yourself that I was right you must allow me to tell you that you are nothing but a couple of fools. You and your cool heads!"

The bargain was struck and I hastened back home and to bed. A wing of chicken which I found—the remains of my child's dinner—was all I ate, and being in a hurry to enjoy the benefit conferred by Morpheus I slipped into bed very quickly. But so much excitement coursed through my veins that whenever I dozed off my legs and arms began to twitch, my whole body shook so violently that it almost leapt in the air, and I awoke with a start.

Here I must mention an incident which I forgot to mention before and which occurred on our way back to town. When we took our seats in the carriage—the Empress, myself, Count Razumovskii, and Prince Volkonskii—in order to rest a while, Her Majesty asked me what she could do for me so as to repay me in some sort.

"Give happiness to my country," I said, "continue to have for me the sentiments which are responsible for my own present happiness, and I shall be content."

"But this is merely my duty," she replied, "and I want to lighten the weight which I feel upon my conscience."

"I never thought," I retorted, "that the service of friendship could be a burden to you."

"Well, anyway," said Her Majesty, "tax me with anything you like, but I shall have no peace of mind unless you let me know this instant what I could do to give you pleasure." She embraced me as she spoke.

"Well then," I said to her, "restore to life an uncle of mine who does not happen to be dead."

"This is an enigma," she said.

"Prince Volkonskii will explain it to you," I replied, for though I was not soliciting this favor for myself it cost me a lot to ask for it.

Prince Volkonskii told Her Majesty that General Leontiev, my husband's uncle, while serving with distinction in the army sent against the Prussians, had been deprived, through his wife's intrigues, of a seventh of his land and a quarter of his furniture and cash—which she should have received at his death (as is the right of widows in Russia). Peter III became all the more readily party to this injustice, as he felt a resentment against all generals who had served well against Frederick.

The Empress admitted the justice of the case, and promised me that this would be one of the first Orders-in-Council she would sign.

"Well, Ma'am," I said, "I shall be excellently rewarded by Your Majesty, as he is my mother-in-law's only brother whom she holds most dear."

I was very pleased thus to give the Prince's mother proof of my attachment to the family and overjoyed at successfully evading the receipt of a bounty, as this went against my principles.

The following day Mr. Panin was granted the title of Count and a pension of 5,000 roubles, and Prince Volkonskii and Count Razumovskii received the same pension. The rest of the conspirators of the first class were to receive 600 peasants and a pension of 2,000 roubles, or else 24,000 roubles in lieu of land. To my great surprise I found myself in that class. I did not want to take advantage of the choice that was given of accepting land or 24,000 roubles, as my mind was quite made up not to accept either. Many of those who had taken part in the Revolution blamed my disinterestedness, but my friends advised me differently. And so, in order not to swell the general outcry or to annoy the Empress, I asked to be given a list of my husband's debts, and as they amounted to about 24,000 roubles, I ordered this sum to be used for buying back the bonds or papers held by the Prince's creditors. This was done by Her Majesty's Private Office on receipt of my order.

The following day Mass was said in the Great Chapel, and we saw Grigorii Orlov wearing the Order of St. Aleksandr. As soon as Divine Service was over I came up to my uncle and Count Razumovskii, who did not expect it, and said to them with a meaningful air:

"With all due respect, you are a couple of fools."

On the fourth day after the accession to the throne, Mr. Betskoi requested a moment's audience of Her Majesty, which was granted—I was the only one to be present, together with the Empress. What was our surprise when he fell on his knees and begged her to tell him by whom she thought she had been raised to the throne.

Her Majesty's answer was: "I owe my accession to God and to my good and faithful subjects."

"Then," he replied, "I can no longer wear this ribbon," and he made to take off the Order of St. Aleksandr with which he was decorated. The Empress would not let him and asked him what the matter was.

"I am," he said, "the unhappiest of men, since you do not know that the guards on that occasion had been posted, and the money distributed among them, by me."

We thought—not without reason—that he was completely mad. The Empress got rid of him very cleverly by telling him she knew how much she owed him, and that therefore he would be the only person to whom she would entrust the responsibility of looking after the jewellers who were to make the great new crown in diamonds to be used on the day of her coronation. He got up in a rapture of very obvious delight, and left us immediately, apparently in a hurry to communicate this great news to his friends. We had a good laugh about it and I admired Her Majesty's inventive spirit which had rid her of a tiring madman.

CHAPTER VIII

❧❧❧

The Petersburg Court presented a great deal of interest at that time. It was composed of new people placed there by the Revolution, and of exiles who had been banished during the reign of Empress Anna, the Regency of Biron, and the reign of Empress Elizaveta.

The name of Empress Anna reminds me of two amusing little stories told about her. It is a well-known fact that in Peter I's reign it was customary to punish nobles who had offended the tyrant by ordering them to become buffoons. The unfortunate victim, however intelligent or knowledgeable, immediately became the laughing stock of the whole Court. He could say whatever he liked, but on the other hand he could also be kicked and beaten without having the right to retaliate. People made fun of everything he said, echoed his complaints as if they were expressions of delight, and repeated his sarcasms as if they were glimmers of intelligence *surprising in a fool.*

The Empress Anna excelled in this barbaric cruelty, but in a manner so amusing that people could not help laughing. She ordered an unfortunate Prince Golitsyn [1] to become a *hen,* in order to punish him for some slight misdemeanor. She had a large basket full of straw brought into one of the reception rooms. A score of eggs was placed in the basket and the Prince was made to sit on them, and obliged, on pain of death, to cackle as if about to hatch a brood of chickens.

The same sovereign was very fond of Countess Chernysheva and often ordered her to come into her presence in order to amuse her with her conversation. The poor lady was very delicate and her legs used to swell

[1] See Index under Golitsyn, Mikhail.—K. F.

whenever she had to stand. The Empress did not want to deprive herself of the entertainment which the Countess's company afforded, and saw her suffer incredible torments without the idea of a subject sitting down in the presence of her Sovereign ever entering her Imperial head. In the end, seeing her friend grow pale, totter, stand on one leg, then on the other, while trying to be pleasant and amiable all the time, she took pity on her and said:

"You lean against the back of that chair and I shall pretend not to see you."

It was the Empress Anna, too, who, curious to see the Russian national dance, had four of the most beautiful married women in Petersburg brought to her in order to see them dance. My mother, who shone at dancing, was one of the four beauties selected for the honor but, intimidated by the Empress's stern gaze, she and her young companions shook so much in every limb that they soon muddled all the steps. Thereupon Her Majesty rose from her seat, came up to them and, giving each of them a slap in the face, ordered them to begin again, which they did more dead than alive.

These anecdotes are perhaps hardly in place here, but they seem to me interesting.

However, to go back to the main thread of my story. The return of all those exiles, recalled by Peter III and now gradually arriving from the various places to which they had been relegated, meant that newcomers appeared almost every day. They were living pictures of olden times, interesting through their misfortunes and able to satisfy curiosity regarding Court and Cabinet secrets of which they had a perfect knowledge, as many of them had occupied important posts.

At last the famous Count Bestuzhev, formerly Grand Chancellor, also arrived. It was the Empress herself who introduced us to each other. And a phrase escaped her which the Orlovs would have stifled had they been able to do so:

"This is Princess Dashkova. Would you have thought that I would owe the Crown to the young daughter of Count Roman Vorontsov?!"

Present-day French writers who pile up remorselessly lie upon lie and thus rob history of any consolation or profit that might be derived from it, have said that I helped Count Bestuzhev to intrigue against Peter III, whereas, in fact, the Count was exiled when I was not yet fourteen. He was unfavorably disposed toward my uncle and I saw him then only once, from a distance, and was struck by the intelligence of his expression as well as by the duplicity and cunning depicted on his face. I asked who he was and was told his name.

Field-Marshal Münnich and Mr. Lestocq, who were fond of my uncle and whom I had, therefore, often seen in my uncle's house, seemed to me animated chronicles, able to give me unfailing lessons in the nature of the human heart which I still saw through rose-colored spectacles. The former, a distinguished old man whose granddaughters were older than myself, became very friendly with me. His intelligence, the firmness of his character, his manner at once courteous and attentive, making him a true gentleman of former times—a contrast to some of our conspirators—rendered his conversation of great interest to me.

This *tableau vivant,* with new objects appearing one after another in quick succession, and indeed, the very disparity of these objects, gave me much food for thought and helped my mind to mature. Soon another person arrived, who, perhaps in all innocence and without even being in the slightest responsible for it, was the source of my earliest and bitter sorrows, a person against whom a woman's courage was not sufficient. She was the Empress's First Woman of the Bedchamber at the time when the Empress was Grand Duchess, and she had gone into exile at the same time as Count Bestuzhev. She was a gentlewoman by birth, had a great deal of native wit about her and, as she had known my mother, people made use of her name to harm me in my father's eyes. However, I shall return to this later.[2]

In the meantime an event occurred which absorbed all my thoughts and filled me with horror and consternation.

When the news was received of the horrible death of Peter III, I was so affected by it and so incensed, even though my heart refused to believe the Empress capable of being the accomplice of Aleksei Orlov's crime, that only the following day could I be persuaded to visit her. When I did, I found her sad and upset. The actual words she said to me were:

"I am shocked by this death, and dismayed."

"It comes too early for your good fame, and for mine," I replied.

That evening in the apartment of the Empress I was rash enough to say

[2] The reference is probably to Maria Zhukova, a great favorite of Catherine's when the latter had just arrived in Russia. Catherine's mother, the Princess of Anhalt-Zerbst, jealous of her daughter's friendship for Maria Zhukova, had her banished from the Court and exiled. She later married a Lieutenant Travin and returned to St Petersburg in 1762.— K. F.

that I hoped Aleksei Orlov would more than ever feel we were not people made to breathe happily the same atmosphere, and that I prided myself on thinking he would never presume to approach me. All the brothers became my implacable enemies; and Aleksei, on returning from Ropsha and for over twenty years afterward, never, for all his insolence, had the temerity to speak to me.

In case anyone presumes to suspect the Empress of having ordered, or connived at, her husband's assassination, I can fortunately advance complete proof to the contrary: the letter of Aleksei Orlov, which Her Majesty had carefully preserved in her strongbox. After her death Pavel had the box opened and ordered Prince Bezborodko to read to him the papers it contained. When Bezborodko came to the letter His Majesty crossed himself as if to thank Heaven and said:

"The few doubts I ever had on the subject have, thank God, been dispelled by this letter."

It was written in Aleksei's own hand, and he wrote like a stevedore. The vulgarity of his expressions, his incoherence (he was dead drunk at the time), his prayers for forgiveness and the sort of surprise he himself showed at the catastrophe made this a very interesting document for those who would like to confute the horrible slanders that have been spread about the Empress, who might have had weaknesses, but was not capable of any kind of crime.

Drunk and terrified, Aleksei sent off that fine epistle to Her Majesty a few moments after Peter III's death. I was rarely in my life so happy and so pleased as when I heard after Pavel I's death that the letter had not been destroyed, and that Pavel had had the letter read out to him in the presence of his wife and of Miss Nelidova, and had ordered it to be shown to the Grand Dukes and Count Rostopchin.[3]

---

[3] This is not quite accurate. The Emperor Pavel destroyed the original letter: he threw it into the fire in a fit of disgust, and for ever afterward repented having done so. However, Rostopchin, to whom the letter had been lent for a quarter of an hour, had time to copy it and later communicated the copy to Simon Vorontsov. It has thus been preserved in the Vorontsov archives and reads as follows:

"My dear Lady, merciful Sovereign! How can I explain or describe what has happened: never will you believe your faithful servant, but I shall speak the truth as before God. My dear Lady! I swear by my life I know not myself how that misfortune happened. We are lost if you do not show mercy. My dear Lady, he is no more. But it never occurred to anyone, and how could it occur to us, to lift a hand against our Sovereign. But, my Sovereign Lady, a misfortune happened. He started arguing at table with Prince Fedor.

My joy at seeing Prince Dashkov again was beyond description. It gave me a fresh lease of life after a spell filled with the most extraordinary events, the physical and mental strain of which was beginning to undermine my rather delicate health. Her Majesty lost no time in celebrating my husband's homecoming by giving him the command of the Cuirassier Regiment of which she herself was Colonel-in-Chief. This regiment which, under the Empress Elizaveta as well as under Peter III, was the First or Life Guards Regiment had been riddled with German officers, and Her Majesty wanted it now to have a Russian nobleman for a commanding officer. This appointment gave Prince Dashkov a great deal of pleasure.[4] Soon he saw young Russians of the nobility flocking to it. He became the soldiers' favorite and spared no expense in horses, etc., etc., to make it into the finest regiment of cavalry.

The first thing we did, the Prince and I, was to move into the apartments that had been set aside for us in the Palace. We dined with the Empress and, as she never had any supper, we made a habit of always inviting ten to twelve people to have supper with us and had it brought up to our apartments.

As the days of my illusions regarding the friendship of Sovereigns are nearly over, I may perhaps be allowed to dwell yet a moment on the graciousness of the Empress at those small, intimate parties.

She could be childishly gay. I was passionately fond of music; she did not care much for it, and though my husband quite liked it, he was in no sense a performer. Sometimes, however, Her Majesty would ask me to sing. On one occasion, as soon as I had finished, she made a sign to my husband and said:

"Come, Prince, let us sing too."

And they began what she called "the music of the spheres," both of them screaming loudly and discordantly enough to frighten anyone, yet

---

We did not have time to separate them before he passed away. We cannot remember what we were doing, but we are all guilty, everyone of us, and worthy of death. Show mercy on me if only for my brother's sake. You have my full confession and there is nothing to investigate. Forgive me or give orders to make a quick end. Life's not worth living: we have aroused your anger and lost our souls forever."

"He" is, of course, the Emperor; "Prince Fedor" is Bariatinskii; "my brother" is Grigorii Orlov, Catherine's lover at the time of Peter's murder.—K. F.

[4] His pleasure must have been considerably enhanced by the opportunity the appointment gave him for enriching himself. Dashkov was notorious for his dishonest deals in connection with purchases of food and fodder for his regiment.—K. F.

with the serious, self-satisfied expression of people who imagine they are giving immense pleasure to others and are delighted with themselves.

At other times it would be "the cats' concert." Then she would caterwaul, taking care to add appropriate words of her own invention, which made us all split our sides with laughter. Or else she would growl, spit, and box her own ears for all the world like two quarrelling cats.

I really believe there has never been anyone in the world, and certainly never any Sovereign, to equal her in the sheer magic of personality, in the resources of the mind, in versatility, and above all in the charm with which she displayed these gifts.

But I must return to the main thread of my story.

A lieutenant in the Guards called Mikhail Pushkin had served in the same regiment as my husband. He was intelligent, and his witty and amusing conversation made him welcome among young people. He and my husband had, therefore, a sort of feeling of attachment for each other, which habit and familiarity had made them mistake for friendship. I had saved him once, having at my husband's request prevailed upon the Marquis de l'Hospital, the French Ambassador at our Court, to stop an action brought against him by the principal French merchant in Petersburg, named Heinberg, and backed by the Ambassador. It was a serious case, for instead of paying the merchant whatever he owed him, Pushkin chased him out of the house and threw him out.

I was still engaged to the Prince at the time, but I saw the Marquis every day in our—that is, my uncle's, the Grand Chancellor's—house, and by dint of imploring him I prevailed upon him to write a note to the officer commanding the regiment, Prince Menshikov, saying in effect that as Heinberg had received satisfaction from Pushkin, he, the French Ambassador, had not only no more demands to make, but requested Prince Menshikov to put a stop to the case and not let Mr. Pushkin be worried any further.

I quote this little story merely to show the character of a man who was responsible for another rather pointless quarrel I had with the Empress. I want to disguise nothing in this narrative. I shall tell of the little differences that cropped up between Her Majesty and myself, and because I shall hide nothing the reader will see for himself that I never fell into disgrace, as has been claimed by several writers who wanted to harm her interests, and that if the Empress did not do more [...] she had an intimate knowledge of me and was quite [...] of self-seeking was entirely alien to my nature.

Besides, my heart remained, in the midst of Court life, so artless, so unspoilt, that I forgave even those who showed black ingratitude, egged on as they were by my all-powerful enemies who managed to turn against me those I had done all I could to help. I have waited forty-two years before venturing to reveal the whole of my experience of human ingratitude, which, however, never made me tired of doing all the good of which I was capable, often at the cost of great financial inconvenience, for my means were more than modest.

Mikhail Pushkin was one of those who repaid my services with ingratitude. His father had been guilty of peculation, lost his place in consequence, and was brought to trial in the later years of the Empress Elizaveta's reign. He was therefore very badly off and could give nothing to his son. Mikhail Pushkin's service pay was very slight and it was my husband's liberality that helped him and his brother out of their difficulties.

In Peter III's reign Mr. Panin had the idea of surrounding his ward with well-educated young men, with a knowledge of literature and foreign languages. The Empress mentioned it to me one day. I told her I knew a young man who possessed all these qualifications to an eminent degree and gave Mikhail Pushkin's name. A few weeks passed after this conversation and in the meantime Pushkin became implicated in a most disgraceful affair. Though I did not like the young man myself, the Empress and I, out of regard for my husband, thought out ways and means of helping him out, and succeeded.

In spite of all these benefits conferred on him both by my husband and by me, he soon afterward played a nasty trick on me. It was after the Empress had already ascended the throne and while we were living in the Palace. He came to see me one day looking dejected and miserable. I asked him what the matter was, and he answered that his wretched fate would never change, for in spite of my promise to obtain a place for him in the Grand Duke's establishment, nothing had in fact come of it. I was confident in my belief that any attempt to comfort a man and revive his hopes could yield nothing but gratitude and a more hopeful outlook on his part. I told him that even if that unfortunate occurrence could jeopardize his chances of becoming a member of the young Grand Duke's household, it should not prevent him from obtaining very favorable employment where his knowledge and his talents could be shown to advantage.

Now, a few weeks before the Empress's accession to the throne, Mr. Panin happened to be a guest of Her Majesty, together with his charge. I was there too, and heard him say that the young Prince was very shy, even a little unsociable, and that this was due to his seeing only few people. He thereupon renewed the suggestion of attaching to his person a number of well-educated young men, among them Mikhail Pushkin. This Mr. Panin did because my husband, before his own departure for the Embassy in Constantinople, had very strongly commended Pushkin to him.

On hearing Pushkin's name, Her Majesty said:

"I am quite ready to believe that that recent nasty story is nothing but slander, but the publicity it has received and the doubt that must persist are quite enough to make it impossible to attach him to my son's household."

I entirely agreed with Her Majesty, but I could not help reminding her that it was well before that affair that I had proposed Pushkin to her, that my uncle, too, must be aware that my husband had made his request before his departure (that is, four months earlier), and that if the whole thing was due to nothing but slander, a poor, but gifted young man, who could be useful to his country, must not be passed over and allowed to vegetate somewhere in a corner.

The Empress and my uncle shared my point of view. That was why in the course of my conversation with Pushkin, which I have already mentioned, I let him understand that he should not set his heart on that particular appointment because, for all her goodwill, Her Majesty might not consider it fitting that he should have it.

And yet what were the consequences of all this? Immediately on leaving me he met Mr. Zinoviev, to whom with the same despairing face he confided his misfortunes, adding that he was the unhappiest of men since he had just heard from me that the Empress believed in the truth of the disgraceful story that was being circulated about him.

Zinoviev offered to take him to the favorite, Grigorii Orlov, with whom he was not only friendly but intimate, and introduced him merely as someone needing his protection. Orlov asked him what it was all about, and Pushkin told him his story with all the eloquence he could muster. Thereupon Orlov, always keen to do me as much harm as possible, assured him that the Empress did not think of him in that way, and that he would speak to her that very evening.

That evening, as we were about to go to bed, the Prince's valet brought him a letter. We could not have been more surprised on seeing that it was a kind of apology from Pushkin, who wrote that Mr. Zinoviev had beguiled him into Orlov's house, that he could hardly remember what he had said there other than that he felt it could have some unpleasant consequences for me, that his sense of obligation to us even more than his sense of fair play made him disavow everything he had said in Orlov's house, and that he would have a written testimonial to that effect ready early next morning to give to the Prince's servant.

My advice was not to send a servant the next morning, but my husband thought it would be a little hard to refuse him the opportunity of justifying himself.

Next morning when I went as usual to the Empress, she immediately enquired why I gave anxiety to her subjects by making them believe she had a poor opinion of them. I had, she said, greatly grieved Pushkin by giving him the impression that she had a poor opinion of him.

I was taken aback by such a welcome, but restrained myself, merely reminding Her Majesty that I had wanted to help Pushkin in view of the friendship which my husband had formed for him in his youth and of which, be it said by the way, he was not at all proud. I let her, I added, be her own judge of his behavior toward me, but surely a sensible and enlightened person like herself did not consider it reprehensible to give such comfort as friendship or pity enjoined upon us; far from telling Pushkin that Her Majesty believed the story so detrimental to his character, I assured him that if he were not appointed to the Grand Duke's household, Her Majesty, I was convinced, would act in some other way to his advantage and he would obtain a post in the State service where his talents could be usefully employed by the Government.

I left the Empress deeply impressed by this conversation, and was not surprised when at home my husband met me with the words: "You have been a better judge of Pushkin than I. He is a rascal. He told my valet he neither could nor dared write the paper he offered to write last night."

"Let us forget him," I said. "He has caused enough trouble and he has never been worthy of your friendship, not even when you were children."

Later, that man enjoyed the protection of the Orlovs and was placed at the head of the Department of Light Industry, where he took advantage of this mark of confidence to have forged bank notes printed abroad. He was deported to Siberia in consequence, and there he finished his days.

CHAPTER IX

Let us now turn our attention once more to public affairs.

In the month of September Her Majesty went to Moscow to have herself crowned. I traveled in her carriage and Prince Dashkov, too, was in her suite. Throughout the journey the Empress had good reason to be pleased with the enthusiastic reception she had from the people of the villages and towns through which we passed.

Before entering Moscow Her Majesty halted at Count Razumovskii's country house, where we found an infinite number of people and all the local officials of the Province of Moscow. My husband went off to see his mother and came back the next morning. I told Her Majesty that I, too, ought to go and see her that morning, and would come back the same evening. The Empress tried to make me change my mind on the plea that all that traveling had already made me tired, but she only succeeded in making me stay till the afternoon, for I was impatient to kiss my little Mikhail whom I had left with my mother-in-law. After dinner the Empress took my husband and me into a room where there was no one, and then, after another attempt at dissuading me from going to town, she told me with all the tender caution of true friendship that my son, my little Mikhail, was dead.

The news distressed me so much that I became insensible to all except my sorrow. My determination to see my mother-in-law was now all the firmer because the house in which my child had lived became a refuge where I could abandon myself to my affliction and my tears. Besides, my mother-in-law had had the child with her ever since his birth and her own grief at the loss of him made her into a sympathetic and an understanding companion.

Marfa Vorontsova, mother of Princess Dashkova.
(From a miniature by an unknown artist)

I did not come back to Petrovskoe (such was the name of Razumov-skii's estate) where the Empress stayed till her solemn entry into Moscow, and thus avoided not only taking part in the procession, which would have been unbearable for me, but even taking possession of the apartments prepared for me in the Palace.

Her Majesty arrived in Moscow a few days before her coronation and I saw her every day. I did not take part in the magnificent public entertainments, yet that was the precise time the Orlovs chose to try to humiliate me by suggesting to the Master of Ceremonies that the Order of St. Catherine (which was mine) did not entitle the holder to any special place. True enough, it gave no definite precedence, but it had for the past fifty years been considered as the greatest distinction the State could confer. Peter I, in order to attract the nobility into the army, had established

German etiquette which in ceremonies and public functions determined precedence according to military rank—in the case of wives and daughters according to that of their husbands and fathers respectively, so that during the coronation ceremony my own had to be that of a colonel's wife. As this was the lowest rank admitted to the cathedral and as the holders of it occupied the last, or rather the top, benches of the sort of scaffolding erected for the public in the cathedral, my friends fancied that I should be deeply hurt.

They therefore entered into what can only be described as *negotiations* with me in order to soothe my feelings, and some of them even suggested that I should not go at all. I replied that I could not help smiling at the meanness of my enemies who found it possible at a moment like that to think of anything but the supreme joy of seeing the religious coronation of a sovereign such as Catherine.

"Besides," I said, "I want to see a ceremony I have never seen before and have no wish to see again. As to the place I shall occupy, it is of such small importance to me and I have so much pride that I fancy in occupying it I shall make it into the foremost in the church. I shall certainly not be the one to be blamed for occupying it. I shall therefore not be the one to blush for it, and I am charitable enough to hope that no one else shall be blamed for it either."

On 22 September, the day of the Coronation, I went to see the Empress as usual, but much earlier that time. The Grand Duke was ill and there was no Imperial Family, so I followed immediately after the Empress as she came out of her private apartments. As soon as we arrived in the cathedral I went with a smile to my humble post, where I suffered no inconvenience other than that of not knowing a single one of those individuals who, like me, were occupying the only places to which they were entitled.

I said to myself that if an opera were being performed and there were no seats apart from the gallery, I should, because I passionately love music, go and sit there rather than miss the performance.

Those who, like me, think that nothing can demean one except one's own behavior, will not be surprised at my attitude toward the whole episode.

On leaving the church, Her Majesty took her seat underneath the Imperial Canopy, and there followed the publication of promotions and appointments, one of the first of which made me a lady-in-waiting—the highest rank at the Petersburg Court, for it takes precedence over

Countess Anna Vorontsova, wife of the Grand Chancellor
Count Mikhail Vorontsov and aunt of Princess Dashkova.
(From a miniature by an unknown artist)

all others except the Imperial Family. My husband became gentleman-in-waiting to Her Majesty, equivalent to the rank of Brigadier, and retained his regiment of Cuirassiers.

Festivities went on for several weeks on end, the whole of Moscow rejoiced and winter passed in universal gaiety and gladness. No sooner was this over than Count Bestuzhev, whom I have mentioned before, circulated among a few persons a document of his own devising in which Her Majesty, in view of the Grand Duke's delicate health, was most humbly and earnestly petitioned to choose a consort for herself. Several members of the nobility signed it, but when he came with this document to the Grand Chancellor, this insane and dangerous idea was brought to nought by my uncle's heroic behavior. He interrupted Count Bestuzhev's reading of it with the request not to rob him of his peace of mind, so indispensable in his then weak state of health. Those schemes, he said, were so dangerous, so ill-digested and so inimical to the peace and happiness of the country that he did not want to listen to any more of it. And turning his back on Count Bestuzhev, he left the room.

As soon as Count Bestuzhev was gone, my uncle, for all his illness, ordered his carriage and went to request an audience of the Empress which was granted immediately. He repeated to the Empress Count Bestuzhev's odd overture to him, and urged upon her the full disadvantage of giving herself a master by taking a husband; it was more than probable, he added, that the nation would not like to see Orlov become her consort.

The Empress assured him that that intriguing old man had acted without her authority. "I am quite aware," she said, "that your frank and loyal behavior was prompted at least partly by your friendship for me personally and I shall appreciate this all my life."

These were the actual words of the Empress. My uncle replied that he had merely done his duty, and it was for her to give some thought to this subject which was capable of producing unpleasant repercussions. On this he withdrew and went home.

The Grand Chancellor's firm conduct brought him universal admiration and respect, but was attributed by Bestuzhev to support from a powerful quarter. In fact, however, my uncle had been prevented by his illness from seeing, and speaking to, almost anyone, though the news of Bestuzhev's proposal had generally transpired and most people were saying that he was the instrument of Count Grigorii Orlov's ambitions.

In the meantime, my husband's youngest sister, the Princess Anastasiia, fell ill. She had an exceptionally strong constitution, but it served merely to delay her death made inevitable by her doctor's lack of skill, and she lived for over a month in great anguish and suffering. Night and day I never left her side, for I alone could bring her mental solace and my presence gave her pleasure. This, added to my own ill-health and advanced state of pregnancy, made me ask my husband not to admit any of our friends who came to see us. The Prince, too, surrounded by a disconsolate mother and a beloved sister who was dying before his eyes, was too distressed to see any but nearest relations. In this way we remained in ignorance of many rumors that went round Moscow and were the talk of the town.

My sister-in-law died in early April and my mother-in-law was persuaded to leave her house for a short time to stay with her brother, General Leontiev. My own grief at the death of that young and charming girl, the sleepless nights passed by her side, the melancholy preparations for her funeral, and my state of health at a very advanced state of pregnancy, finally brought me to bed.

These domestic misfortunes saved me from frequent visits from Khitrovo, who came to consult me on what should be done to prevent the Empress's marriage to Grigorii Orlov, which was expected to take place in the near future; the Emperor of Germany himself had just made him a Prince of the Empire. Mr. Khitrovo had been one of the most disinterested of the conspirators against Peter III. His honesty, his good looks, his polite and dignified manners had also helped, perhaps, to excite the jealousy of the Orlovs. A cousin of his, Mr. Rzhevskii, who had been one of the conspirators together with the Orlovs and Khitrovo, repeated to Aleksei Orlov his cousin's suggestion that all those who had played a part in Her Majesty's accession to the throne should jointly petition her not to give effect to Bestuzhev's plan, and that if the Empress approved or took steps to implement that plan they should sacrifice their own lives by taking that of Grigorii Orlov. Khitrovo was arrested and questioned by Aleksei Orlov who, it was even said, subjected him to brutal treatment. But he denied nothing and proudly answered that he would be the first to thrust his sword into Grigorii's breast and himself suffer death in consequence rather than live with the humiliating thought that the only result of the Revolution had been to bring about the dangerous rise of Orlov.

In the course of the more official examination by Mr. Suvorov (father of the famous field-marshal of that name), he was asked whether he had ever spoken to me about his scheme or knew what my thoughts were concerning it. His reply was:

"I took the liberty of calling three times on the Princess to ask her advice and even take her orders, but I was not admitted and learned afterward that she was receiving no one. Had I had the honor of seeing her I would have presumed to reveal to her what I thought on the subject and I am convinced that her reply would have been dictated by sentiments both high-minded and patriotic."

I do not know how to explain Mr. Suvorov's conduct, but on meeting my husband at Court next day he told him confidentially that he was glad to repay the kindness shown to him by Prince Dashkov's father by informing him of what had been said at the examination I have just described.

On 12 May, old style, I gave birth to a son, and on 13 May my husband was taken ill with the quinsy, a complaint he had nearly every year, and which gave him a very high temperature. Such was the state of things when three days later a letter from the Empress to the Prince was brought by Her Majesty's first secretary, Mr. Teplov. Whether it was that he had been ordered to remit the letter privately or that he did not wish to meet the two Counts Panin in our house, I do not know, but anyway Teplov sent up a message asking my husband to come down into the street as he had a reason both for giving him that little trouble and for not coming up himself.

The Prince, who was in bed in a room next to mine, got up without making the slightest noise, put on his coat and went out to meet Mr. Teplov in the street. The contents of the letter incensed him. It expressed "Her Majesty's wish not to be forced to forget all she owed me; she, therefore, begged Prince Dashkov not to let me forget myself either, for she had heard that I had had the effrontery to threaten her."

I knew nothing of Mr. Teplov's message until evening when our cousins, the two Counts Panin, arrived and I heard them speak in a low voice as if afraid of being overheard by me. As my sister-in-law, Princess Aleksandra, came into my room through that of her brother, I asked her who were the people sitting in that room. She said there was no one there. At that I became alarmed, thinking that my husband's illness had taken a turn for the worse, and I was about to jump out of bed and go to see him. To prevent me doing this the Princess admitted that her two cousins, the Counts Panin, were there, that she did not know what it was all about, but that they were having a very earnest conversation with her brother, who felt much better than he did the day before.

I begged her to tell our cousins that I wanted to speak to them. They came presently and informed me of the message brought by Teplov. I was more vexed at him for having made my husband leave his bed and come out into the street than I was at the Empress's injustice, for the hostility of the Orlovs made me expect things like that.

I asked to see the letter, but General Panin said: "The Prince did what I should have done myself—he tore it up, and gave a firm and dignified reply."

I must confess that I was much less worried than any other person might have been in similar circumstances and I begged Count Panin (the Grand Duke's tutor) to ask Her Majesty if she wanted to attend my son's christening since she had herself suggested that she should be godmother to the child I was then expecting.

"You will see," I said, "she will never presume to refuse it."

He promised to ask her the following morning and let me know her answer.

When my cousins were gone my husband left his bed, which had to be remade for him, and came into my room. So pale was he that he was quite unable to convince me that he was feeling better. I did not let him stay with me for long, but implored him to go back to bed and take a little broth. His pallor distressed me beyond measure and prevented me from falling asleep at my usual hour.

I had hardly dozed off when I was suddenly awakened by the songs, or rather yells, of drunken revellers. These were weavers whom the Orlovs used to invite to their house—Grigorii Orlov was the only one to live in the Palace—and make drunk just for the fun of it. They then made them dance and sing and turned them out into the streets in that condition. On their way back the weavers had to pass by our house, and unfortunately my bedroom had a window opening on to the street.

I awoke with a start, feeling as if my bowels were turning to water and myself ready to faint. Suddenly I realized that one hand and one foot were paralyzed. I despatched the old woman who slept in my room to the regimental surgeon, living in the same house as us, with instructions to wake him up and bring him to me through a room other than that of the Prince.

The surgeon, on seeing me, lost his head and wanted to send for the doctor and wake up the Prince, but I did not let him do either. However, at six o'clock in the morning I felt even worse and fancied I was really at the point of death. I then called for my husband, blessed our children and entrusted them to him, murmured a few words to him about their upbringing, and feeling myself grow even weaker, kissed him and said good-bye by signs rather than words.

The look he gave me remains in my memory to the present day and that moment seems to me now to have been a moment of happiness. But it pleased God to prolong my melancholy life and let me survive the dear friend who made it worthwhile.

The Empress and the Grand Duke held my son at the baptismal font. On the day appointed by Her Majesty the Countess Panin went to Court and presented him, but Her Majesty *did not even inquire after my health*.

Soon after, the Court left for Petersburg.

My recovery was extremely slow. I stayed in Moscow and took baths every day without getting any stronger. My husband went to Petersburg in July and thence to Dorpat, where his regiment was stationed, while I went to live in our country house, less than five miles away from Moscow. Miss Kamenskaia and her sisters came to share my solitude.

The wholesome air, cold baths, and the regular and uniform life I led brought about an improvement in my health, and in the month of December I left for Petersburg accompanied by Miss Kamenskaia. There my husband rented the spacious and newly appointed house belonging to Odart. It may appear strange that I did not own a house myself and was obliged to rent that of my protégé who himself owed it to the generosity of the Empress, but such is the truth.

CHAPTER X

The death of August, King of Poland and Elector of Saxony, left vacant the throne of Poland and hence a vast field for political intrigue. The House of Saxony wanted to keep the Crown of Poland to itself; the King of Prussia had contrary ambitions. A part of the Polish nobility, won over by bribes and high positions which they owed to the House of Saxony, were inclined to favor its interests. Others, moved by more patriotic motives, were afraid that this might result in making the Crown, contrary to the Constitution, almost hereditary in the Saxon House, and therefore wanted national elections. The Court of Vienna, very anxious to gain the confidence and friendship of our Court, declared itself unhesitatingly for a national election; possibly it had in view one of the Princes Czartoryski. The Empress had not yet announced that it was Poniatowski she wanted to raise to the throne of Poland and had merely declared herself in favor of national elections in accordance with the Constitution. But she made her intentions known in Council. Prince Orlov put forward what he claimed to be very powerful reasons against the elevation of Poniatowski. The Minister of War, Count Zakhar Chernyshev, and his brother Count Ivan, on perceiving the extent to which Orlov was able to sway Her Majesty's mind, went over to his side (though not quite openly, truth to tell) and did everything possible, short of manifest disobedience, to control the movement of troops in Poland, hamper the military operations, and bring about the failure of the plan favored by the Empress.

The time appointed for the Diet was approaching, and she came to the conclusion that the man to be sent at the head of the troops must be someone whose zeal and energy were not handicapped by too much consideration for the favorite. Her choice fell on my husband. She kept her conversations with him so secret that by the time his mission became known he had already left town.

The Prince was flattered by the Empress's trust in him. He left immediately and triumphed over all the obstacles put in his way. Prince Volkonskii, Commander-in-Chief of the Army which had to enter Poland in order to maintain the Constitution and give support to the Patriot party, received the order to halt at Smolensk. My husband had under his command all the regiments necessary to carry out his mission, and the full powers with which he was vested helped to smooth out any difficulties. Generals and brigadiers senior to him in the service were placed under his orders, and he was accountable to no one but Her Majesty and her First Minister, his cousin Count Panin, until he reached Warsaw.

My husband's departure and my daughter's illness affected me to such an extent that I thought it necessary to have a change of air. But not wishing to live far from Petersburg where news of the Prince could reach me quickly, I obtained my cousin Prince Kurakin's permission to settle down in Gatchina, which is now so beautiful and magnificent, and was then his main residence in the country. It stood some forty miles distant from Petersburg at the time, for the fine road which since has considerably shortened the way to the Capital, and which Her Majesty had built when she bought Gatchina after Prince Kurakin's death, did not yet exist.

I stayed there with Miss Kamenskaia and my two children till the Empress's return from Riga, in complete seclusion, never going out except to ride in the neighborhood for the sake of fresh air and exercise.

A few months previously General Panin had been appointed Senator and Member of the Council. As he had no house of his own and mine was very spacious, I offered it to him, and myself moved into one of its wings which contained a bath so that my children could bathe as prescribed by the physician. This suited me all the more as I wanted to see no one and limit my expenditure as much as possible during my husband's absence.

General Panin occupied my house until the Empress's departure for Riga whither he accompanied her. In his capacity as Senator he received almost every morning a great many petitioners and plaintiffs appealing against court decisions, but as we each had an independent entrance, separated the one from the other by the whole length of the house, and as anyway they all came in the very early morning, I never saw them and did not know who they were. Among them was the famous Mirovich, notorious for his criminal and stupid project for restoring the Crown to Ivan, who had been held prisoner since infancy in the fortress of Schlüsselburg.[1]

That story brought me a great deal of sorrow as a result of the undeserved suspicion that attached to my name and the unfair and unjust treatment to which I was subjected in consequence. Worry and sorrow are the necessary outcome of a high position at Court, but unfortunately my very principles were misunderstood. I had done too much for the Empress and against my own interests not to be exposed to malice and slander.

The Court returned to Petersburg and I, too, came back a few days after. My cousin, General Panin, was, by then, living in his own house together with his wife who had arrived from Moscow. That worthy woman was a sincere friend of mine, and apart from qualities that made her the envy of our sex, she was sweet and gentle as few women are. Unfortunately she suffered from a disease of the lungs and her complaint had grown worse since we last saw each other in Moscow. Her husband, the General, was obliged to spend much of his time at Court and went out a great deal, leaving me with her.

One day, my cousin told me that Her Majesty's first intimation of the tragedy which had befallen Ivan was contained in a letter from Aleksei Orlov which she had received in Riga. It was a great shock to her and she immediately informed her First Secretary, Mr. Elagin. The letter had a P.S. added to it which said that Mirovich had several times been seen entering my house very early in the morning. Elagin assured Her Majesty that it could only be a mistake, and that Princess Dashkova, who did not go out and admitted practically no visitors, was not likely to receive a completely unknown and apparently crack-brained individual.

The impulse which made Mr. Elagin speak thus to the Empress was dictated by a sense of honesty and fair play. But not content to leave it at that, he immediately went to see General Count Panin and repeated the whole thing to him. The latter told Mr. Elagin he could inform Her Majesty that Mirovich might indeed have been seen entering the Princess's house, but that these visits were intended for him, Panin, in connection with a case due to come up before the Senate. He could also inform Her Majesty that since Mirovich had been his regimental adjutant during the Seven Years War, he, Panin, was better qualified than anyone else to give the Empress, should she so desire, particulars of his character.

[1] The Emperor Ivan VI—see Index.—K. F.

Mr. Elagin immediately went to the Empress and told her she could gratify her extreme curiosity concerning Mirovich since General Panin knew him personally. The Empress lost no time in sending for Count Panin. He told her all he knew, and if on the one hand he completely allayed the Empress's suspicions regarding my supposed connection with that wretched man, he could hardly, on the other, have given her much real pleasure by making his description of Mirovich fit precisely that of Grigorii Orlov. He was, he said, presumptuous through ignorance, and enterprising through incapacity to comprehend with his mediocre brain the scope and depth of what he thought would be so easy to accomplish.

All this was a source of great grief to me. I saw that my house was besieged by the spies of the Orlovs, and was sorry that the Empress should have been misled sufficiently to suspect even the most patriotic individuals; and when Mirovich was executed, far from regretting him as an accomplice, I thanked my stars that I had never seen him. For he was the first man to have had the sentence of death passed on him since the day of my birth, and the impression his execution made on me was such that his face and figure would certainly have haunted me in my sleep had I known what he was like.

This unfortunate incident had no repercussions. Mirovich's trial and examination, held with the utmost publicity in full Senate and in the presence of the Presidents and Vice-Presidents of all Departments as well as of all Generals commanding Army divisions stationed in the Petersburg Province, left no doubt in Russia as to the truth of the case. It was obvious to everyone that the apparent ease with which the fall of Peter III had been brought about had left Mirovich's sick brain with the impression that he could do the same thing in Ivan's favor.

Abroad it was believed, or at least people affected to believe, that the whole thing was a horrible plot by the Empress, who had prevailed on Mirovich by the promises she gave him to do what he did, and then sacrificed him. During my first tour abroad in 1770, I had great difficulty, particularly in Paris, in clearing Her Majesty's character of a reputation of having double-crossed both sides. All Governments, jealous of the preeminence Russia was likely to enjoy under an enlightened and energetic Sovereign, clung to the slightest scrap of gossip which might feed their slander and flatter their jealousy. I said in Paris (and before that in Spa to Monsieur and Madame Necker) that the French, who had had Mazarin as Minister, should be the last to accuse Sovereigns and their Ministers of such conduct in trying to rid themselves of suspect characters; they knew, I said, that the effects of a dose of poison mixed in a drink are speedier and more easily covered up.

Count Rzewuski, Ambassador of the King and Commonwealth of Poland, was the only foreigner I used to see, because he was able to give me news of my husband. He told me how, thanks to the energy displayed by the Prince, the success of the Empress's plan was not in doubt, how popular he had become through the order and discipline of the troops under his command, and how much Count Poniatowski in particular was beholden to him. The Empress, too, spoke highly of my husband and called him *her little Field-Marshal.*

But fate did not let him enjoy the fruit of his labors and of his noble and selfless devotion to duty. The courier announcing the election of Poniatowski to the throne of Poland arrived in September. He was closely followed by another from the Russian Ambassador in Warsaw, Count Keiserling, with the news that my husband had finally succumbed to the lack of rest and the forced marches he had imposed on himself despite his high fever, a victim to the zeal which he applied to the fulfilment of the Empress's wishes.

This terrible catastrophe, which marked the saddest crisis in my life, was deplored by everyone. And yet I knew nothing of it until my cousin, Countess Panina, came in one morning, all pale and dejected, and proposed I should go out with her in her carriage to take the air and then stay for dinner with her. I thought she was ill, and never dreamt it was I who should have been pitied. I dressed quickly and when I arrived at her house I found there the two Counts Panin, looking so embarrassed and dismayed that I became apprehensive. And when after dinner, and taking every precaution their friendship for me could devise, they finally revealed to me the dreadful news of my husband's death, I fell back in a faint and remained unconscious for several hours on end. When I came to I was indeed a pitiful sight and my distress beyond all description. My children were brought to me and I trembled and shook all over as I took them in my arms. For about a fortnight I hovered between life and death and my limbs hung from their sockets like useless pieces of wood.

My dear cousin forgot her own weakness and, helped by Miss Kamen-skaia, looked after me night and day. My doctor, the excellent Mr. Kruse, saved my life by his skill and care, but I contemplated the future through a shroud of death. My children and their nurse, my personal maid, and all the things necessary to me were brought across to the Panins' house before I had recovered consciousness, and I was established in my cousin's apartment without the slightest effort on my part, while she kept only a small study for herself where she slept. A fortnight later she became very ill and no longer left her bed. For a week she held on, while I was carried into her room every day, and then I had the misfortune of losing for ever that dear and loving friend. The very next day after her death I asked to be taken back to my own house.

For quite a long time I remained in ignorance of the unsatisfactory state in which our finances—my children's and mine—had been left by my husband when he died. In his efforts to save the poorer officers under his command from having to harass the local inhabitants, he helped them generously, to the point, however, of himself running into debt, and as these debts had to be settled they could not possibly remain hidden from me. My brother, Count Aleksandr, whose friendship for me had never faltered, was abroad as Minister Extraordinary and Plenipotentiary in Holland, and the rest of my family had abandoned me. I could, therefore, expect help and advice only from my cousins, the Counts Panin. As he lay on his deathbed my husband wrote with his own hand to Count Panin, the Tutor and Minister, admitting to having left his affairs in a muddle and begging him to put some order in them, not to abandon me and the children, and to try to pay off the creditors without depriving us of some measure of financial independence. He made Count Panin guardian of his children and his property. The latter prevailed on his brother the General to become joint guardian, and showing me the letter gave me to understand that being both of them through their employment resident in Petersburg, it was absolutely essential that I should become a guardian too. I could then, by going to Moscow and visiting my estates, see better for myself and do more than they could, however much they tried to be helpful.

The elder Count Panin thought that as soon as Her Majesty had learnt the straits to which my children and I had been reduced, she would hasten to help me. He therefore asked her for an administrative order giving the guardians the right to sell land in payment of debts. This greatly annoyed me, and when I was shown the Order I said I should never make use of this Imperial favor and should sooner content myself with a dry crust all my life than sell the heritage of my children.[2]

---

[2] Princess Dashkova preferred to solicit the Empress for aid which would not entail the sale of property and would thus be more profitable. Her petition is couched in very humble terms, somewhat at variance with the proud tone of the *Memoirs,* and includes

Hardly had I begun to lead a somewhat more normal existence and get up from bed for a few hours every day than my son fell ill with an internal abscess which required a risky and painful operation, and it was due to the care taken of him by Mr. Kruse and to the skill of the surgeon Kelchen that I owe the preservation of his life. This illness delayed my recovery still further, so that I was only able to leave Petersburg at the beginning of March 1765, in spite of my intention to make the journey to Moscow before the thaw (which begins in March every year) had made the rivers very dangerous to cross.

Before leaving Petersburg I handed over to my husband's three principal creditors his entire dinner service as well as the few jewels I possessed, keeping back nothing but some forks and spoons sufficient for four persons only, and left, firmly resolved to pay my husband's debts without the sale of landed property or the Crown's assistance.

After my arrival in Moscow I wanted to go and live in the country, but was informed that the house had collapsed. I had another timber house built, smaller than the old one, and went to live in that humble abode the following spring. I reserved for my children and myself a mere five hundred roubles a year, but, on the other hand, my savings as well as the sale of the jewels and the dinner service enabled me to pay off all my debts in five years. Had I been told before my marriage that, accustomed as I was to luxury and expense, I should be capable, after becoming a widow at twenty, of stinting myself for several years of everything save the simplest clothes, I should never have believed it. But I wanted to be as good a steward of my children's property as I was their governess and their sick-nurse, and no price was too high.

The following year brought with it more trouble and embarrassment. My mother-in-law discovered that the deed of sale of our Moscow house brought to her by her husband contained a loophole which gave her the right to dispose of it as she wished. She, therefore, gave it to her granddaughter, Miss Glebova, and I remained without a home in town. Far from complaining, I decided never to mention the word *house* in my mother-in-law's presence, and paid her out for the harm she had done my children by behaving to her with tactful kindness in the following predicament.

I bought a piece of ground in the same street, with a building on it

---

the following passage: "My infants and I throw ourselves at your Royal feet. Cast a glance of compassion, most merciful Sovereign, at a weeping widow and her two orphans, show your generosity in our misfortune and save us from poverty."—K. F.

which looked as if it was about to collapse, and had a timber house erected at one end of the site, as a provisional dwelling till I was in the position to build a stone house for myself. Now, three years later it so happened that my mother-in-law had to leave her apartments in a convent where she had withdrawn after her son's death, while repairs were being carried out. She was not allowed to stay in her son-in-law's (Glebov's) house, and thus came to live with me in a house next to mine which I had bought the year before on very favorable terms.

CHAPTER XI

❧❦❧

In the year 1768 I applied—in vain, however—for permission to travel abroad, in the hope that change of air and the actual traveling would benefit my children who suffered from rickets and had poor health. My letters remained unanswered. I went to Kiev, a journey of about 1,300 miles there and back, for I made detours in order to see different cities and particularly the German colonies which the Empress had established and which were of great interest to me.

I greatly enjoyed my stay at Kiev. The Governor, General Voeikov, a relation of my husband's, was a highly educated man who had from his youth upward been employed in foreign affairs. He had been entrusted with delicate negotiations at various Courts and had thus traveled a great deal and seen much—both men and things. The gaiety which he had kept in his advanced age made him as pleasant a companion as he was an instructive conversationalist. We passed all our days together and he even accompanied me on my tiring excursions to the catacombs.

The many caves hollowed out of the hill on which part of the city is built make it a very curious place. In several such grottoes or recesses can be seen, incredibly well preserved, the bodies of saints who had lived and died there. The Cathedral in the precints of the Pecherskii Monastery is remarkable for the ancient mosaics on its walls. There are fresco paintings in one of the churches representing the different Councils held before the separation of the Eastern Church. These frescoes are of extraordinary beauty and must have been painted by great artists.

For many years past Kiev had had both an academy and a university where hundreds of students received free education. It was still their custom, when I was there, to go and sing canticles and church hymns every evening under the windows of the local inhabitants who took their ease at that hour and rewarded the students liberally with money, which the students afterward handed over to their masters.

Learning had traveled from Greece to Kiev much earlier than it had to many a European nation now so quick to saddle the Russians with the name of barbarians. Newton's philosophy was brought into its schools at the time when the priestly rabble of Catholic faith did not allow it in France. Many of its churches and monasteries are well worth seeing for their antiquity alone.

My trip lasted for about three months and I had the satisfaction of seeing that it had been excellent for my children's health without at the same time involving me in a lot of expense, for I had traveled throughout with my own horses.

The following year I went to Petersburg quite resolved to obtain permission to travel abroad. As a member of the gentry class I had full right to do so without asking permission first, but as lady-in-waiting I had to have the Empress's agreement. I put off mentioning it to her till the anniversary of her accession to the throne was celebrated in Peterhof, but in the meantime told everyone without distinction that I wanted to go on a journey to foreign parts, and when asked whether I had already applied for permission I answered that I had not done so yet, but it could not possibly be refused since I had done nothing to lose the right of traveling which every member of the gentry possessed.

On the day of the anniversary, at the ball, I joined the group of foreign Ambassadors and was chatting to some of them before Her Majesty had time to come up to them. At last the Empress approached, spoke to them and said a few words to me. I replied, and then in the same breath, so as not to lose the opportunity, requested Her Majesty to grant me the permission to travel abroad for the health of my children. She was careful not to refuse and said:

"I am sorry this should be the reason for your travels, but you are certainly free, Madam, to leave whenever you like."

Her Majesty moved on, but had not gone more than a few steps before I was already asking the Chamberlain, Talyzin, to go and tell my cousin, the Minister Count Panin, to make out a passport for me as I had just obtained the Empress's permission to go abroad. (My cousin had an intrigue with Talyzin's wife, which did not prevent my enemies from saying sometimes that I was Count Panin's daughter, and at other times that I was his mistress.)

So far my plan had succeeded. A short time later I left Petersburg to go to Moscow and Troitskoe and had everything ready for going abroad as soon as the roads allowed it. When Count Panin and other people who took an interest in me asked me how I should be able to afford the expenses of the journey, I answered that I should be traveling under another name and my expenses would be limited to horses and food.

In December I was back in Petersburg from Moscow, and hurried so much that in that very same month I was able to leave for Riga. A few days before my departure an Under-Secretary of the Empress's Council brought 4,000 roubles to me on Her Majesty's behalf, and showed me the order he had received. I did not want to exasperate the Empress by refusing to accept this ridiculous sum, but asking the gentleman to wait a little, I fetched and showed him the bills I had received from my saddler and from my jeweller who had made silver saucepans for my journey.

"You see, sir," I said, "what these bills amount to, and I have not paid them yet. Would you please leave the equivalent amount on the table and take the rest yourself."

At last I was able to leave, and went by post-horses as far as Riga. There I stopped for a few days and thence hired horses to take me to Berlin. In Koenigsberg I found Countess Keiserling, who prevailed on me to stay there for six days.

In Danzig, I stayed at the best inn, the Hôtel de Russie, which was frequented by all Russians and all really distinguished travelers. Consequently, I was all the more shocked at seeing in the main room two pictures representing two battles lost by the Russian troops, who were shown wounded, dying, or standing on their knees before the victorious Prussian troops.

I asked our Chargé d'Affaires, Mr Rähbinder, why he put up with it. He replied that he could not interfere and that Count Aleksei Orlov, when on his way through Danzig, had been most annoyed at seeing those pictures.

"What!" I exclaimed, "and he never bought them to throw them into the fire afterwards?! I am very poor compared to him, and cannot afford to make silly purchases like that, but I shall know how to deal with this."

As soon as the Resident was gone, I asked in the greatest confidence the Secretary at our Legation, Volchkov, and the Counselor, Stählin (who was accompanying me as far as Berlin where he was posted), to go and buy oil paints for me—blue, green, red, and white. After supper we locked and bolted the door to avoid being caught at what we were going to do, and then the two gentlemen who knew how to handle a brush, and myself, made the troops exchange their uniforms. The Prussians—supposed to be victors in the two battles—became Russians, and the defeated were given Prussian uniforms.

We spent nearly the whole night at that work. I do not know what my host and the servants thought of my being locked in with those gentlemen in a room with the lights on, but I was as happy and as nervous of not being allowed to finish my boyish prank as a naughty child in dread of his parents' return. The following day I had my trunks unpacked amidst the confusion in my room, and on this pretext did not let in either mine host or any of the servants. I left Danzig the day after, but before leaving I showed our Resident the metamorphosis I had wrought. I was very proud of my feat, and when we had left the Hôtel de Russie behind us we laughed a great deal at the thought of what mine host would say when he saw that the Prussians had lost the two battles which the painter had made them win.

Miss Kamenskaia, my two children, and my cousin, Mr. Vorontsov, who was attached to our Legation at The Hague, came with me. I stayed for two months in Berlin. Prince Dolgorukii was our Minister there; he was universally liked and esteemed, and fully deserved it. He treated us in the easy, friendly manner so typical of him, a blend of eagerness and spontaneity.

I had no idea whether people wanted to see me merely because they were curious to see an unlicked bear cub (as I often used to call myself in order to irritate my friends), but anyway the Queen, the Princesses, Prince Henry, and his worthy spouse simply besieged Prince Dolgorukii with entreaties to persuade me to go to Court.

I knew that Berlin etiquette forbade private individuals to be presented under an assumed name, and I took that of Madame Mikhalkova (from the name of a little property near Moscow belonging to my children), because I wanted to avoid the expense of going to Court. I therefore replied that I could not go to Court under the name of Madame Mikhalkova and that if I changed it only to adopt it again immediately afterward I should really give the impression of an adventuress.

The Queen and the Princesses spoke to the Minister of Foreign Affairs, Count Finkenstein, who spoke to the King. The great Frederick was at Sans-Souci, and his reply was: "Etiquette is a foolish thing; Princess Dashkova must be received under any name and in any way she wants." That day I dined with the English representative, Mr. Mitchel, with whom

I also met Count Finkenstein. He told me both of the Royal Family's desire to know me and of the King's decision. There was, therefore, no longer any way of escape for me. I put myself to the expense of buying a new black dress, for I was still wearing mourning as was the custom for widows in Russia at the time, and off I went.

Her Majesty the Queen accorded me the most distinguished welcome, and I was invited to stay for supper; the Princes and the Princesses vied with each other in showering upon me tokens of their interest and esteem, and soon I was unable to go to suppers given for me by foreign Ministers and private individuals, for I was continually invited either to the Queen's Court or to her sister's. Both these Princesses stuttered and mumbled as they spoke, and my greatest merit in their eyes consisted in an ability to understand them in spite of their defect, so that the chamberlain who was always placed next to a stranger never had the time or need to act as a kind of interpreter. I understood them and answered them at once. This put Her Majesty and her sister at their ease with me.

This sister of the Queen's was the widow of the Prince Royal and the mother of the Princess of Orange and the Prince who became King after the death of the Great Frederick. If outstanding genius as well as constant and unflinching zeal in working for the benefit of one's subjects make for greatness, Frederick was unquestioningly one of the greatest of kings.

I shall always remember my stay in Berlin, and the kindness shown to me there, with pleasure and gratitude. I was sorry to leave, but I wanted to take advantage of the early season and of the baths and waters of Aachen and Spa.

We crossed Westphalia, which I did not find as dirty as is alleged by Baron de Bar, the pleasant author of a number of letters. At Hanover we stopped just long enough to repair our carriages. On learning on the day of our arrival there that an opera was being given that same evening, Miss Kamenskaia and I went to hear it, while Mr. Vorontsov felt indisposed and stayed at home. I allowed only one Russian servant to accompany us, but he knew no language but his own and therefore could not tell people who we were. I took that precaution because Prince Ernest of Mecklenburg told me that his elder brother, the Governor of Hanover, wished to know when I should be in Hanover, and I did not want to make my presence known.

In a box, where there was just enough room left for us, we found two ladies who tried to give us a little more and who showed us a great deal of courtesy. During the second act I saw a young officer leave the Prince's box to come to ours. After a few words addressed to us and none to the two ladies, this dashing young blade said to us:

"Both of you ladies are foreigners, are you not?"

"Yes, sir."

"His Highness desires to know to whom I have the honor of speaking."

"Our names," I replied, "are of little consequence to you or to His Highness, and being women we are privileged not to divulge them even in a fortress, so you would be kind enough, I hope, to let us conceal them from you."

He appeared a little put out, and left us. The two ladies looked at us with some surprise. I had, indeed, been somewhat stern, but then I have never been able to suffer fops gladly. During the last act, after warning Miss Kamenskaia in Russian not to contradict me, I told the ladies that though I had refused to let the Prince's A.D.C. know who we were, I should not conceal from them, since they had been so good to us, that I was a singer and my companion a dancer and that we had come in search of profitable employment. Miss Kamenskaia opened her eyes wide in astonishment, and the two ladies who had been so courteous to us before were so no longer, and could not even refrain from moving slightly away from us, as much as the box would allow, so as to give the impression they were turning their backs on us.

My stay at Hanover was very fleeting and I was not able to see anything. I noticed, however, that the horses of that country, even the peasants' horses, were of a fine breed, and the land well looked after. That is all I can say about the place.

On arrival at Aachen I took a house opposite the Assembly Rooms and the Baths. Two Irishmen who had served in Holland, had retired and were now permanent residents there, became our daily companions. One was Mr. Collin and the other, Colonel Nugent, father of the General who had been Minister representing the Court of Vienna at Berlin. Their cheerful disposition and courtesy made their companionship very pleasant.

At Spa I made friends with Mrs. Hamilton, daughter of Mr. Ryder, Archbishop of Tuam, and with Mrs. Morgan, daughter of Mr. Tisdal, Solicitor-General in Ireland, where he enjoyed great regard and esteem. Ever since that year, 1770, these feelings of friendship have continued, as anyone who knows us can testify, proof against all vicissitudes of fortune.

In Spa I also met Monsieur and Madame Necker, but only with the English did I live on terms of friendly intimacy. Lord and Lady Sussex came to see us every day, and with the help of French and German I was able in three weeks to understand all I read in English, even Shakespeare. My two friends took turns every morning to come and read English books with me; they corrected my pronunciation and were the only teachers I have ever had in that language, with which I soon became fairly familiar.

I resolved to go to England, if only for a few weeks, together with the Tisdal family, and promised Mrs. Hamilton to spend the winter with her in Aix-en-Provence where her father, the Archbishop, had been ordered to go by his doctors. We crossed the Straits of Dover in the same boat, and it was the first time I found myself out at sea. I was ill all the time and my charming friend looked after me to the best of her ability.

When I arrived in London I found that our Minister, Mr. Pushkin, had already prepared a house for me in a part of town near his. His wife (she was his first) was, I discovered, the pleasantest and most estimable woman one could wish for a friend, and she quickly became mine.

Throughout Mr. Tisdal's stay in London I divided my time between Mrs. Morgan and Madame Pushkina, and when the former left for Dublin with her father, I went off to visit Bath, Bristol, and Oxford, and made excursions in the country around them.

The trip lasted only thirteen days, during which my son remained in London in the care of our Minister, whose wife was particularly worthy of such trust. Every other day I received news of the child together with a note from him in which he boasted of having seen such or such thing. This was our first separation; we both felt it keenly, and in order to console him, Countess Pushkina took him to horse races as well as to visit the Duchess of Queensberry. In his last note to me he described this expedition exceedingly well for a boy of not quite seven.

I came back to London, but only stayed there for about ten days, during which I met the Duke and Duchess of Northumberland, but did not go to Court, and devoted my time to sight-seeing.

CHAPTER XII

Our crossing from Dover to Calais was not very pleasant. There was a terrible wind, which might have been favorable for those going to India, but for us merely represented twenty-six hours of constant danger, with the waves splashing water over us even in our cabins.

My children were quite terrified and sobbed their hearts out, while I took advantage of all this to make them feel how much courage was superior to cowardice. I drew their attention to the behavior in such a critical situation of the English captain and sailors, and after impressing upon them that the Divine Will demands submission and is always wise, I bade them be quiet. I was obeyed beyond all expectation, for soon, as I was happy to see, they were peacefully asleep in spite of the raging storm. We were obliged to close and bolt the entrance to the cabin which made me even more nervous, though I did not show it.

However, no mishap in fact occurred and at last we arrived at Calais. My cousin Vorontsov proceeded straight to Aix-en-Provence to make ready a suitable place for me to live in, while I went first to Brussels and Antwerp, where I stayed only a short time on the way to Paris. My stay in Paris, too, was very short—only seventeen days—during which I wanted to see no one except Diderot. I went round churches and monuments, and visited the studios of famous artists, as well as theaters where I always sat in the gallery among the humblest members of the audience, wearing an old black dress and shawl and a close cap in order to escape all notice.

One evening as Diderot and I were sitting alone together, the servant announced the visit of Madame Necker and Madame Geoffrin. Quick as lightning, Diderot ordered my servant to tell the ladies I was out.

"Come, now," said I, "I knew Madame Necker at Spa, and the other is in correspondence with the Empress, so that it could do me no harm to know her."

"You have only about nine or ten days more left in Paris," replied Diderot, "and as they would, therefore, see you only two or three times they would not understand you, and I hate seeing my idols blasphemed. Were you to stay here for another two months, I should be the first to acquaint you with Madame Geoffrin. She is an excellent woman, but one of the trumpets of Paris, and I do not want her to form a friendship with you that can be no more than casual."

And so I sent my servant to say I felt somewhat feverish. However, that was not the end of the affair. The following day I received a very flattering note from Madame Necker saying that Madame Geoffrin hated the idea of living in the same town without seeing me, and such was her high opinion of me that she would never get over the fact of having missed me.

In replying to Madame Necker I pleaded my desire to preserve the esteem of the two ladies, and added that in my present condition I could hardly expect to justify their favorable and probably undeserved opinion of myself; therefore, I said, I had to deny myself the pleasure of seeing them and must ask them to accept my regrets.

And so that day I had to keep to my room. Ordinarily, my morning excursions, which lasted from eight o'clock till three in the afternoon, ended at Diderot's door. I took him home in my carriage to dine, and often the two of us would talk till two or three o'clock in the morning.

One day he spoke of what he believed to be our peasants' slavery. "You will agree," I said, "that though I have not the soul of a slave, neither have I that of a tyrant. I therefore deserve your confidence on that subject. At one time I held the same opinions as you, and thought of giving more freedom to my peasants and making them happier. I changed the administration of my estate in the Orel Province with this end in view, and yet I found they merely became more liable to be pilfered and robbed by every little employee of the Crown. The welfare and wealth of our peasants create our own prosperity and increase our revenues. A landowner would have to be crack-brained to want to exhaust the source of his own riches. The gentry serve as intermediaries between the peasants and the Crown, and it is in their interest to defend the peasants against the rapacity of Provincial governors and officials."

"But, surely, Princess, you cannot deny that freedom would increase their knowledge and understanding, and that these would later give rise to abundance and riches?"

"If," I replied, "by breaking a few links of chain that ties the peasants to the gentry, the Sovereign were also to break a few links that keep the gentry chained to the whims of their Sovereign, I should cheerfully sign with my blood the declaration of the peasants' freedom. But, in stating your case, you have, if you will forgive my saying so, confused cause and effect. It is knowledge and understanding that produce freedom; the latter without the former would produce nothing but anarchy and confusion. When the lower classes of my fellow citizens become more enlightened they will deserve to be free, because they will know how to enjoy freedom without detriment to their fellows and without prejudice to the order and obedience essential to every government."

"You argue well, my dear Princess, but you have not convinced me yet."

"Our basic laws," I replied, "contain several kinds of antidote to the tyranny of the gentry. Peter I, it is true, abolished several of these laws, including those which empowered the serfs to complain against their masters, but in the present reign a Provincial governor can, by agreement with representatives of the gentry and their Marshal, take peasants away from a tyrannical oppressor and have both land and serfs administered by a board of trustees chosen from among the gentry themselves. I am afraid I cannot explain my meaning as well as I should like, but what I always think of in this connection is a blind man on a steep cliff surrounded by a yawning chasm. He is unaware, thanks to his defect, of the dangers of his situation, and being unaware of them he is gay, he eats and sleeps with perfect unconcern, he listens to the singing of birds and sometimes sings himself. And then up comes a wretched oculist who gives him back his sight without being able to save him from his plight. So there is my poor man, his sight fully restored, feeling as unhappy as could be. He sings no more, he hardly eats or sleeps, he is afraid of all—of the abyss that surrounds him, of the waves which lash against the rock and which before he knew nothing about—and he ends by dying in the flower of his youth from fear and despair."

Diderot jumped up as if my little story had touched off a mechanical device to propel him out of his chair. He walked up and down the room and spat on the floor in a kind of anger. "What a woman you are!" he burst out. "You have upset ideas I have cherished and upheld for twenty years."

I admired Diderot in all he did, admired him, too, for those outbursts of his caused by his warm-hearted way of feeling and looking at things.

His sincerity, his loyalty to friends, his shrewd and profound mind, and the interest and esteem he invariably showed me, were all traits that won me over for life. His death was a great grief to me and I shall always regret him so long as there is a spark of life in my body. This extraordinary man was but little understood. Virtue and truth were the well-springs of every one of his actions, and the general good was his ruling passion and constant pursuit. The very liveliness of his mind sometimes led him into error, but he never ceased being sincere, for he was his own dupe. However, it is not for me to attempt a eulogy worthy of him. Other pens, better qualified, will not fail to do so.

Another evening, when he was sitting with me, Monsieur de Rulhière was announced. He had been in Petersburg, attached to the French Embassy at the time when the Baron de Breteuil was Ambassador. I used to see him very often in my house then, and even more frequently in Moscow in the house of Miss Kamenskaia. I did not know that on his return to Paris he had written an account of the 1762 revolution in Russia and given readings of it at large social gatherings. I was about to tell my servant to let him in, when Diderot interposed. He took my hand and pressed it vigorously. "Just a moment," he said. "Do you intend going back to Russia ever again?"

"What a question!" I replied. "Have I a right to deprive my children of their country?"

"Well, then, send your man to tell Monsieur de Rulhière that you cannot receive him now, and I shall explain my reasons to you."

His manner made it obvious that he had my interests at heart and was entirely motivated by feelings of friendship, and such was my faith in his integrity that I refused my door to an old acquaintance whose wit and erudition had always made his company very pleasant.

"Do you know," said Diderot, "that he has written an account of the Empress's accession to the throne?"

"I did not," I replied, "and that is all the more reason why I should want to see him."

"I shall tell you," said Diderot, "all you can find out in his book. He gives you a very fair deal, and credits you with all the gifts and virtues of our sex in addition to those of your own, but he does not treat the Empress in the same way. She therefore made offers, through the intermediary of Betskoi and your Chargé d'Affaires Prince Golitsyn, for the purchase of this book. The negotiations were so clumsily conducted that Monsieur de Rulhière had time to make three copies of his account, one of which he deposited with his Foreign Office, one with Madame de Gramont and one with the Archbishop of Paris. Having failed to purchase the book, Her Majesty did me the honor of commissioning me to negotiate with Monsieur de Rulhière, but all I could obtain from him was an undertaking not to publish his account in his own or the Empress's lifetime. The King of Poland, by the way, he treats just as unkindly, and describes in detail his love affair with the Empress when she was still a Grand Duchess. So you see, by receiving Rulhière you would be giving your approval to a work which is a source of embarrassment to the Empress and which is widely known since it has been read everywhere, including at the receptions of Madame Geoffrin. These receptions are attended by all the best people and by all distinguished foreigners and travelers, but this does not deter this good lady, in spite of the friendship she professes for Poniatowski, to whom she refers in her letters as her son."

"But how can this be reconciled with her behavior?" I queried.

"The fact is, simply, that we are thoughtless and age does not seem to change us, whether we are sixty or eighty."

I thanked Diderot for this mark of friendship which saved me from getting myself quite innocently into trouble Rulhière called again twice, but I refused to receive him, and on my return to Petersburg fifteen months later I had good reason to appreciate Diderot's advice. For I was informed by a person high in Count Fedor Orlov's confidence and to whom I had had the good fortune of rendering some service in the past, that Diderot wrote a letter to Her Majesty in which, after speaking a great deal about me and my affection for her, he said my refusal to see Rulhière had done more to undermine confidence in his book than anything that could have been done by ten Voltaires and fifteen miserable Diderots. He never told me he intended to write about this to the Empress and credit me with wise conduct, though all I had done was to follow his advice. This natural tact and warmth of feeling for his friends will always make his memory dear to me for as long as I live.[1]

I wanted to see Versailles without letting others know I was going to

---

[1] Diderot's account of Princess Dashkova's first visit to Paris tallies very closely with the Princess's own version. However, he makes no mention of his rather improbable conversion to the advantages of serfdom, and states that he saw her four times only, each time from five o'clock in the afternoon till midnight.—K. F.

be there. Our Chargé d'Affaires, Mr. Khotinskii tried to convince me that it was impossible, since the movements of every foreigner, however unimportant, were watched by the police, and I could therefore expect to be closely followed. I assured him that I should succeed in my intentions, provided he was willing to do just one thing for me—have his pair of horses ready and waiting, one of these days, out of town, but not beyond the toll-gate leading to Versailles. Then, on the day appointed, I sent off my hired servant on enough errands to last him several hours, and taking my Russian footman who spoke no language other than his own, I set out in my carriage together with my children and an old Major Franz who had known me from childhood and who happened to be in Paris. I ordered the coachman to drive out of town so I could have some fresh air, and made him go to the place where Mr. Khotinski was waiting for us. The latter's horses were added to ours and we told the coachman to drive up to a gate of the Versailles park, where we alighted and walked about till the King's dinner time. As the public was admitted to view the King sitting at table, we mingled with the crowd which was anything but fashionable and grand, and entered with it into a room which appeared to me very dirty and very squalid. Louis XV, the Dauphin, the Dauphiness, and the Princesses Adelaide and Victoria came in and I saw them take their seats and have a hearty meal.

Whenever I passed any comments, as I did, for instance, on noticing Princess Adelaide drink her soup out of a mug, the ladies around me immediately asked questions:

"Do not your King and Princesses do the same?" they would say.

"There are no King or Princesses in my country," I replied.

"Then, Madam, you must be Dutch."

"Perhaps so."

As soon as the meal was over we hurried back to our carriages and returned to Paris without anyone knowing about our excursion, which often afterward afforded me great amusement at the thought of having escaped the vigilance of that famous police force. The then First Minister of the Crown, the Duke of Choiseul, could hardly be persuaded of the truth of the story. He paid me many handsome compliments through our Chargé d'Affaires, invited me to his house and assured me that if I came he would give a magnificent reception in my honor. However, he was an enemy of our Cabinet and spoke slightingly of the Empress on every possible occasion, thus earning Her Majesty's dislike. I therefore had it conveyed to him that though Madame Mikhalkova thanked him profusely for his invitation, she could neither receive people nor attend entertainments in other people's houses, but wished on the present occasion to see nothing but local color and things of local interest rather than distinguished personages for whom she had esteem and regard.

CHAPTER XIII

After spending seventeen days in Paris, of which the last ten or twelve to my great delight were, apart from morning expeditions to see the sights, almost entirely in Diderot's company, I left for Aix-en-Provence. Here the house of the Marquis de Guidon was rented for me, facing the square and the fountains. I was very pleased with my accommodation, but was happier still to find my friend, Mrs. Hamilton, staying in Aix together with her father the Archbishop, her brother, and her aunt, Lady Ryder. There were also Lady Carlisle, her daughter, Lady Oxford, and other English families.

As the Parliament of Provence had been dissolved, the best accommodation was at our disposal and we spent a very agreeable winter. I was busy improving my English, and whenever I made excursions to Montpelier, to Marseilles, to Hyères and along the Royal Canal, I was accompanied by my friend Mrs. Hamilton. I received my letters regularly, even those from Paris, in spite of the anxious suspicion with which the Government regarded the correspondence of Parisians with the inhabitants of Provence's capital, which had been the seat of the provincial parliament.

I must not omit from mention the letters of Diderot with their many expressions of trust and esteem. One of them, especially, deserves to be known because it displays the depth and the acuteness of his genius. It was written at the time of the dissolution of parliaments, and the picture he draws of the feeling which that event had produced in serious and well-intentioned minds, of the motives behind it and of its inevitable consequences, make this letter into an accurate forecast of what has since happened in the French Revolution.

When in the spring we proposed to visit Switzerland we could not get all the horses we needed, and the post-master would only let us hire or otherwise procure some by paying him as much again as to the eventual owner of the horses. He said he had the right to do so because it was not his fault his horses had been commandeered for the Princess of Piedmont, who was then betrothed to the Count of Artois; he paid a lot to the King for the privilege of being post-master and he had no intention of losing the profit he made on travelers. In view of the number of servants traveling with me, we had to have sixteen horses, and as we had to pay double—once to the post-master and again to the person from whom we hired the horses—this involved us in considerable expense.

Mrs. Hamilton and her aunt, Lady Ryder, who wanted to accompany me, agreed to put off the journey for a few days, during which we persuaded the post-master to let us have five horses and four oxen, for which I paid him the equivalent of the hire-money for sixteen horses. My friend's father and aunt followed later in an ox-cart after paying for it at proportionately the same rate.

Lady Ryder wanted to be at Lyons for the festivities in honor of the Princess, who was due to pass through the town. Personally I was not very interested, but I did not want to forgo the pleasure of visiting Switzerland in the company of my friend, and I therefore gave in to her aunt's wish. Lady Ryder was a little old lady of between sixty and seventy, interested in everything, very charming, witty, and good-humored, combining all the qualities that command respect with the cheerful disposition of the first flush of youth.

Our journey to Lyons is not worth describing and I shall therefore not dwell on it. But in Lyons itself we saw all the best products of its factories, prepared either as gifts to the Princess or as public exhibits.

The Captain of the Guards, the Duke of ———, sent by Louis XV, had already arrived, and on learning I was due to come forbade members of his suite to occupy the lodging prepared for me. As soon as he heard of my arrival, he paid me a visit and offered me a box in the theater for the spectacles to be given in honor of the illustrious traveler. The Duke was very civil toward me and I feel guilty at having forgotten his name.

At last the Princess appeared. All the inhabitants longed to be presented, and be able to admire a future member of the family of Louis, formerly known as "the Well-Beloved," and afterward dubbed by wags "Louis the Misnamed." At that time, however, most of the population considered it their duty to worship their kings, and the thought of guillotining them would not have occurred to them in their wildest dreams.

We went, all four of us—Lady Ryder, Mrs. Hamilton, Miss Kamenskaia, and myself—to the very first spectacle that was being given. But my astonishment was great indeed when I found in our box four Lyonese ladies, so ill-bred that when the person ushering us in said that the Duke had reserved the box for foreign ladies of distinction they behaved like deaf-mutes, and neither moved nor answered. I told our guide not to worry; I did not, I said, particularly care for the spectacle and should go back home. Lady Ryder and Miss Kamenskaia remained standing behind the two impertinent women, while I left together with Mrs. Hamilton.

In the foyer other incidents, unpleasant and even dangerous, were lying in store for us. A detachment of Life Guards were using the butt-end of their muskets to defend the doors of the auditorium against a crowd which wanted to force its way in because the spectacle was being given free of charge.

Whether out of excessive zeal or a misplaced sense of humor, these gentlemen were dealing out blows to persons going out as well as to those who were trying to come in, and I received a blow even though I belonged to the former—and more reasonable—category. I might perhaps have been knocked down altogether before reaching the street, had I not given my name of Princess Dashkova—proof enough that the alleged civility of the French does not come from the heart. The guardsman, or constable, or whoever he was, thereupon made the silly excuse that he had been unaware of my rank. I replied that my skirt should have been sufficient protection, apart from the fact that I was trying to leave and not come in. He was afraid I might complain to the Duke, made profuse apologies and escorted me as far as one of the side streets beyond the long row of carriages. There I dismissed him, promised I should not lodge any complaint, and advised him not to strike women, several of whom, at least, must have been saved by his absence while accompanying me, since there was one brute less in the foyer.

At last Lady Ryder let herself be talked into going with us to Switzerland. I shall abstain from describing that country, for more skillful pens than mine have done so, contenting myself with naming persons I had the privilege of meeting there.

The day after my arrival at Geneva I sent to beg Voltaire's permission for me and my companions to see him the following day. He was very ill, but all the same sent a message to say that he would have great pleasure in seeing me, and that I could bring anyone I liked to see him, entirely at my own discretion.

In the evening of the day appointed I went to see Voltaire together with Mrs. Hamilton, Lady Ryder, Miss Kamenskaia, my cousin Vorontsov, and Mr. Campbell of Sheffield. The night before, Voltaire had lost over sixteen ounces of blood, but he would not let anyone know this for fear I might not come. On entering his room I found him stretched out in a lounge chair, weak and ailing. I told him I was all the sorrier to see him in that condition since by asking me to postpone my visit a day or two he would have paid me the compliment of supposing me capable of appreciating how precious was his health and his life.

He raised both his arms, as is done on the stage, to mark his astonishment and said:

"Good Heavens! Even her voice is the voice of an angel!"

(I would remind my readers that this will only appear after my death, so they cannot tax me with vanity because I repeat things as they were said.)

I felt disconcerted, for I really wanted to hear and admire him, and it never so much as entered my head that he would flatter me to that degree. I more or less told him so, with the result that after paying me another compliment he spoke of the Empress.

When, an hour or two later, I wanted to leave, he would not let me, but asked me to pass into the apartments of his niece, Madame Denis, and stay to supper in his country mansion. "Which," he said, "as from tonight, will deserve to be so called," and where he would join me later if he could be allowed to kneel on an armchair next to me, as it was impossible for him to stay on his feet. And indeed I did not remain alone long with Madame Denis—a slow-witted woman, by the way, for a niece of so great a genius—before Voltaire, supported by his valet, came to join us. He faced me kneeling in an armchair whose back was turned toward me, and remained throughout supper in that posture, made necessary by his complaint, which was that of bleeding piles. All this and the presence of two rich farmers-general from Paris, whom I recognized as the originals of the two portraits in Madame Denis's drawing room, and to whom the niece and sometimes the uncle paid flattering attention, disappointed my expectations of that visit.

As I was leaving, Voltaire asked me whether he would have the pleasure of seeing me again. I begged to be allowed to come in the mornings so as to spend them en tête-à-tête with him. He agreed, and I took advantage of his permission during my stay in Geneva. He was very different then and, alone with him in his study or his garden, I found him to be such as I had imagined and pictured him to be from reading his books.

In the first few days I spent in Geneva I made the acquaintance of all its most distinguished citizens, including that of Monsieur Hubert, nick-named "The Fowler." He was a man of remarkable intelligence possessing all the agreeable talents; he was musician, painter, poet, and to immense sensibility he added gaiety and good breeding. Voltaire was afraid of him, because Hubert was well aware of his little foibles and painted a portrait of him in which Voltaire recognized some of them. Besides, Hubert often put him into a temper by winning every game of chess they played together. Moreover, he had a dog to which he used to throw a piece of dry cheese; the twists of the dog's mouth as he tried to munch it gave a striking resemblance to Voltaire, almost like a miniature copy of the bust by the famous sculptor Pigalle.

In the evenings all our party used to go out boating with M. Hubert on the beautiful Lake of Geneva. With the help and explanation of my cousin Vorontsov, Hubert paid me the compliment of hoisting the Russian flag on the largest of the boats. He was thrilled with the airs of Russian music which he heard Miss Kamenskaia and me sing, and thanks to his good ear soon learned them and was able to sing them himself without our assistance.

It was with deep regret that we left Geneva and the friends we had made there, including a Russian—Mr. Veselovskii—and his family. In order to avoid the brutal anger of Peter I who had recalled him home after employing him in Vienna, Mr. Veselovskii had escaped to Holland, married there, renounced his country and finally settled in Geneva. His eldest daughter was married to Mr. Kramer, famous as a printer, and more famous still for his friendship and his quarrels with Voltaire.

On our way from Switzerland we went down the Rhine on two large boats, one of which held our carriages and kitchen furniture, while the other we fitted up with wooden partitions to make cabins where we slept and which we decorated with pretty wallpaper. The gentlemen found sleeping accommodation in the villages close to the river, leaving us under the safeguard of only our two boatmen and my servants.

We stopped and went ashore whenever the towns past which we sailed seemed worthy of a visit, Miss Kamenskaia and I clad simply in black dresses and straw hats and accompanied by only one Russian servant who knew no language but his own. We thus remained completely unknown and often by way of amusement bought our own provisions for the dinner prepared on board. Lack of practice made me too shy to speak German, and Mr. Campbell took it upon himself to be our spokesman in that

[handwritten note: -Princess Dashkova is very popular, to whereve she's traveling]

language whenever ███████ it to the point of
unintelligibility, wh ███████ general interpreter
for the rest of the j█████

We hired two ca███████████████ famous Karlsruhe,
but scarcely had we reached the inn when the Grand Master of the Court
of His Highness the Margrave of Baden arrived with a complimentary
message from Their Serene Highnesses and an invitation to the Palace. I
excused myself on the plea that we had none but traveling clothes with us
as we had intended staying only a few hours to admire the park and the
garden. He left us, but an hour and a half later we saw Their Highnesses'
Master of the Horse arrive in a fine carriage drawn by six horses, to tell
us that the Margravine knew Madame Mikhalkova was none other than
Princess Dashkova, whose acquaintance she wanted to make, and as Her
Majesty the Empress of Russia had made her Knight of the Order of St.
Catherine she thought that bond of relationship between us might lead to
a visit; if, however, I absolutely refused to come to the Palace she would
beg me make use of her landau to avoid fatigue while driving about the
very extensive park; in the meantime her Master of the Horse would show
us all there was to be seen.

It was impossible to refuse this latest mark of kindness and I therefore
accepted the offer. We seated ourselves in the magnificent carriage and I
tried to convey to the Master of the Horse how much I appreciated the
kindness of a Princess so distinguished for her natural intelligence and her
education, for Her Highness entertained a correspondence on scientific
subjects with scientists from different countries, who all admired her.

Scarcely had we entered the first drive of the park when we saw another
carriage, similar to ours, emerge from one of the side drives and stop in
front of us. It contained Their Serene Highnesses, the Crown Prince, and
several persons of the Court. The Margravine with all her usual grace and
wit said to me:

"You will allow us, Madame, I am sure, at least to show you some of
the more beautiful spots in this park of which we are very fond."

I got out of my carriage and changed places with the Crown Prince. We
spent over an hour driving over that charming plantation, during which
time I could not sufficiently admire Her Highness's great gifts. Our drive
finished at the steps of the Palace, and I had no choice but to come in and
pay my court, something I have always done very badly, but Their Serene
Highnesses were extremely indulgent.

A delightful concert, a magnificent supper and, above all, the conversation of our illustrious hosts made this into a pleasanter evening than I could have imagined. We were shown most cordial politeness, and when I made to leave, the Margravine said that our servants were in the Palace and she would not allow us to spend the night in a bad inn; in order to oblige me, since I was in such a hurry, she agreed to my leaving the next morning as early as I liked without seeing my hosts. All I had to do was to tell her the time at which I wanted breakfast, and the post-horses would be ready for me.

My friends and I were magnificently lodged and, what is more, comfortably too. The following morning we left so early that the whole Palace was, I believe, still asleep.

I shall say nothing of the beautiful country through which we traveled or of the pleasure that can be derived from seeing the landscape of the Rhine. Better pens than mine have described it all before. I have no desire to give an account of my travels, the towns I have seen, etc., etc., but would just mention that in Düsseldorf, while admiring the magnificent picture gallery, I could not refrain from pointing out to the Director that he had a beautiful 'St. John' by Raphael hung in an embrasure of a window, because he failed to recognize in it the work of that great master who had painted it in his last manner.

In Frankfurt I had great pleasure in seeing Madame Weynacht, the widow of a merchant who had spent over twenty years in Russia. I had known her in my childhood, and I stayed for her sake one day more in that town, for my life as a child was less unhappy than it later became and it is natural for us to hark back to happier times.

I also made the acquaintance of the youngest of the Orlovs, Count Vladimir, a man of shallow mind who had derived from his studies in Germany nothing but a pedantic tone and an entirely unfortunate conviction of his own deep learning. He entered into long arguments with me for the simple reason that that was what he always did as soon as anyone spoke to him; he regarded every sophism of Jean-Jacques Rousseau as a profound truth and adopted every rhapsodical statement of that eloquent but dangerous writer as if it were his own.

Little did I foresee then that he would be placed at the head of the Petersburg Academy of Sciences, that he would be followed as Director by Mr. Domashnev, a creature of the Orlovs and quite as inefficient as himself, and that I should be their successor.

CHAPTER XIV

At Spa I made the acquaintance of Prince Ernest of Mecklenburg-Strelitz and of Prince Charles of Sweden, since Duke of Sudermania, who had occupied part of the house I had rented at Aachen.

Prince Charles, who was suffering from rheumatism, came to Spa accompanied by his tutor, Herr von Schwerin, a Captain Hamilton, and another junior officer. Schwerin would not let him incur any expenses, for the Prince's traveling allowance was not, I believe, very considerable. We saw a great deal of each other every day, and I got to know him really well. He did not like either the Queen, his mother, or his elder brother, and would often say that he had a good chance of becoming King, as his brother, according to him, could not have children. Therefore later, during our war with Sweden, when he, as Duke of Sudermania, was commanding the Swedish Navy, I told the Empress what sort of person the Prince was and how easy it would be to make him turn against his brother.

As the time was approaching when my friends had to leave Spa and I return to Russia, we all felt sadder and sadder. One evening, as we were strolling along the Promenade de Sept Heures lamenting the necessity for our separation, we observed a fairly large house, which was then still being built.

"Before five years are over," I said to my friend, Mrs. Hamilton, "I promise I shall come here and occupy this very house together with you. If you arrive before me, rent it for us both" (for the house looked big enough to contain both our families easily). I kept my word and, in less than five years came back to Spa where I welcomed Mrs. Hamilton in that very house, which my banker had in the meantime rented for me.

On my way back from Spa I went through Dresden, where I stopped for a few days, all of which I spent almost entirely in the beautiful picture gallery admiring and studying the pictures, for which, indeed, a lifetime would not suffice.

It was not, however, worth spending much time on the Electoral treasure, most of which had been pledged to Holland to finance the expenses of State and Court.

My reception at Berlin was just as gracious as the first time. Our Minister, the excellent Prince Dolgorukii, was a great friend of mine and I valued his company for his good nature and kindness as well as for his distinguished mind. Thence I went straight to Riga, where I received letters from my brother Aleksandr which threw me into consternation. The plague had broken out in Moscow and he had left to seek refuge in Andreevskoe, a magnificent estate some ninety miles from Moscow which had belonged to my mother. My steward wrote that forty-five of my servants had died, and that as my house had been infected with the plague he would not be able to send anything to me in Petersburg before my own arrival, for the sending of things was forbidden and even those servants who felt quite well were subjected to a six weeks' quarantine.

But it was worry for my brother, far more than anything else, that affected my health. I fell dangerously ill, and remained for about three weeks in Riga. Ten whole days passed before I suddenly realized that I had nowhere to go and nothing to set up house with. Then I wrote to my sister Madame Polianskaia asking her to give me shelter in her house till I could rent one myself and obtain servants. My own house was sold in my absence by Count Panin acting on my behalf, in the hope that the proceeds of the sale would cover the expenses of our journey, as my own income, or rather the income I shared with my children, would not have sufficed. However, Madame Talyzina, who was then my cousin's favorite, successfully persuaded him to sell it at half price to a friend of hers.

I arrived at last in Petersburg and went to stay with my sister, while Miss Kamenskaia went to stay with hers. Her Majesty was kind enough to ask after me, and sent me 10,000 roubles for my immediate needs.

I also had the comfort of seeing my father, and though he gave me no help at all, he did something more, something that was of greater value to me: he treated me with kindness and esteem, as he had not for some time because of all the malicious gossip and tittle-tattle. I have already said in these memoirs when speaking of Madame ————, a former personal maid of the Grand Duchess who had come back from exile, that she had exercised—perhaps unwittingly—a certain influence on my life.[1] She is supposed to have stated that prior to his departure abroad as Russian Minister Plenipotentiary, Count Panin had a liaison with my mother, and that I was his daughter. I should like to believe that this is noting but ghastly slander and that the veneration I have always had for the memory of my mother (whom I never had the happiness of knowing, since I lost her at the age of two) was as well-deserved as it was profound. The Orlovs, who at that time had some social connection with my father, had it insinuated to him through certain sycophantic individuals they all knew, that I went about boasting of it, though at the same time they tried to make people believe that I was having a love affair with that same Count Panin, who, so far as his age was concerned, could certainly have been not only my father, but even the father of my elder sisters, for he was several years my father's senior.

I hope that at the bottom of his heart my father did not believe me capable of such horribly immoral conduct, but anyhow, for a very long time he absolutely refused to see me in spite of all my attempts at reconciliation. However, I do not wish to expatiate any further on this subject; I merely thank Heaven that I was able to enjoy—even if rather belatedly— my father's trust and esteem. His regard would have been precious to me even had he not borne the sacred name of father, for he was a man of very superior parts, with a distinguished mind and a generous and charitable soul, a stranger to all vanity and meanness—so characteristic, I always think, of persons of small merit. I want to forget all the rest.

To return to my arrival at Petersburg. I was weak and could not go out, but a brighter future seemed to lie in store for me, since Prince Orlov was no longer favorite, and when I appeared at Court Her Majesty treated me with kindness. I could not so much as think of going to Moscow for months yet, as several servants of mine had died of the plague in my house, and therefore, as soon as some of them arrived at Petersburg I rented one—a rather indifferent one, at that—bought furniture, linen, kitchenware, etc., etc., and hired more servants. And I cannot fairly say that I either enjoyed it all or found it convenient.

Shortly afterward, the Empress sent me 60,000 roubles with which to buy a property of my own in the country. Possibly she had no idea till then that except for a piece of marsh near Petersburg and a timber house in Moscow I had nothing that belonged to me personally, or else, being

[1] Probably Madame Travina, formerly Maria Zhukova, see note on p. 92.—K. F.

no longer subjected to the influence of the Orlovs, she wanted to help me by making me easier in my circumstances. But, whatever the reason, I was astounded, for it was most unlike the manner in which I had been treated during the ten years that had passed since she had ascended the throne.

I had the pleasure of helping my father out of a difficult situation, as he needed 23,000 roubles to satisfy a claim which the Crown had against him.

In the Spring I established myself in my little country place where my son, soon afterward, fell ill with an extremely high fever. I was worried to death, for unfortunately, both Mr. Kruse and Mr. Kelchen, who had attended him ever since he was a child, had followed the Court to Tsarskoe Selo. I was nearly out of my mind with despair when Admiral Knowles's wife came on a visit and, seeing me in that state, recommended to me a young doctor Rogerson, lately arrived from Scotland. She did more; she offered to go at once and send him to me.

He came at midnight, and though he did not disguise the full extent of the danger, he assured me there was no need to despair of my son's recovery. Seventeen days, oblivious of food and drink, I passed by his bedside, but God took pity on me, and Mr. Rogerson's great skill and care gave me back my son. Ever since, this worthy doctor has been a close friend, and our friendship, based on esteem, remains unshaken.

But no sooner was my son restored in health than nature demanded her due. Fatigue, worry, sleepless nights finally forced me to take to my bed. Just then, Prince Potemkin, who had at the time the rank of Major-General, arrived from the Army with news of our complete victory over the Turks and their desire to make peace with us at any price.

I could not go personally to congratulate the Empress on the brilliant success of her Armies, but I wrote to her and sent her a fine picture of a beautiful Greek girl by Angelica Kauffmann. In my letter I alluded both to my own condition and to the liberation of the Greeks, or at least, to the improvement of their lot. The work of that charming artist and charming woman was not yet known in Russia, and the picture gave Her Majesty great pleasure.

In the autumn of the following year, 1773, I went to Moscow and found my mother-in-law astonishingly well for a person of her age. I placed the money the Empress had given me in safe hands, so that my daughter might eventually have it instead of squandering any more of her father's fortune, which I wanted my son to get intact. After making other necessary arrangements I left for Troitskoe, whence I took my children every fortnight to see my mother-in-law, so to avoid any complaint on her part that I prevented her from seeing them.

During one such visit to Moscow in the house of a cousin of mine, General Eropkin, I met General Potemkin who later was so powerful in Russia and was created Prince by the Emperor of Germany on becoming the favorite, nay, more, the friend, of his Sovereign. The acquaintance I formed with him at that dinner was only slight, but I remembered then being told in confidence by Levashov, who was under some obligation to me, that Potemkin was hastening back to Petersburg because he was in a hurry to occupy the place of favorite. I gave him a certain piece of advice which he followed and thus avoided scandalous public scenes, which the Grand Duke (later Pavel I) would not have failed to make in order to injure Potemkin and annoy his own mother.

CHAPTER XV

C ount Rumiantsev was invested with full powers to impose peace conditions and in the course of the following summer, 1785, the Empress came to Moscow to celebrate the event with splendid magnificence. Rewards were heaped with unexampled generosity and profusion on Field-Marshal Count Rumiantsev as well as on the other generals and the Army as a whole. My brother, Count Simon, was promoted and his regiment—the Grenadiers—received the honor of becoming a Guards regiment.

The Empress toured the country and on one occasion visited Kaluga, where she stayed at the superb country seat of my uncle, Count Ivan Vorontsov.

I did not take part in all this because my mother-in-law was dangerously ill. During the three weeks that her illness lasted I spent most of the day by her bedside, in spite of being myself racked by a relapsing fever. My mother-in-law was good enough then to show me a great deal of esteem and affection and whole-hearted approval, particularly of all I was doing for the upbringing and welfare of my children. She died in my arms, after signifying her desire to be buried in the Monastery of Our Savior by the side of her husband and her husband's ancestors. I asked for permission to do so, but all in vain, as that year the monastery was not the one in which burials took place. According to a new regulation issued by the Empress, the dead were to be interred either outside the city walls or else in one only of the many monasteries, each of which, in order to equalize profits, took its yearly turn in rotation to bury the rich and superstitious who did not wish to leave the city on their last journey.

Being unable to fulfill exactly my mother-in-law's last instructions, I resolved, though still weak, personally to accompany her remains and see them deposited in a monastery forty-four miles out of Moscow where Prince Dashkov's ancestors were also buried. I had made it a rule for myself, from which I never deviated, to behave toward members of my husband's family in the way in which I thought he would have behaved, and therefore did not regard this melancholy journey as a hard task.

On Her Majesty's return I asked permission to go abroad in order to give my son a classical and university education. This permission I obtained, but it was given to me with unbelievable coldness because Her Majesty did not like my leaving Russia. On learning that I had not even been privileged to take leave of Her Majesty otherwise than by kissing her hand at a general audience granted to all and sundry in one of the great apartments on the occasion of the Empress's imminent departure for Petersburg, the Prince of Anhalt-Bernburg told me he was delighted that all pretence had been dropped in the attitude adopted toward me, which was of a piece with all the rest, but I could be sure, he added, that the time would come when things would change and greater fairness would be shown to me.

I returned to Troitskoe where I married my daughter off to Brigadier Shcherbinin. The bad treatment he had received at the hands of his parents had left him with a melancholy, though gentle, disposition, and I hoped my daughter would have a quiet and peaceful life with him. Thanks to a certain physical defect, she was not yet fully developed and I could not expect a younger and more dashing husband to remain loving and submissive.

The consideration that decided me on this marriage was the nine, or perhaps ten, years that my son's classical and university education abroad would take. It may not have been the best I could have wished for my daughter, but at least it offered me the inestimable advantage of having her with me and being able to keep an eye on her while she was so young.

Mr. Shcherbinin's father agreed all the more readily to letting his son go, as he had my assurance that it would cost him nothing and that the capital I should give my daughter would yield sufficient interest to cover the expenses of both of them if they lived with me in my house.

Criticism and malicious gossip, which I could treat with contempt in the perfect confidence that I was acting as a good mother should, were not, unfortunately, the only sorrows that that marriage brought me.

But I am determined to pass over in silence the most bitter of all the unhappy experiences I have had in my life, and shall continue with my narrative.

We set out on the road to Pskov to pay a short visit to the magnificent property belonging to Shcherbinin's father situated in the province of that name. An accident occurred on the way which alarmed me considerably. A servant of Madame Taneeva, who was traveling with me, fell and two of our carriages went over him. There was no surgeon to be found at the end of the first stage, and none at the second. The man had no broken bones since our carriages were light and placed on runners, but his left arm and almost the whole of his left side were so bruised and swollen that his shirt could be taken off him only after cutting his sleeve open from one end to the other. He could not have endured the rest of the journey and would inevitably have died as a result of his accident, if I had not suddenly remembered that my son had a lancet in his English brief-case. I asked, I begged, everyone, including even the servants, to bleed the poor man, but all in vain—no one was brave enough. I was obliged to perform that operation myself. I opened up his vein successfully, but had violent palpitations afterward. However, I did not mind this, since I had had the good fortune to save the man's life.

I was extremely bored in the country in the company of Shcherbinin's parents, and therefore cut short my visit and continued my journey.

Just before we arrived in Grodno my son gave me a mortal fright by catching measles. There was no help to be obtained from anywhere in that semi-barbarous country, where peasants have none of the Russians' resourcefulness and hospitality, and where poverty and filth reign supreme. The roads were impassable for anything but their kind of light carts (*brichki*), and my carriages could advance only with the help of thirty Russian cossacks who went half a day's journey ahead of me and felled trees in order to widen the road through the immense forests.

On arrival in Grodno I was fortunate enough to find an excellent physician who had come from Brussels on the King's invitation, and was attached to the Cadet Corps which the King had founded.

There I stayed for five weeks, because my daughter, who refused to leave her brother's bedside, caught the measles in her turn. At the end of that period I went to Warsaw by way of Vilno. It was the year of the Jubilee, and though the entertainment we were offered was not of the noisy sort, I had the satisfaction of frequently enjoying the King's pleasant and instructive conversation.[1] His Majesty came to see me two or three times a week, and we spent hours on end talking to each other, while

[1] See Index under Poniatowski, Stanisław-August.—K. F.

his nephew Prince Stanisław,[2] a pleasant and highly educated young man, and General Komarzewski and the rest of his suite remained in the other rooms with my children.

I was, I must say, frequently struck with the King's great qualities. He had a noble and compassionate heart and a distinguished mind, and his taste for the fine arts, of which he had a connoisseur's appreciation, made his conversation as varied as it was interesting. He deserved to be happy, and the Crown of Poland was for him more of a curse than a source of happiness. As a private citizen, pleasant and esteemed, he would have made the most of those qualities and gifts which Nature had lavished on him and education had improved, and he would have been loved; as King of a turbulent nation, the incoherent constitution of which could only produce contradictions in the character of the people, he was not liked because he could not be appreciated; as a neighbor of two great Powers he was often forced to act against his principles and his own inclination, while the intrigues of the Polish magnates were partly responsible for his being blamed for faults he never had.

It was with regret that I left Warsaw. The King, his nephew Stanisław, and the veneration in which my husband's memory was generally held there made me feel very attached to it.

In Berlin I was received as kindly as before. From there I wrote to my banker asking him to rent for me the newly built house in Spa on the left-hand side of the Promenade de Sept Heures. I arrived there before Mrs. Hamilton, and thus was able to keep my promise to her in all respects, as she found me already installed in the whole house.

Mr. Shcherbinin in the meantime received letters from his father and mother urging him to return to Russia; he therefore left us in Spa, even though he felt both irresolute and unhappy about it. My daughter refused to accompany him and stayed with me.

[2] See Index under Poniatowski, Stanisław, Prince.—K. F.

CHAPTER XVI

I t was from there I wrote to Robertson, the historian and Principal of Edinburgh University, to tell him that I was coming to Edinburgh in the autumn in order to settle there for the duration of my son's studies. I told him my son was only thirteen, and that I should in all likelihood need his guidance during the several years of the course. I begged him, therefore, to give me all the information he thought necessary. When I received his answer, in which he advised me to postpone my son's entry into the University for a few years while I prepared him for it, I was able to assure him in all honesty and with a true mother's pride that my son was entirely fit and able to be a student since he had a perfect knowledge of Latin, mathematics, history, geography, French, and German, and had sufficient command of English to understand everything, though he did not speak it fluently enough yet.

As soon as the season at Spa was over I went to England. I stopped in London for a very short time and then proceeded to Scotland, breaking the journey, at the invitation of Lord and Lady Sussex, at their place in the country. It was there I had the pleasure of meeting Mr. Wilmot, the father of my young friend for whose sake I have overcome my repugnance at the idea of writing these memoirs. He was a relation of the Sussexes and stayed there all the time I was there.

I went thence to Edinburgh, where I spent several years, and lived in one of the apartments of Holyrood House, the ancient palace of the Sovereigns. Often did I have occasion to reflect on the fate of the rash but all-too-unfortunate Queen Mary, whose study and the stair down which her Italian favorite was thrown were adjacent to my apartments.

To my great satisfaction Mr. Robertson found that my son was fully qualified to enter the University for his classical studies. I made the acquaintance of the University professors, all of whom were generally esteemed for their intelligence, intellectual distinction, and moral qualities. Strangers alike to envy and to the pretentiousness of smaller minds, they lived together in brotherly amity, their mutual love and respect making of them a group of educated and intelligent people whom it was always an immense pleasure to see and whose conversation never failed to be instructive.

The immortal Robertson, Blair, Smith, and Ferguson came twice a week to spend the day with me. The Duchess of Buccleuch, Lady Francis Scott, Lady Lothian, and Lady Mary Irwin contributed to make my life pleasant; indeed, this period of my existence was both the happiest and most peaceful that has ever fallen to my lot in this world. During the summer vacations when my son was free of his University lectures we made a trip to the Highlands. My friend Mrs. Hamilton came too and her presence increased the total sum of happiness which even the violent bouts of rheumatism I had caught in the mountains could not affect. For I had become hardened to physical ills and lived entirely outside myself— that is, wholly for others and for the sake of my love for my children— with the result that I was able to laugh in the midst of acute pain.

The following year I went on the orders of my doctor, the famous Mr. Cullen, to take the waters at Buxton and Matlock, and then to bathe in the sea at Scarborough. I undertook this cure because I could go through with it and finish it during university vacations. My friend Mrs. Hamilton accompanied me, and I probably owe my life to the tender and tireless care she took of me when I was lying on my deathbed in Scarborough.

As soon as Lady Mulgrave, who after her husband's death was living alone in the country, had heard from a friend that I was dangerously ill, she came to Scarborough to see me in spite of her gout and in spite of still suffering from the shock of her own great loss. She stayed till she was quite certain that I was out of danger. I really cannot forbear saying a few words on the subject of that excellent person and her generous, indeed touching, behavior. She had just lost a dearly beloved husband whom she had nursed throughout a long illness which made him all the dearer to her heart. She tore herself away from her sorrow in order to look after me in the kindest way possible; and thinking me to be on the point of death, she showed sympathy and understanding and tried her best to set my mind at ease, as I lay worrying about my children alone and inexperienced in a strange land, far away from their family. She promised to take them and look after them like a mother till such time as their guardians came to fetch them back to Russia. The story of this characteristic gesture of hers is, I think, the greatest praise I can give her. My own feelings and gratitude are beyond expression.

I had at the time a dog which always lay on my bed. As soon as I became seriously ill the little animal hid under the bed and refused to come out for anyone in the world. It would not eat or drink and refrained from satisfying its natural needs, since it had learned never to make a mess in a room. During the night it would sometimes leave its voluntary prison, would look at me and then go back to it again. Woe betide anyone who ventured on these occasions to take it in his arms in order to put it out of the room: it would immediately show its teeth. On the very day that my illness took a sharp turn for the better, Favori left his retreat, was pleasant and gentle with everyone and behaved in his normal way. All this lasted three days, during which even my son failed to obtain obedience from him, though, in fact, the little dog was very attached to him. Such proof of a dog's devotion may not be very extraordinary, but I have a great fondness for dogs and recall this with pleasure.

Lady Mulgrave prevailed on me to spend a few days with her at her friends' house on my way back to Edinburgh. I promised to do this, and as soon as I had regained sufficient strength to undertake the journey I left Scarborough and went to see her. I stayed two restful days with Lady Mulgrave and her friend and then resumed my journey to Scotland, where I arrived before the beginning of term.

Although I was still suffering from rheumatism in the knees and my digestion was out of order, I was glad to be able to fulfill the duties of a mother and a mentor to the best of my abilities and never sparing myself. My quietly cheerful and gentle disposition amazed all those who came to see me.

By way of amusement and exercise for my son I gave a dance every week; I also made him go to a riding school, and an excellent fencing master who happened to be living in Edinburgh gave him lessons every other day. Not only was I thus able to preserve his health, but he acquired great vigor and became surprisingly strong.

Personally, I had to suffer constant privations, but was perfectly indifferent to them: my life was dedicated to the love I bore my children, to my duties and my friends, and in the midst of all my suffering I was able to enjoy my friends' company with a gaiety of spirit which surprised them, but which was due to the happiness I felt at being able to fulfill my duty.

Absorbed as I was in trying to give my son the best possible education, the modesty of my children's fortune and my own poverty affected me not at all, and as life is not very expensive in Scotland, I realized that with a little economy my income would suffice, except that I should have to draw upon my credit with my bankers, Sir William Forbes and Mr. Hunter— whom I knew intimately—if I was to undertake the journey to Ireland after the completion of my son's studies. And in fact, I did avail myself of their offer on the eve of my departure and borrowed £2,000 from them, which I repaid a few months later from Holland. So much for my financial debt, but what I can never repay is their friendship, kindness, and zeal.

In the month of May 1779, my son sat for a public examination at the University. The audience was prodigiously numerous, and so amazingly successful were his answers to the questions on all his subjects that the audience could not refrain from clapping (even though this is forbidden). He received his degree of Master of Arts, and my joy at his success can only be appreciated by a mother who, like myself, has fulfilled the functions and duties of a tutor.

We left for Ireland at the beginning of June, landing at Donaghadee where I was met by my friend, Mrs. Morgan. We went to Coleraine and also saw the Giant's Causeway, which is indeed well worth a visit. On arriving in Dublin I found a large, fine house all ready for me. My stay in Dublin even now seems to me like a happy dream which lasted a whole year. But my enjoyment of it was no illusion, for the care and affection of my two friends, Mrs. Hamilton and Mrs. Morgan, and the attentions and respect of their families anticipated my every wish and made my days flow in peace and contentment.

I found in Dublin an excellent dancing master recently returned from Paris, and I engaged him to come twice a week to give lessons to my son. Another man came to teach him Italian and Mr. Greenfield coached him every morning in the subjects he had studied in Edinburgh, and read Greek and Latin classics with him. His days were thus fully occupied in useful pursuits.

In the evenings we went out. Dublin Society was then distinguished by its elegance, its wit, and its manners, and enlivened by that frankness which comes naturally to the Irish. Often we went to the theater, and every week I gave a dance which kept my children cheerful and healthy.

I was fortunate enough to gain the love of Lady Arabella Denny, the most estimable woman in the world and the most esteemed, for Parliament had sent her a deputation to thank her for her public services and the useful establishments she had founded and was still superintending despite her great age. We often used to visit her for tea; her good sense, serene temper, and charm of manner—qualities she possessed to an eminent degree—won the hearts of all who were fortunate enough to know her well. The Magdalen Hospital, which thanks to her was both useful and efficient in a very real sense, greatly interested her; she took me there several times, and as she had formed too favorable a notion of my poor abilities, she begged me set to music a favorite hymn of hers to be sung by the inmates. I could not refuse, for her every wish was my command, and I composed music for four voices. She had it rehearsed several times, and a fortnight later had it sung in church in the presence of a numerous congregation drawn by curiosity to hear what a Russian bear could have composed. The collection was very considerable. Lady Arabella, when I saw her that evening, was charmingly gay, gave me a full account of the morning service, and ascribed the profit made by her Magdalen establishment to my music. Then she gave me her blessing as affectionately as a mother.

I often visited Parliament to hear the better speakers, among whom Mr. Grattan was the most brilliant. Concerts and books which I frequently read with my two friends so filled my time that a whole year was, so to speak, spirited away. But duty called, and I left Dublin with sorrow and reluctance to set out on further travels before returning home to present my son to his Sovereign. We made excursions to see Kilkenny and its castle, Killarney and its beautiful lake, Cork and its fine harbor. In the neighborhood and in a truly magnificent setting, Mr. Rogers, great-uncle of my young friend, then had his superb country seat called Lota. He gave a small but very elegant reception in my honor, and the morning I spent there was made delightful for me not only because I enjoyed the natural beauties of that wonderful place, but also, and mainly, because of the varied and very superior accomplishments and the distinguished and attentive manners of every member of his family.

Then we proceeded to Limerick and visited the magnificent country round it as well as other places.

Early in the year 1780 we left Ireland and landed at Holyhead. The way to London is, all of it, very interesting, and there are many most romantic places in Wales. Upon my arrival in London I was presented to Their

Majesties who received me with their usual kindness and affability. I told them I had rarely enjoyed such untroubled happiness as I had in their dominions; my son, especially, had derived great benefit from the education he had received, and I, as a mother, was deeply thankful for this. In saying it, I added, I wanted to give full expression to the sentiments of mingled respect and gratitude I felt for Their Majesties.

"I have always known," said the Queen, "that there are few mothers like you."

I replied that I had no such pretensions, but knew what an excellent mother she was herself, and her fine family justified all the affection she lavished on it. The Queen spoke of her children, saying she had a great number of them and doubted I knew them all. When I told her I did not, and expressed the desire to see them, she very kindly replied that she would have them all come from Kew expressly to see me. Her Majesty then turned to Lady Holderness and ordered her to fetch them the morning after next for dinner in London, and to inform me of their arrival. I expressed as best as I could how much I appreciated Her Majesty's kindness. I afterward saw those beautiful children, who really were quite angelic.

We visited all the Royal castles and houses, made excursions to Bath and Bristol, and after a farewell audience with the King and Queen went to Margate and sailed for Ostend.

From Ostend we proceeded to Brussels, stayed there for a few days and then, leaving behind us our carriages and some of our servants, continued into Holland by way of Antwerp, visiting Rotterdam, Delft, the Hague, Leyden, Haarlem, Utrecht, and the establishment of the Hernhutter brothers.

In Haarlem I received a letter from Prince Golitsyn, our Minister at The Hague, which made us laugh a lot. I must explain first that I hired an entire cabin in a *trekschuit* to travel down the canals. *Trekschuits* are long barges pulled by one or two horses. They contain a small and very clean cabin which can be hired by the well-to-do or the gentry, and a large or common cabin where people pay a modest sum at so much per head. The roof of these two cabins corresponds to the upper deck of a coach in other countries, and a place can be obtained on it at a still lower price. These barges leave at a certain fixed time every day, and their arrival at any place also takes place at regular intervals and at stated times.

At the precise moment when my *trekschuit* was about to leave, a man appeared who was obviously in a great hurry. He could only find a place with servants and peasants on the roof, and I noticed he was worried. I therefore suggested that he should come into my room, and he accepted the offer with alacrity. He told me half in Dutch and half in Low German that business required his presence at The Hague on a certain day. Thereupon I suddenly thought of concealing my name from him and asking him to tell our Minister (whom he told me he knew) that the Russian woman to whom he had given his protection presented her compliments and begged him kindly to send her letters on to Amsterdam. He promised to do what I asked him. Soon we had to go up another canal by a boat which left a whole two hours after the arrival of our own. I asked him what the peasants did and where they went to during these two hours.

"The natives," he replied, "who have business to transact have either their own houses or their friends' houses to go to, but as you are a stranger, I shall take you to a tavern quite close to the place where you have to embark."

It was my turn to accept his offer, and we thought we should burst out laughing when he presented us with a mug of beer, a piece of bread, and some cheese.

After the journey my friend did not omit to go to Prince Golitsyn and tell him that the Russian woman who was indebted to him for her travels presented her most humble duty, etc., etc. The Prince at first took him for a madman; then suspecting the truth, questioned him more closely, saw through the little hoax, explained it all to him and had infinite amusement out of the good man's astonishment and the way in which he expressed his embarrassment at the familiarity with which he had treated me. The Prince's letter gave a very lively and witty description of that practical joke.

On my return to The Hague I again saw the worthy Princess of Orange, whom I sincerely loved and esteemed. Both times I stayed at The Hague she insisted that I should visit her, although I had only my traveling clothes. At her first invitation I excused myself on that score, but she sent Mrs. Dunkelmann to see me; Mrs. Dunkelmann was her governess in charge of her education, enjoying the full confidence of the Princess's mother. I shall not stop to give that lady all the praise she deserves, but shall merely mention that she was in correspondence with the great Frederick, King of Prussia and uncle of the Princess of Orange.

At her insistence, I overcame my scruples, as indeed nothing was infringed but sartorial decorum, and off I went to the Palace, together with my son and daughter, in Mrs. Dunkelmann's carriage.

We supped with the Princess, which we did every night throughout our short stay at The Hague, both before and after the little excursion I mentioned above. The Prince of Orange was also present, and though ordinarily he fell asleep at table however early the hour, that time I was sitting by his side and did not even see him doze. He did me the honor of saying that he liked falling asleep at table, but I was so charming that I had been able to chase Morpheus right away. I replied that I was sorry he had made such a sacrifice for my sake, and when the Princess asked me what it was the Prince was telling me I was fairly embarrassed at having to repeat his witty little speech, and merely replied that her consort was paying me compliments.

I have omitted to say that when I went to Leyden to see some friends I had made during my first journey, I did not want to remain for more than two days and therefore agreed to stay with a cousin of mine, Prince Shakhovskoi. Immediately on arrival I went to see the famous physician, Gaubieus, for whom I had infinite esteem. I knocked at the door, which was opened by his old servant with the words that he was not at home. As I knew he never went out I said to the cook: "I know the doctor never leaves the house, and I flatter myself that he would be sorry to have missed me. I must ask you, therefore, to tell him that Princess Dashkova wants to take leave of him."

He was in the next room and, on hearing my voice, came out into the hall. As the servant opened the door I saw that the doctor had with him Prince and Princess Orlov, who had, apparently, come to seek his advice.[1] My surprise was all the greater as I had no idea they had left Russia. My few correspondents gave me hardly any details; convinced that Russia under Catherine II could do nothing but prosper, and entirely absorbed as I was by the one aim and desire which shaped all my actions—that is, my son's education—I asked them to write only of themselves, my relations, and my friends.

It gave me great pleasure to see Gaubieus again. He, too, appeared pleased, but I did not want to interrupt him in the middle of his work, and so remained outside in the hall and then left after as brief a visit as possible, returning home on foot.

We had hardly sat down to dinner when Prince Orlov came in. Whether it was that the expression of my face, which to my own great detriment always revealed my feelings, gave him to understand that his visit was

[1] Grigorii Orlov and his wife Catherine.—K. F.

neither expected nor particularly relished, or whether he merely uttered the first thing that came into his head, I do not know, but what he said was:

"I have come not to make war, but as a friend."

No one made any answer.

It may be that he was smitten by conscience at the thought of all the wrong he had done me; in any case he stared at my son and then said to me:

"I see by your son's uniform that he is still in the regiment of Cuirassiers; I am traveling for the benefit of my wife's health, but I have not quitted the service and am still, therefore, in command of the Horse Guards. I shall, if you wish, Madam, write to the Empress asking her to transfer your son to my regiment, thus promoting him to two ranks above his present one."

I thanked the Prince, saying that on that subject I must speak to him in private. Then I rose from the table and after asking the others to remain seated and not wait for me to finish their meal, I invited Prince Orlov to follow me to my room. I did not know whether he fully appreciated my tact, but after thanking him once again for his kind intentions I begged him not to act upon them for a while, as I had already written to Prince Potemkin, as Minister of War, to inquire what I could expect for my son, whom I intended for a military career and to whom I had given an education which should enable him to serve with distinction. In the circumstances I could not let him be transferred from one regiment to another without prior consultation with Her Majesty, who was his godmother, and besides, such precipitate action on my part might also give offence to Potemkin and be interpreted by him as lack of respect.

Orlov replied that he could not understand how my behavior could be interpreted as lack of respect. I knew that both Princes were on very bad terms with each other, and therefore thought it my duty to tell him that my letter to the War Minister had already been sent. I saw, too, that I should merely be wasting my time trying to explain my motives to him, and therefore put an end to our interview with the request to let me know where I should address my letter informing him of the answer when I eventually received it from Petersburg. I said I hoped he would continue to be well-disposed toward my son, and added that I might perhaps take advantage of this later.

"That I can promise you," he replied, "for it would be difficult to find a finer-looking young man than Prince Dashkov."

This observation about his good looks made me angry at the time and proved to be a source of great worry later.

I saw Prince Orlov again at Brussels, where he stopped before going on to Paris and then to Switzerland to have his wife treated by Tissot. He was accompanied by Mr. Melissino, Principal of Moscow University, by his wife who had her nephew with her, by Miss Protasova, maid-of-honor to Her Majesty, and by Miss Kamenskaia. Before ever I knew they were in Brussels I had my room flooded out by the entire party, but it was only old Melissino with his well-stocked mind, his pleasant, even temper, and his charming manners that I was delighted to see again; for many years he had been in the habit of visiting me every other day.

But my attention was perforce divided at that moment, and Prince Orlov soon caused me acute embarrassment by looking at my son straight in the eye and saying:

"What a pity, Prince Dashkov, that I am not likely to be in Petersburg at the time of your arrival there, for I have no doubt at all that you will supplant the present favorite, and as for some time now it has been my function to look after and console those that have been dismissed, I should do it with great pleasure if it meant making room for you."

Those astonishing words made me regret my son's presence, and I hastily sent him out of the room before he had time to answer, with the request that he should write a note to Dr. Burtin reminding him to come at nine o'clock the next morning so that we could make an expedition to the neighboring hills where a number of fine fossils were to be found.

As soon as my son had gone out I told Prince Orlov it was inconceivable to me that he should say such things to a boy not yet seventeen years of age, and compromise his Sovereign to that extent; never, said I, had I been acquainted with any of the favorites, and if some of those General A.D.C.'s did occupy apartments at the Palace, I ascribed this to their official functions and to the confidence Her Majesty reposed in them. I asked him not to speak thus in my presence and still less in that of my son, whom I was trying to bring up in absolute respect to, and reverence of, his Sovereign and godmother, and I expressed the hope that he would never be anyone's favorite—unless it were of people virtuous in all respects.

Prince Orlov's answer was in his usual style and is not, therefore, worthy of being recorded here.

A few days later, I had the pleasure of seeing him leave for Paris, while I stayed on for a short time in Brussels as I had made arrangements for my money to be transferred there. Every morning Dr. Burtin and I went off botanizing together in the neighborhood of the city where I found several plants we had never seen at home.

As soon as my remittances arrived we set off to Paris. I only stopped for two days at Lille and made the greatest haste possible to arrive in Paris, where the Hôtel de la Chine had been rented for me.

I learned with pleasure that Prince Orlov and his followers had gone by then. That boring set was out of the way, and I was delighted that excellent old Mr. Melissino and his wife had remained in Paris. I was overjoyed, too, to see my friend Diderot, who threw his arms round me with that lively cordiality he always showed his friends. I found, too, that Monsieur de Malesherbes and his sister, as well as Madame Necker and a few other old friends, were quite as willing to extend their friendship to me as they had been during my first stay.

There were many Russians in Paris at the time, including Count Salty-kov (later Field-Marshal and Governor-General of Moscow) and his wife, Mr. Samoilov (Prince Potemkin's nephew), and Count and Countess Andrei Shuvalov. The latter had been in Paris for two whole years but had never earned any respect. As he had, if only for a few moments, contrib-uted to make me feel acutely worried, I think it would not be out of place to sketch a portrait of him. He was an intelligent man, spoke French per-fectly, wrote verse with astonishing facility, and was fairly well informed on a variety of subjects, particularly with regard to French poetry which he knew very well; very ambitious and proud, harsh to his inferiors, mean and obsequious to those in power, making an idol out of the Empress's current favorite, capricious and precipitate in his opinions, he often fell wide of common sense, for he lacked the solidity of mind essential for a sound and steady judgment. Finally he lost his reason and died insane unlamented by anyone—even by his own family.

CHAPTER XVII

Many people came to visit me in Paris and I had, therefore, many visits to pay back. I regretted the time thus spent, for I did not want to remain long in Paris and still less did I want to waste any time.

I was given to understand that I should do well to go to Versailles; my reply was that I was never so much out of my element as at Court. I always felt such a simple little soul when I was there, for all that I was Countess Vorontsova by birth and Princess Dashkova by marriage. Then I was spoken to in clearer terms: the Queen, they told me, wished to make my acquaintance. I replied in terms just as clear that I did not mind what kind of seat I sat on, provided it was not too uncomfortable, and that I attached scant value to high birth and could view with complacency a French Duchess, herself a daughter of some rich tax farmer, occupying the "*tabouret*"—considered a seat of honor at the Court of Versailles— but as lady-in-waiting to the Empress of Russia, I could not be responsible for any slight to my rank.[1]

A few days later, Madame de Sabran, with whom I was lunching at the house of the Abbé Raynal, informed me that Her Majesty the Queen desired me to come to Versailles to the house of Madame de Polignac; she would be there herself, and in the absence of any etiquette we should both be more at our ease.

I often lunched at the Abbé Raynal's, and Diderot, though in weak

---

[1] The reference is to the French rule of Court etiquette according to which French peers and peeresses took precedence over foreigners of equal rank. Princess Dashkova would not have been entitled to sit on a *tabouret* (literally—a stool) which was the prerogative of French Duchesses, and would thus have considered herself slighted.—K. F.

health, visited me almost every day. My house was open to my friends on such evenings as I stayed at home, and my mornings were occupied in visiting the studios of the best artists, except on days when Gardel gave dancing lessons to my children and a pupil of d'Alembert coached my son in mathematics and geometry.

Houdon, too, took up much of my time for, at my daughter's request, he made a large bust of me in bronze. I could not help remarking on seeing it that French artists had too much taste to make a likeness of me, for he would not let me be as God had shaped me, but had made a French Duchess out of me, wearing a dress with a low-cut neck, instead of the simple, unaffected woman I really was.

At Madame Necker's I made the acquaintance of the Bishop of Autun as well as of Monsieur Guibert, author of a book on tactics which had earned so much fame; and there, too, I met Monsieur de Rulhière whom I had known in Russia at the time of the Empress's accession to the throne. I saw he was embarrassed, perhaps because he remembered that I did not want to see him during my first stay in Paris. I came up to him and said that I had too favorable an opinion of him and too much pride to imagine that the friends I had in 1762 were friends no longer; I was, I said, delighted to see him again and esteemed him too much not to appreciate his company; if Madame Mikhalkova (the name under which I traveled the first time) had sacrificed the pleasure she would have had in seeing him to her desire to see no one, there was no reason for Princess Dashkova to do likewise; I should be delighted, I added, to see him in my house at any time he wanted to come, and the only sacrifice I should impose on myself this time would be that of not reading or listening to his book which, however, should, for several reasons, be interesting for me.

Rulhière seemed pleased with this reception and visited me several times. Monsieur de Malesherbes, his sister, and a number of other people, including, particularly, Diderot, whose natural sincerity and lively friendship for me inspired belief in anything he had to say, assured me that Rulhière had given me perfectly honorable treatment throughout his book. They did, however, quote some passages about the Empress to which I could give no credence. My astonishment can be imagined when twenty years later at a time when everything in France was overthrown, at a time when slander, indecency, and rage—fruits of prejudice and discord—made it possible to say, publish, and do anything that hatred prompted, my astonishment, say I, can be imagined on reading in a pamphlet entitled *A Memoir on the Revolution of 1762* by Rulhière, that I had been the mistress of Count Panin, a respectable old cousin of my husband's who could have been his father let alone mine, that I was pregnant with a child from him at the time (I should have had to be pregnant for eleven and a half months, for it was on the 12th May, old style, that I gave birth to my son) and many other lies.

But when I reflected that Monsieur de Rulhière had worked for many years at the office of foreign affairs and with his gifts and intelligence could not have stated that the marriage contract of Peter III and the Princess of Zerbst (later Catherine II) had stipulated that in the case of Peter's death she would inherit the crown—something an absolute novice in diplomacy would never have asserted in the face of all known truth—when I reflected on all this, I felt somewhat comforted, and I exonerated of all blame a man who, since he saw me almost every day, must have known how fond I was of my husband and what my morals in general were, and I could no longer doubt that Rulhière's alleged book was entirely apocryphal.

On the day appointed to see the Queen, my children and I went to Versailles. The Queen was waiting for me in the apartments of Monsieur Jules de Polignac. Her Majesty came forward to meet me, was so good to me and spoke so graciously that I was profoundly affected. She talked to my children about dancing and said she knew they were very good at it. She added that to her great regret she would soon have to give up this type of amusement which she owned she greatly enjoyed.

"And why?" I asked.

"Because," answered Her Majesty, "in France people are not allowed to dance after reaching the age of twenty-five."

Quite oblivious of the Queen's reputed love of the card table, I replied with my usual artless candor that people should continue to dance for so long as their feet would let them and that it was a much more natural amusement, or task, than passion for play. Her Majesty said she was very much of the same opinion as myself, and when I afterward reflected on my stupid blunder, I could not recollect the slightest trace of displeasure on her part, and we continued to talk as frankly and pleasantly as ever.

The following day in Paris I learned that my unfortunate remark was being repeated in every drawing room. This may, perhaps, have been a proof of my importance in the eyes of the Parisian public, but it did not make up for my distress at hearing it repeated, for it appeared as if I had tried to lecture the Queen.

Her Majesty continued to show me great kindness, and Madame de

Polignac and Madame de Sabran never came to Paris without gracious messages from Her Majesty. Besides, it was through her that I afterward obtained permission for my son to see the St. Cyr establishment where men were generally not admitted.[2]

I heard from Diderot that Falconet and his pupil Mademoiselle Collot were both in Paris, and I asked him to tell them that they would give me great pleasure if they came to have tea with me. They did come, and Mademoiselle Collot told me that only the day before at a friend's house she had met the former governess of Count A. Shuvalov's children, and had a lively argument with her about my son and me. The governess received a small pension from the Count and frequently visited his house, but I did not know her and had never had anything to do with her. I was therefore both astonished and curious to know what she could have said about us, and asked Mademoiselle Collot to tell me more about the argument.

In the childish idea behind the governess's story I recognized the malevolent spirit of Count Shuvalov. My plan, she maintained, was to inspire my son with the ambition of becoming the Empress's favorite, but she knew with absolute certainty that it sufficed to make such a project generally known for it never to succeed. Mademoiselle Collot, whom I had often seen in Falconet's studio as well as in my own house during her stay in Petersburg, felt indignant at these insinuations for she knew enough about me to know this was not true. She knew my principles and therefore knew that I, of all people, would never propose Prince Dashkov as a candidate for the place of favorite, and being the boy's mother I should be even less likely to do so. I had always avoided those who had occupied it, and the great Catherine had sufficient respect for me to show some restraint in her attitude to those gentlemen in my presence. Indeed, on occasions when the three of us—the Empress, her favorite, and I—were alone together, she condescended to treat him merely as a general who enjoyed her confidence and esteem.

Mademoiselle Collot's story made me feel more uneasy than I can say. It was certainly not the fear that my son would not become the favorite that worried me; what threw me into a panic, all the more pardonable as I had already experienced the power those gentlemen wielded on occa-

---

[2] St. Cyr was still at that time the rather genteel girls' school founded by Madame de Maintenon in the previous century. It was closed down during the Revolution and reopened in 1802 as an officers' training college.—K. F.

sions like this when they concealed their ambitions under a semblance of love, what threw me into a panic, I say, was that the favorite's jealousy would prompt him to allege some pretext to keep my son away from the Empress and to refuse him advancement and honors on the plea that his mother had nursed a project offensive to Her Majesty.

Mademoiselle Collot was surprised to see how worried I was. But she found it natural when I had explained to her the reason for it, and she was sincerely sympathetic.

My apprehensions were all the greater because I had not received a reply to my letter to Prince Potemkin, and I admit that a certain degree of vanity made me think that despite all his negligence Potemkin wold never have dared behave in this way if he had not been sure of the Empress's indifference to me.

As soon as Mademoiselle Collot had left, I sent a message to Mr. Melissino saying I wanted to speak to him, and would he please come and see me that same evening. I told him, when he came, the subject of my worries, and he was able to comfort me.

"You are wrong, Princess," he said, "to worry over a remark which I can trace to its origin and bear witness to your indignant rejection of the same fanciful suggestion when it was made by Prince Orlov in Brussels. I was present at the dinner in Shuvalov's house when Prince Orlov said he was willing to take on a ten-to-one bet that Prince Dashkov would become favorite; and, besides, you can nullify the whole effect of Count Andrei Shuvalov's remark by quoting it in all confidence, to Mr. Samoilov. He has been to see me today and said he would call on you tomorrow. With your permission, Madam, I shall call at the same time, and without letting it appear that I have already been informed by you of that silly piece of gossip, I shall quite naturally repeat all I know, stressing the fact that I have personally been able to follow the progress of Prince Orlov's piece of scandal and have been present on the occasions on which he repeated it, including the time in Brussels when you rebuked him sharply for doing so."

I followed Mr. Melissino's advice, and told Mr. Samoilov the following day how shocked I was to discover that a crazy idea of Prince Orlov's was being repeated and could, if only it gained credence, prejudice my son's career. Mr. Samoilov assured me that Prince Orlov as well as Count Shuvalov (however good a poet the latter might be) were well known for their habit of saying extraordinary things and voicing opinions that could be shared by only a few people.

"But," said I, "how can the public be informed that the scheme which set wagging Shuvalov's dangerous tongue was but a child of Prince Orlov's imagination? And how can it be made generally known, without spreading rumors unworthy of the Empress and, if I may say so, of me, that far from having such absurd ideas, I deplore them?"

"The Empress knows you too well," replied Samoilov, "to ascribe them to you. Anyway, I shall soon be back in Petersburg, and you will only be there in about a year's time; I shall, if I may, faithfully repeat all I have just heard to my uncle, Prince Potemkin, and shall be happy to give you proof of my respect and gratitude by warning him of the slander of which you are the victim."

I thanked him for this show of good will and accepted his offer, adding, however, that I was not used to seeing my letters remain without an answer; I had not had one, I said, from Prince Potemkin, though crowned heads themselves, as he well knew it, treated me very differently.

He protested vigorously that his uncle could not have acted thus and assured me that his letter must have got lost.

Mr. Samoilov had wanted to see models and plans of fortifications which could not be viewed without special permission from the Court. For eight months Shuvalov had given him to think he would obtain it for him, but to no avail. I told him I had obtained it for my son and he could go there the following morning with him; there was, I said, no need for them to hurry over the examination of these plans, for I should not expect them back before dinner, after which he could, if he wished, accompany me to the opera. I was very happy to have been able to give him pleasure, and he seemed delighted with it all.

Both at the opera and in the theater I could, whenever I wanted, occupy the box belonging to Marshal de Biron—a most courteous old nobleman with manners that were traditionally typical of the French Court in former times. He took a great fancy to my daughter, who made him do anything she pleased, so much so that I several times saw him in my house capering round the room and singing: "Quand Biron voulut danser, quand Biron," etc.

CHAPTER XVIII

W̲e left Paris at the beginning of March and went to Switzerland by way of Verdun, Metz, Nancy, and Besançon, stopping at all garrison towns to enable my son to learn what he could about French military science. The orders we carried, signed by Court officials, made it possible for us to examine freely all we wanted to see, and at Lunéville a review of the gendarmerie was held especially for us—something never done for a private individual.

I saw some old friends again at Berne, and met Monsieur and Madame Kramer in Geneva, as well as Monsieur Hubert, nicknamed the Fowler for his love of falconry and minute knowledge of the natural history of every bird. That man, with his exceptional gifts and intelligence, had feelings of real friendship for me. He made me a present of Voltaire's portrait painted by himself, and we separated with much regret.

Osterwald, famous for the court actions which he brought as Knight Banneret against Frederick the Great in defence of the people's rights, accompanied me from Neufchâtel into the interior of the country to see those interesting villages La Locelle and La Chaux de Fonds and their romantic environs. We traveled in local carts, for the roads are a little narrow there. The good sense, extensive knowledge, and pleasant manners of that worthy old man were responsible for making it a delightful excursion. His daughter helped him to manage his printing works. I bought several books from him and asked him to send them to my bankers, Pye, Rich and Wilkinson at Amsterdam.

I saw Geneva and Lausanne again with a mixed feeling of pleasure and sadness, for these two places reminded me of happy days passed in the company of my dear friend Mrs. Hamilton.

We traveled by way of Savoy and Mount Cenis to Turin, where I was very well received by Their Majesties the King and Queen of Sardinia and all the Royal family. There was no Russian Minister in Turin at that moment and I was presented at Court by the British Minister, son of Lord Bute and nephew of Mr. McKenzie whom I had known very well in London. I saw the Military School, and was shown by order of the King everything that was worth seeing.

There was in Turin a young Baron Elmpt, a Livonian subject of the Empress and son of General Baron (later Count) Elmpt. He was studying at the Royal Military Academy, but behaved badly and was guilty of some foolish things which could have resulted in his expulsion and disgrace. I obtained his pardon, but lectured him unmercifully and begged the British Minister, Mr. Stewart, to look after him till his father, who enjoyed great consideration in Russia and to whom I promised to write, should recall him home.

The King of Sardinia prided himself exceedingly on the fortifications he had built at Aleksandria, especially the citadel which was not shown to foreigners without a special order signed by His Majesty. The King was kind enough to command that on our way through Aleksandria the citadel and everything in the fortress should be shown to my son.

From Turin our route lay through Novi and Genoa, where we halted a few days and took the necessary time to examine Milan and the country round it. Count Firmian, a Minister of the Emperor and Governor of that Duchy, was a most enlightened and virtuous person adored throughout the province. I greatly enjoyed his company and was grateful to him for his efficient help in the excursion I wanted to make to the lakes Maggiore and Lugano as well as to the islands of Borromeo. There were no posts or relays of horses along that route; he therefore provided such relays, and we made a delightful tour without any inconvenience or hindrance of any sort. So enchanted were we with the beauties of nature that we found it hard to leave a place which seemed to us to be a paradise upon earth. Orange and lemon trees grew there in the open like birch and lime trees in Russia, and we saw some of them in flower and others already bearing ripe fruit.

The huge edifice, started by a member of the Borromeo family and only half finished, would have been too vast a country house even for a Sovereign. It can only be explained or excused by the fact that he was nephew of a Pope who, in those remote times, could afford all kinds of prodigal magnificence.

We allotted two days each to Parma, Piacenza, and Modena, and made a longer halt in Florence.

There we spent over a week very pleasantly, visiting the famous picture gallery, the churches (also full of the most lovely pictures), the libraries, and the Grand Duke's Cabinet of Natural History. His Royal Highness had ordered that I should be given any duplicate specimens of petrified objects I might desire, and I thus obtained some beautiful samples not only of Italian origin, but also coming from other parts of the globe, as collected by the great Cosimo who had revived and fostered the sciences in Italy.[1]

We went on to Pisa—a fine city of about 15,000 inhabitants, considered as the second greatest in Tuscany. According to Strabo it was founded by the Arcadians on their return from the Trojan war, while others assert that it had been built by the Greeks long before that, the real founder being Pelope, daughter of Tantalus, King of Phrygia. Anyway, Pisa was one of the twelve principal cities of the Etruscans, and at the fall of the Empire in the eleventh century it was the mistress of the seas. In 1509 it ceased to exist as a Republic, and the Medicis, in their search for security from the Pisans (who, apparently aspired to independence in 1609), constantly tried to weaken it.

The city itself is big and well-built, but because of its great size relative to the small number of its inhabitants, it struck me as, in a way, somewhat deserted. It had no trade, though the river Arno which crosses it from one end to the other should have been able to foster some. All it had was a manufactory of steel products. The city's most remarkable building is the cathedral, built in the eleventh century and decorated with the booty brought by the Pisans from the Saracenic wars. It has three beautiful bronze doors wrought by Giambologna and representing the mysteries of the Passion. Its walls are covered with marble and adorned with four pictures by Andrea del Sarto, while seventy-four pillars, of which sixty-two are of oriental granite and two of porphyry, enhance still further the beauty of the place. One of the small pillars supporting the pulpit is most remarkable: it is made up of several different kinds of porphyry.

The Prefect gave me a magnificent dinner after which he took us to the courtyard of a house belonging to a Madame Rosalmina to see the

[1] Princess Dashkova's collection of natural curios, which she so assiduously assembled in all the countries she visited, came finally to consist of 15,000 objects valued at 50,000 roubles. On the death of her son in 1807, she presented it to the University of Moscow; it perished in the Great Fire of 1812.—K. F.

game of *il juoco del ponte,* which was ordered especially for me. Two sides, each bearing the name of its parish—Santa Maria and Santo Antonio—were set against each other on the great bridge in helmets and cuirasses, with a long robe covering their armor. Their only weapon, both offensive and defensive, was a kind of flat mace with two handles underneath to hold it by.

The Pisans are so passionately fond of this game that the gentry frequently take part in it. It used to take place once every five years, but is now being neglected, since the Grand Duke, without entirely forbidding it, has put obstacles in its way by making the forty-eight representatives of the two sides responsible for its consequences, pay for any damages that might ensue, and provide for the families of all victims, not only from Pisa but from Florence and Leghorn too.

The game would often end in a dispute leading to duels. All the nobility took part in it, including the ladies who wore on that day the colors of their parish. Mothers would quarrel with their daughters in cases when marriage had placed them in different parties.

The hot months, when malaria is rife and it becomes dangerous to travel, I spent at the Baths of Pisa.

While still at Pisa we lodged very comfortably with our Minister, Count Mocenigo, who had his own house. That worthy man lived in the bosom of his family as people did in the good old days; he, his wife, and his daughter all occupied the same room, his son had another. All he had kept for himself, apart from these two rooms, was his study; the rest of the house was put at my disposal. But at the Baths of Pisa I rented the best house there was. I could borrow any books I wanted from the Ducal, public, and conventual libraries, and I determined on a regular course of reading which followed a certain chronological order by subject matter. At eight o'clock every morning, after a light breakfast, my children and I went to sit in the biggest room facing north. At eleven we closed our shutters and took turns at reading to each other by candle-light till four in the afternoon. Then we washed and changed, and dined at five. Another hour of reading after dinner brought us to the time when we could without dying of heat open the windows and go for a walk along the banks of the canal. This was the only place where we could enjoy fresh air, but it was derelict and choked up with all kinds of filth. I therefore had it cleaned at my own expense, made a gravel path and had some benches placed.

The heat and lack of air were stifling, and though at night there was no sun to scorch us, yet it seemed to me as if some malevolent being was busily pumping out with a pneumatic machine all the air there was in Pisa.

In spite of this inconvenience I shall always think with pleasure of our stay at the Baths, for I must say, without undue presumption, that in the course of those nine weeks my son had done more reading with my help than an average young man would have done in a year, and such was his diligence that I can frankly say few people of his condition would have drawn as much profit from their studies.

On June 28, old style, the anniversary of the Empress's accession to the throne, I gave a great ball in the public rooms, which was attended by all the nobility of Pisa, Lucca, and Leghorn. There were at least 460 persons present, yet the expense was not great, for all that was needed was torches in the courtyard and candles. On the whole, however, no variety came to disturb our lives at the Baths except for the entertainment I have just described, a trip we made to see the illuminations of the Cathedral—a most striking sight—and the boat race on the Arno. The prize given to the winner of the race is a piece of crimson damask with about fifty ducats, handed over with some ceremony by the City Magistrates, of whom one group is present at the start and another at the finish. We were greatly scandalized at the sight of the oarsmen, who wore no shirts, merely a pair of breeches and no other clothes.

From Pisa we went to Lucca. There the first thing we did was to visit the Cathedral, a building of no great beauty outside, but inside of an agreeable Gothic style. The vaulting over the choir is decorated by paintings by Colli and Sancasciani, two native Luccan artists. In the middle of the left aisle there is a small chapel, shaped like a rotunda, in which is kept the miraculous crucifix of the Volto Santo. Formerly it was in the church of San Frediano, whence, it is believed, it came over entirely by itself to the place where it now is. The Volto Santo is uncovered but three times a year, or whenever there is a State emergency or other pressing need for it.

The Palace of the Republic is the most remarkable building in the city. The form of government is aristocratic but members of the Council must not be less than twenty-five years of age, and at the time when I was there, there were about 240 nobles who had reached their majority. The nobility is hereditary, but the patent of nobility is sometimes obtained through merit or on payment of a sum of money. The nobles are divided into two "congregations," each consisting of ninety members and thirty deputy-members. The two Congregations succeed each other annually on the Council, and proceed to elect the members of the new Congregation, who cannot remain members for more than one year at a time. The Magistrates are likewise chosen from among the nobility at annual elections, except for the Supreme Magistrature consisting of nine "Ancients" (Anziani) and the Gonfalonier who are changed every two months.

The election of those who will eventually become Gonfaloniers takes place once every three years by thirty-six special councillors whose duty it is to elect several other Magistrates concurrently with their eighteen deputies. These elections take place with great solemnity and are called Rinnovazione della Tasca, because of the new ballot boxes. This renewal of the ballot boxes takes place every two and a half to three years depending on the number of members. Up to 180 nobles are chosen, including the nine responsible for managing the elections, and are known as the Assortitori. They first of all elect the Gonfalonier and then proceed to select the Magistrates who form the Supreme Council (Supreme Magistrato) for two months at a time. The Assortitori carefully put in the appropriate box the names of those they have selected. Every two months ten names are taken out to make up the nine "Ancients" and the Gonfalonier.

The legislative and the supreme powers are vested in the council consisting of the two Congregations. Most of the decrees cannot be passed unless approved by three-quarters of all members present, of whom there must not be less than eighty apart from the Grand Magistrates and the Gonfalonier. They have the right to propose subjects for deliberation and discussion. The Gonfalonier is the first proposer and the first representative. This is what his power is in fact reduced to. He has the title of Prince and the honors of a sovereign, and seventy Swiss soldiers, kept and paid by the State, mount guard at his door, or rather that of the Palace of the Republic, but he is not in the position to take undue advantage of all these prerogatives.

The executive power is vested in the "Ancients" and the Gonfalonier, but partly also in the various magistrates, each within his sphere of action.

The third power of the State is that of the Judiciary, exercized almost entirely by five "Auditors." One—called Podestà—is in charge of criminal cases. The four others deal with civil matters. As in other Italian cities, these judges are always foreigners, to avoid their having relatives or friends who might prejudice their decisions. When the Podestà passes a sentence of death he refers it to the senate which either executes it or exercises its prerogative of mercy. Whenever the Podestà takes part in a ceremonial procession he carries a silver rod, bearing on it the motto of the Republic—"*Libertas*"—and surmounted by a panther, symbol of strength.

The police has its headquarters in Lucca and is subject to very rigid discipline. It numbers forty *sbirri,* from whom two squads are formed to patrol the streets at night. Each squad is accompanied by an attendant dressed in the livery of the Prince of the Republic, whose duty it is to serve as witness in case of need. As the bearing of arms is forbidden, any citizen found carrying side-arms is the very next day condemned to the galleys, but as the Republic of Lucca has none of its own, the condemned men are sent to Genoa where they are received without any difficulty. If a man is found in possession of firearms he is also sent to the galleys, but in addition he is punished with the *strappado.* An exception is made for foreigners, who for some years now have been allowed to wear a sword in the city.

The Republic contains over 120,000 inhabitants, including 26,000 to 29,000 within the city, which is equivalent to 5,203 persons per square league, compared to only 900 in France.

Agriculture is in a most flourishing state. The soil yields fifteen- to twenty-fold, and three harvests are gathered from the same field every two years. The Republic produces the best and the most highly reputed oil, and is also famed for its silk manufactures.

Most of the produce of Lucca is sent by road to Leghorn, and some of it to Viareggio, the port of the Republic four leagues distant from the city. Strangers are made extremely welcome, and if ever the city has a spectacle, the subject, they tell me, is always excellent.

From Lucca we went on to Leghorn—not a big city, but densely populated then, with its 43,000 inhabitants. The fact that it is a free port and a few other advantages make it into a very busy place. I spent some little time there, and greatly admired the new quarantine hospital, built by the Grand Duke Leopold. (The Grand Duke had, I think, more judgment and discretion than his brother, the Emperor Joseph. He was much beloved of his subjects, who greatly esteemed him. As a result, he was able to forbid, without raising the slightest protest, the reading in church every Passion Thursday of Gregory VIII's Bull *Incenum Dom,* which claims for the Pope supreme authority over all sovereigns.)

But to return to the quarantine hospital, an institution so humanitarian in its purpose and which interested me immensely. I was struck by the order and cleanliness that reigned within it. There was, it so happened, several persons there who had come from places where an epidemic was suspected. I, therefore, sprinkled my children's handkerchiefs with Marseilles vinegar, and all the time we were in the building made them sniff a mixture of that vinegar and spirits of camphor. The Commandant who accompanied us, and who, being ordered by the Grand Duke to do all he could for me, could not refuse me permission to inspect that noble edifice so beautifully administered, thought me very courageous.

He had been told, apparently, to report all my remarks, as in the case of every distinguished stranger who came to visit the hospital. I expressed my admiration for that very humanitarian establishment, and said that as our Sovereign's constant conquests gradually brought us nearer countries whose climate was favorable to epidemics, I should like to present to Her Majesty the institute's plan and rules as well as the history of its administration.

I said all this more in the spirit of a compliment than in the expectation of really being able to do anything about it. However, in a few days' time the Commandant brought me the plan of the hospital with full details of its administration, saying that he did so on the Grand Duke's behalf. I charged him to offer my most humble thanks to His Royal Highness and tell him that I should transmit the whole to the Empress, my Sovereign, at the very first opportunity.

I took advantage of Mr. Lvov's return to Petersburg to do so a few days later. I also wrote to Her Majesty and, being confident of her indulgence, told her that I had written eight months before to her War Minister, Prince Potemkin, recommending my son to him and asking him whether my son had been promoted "according to his seniority," as Her Majesty's decree put it when he had first received his officer's commission in the Life Guards twelve years ago. I had not, however, received a reply from Prince Potemkin; I was, I confessed, too proud to feel humiliated, but at the same time I experienced a far more painful feeling, the apprehension that Her Majesty had become indifferent to my children and myself. I therefore implored her to set my mind at rest by granting advancement and protection to my son. I had, I said, taken immense pains to give him a good education so that he could be useful to his country and could gain distinction as much through his zeal as through his natural aptitude. And I ended boldly and frankly by begging her to let me know what precisely

I could hope for, for a son who was the object of all my solicitude and who ought not, on returning to his native country after acquitting himself with so much credit everywhere we had been, find himself in a position of inferiority through holding a rank he had had since he was four years of age.

CHAPTER XIX

❧❦❧

We went to Rome by way of Siena. Among the people most attentive to us there was the Cardinal de Bernis. His gentleness, his polished manners, and his wit appealed to every heart and mind. I often dined in his house, and he came and visited me in mine. I took great pleasure in his society, and he seemed flattered when I quoted to him one of his epistles out of a book published under the name of Works (or Poems) of the Abbé de Bernis.

I made the useful acquaintance of Mr. Byers, a highly educated and well-informed Englishman, passionately fond of the arts and resident in Rome for over twenty-five years. Under his guidance I had no need for a *cicerone* as other foreigners always have.

I saw Pope Pius VI in St. Peter's Church. His Holiness spoke to me with much kindness and appeared pleased to hear me praise—as indeed it well-deserved to be—the noble undertaking which he had planned and was carrying out with all speed, and which consisted in reclaiming in its entirety the Via Appia passing through the Pontine Marshes.

I told His Holiness I was absolutely bent on seeing it and, moreover, wanted to have the glory of being the first to travel along that road on my way to Naples.

"You must warn me then," he said kindly, "a few days before your departure, so I can have relays of horses stationed for your convenience, as there are no posts or accommodation for travelers established as yet."

He spoke to me for a long time of the precious monuments of art which existed in Rome, and spoke as a lover of the arts and a connoisseur. He was the first to think of forming a Museum in the Vatican, and he had already been able to collect several fine statues, vases, pictures, and so on.

I spent my time very agreeably in Rome without wasting it on a social life, receiving and paying visits. Every morning at eight o'clock and sometimes even earlier, we drove out to see and admire all sorts of masterpieces in the city or its environs. These excursions lasted till three o'clock in the afternoon, when I had a hasty dinner, and was ready to receive various artists who came for a cup of China tea sent to me especially from Russia. The two Hackerts, one with his burin, the other with his pencil, and Hamilton with his crayons sat down to work and converted my room into a most pleasant studio. We talked of this and that, I asked their opinion on the various masterpieces I had seen in the morning, and my son took lessons in etching from Mr. Hackert.

I was also fortunate enough to form the acquaintance of Mrs. Damer, who was traveling with her aunt, Lady William Campbell. She was a person of extensive knowledge, to which she added excellent good sense, natural gifts, and a modesty which inclined her to hide her natural superiority. She was a sculptress much above the average who had made a reputation for herself, and had, besides, a knowledge of the Greek and Latin languages.

I went to Tivoli twice, and also to the Villa Augusta. Every spare moment I had I spent in the Church of St. Peter, whose noble proportions I could never cease to admire, for architecture was of all the arts the one I had most taste for.

One day I happened to meet a young Russian painter there, a pupil of the St. Petersburg Academy of Fine Arts, and obtained for him the permission of certain noblemen who had a fine collection of pictures to study these pictures and copy them.

In the course of one of my morning excursions in the company of Mr. Byers, I looked at my watch, and seeing it was too early yet to return home—"Where shall we go?" said I, "We have fully an hour left before it is time for dinner." He suggested we should visit the Villa Farnese. I had been there before, but he doubted I had ever gone down into the cellars, and said I should there find masterpieces of sculpture, mutilated, it was true, but worth more, in his opinion, than many a whole work now so much admired.

I ordered my coachman to drive us there, and as soon as we arrived we went to see the cellars. As we were walking along I hurt my foot against a stone which I took for a large piece of serpentine, and said to Byers with a smile:

"I do declare this stone is not worthy of the honor of wounding me."

"I am sorry about your little mishap," said he, "but if you think this is a block of serpentine, you are mistaken; it is a matrix of emerald brought from Africa for the great Cosimo by one of the scientists he despatched all over the world to bring him back their most curious finds, and it is through the Farnese succession that it came to belong to the King of Naples. You ought to buy it, for they do not know what it is and they will sell it for verd antique, or serpentine perhaps."

"And what shall I do with it?"

"I shall, if you let me," said Byers, "saw it in two and make two tables for you such as no Sovereign has in his possession—nor ever will," he added. "A small service indeed, but I shall thereby repay you, however slightly, for all I owe you."

I had been able, to my great satisfaction, to obtain for Mr. Byers the sale in one lot of his collection of antique *pierres gravées,* which he did not want to disperse and sell one by one. It was Her Majesty the Empress who, on my recommendation, made the purchase.

It occurred to me that I might present the tables to the Empress, and I therefore agreed with his idea and asked him to buy the matrix. In 1807 I presented the two tables to His Majesty the Emperor Aleksandr, and they now form part of the Imperial collection of treasures in the Kremlin.

After thoroughly examining all that was worth seeing in Rome and its environs, without omitting the horse races which appeared to me very ridiculous, and the theater which was somewhat disgusting since men acted female rôles, we went to Naples traveling by the new road. At Terracino we left the carriage to explore the harbor which had been cleared of the mud and the marsh that had silted it up for so long. A handsome stone wall had polished brass rings attached to it at regular intervals for tying up boats, and would have appeared of recent construction if it did not strike the observer that it was situated much further from the city than described by contemporary historians. A drawing, made to scale, seemed to me of interest, and I wrote to the excellent Mr. Byers asking him to have it copied secretly because the Pope himself had not one yet. The copy I intended to send to the Empress.

On arriving at Naples, I was delighted to find that a very good house had been prepared for me with a charming view of the bay and of Vesuvius opposite. I found, too, many old friends, our Minister and Envoy Extraordinary, Count Andrei Razumovskii, Mrs. Damer, and her aunt, and that worthy old man the Chevalier Sacromoza.

I met the King of England's Minister, Sir William Hamilton and his

wife—I mean his first wife—the Abbé Galiani, and several artists and
men of letters. Sir William Hamilton's collection of antiquities was very
precious, but I envied him only his star-stone ring. This stone, although
so well described by Pliny, was, because an example of it could not be
found, long considered as imaginary, and the great naturalist was believed
to have dreamed up his description of it. Such is men's attitude to things
whose truth they are too lazy or too ignorant to demonstrate, for the
most convenient and the shortest way of dealing with what one does not
understand is to deny it.

The mornings we spent in sightseeing and excursions which usually
ended at Mrs. Damer's studio. For it was not in her boudoir that her
friends found her—rather did they find her wrestling with a block of
marble, trying to impart to it the shape she wanted. But it was a sanctum
open only to her closest friends. She was very modest by nature and would
never parade her talents and her learning. And so one day I disconcerted
her by discovering a book of verse by a Greek poet, the margins of which
were filled with annotations in her own handwriting.

"You know Greek, then, my fair lady?" said I. "And you hid it from
me! Is it because you were afraid of humiliating me? But I have told you
before: I am very ignorant."

She blushed and looked just as embarrassed as if she had been caught
out in something really reprehensible.

The Court was at Caserta, and there we were received with great kindness by Their Majesties, after being presented by the Duchess of Ferolete,
who became my "chaperone" in accordance with the custom of the country which requires every distinguished stranger, if she is a lady, to be
accompanied by a Neapolitan lady of rank.

I was out morning and afternoon sightseeing and buying things, among
which was a number of works in marble, pictures, and prints; but I never
felt tired—on the contrary, the days seemed too short. My son sometimes accompanied the King on his hunting parties, and my daughter and
I always spent our evenings at Lady Hamilton's. Her conversation and
Mrs. Damer's, pleasant as it was, enabled us to enjoy all the advantages
that enlightenment, friendship, and polite intercourse give to Society.

It was with immense interest that I viewed the invaluable treasures
found in Herculaneum, Pompeii, and other places, and now stored in Por-
tici. I took the liberty one day of saying to Their Majesties that the small
number of workmen employed in excavating Pompeii and other places
ought to be trebled, and when Pompeii was finally clear of its ashes, every

piece of furniture, every utensil found there ought to be put back in its original place, and soldiers stationed to guard the town and its treasures, and when that was done it ought to be publicized all over Europe that there was a true picture to be seen of the habits and customs, utensils and instruments of the citizens of one ancient town containing streets, houses, and taverns with their sign-boards and posters, all of which could be viewed on payment of so much per head. The revenue His Majesty would derive therefrom would far surpass any expenses in connection with the scheme, for experts, sightseers, and simple idlers with nothing better to do would flock in crowds to enjoy a sight no description could bring to life in quite as convincing a manner. People would have the impressions of actually beholding the inhabitants, seeing what they were like and how they lived, and His Majesty would have performed a feat of magic in rescuing from the effects of time and oblivion an image at once so interesting and so alive.

The King, forgetting apparently that I knew Italian, said to the gentleman standing next to him:

"She is a clever person, I believe she is right, and all these antiquaries who make a worship of such things were never able to think of it."

I saw that His Majesty did not take offence at my little speech, for without replying to my suggestion he turned to me and said:

"There is a publication in several volumes with engravings showing all that has been discovered up till now. I shall order it to be given to you."

I thanked the King most sincerely for this gift which I valued far above expensive ornaments and jewels.

My visit to the top of Vesuvius very nearly proved fatal. I had not felt well for several days before, and was overcome with such tiredness in making the attempt that my life was in danger. I did not want to call in Neapolitan doctors, for my general lack of faith in the medical profession as such was, in their case, confirmed ten times over, but yielding finally to the pleas of my children and Mrs. Damer I agreed to call in Mr. Drummond, an Englishman who, though not a professional physician, attended his compatriots and his friends with considerable zeal and devotion. He, very properly, administered castor oil, thus allowing my bowels to resume their natural function, and saved my life. Climate and a special diet soon gave me back the strength to set out on those drives and rambles which my natural curiosity led me to undertake.

Shortly after, I had the benefit of an even more efficacious restorative. A courier brought me a most comforting letter from the Empress, in which Her Majesty assured me she would never cease taking a sincere interest in my children; on our arrival in St. Petersburg she would, she wrote, place my son on a footing which would be satisfactory to me, and in the meantime she would appoint him Gentleman of the Chamber, which carried with it the rank of Brigadier. She thanked me for the plan and the rules and regulations of the Leghorn hospital, and her letter was, in general, couched in very gracious terms.

I did not lose a moment in replying, and while expressing my most lively appreciation of her offer I begged her not to give my son a Court function. I told her the education I had given him was not calculated to make a courtier out of him, but she would fulfill all my wishes if she entered him in the Guards so that he could pursue a military career, in accordance with his natural aptitude. I ended my letter by assuring the Empress that before the year was out I should have the happiness of paying her my humble respects.

From that instant I was determined not to waste any more time. We went to see what remained to be seen, then I took leave of Their Sicilian Majesties and returned to Rome. Monsieur Azara, the Spanish Minister at the Holy See, presented me both with his own works and those of Winkelmann. Also I had the very great pleasure of seeing my friend Mr. Byers and the Cardinal de Bernis once again, and had a longer time than I had hoped in which to enjoy their company, for the courier traveling in advance of the Grand Duke Pavel and his spouse had arrived, and they were expected in Rome very shortly, so that I could not decently leave the city yet.

In fact Their Imperial Highnesses came three days later, and I paid my respects to them and presented my children. Their stay in Rome was short, for it was their intention to remain there somewhat longer on their way back from Naples.

I spent only a few more days in Rome after the Grand Duke's departure for Naples, and then left too. We went through Loretto, where I stopped a mere thirty-six hours to see the treasure and wardrobe of the Madonna, whose clothes were changed for her almost every day, and admire the beautiful emeralds crystallized in little columns set in a matrix of gold, presented to her by a King of Spain.

I stopped in Bologna for two and a half days to admire the masterpieces of that school. I also halted for two days at Ferrara on my way to Venice.

On my arrival there I found that our Resident at that Republic, the Marquis Maruzzi, had prepared his house to receive me with a great display of refinement and magnificence. I attributed this to the fact that he was greatly beholden to my uncle, the late Chancellor, Count Vorontsov, and to the man's innate vanity. He had just been decorated by our Court with the order of St. Anne, and either its ribbon or its star was represented in sculpture or in paint on door lintels, over the main entrance, and on his carriages. But I am very willing to forgive him his vanity because of his generosity, to which I owe two Canalettos which he gave me.

I bought some old engravings by the earliest masters in order to have a series showing the gradual development of the art till it finally reached its present degree of perfection.

The churches and convents of Venice possess many fine pictures: I went to see several of them, using gondolas for the purpose. These have a somewhat gloomy appearance, but provide very pleasant excursions.

I shall say nothing on the subject of either the government or the buildings of Venice, and shall avoid encroaching, as I have throughout this story, on the travelers' prerogative of sparing us no details. Faithful to this principle, I shall pass on at one swoop to Vienna without a glance at Padua, Vicenza, and Verona on the way.

CHAPTER XX

We had to cross some of the Tyrolese mountains, but the friendly and considerate welcome accorded to us by our Ambassador at Vienna, Prince Dmitrii Golitsyn, soon helped us to forget the fatigue of the journey. He provided for us all the comforts and amenities we could desire. Long residence in Vienna had turned him almost into a native of the place, and he was generally liked there. His manners were such as Louis XIV's courtiers reputedly had, and the mediocrity of his natural abilities was obscured by perfect breeding and worldly polish. Through him we soon became acquainted with all the High Society of Vienna.

The Emperor Joseph was suffering from an affliction of the eyes which compelled him to avoid exposure to too much light and prevented him from going out. I thought, therefore, that I should not see him, though Count Keglovich, who had known me as a child when he was attached to his Embassy in Russia, and who now spent every evening with the Emperor, told me His Majesty was keen to see me and was wont to say, in his impatience: "It would be incredible, absurd, if I missed seeing such a historic personage as Princess Dashkova, now that she has come to Vienna and that I happen to be there too."

The Emperor's First Minister, Prince Kaunitz, left a visiting card at my door, something he never did for anyone. This vain man, ready, outside his hours of work, to gratify nothing but his own desires, was the spoilt darling of the Empress Maria Theresa who was willing to humor him because she knew he had no equal for sheer ability and knowledge of politics. The Emperor had the greatest regard for him, and he was accustomed not to stand on ceremony with anyone. During his stay in Vienna Pope Pius VI was invited to dine in Prince Kaunitz's house. The very day of the dinner Prince Kaunitz, unwilling to modify in any way his habit of going to his country house for some exercise in the riding school, stayed there longer than usual, made the Pope wait and then turned up at five o'clock in the afternoon in his riding boots, whip in hand, using it to point out to his illustrious guest the pictures he appreciated most.

I returned his visit, and he invited me to dinner. This invitation I accepted, on condition he did not take offence if, once in his house, I did not wait for him beyond four o'clock in the afternoon, after which I should leave and have dinner in my own house, for as I never had breakfast I could not continue without food till a later hour.

On the day appointed I went to see the Prince at half-past three and found him waiting for me in his drawing-room. I believe, however, he was not a little astonished, and even bore me a grudge because I had appointed my own time and refused to be at the mercy of his whim regarding the dinner hour.

At table he spoke all the time about my country, and, turning to the subject of Peter I, said the Russians were very much in his debt, for he was the creator of our nation. I denied the truth of that statement and told him it was foreign writers who gave Peter that reputation because he had invited several of them to come to his country, and they, out of sheer vanity, called him the Creator of Russia, imagining themselves or their compatriots to be his partners in the alleged creation of the country. Long before Peter I's birth, the Russians had conquered the Kingdoms of Kazan, of Astrakhan, and of Siberia. The most warlike of nations, known under the name of the Golden Horde (because it possessed great quantities of gold and the weapons of its people were decorated with it) was also vanquished by the Russians. Long before Peter I's ancestors had been called to the throne the arts had found a home in Russia, and pictures which are masterpieces of painting and date back to those distant times can still be found in our monasteries. We had historians who left more manuscripts than all the rest of Europe put together.

"Four hundred years ago, Prince," I added, "we had our churches, which were covered with mosaics, destroyed by Batyi."

"Do you count for nothing," replied Prince Kaunitz, "the fact that he drew Russia nearer to Europe and that it is only since his day that she has become known?"

"A great Empire, Prince, with all the resources of wealth and power, such as Russia possesses, has no need to be drawn nearer to anything.

When a body as formidable as my country is well governed, it draws others toward itself. If Russia remained unknown till the period you mention, you will forgive me, Your Grace, if I conclude that this only proves the ignorance or folly of the European countries which remained indifferent to the existence of so formidable a Power. And to prove to you that I am not in the least prejudiced against the Emperor Peter I, let me give you my sincere opinion of that extraordinary man. He had genius, energy, and zeal for improvement, but his total lack of education had left him with unbridled passions which completely swayed his reason; quick-tempered, brutal, and despotic, he treated all people without distinction as slaves who must bear with everything; his ignorance did not allow him to see that many reforms introduced by him through violence were being introduced quietly and peacefully by trade, exchange, the passage of time, and the example of other nations. He would not have destroyed that priceless heritage which was our ancestors' character if he had not valued foreigners so much above Russians; he would not have weakened the power of the law and the respect which is due to it if he had not changed laws so often, including even his own; he sapped the very foundations of his father's code and decrees and substituted for them a number of despotic laws, only to abolish some of them again; he almost entirely abolished the freedom and privileges of the gentry as well as of the servants, who had a tribunal to which they could apply against persecution; he introduced a military form of government which is certainly the most despotic of all governments, and the vainglorious ambition to be a creator pushed him on toward the building of Petersburg with all haste and with means most tyrannical: thousands of workmen perished in that marsh, while he thrust upon the nobles the burden of finding and supplying more workmen, and forced them to build brick houses for themselves in accordance with *his* plans, regardless of whether they needed houses in Petersburg or whether they did not. That must have been horrible. He had an Admiralty built in that town, though the waters of the Neva are so shallow that only hulks of warships could be built in the dockyards, to be transported later to Kronstadt at the cost of much labor and money. This he should have avoided, knowing as he did that even merchant vessels, if they were of any size or heavily loaded, did not call at Petersburg. Under Catherine II the area of the town has expanded four-fold and official buildings are far more magnificent, and all this has been accomplished without any taxation and without discontent."

I noticed that my words made an impression on Prince Kaunitz. He apparently wanted to make me talk, for he said it was pleasant to see a monarch work personally and for a long time in a dockyard.

"I am sure, Your Grace," I replied, "you are saying this in jest, for you know better than I do that a Sovereign must not spend his time performing the work of a simple laborer. Peter I could have engaged not only carpenters and shipwrights, but admirals too, had he wished. He was failing in his duties and in the important work and cares of State for which he was responsible by staying in Saardam, becoming a carpenter and mutilating the Russian language with Dutch terms and word-endings which invade his edicts and all naval phraseology. There was no necessity for him to send his nobles abroad to learn how to be a gardener, a farrier, a miner, etc. Any noble would with pleasure have sent three or more of his serfs to learn these trades."

Prince Kaunitz let the matter drop and changed the subject. I was much relieved, as it suited me not to have said all I felt regarding Peter I's exaggerated reputation.

Count Keglovich told me that Prince Kaunitz had sent up to the Emperor a little note of our conversation on the very same day on which I had dined with him. I replied that I had never had a sufficiently high opinion of myself to imagine that my conversation could interest a Minister with so distinguished a mind as Kaunitz, nor serve as entertainment for an intelligent and broad-minded Monarch. If I had sharply criticized the Prince's ideas it was because I loved truth and my country in equal measure.

From that moment Count Keglovich inquired every morning after my plans for the day. On the eve of our departure he again urged me to stay a few more days in Vienna because the Emperor had not yet quite recovered from his illness. I told him I was not traveling for pleasure, but because I had, both as mother and as mentor, drawn up a plan; all my movements had but one object, which required the service of all my faculties: it was the completion of my son's education. I had written, while still in Italy, to His Majesty the King of Prussia, begging him to grant my son permission to follow his maneuvers, and he had been graciously pleased to grant it to me, so that my time was limited; that evening, I said, I wanted to visit once more the fine natural history collection in the Imperial Gallery, and should then have supper at Prince Golitsyn's. I asked him to come, too, as that would be the last time I should see him, for I was leaving the following morning at crack of dawn.

Immediately after dinner we went to see the Imperial collection, but hardly had I begun to examine it when I saw the Emperor come in, wearing a green taffeta shade over his eyes. His Majesty spoke very kindly to me and in such a way that, though I felt he was being too flattering and I did not deserve all he said, nevertheless I was not abashed. He was kind enough to tell me how sorry he was to have missed the pleasure of my company and how much he had lost thereby. He spoke with reverence of my Sovereign, and the sentiments he expressed in her connection rendered the few hours I spent with him highly enjoyable.[1] Finally, he offered me any duplicates I might choose from his gallery, and then took his leave saying that, knowing my taste for natural history, he did not want to presume any more upon my time. I selected—with great moderation—a few specimens from the mines of Hungary and from a number of different provinces.

We supped with our Ambassador and left the following day for Prague, where we stopped just enough time to let my son get acquainted with the details of the Austrian army in general and obtain information on the garrison stationed at Prague, as well as on the town itself, which constituted a fortress designed to protect Bohemia.

I, in the meantime, formed a small collection of petrified wood and of a few specimens of marble, obtainable at a very moderate price.

After that we went to Saxony. I made a halt of a few days at Dresden, where Prince Sacken entertained us in magnificent style. We visited the wonderful picture gallery several times and found it as inexhaustibly interesting as ever. Count Brühl's gallery of pictures was no longer there; it had been bought by Catherine the Great, who loved and encouraged the arts and obtained for Russia some masterpieces of painting and sculpture such as it never had before.

The time for the King of Prussia's reviews and maneuvers was drawing near, and I could not stay long in Dresden. We arrived in Berlin, where I was treated by the whole Royal Family with the same kindness as before.

Our Minister had not been transferred elsewhere and we were very pleased to see our dear Prince Dolgorukii still at his post. His friendship for my children and myself was both sincere and active, and he introduced my son to all the Ministers.

[1] To his intimates, such as Kaunitz, the Emperor spoke of Catherine with much less reverence. During his visit to Russia, he said, he found her in a state of perpetual excitement—"*une femme exaltée,*" he called her—and accused her of being interested only in herself, to the exclusion of everything else, even of Russia.—K. F.

My son, who was already acquainted with all the Royal Family, went to Potsdam to be presented by Count Goertz, the Adjutant General, to the Great Frederick. His Majesty received him graciously, and told him he would be delighted to have him at his maneuvers.

Soon afterward the King came to Berlin and reviewed his troops, amounting to 42,000 men, in the park of the city.

During these military reviews the King never had any ladies presented to him. However, he was good enough to express the desire to see me and speak to me, and said that if I was curious to see the review in the park, the Princess Royal, wife of the Heir Presumptive, would take me there and enable His Majesty to meet me. Count Finkenstein was commanded to explain to the Princess the day, the time, and the place at which the King would come up to me.

On the morning appointed for the event rightly calculated to flatter me, the Princess (since Queen of Prussia) came to fetch me at my hotel. What was my surprise when, upon arrival at a certain place in the park, the carriage halted and the Princess said:

"This is where you should alight, my dear Princess. It is here my old uncle will come and speak to you; I shall continue the drive as I have no desire to see the old monkey."

To my great joy, as I left the carriage, I saw Prince Dolgorukii, who had been posted at the same place. Half an hour later the King, without dismissing the troops, rode up to me, got off his horse and, hat in hand, spoke to me—to the great astonishment of his troops, for never before had His Majesty been seen speaking to a woman at a review.

When the King left me, the Princess came back to fetch me. The following evening I supped with the Queen, who treated me, like the rest of the Royal Family, not only as a distinguished individual, but with affection as an old and esteemed friend. The Princess Henry said to me during supper that history will record me as a person for whose sake the King had made an exception to the rule.

Soon after, my son accompanied the King for the review of troops. I was sorry to leave Berlin and hurried so much to catch up with my son that my carriage was entering the city gates of ———— just as the King was driving out of it. He waved to me affectionately and said afterward to Prince Dolgorukii that it needed all of a mother's love to be able to calculate so exactly and not lose a moment of time for seeing one's son. I found him in perfect health, enthusiastic in his admiration for the King, and eager to give their due to Prussian officers whom he was trying to get to know.

After resting that day, we took the route of Koenigsberg, where General Mollendorff assured me that His Majesty had referred to my son as to a promising young man who was likely to become a distinguished soldier. The King (as I learnt afterward) wrote the same thing to his Minister Resident in St. Petersburg.

After a few days rest, we went to Riga, by way of Memel. The Governor General, Browne, prevailed upon me to stay two days in Livonia's capital where my father's name was revered; he had always defended in the Senate the privileges of the Livonian nobles, and had always with success opposed the ideas of some of his colleagues. He was too enlightened and too generous a man to desire, like them, the abolition of the privileges confirmed to the Livonian nobles by one after another of our Sovereigns, simply because the Russian nobility had themselves been deprived of these privileges. Catherine the Great granted them to him and we are now the equals of Livonian nobles who, during the reign of the Empress Elizaveta, made him a member of their corporation.

After leaving Riga, we only stopped at night and arrived at St. Petersburg without mishap.

Thus ended a journey undertaken with modest means and requiring all the courage which a mother's love can give. My son's education had been my dearest aim; I had wanted to preserve his principles intact and keep him away from the innumerable temptations which always lie in wait for a young man in his own country. After much thought I had decided to take him abroad. My choice of country had not been difficult: I believed his happiness would best be served by giving him an English education and, consequently, that became the goal of my ambitions. The few debts that were incurred as a result I had foreseen in advance, and I was only too pleased to be able to discharge them by depriving myself of a few things and living very economically in the country where I wanted to bury myself for a few years. This decision made me happy by helping me realize all my wishes.

PART II

CHAPTER XXI

I arrived in Petersburg in July 1782, but as I had no house in town I went to live in Kirianovo, my country house two and a half miles away. My sister, Madame Polianskaia, and her daughter were the first to come and see me. They were practically the only members of my family to be in Petersburg. My dear father was in Vladimir of which he was Governor, or rather Viceroy, for he ruled over two provinces. Two days after my arrival, having learned that Prince Potemkin came daily to visit his niece, Countess Skavronskaia, who was recovering from her confinement in a house near mine, I sent my servant with a request for a small favor from His Grace. I asked him to send me one of his nephews who would pass on to him a message I did not want to entrust to anyone else. The next day, while my children and I were out on a visit to Count Panin, Prince Potemkin came himself, and I was very annoyed at having missed him.

He sent General Pavel Potemkin to see me the following day. Through him I begged the Prince's services in obtaining Her Majesty's permission to come to Tsarskoe Selo and present my children (for no one was allowed there without special permission). I also requested the General to ask his uncle whether Field-Marshal Count Rumiantsev's application at the War Office to have my son, Prince Dashkov, appointed his A.D.C. had had any result; finally I asked him to let me know what rank my son would now have.

Two days later General Pavel Potemkin came to tell me that his uncle the Prince had informed Her Majesty of my arrival, that she had been pleased to command my presence and that of my children at dinner the following Sunday at Tsarskoe Selo, and that I should there hear from Prince Potemkin all the particulars regarding my son.

Count Mikhail Vorontsov, Grand Chancellor, uncle of Princess Dashkova.
(From a miniature by an unknown artist)

I was unable to take advantage of the Empress's gracious permission, for on the very eve of that day my son had a violent attack of fever and was delirious all night. Distracted with worry, fearing for his life, I forgot that I had rheumatism in the knees and stayed by his bedside all night in my bare feet. All I could bring myself to do was to see General Pavel Potemkin, and then only because it was in connection with the Empress and because I thought I might learn something with regard to my son's promotion. I did not want to receive or see anyone apart from my sister, Madame Polianskaia. On the fourth day of his illness, Dr. Rogerson, that good, and indeed, excellent doctor, declared my son to be out of danger. That very night my own rheumatic pains began, this time in my intestines, and I was in real danger until saved by the skill of Dr. Rogerson. As he went to Tsarskoe Selo every Sunday I asked him to inform Her Majesty of my son's and my own state of health which prevented me from taking advantage of Her Majesty's gracious permission to let me pay my respects and present my children to her. My convalescence dragged on for over a fortnight and was made painful by spasms in the stomach and by fits of vomiting that continued to recur, even though less frequently, I bore my sufferings all the more impatiently as my sickness delayed my journey to Tsarskoe Selo and, therefore, the advancement and promotion of my son, who had completely recovered.

When at last I went to Tsarskoe Selo it cost me the greatest possible effort. I was still very weak, and whenever the carriage gave a particularly nasty jolt the pain made me break into a cold sweat. I would then halt the carriage to recover my breath. What will not a mother's love accomplish!

We arrived at Tsarskoe Selo just before Mass, and as Her Majesty was passing on her way to church through the Assembly Hall where I was standing, I came forward to meet her, or rather she approached me first, said kind things to me and expressed her pleasure at seeing me back. As lady-in-waiting I was able to present my daughter myself, while the Court Chamberlain performed that service for my son. Although the pleasure of seeing Her Majesty and her gracious welcome made my spirits rise and caused me to forget that I was only just beginning to convalesce, I was still too weak to keep up with the Empress on her way to the Chapel (which, indeed, was at the other end of the Palace). She was therefore good enough to walk slowly for my sake and sometimes to stop in order to speak to me. As we left the Chapel I felt extremely tired and even less able to keep up with Her Majesty, so that we became separated by the whole length of a room. I therefore asked those of her suite who were too polite to pass me, to go ahead and not bother about me.

When I reached the Grand Hall Prince Potemkin came up to me and asked me what rank my son now held in the army, and what it was I desired done for him. I replied that the Empress knew herself what I desired. "As to his rank," I said, "you, Prince, as Minister of War ought to know what it is better than I. It is twelve years since he has received Her Majesty's commission as ensign in the regiment of Cuirassiers, with order to promote him when his turn came, but I do not know whether he has been. Field-Marshal Count Rumiantsev has asked the War Office to appoint my son his A.D.C. Has this been done or not? That, too, I have been kept in ignorance of."

The Prince took leave of me and I was a little worried to learn that

*A draft page of Princess Dashkova's memoirs
in her own handwriting.*

he immediately left for town. The Grand Marshal of the Court then approached me to say that Her Majesty commanded that my children and I should dine with her. Since Peter I had introduced an entirely German etiquette according to which privileges were granted or withheld depending on military rank, it never entered my head that my son, as ensign in the army, could have the honor of dining with his Sovereign. (I discovered afterward that the Grand Marshal had asked the Empress what he should do about Prince Dashkov, and she had replied: "He will certainly dine with me.")

In order to rest a little, I remained in the room next to that in which Her Majesty played chess before dinner. As she crossed the room on her way to dinner she came up to me and said in a very loud voice, apparently so that everyone there should hear her:

"I wanted your son to remain ensign for just today and have dinner with me to prove that I shall always make a distinction between your children and others." These few words deeply touched me. Indeed, no one but her could, with so much subtlety and tact, have turned the forgetfulness of a promise into such a flattering compliment.

At table I was placed next to her. She devoted all her attention to me and spoke to me throughout the whole dinner. I felt well and strong, but could eat nothing, which she noticed and said: "A room has been prepared for you, so you can rest there."

After dinner, I took advantage of the solicitude thus shown to me and which I deeply appreciated.

I accompanied the Empress during her evening walk. She was kind enough to slacken her usual pace and occasionally to stop and make me sit beside her. As soon as the walk was over I went back to town, as I was afraid of falling ill at Tsarskoe Selo. The following day, I received by Her Majesty's command a copy of the order with my son's promotion to the rank of junior captain in the Semenovski Guards, which was equivalent to the rank of lieutenant-colonel. My son and I were overjoyed.

I remained ill and weak for some time, but the good weather and the peace of mind which was now mine restored me to health sooner than I had expected.

The Court came back to town earlier than usual. I went to thank the Empress for my son's promotion and was kindly received. She invited me to come and see the play at the Hermitage, to which very few people were allowed, as the new apartments bearing the same name were not yet finished and the theater which formed part of them was small.

The following day my children and I dined with Count Panin, the First Minister, the short distance separating his estate from mine permitting me to make that journey. After dinner, Prince Potemkin's A.D.C. brought me a letter in which he informed me, in accordance with the Empress's instructions, that she had made it a rule never again to give away any Crown lands, but desired me to find a suitable piece of land for which she would pay the price.

I informed the Prince how appreciative and grateful I was and yet how unwilling to make the choice myself; I should be perfectly well pleased with anything Her Majesty thought fit to give me. Two days later I received another letter from the Prince, informing me that the Empress had not restricted her freedom of action in respect of Crown lands in Belorussia, that, on the contrary, she wanted them to belong to, and be administered by, Russian gentry, that if I wished to own property there, some land was not yet disposed of by Her Majesty and finally, that he advised me to choose a piece of land there as it was more productive than in Russia proper. I replied that my sole objection to landed property in Belorussia was my firm conviction that if members of the gentry who had owned serfs for centuries became responsible to the Government for their administration, I should feel the weight of that responsibility all the more for having incurred it in consequence of my Sovereign's favor. I said that I had supervised my children's property for about twenty years, and had had the satisfaction of seeing that my administration had rendered the peasants more industrious, richer, and happier than they had ever been before, and that I should continue to be guided by these principles; but that I would not be able to have the consolation of expecting an equal success with peasants who were half Polish and half Jewish and of whose customs and language I was quite ignorant.

A few more letters passed between the Prince and me on this subject, and I put an end to the correspondence by declaring that I should regard any piece of land Her Majesty was pleased to give me as an unexpected kindness.

Some days later I received a letter from the Empress's First Secretary, Count Bezborodko, enclosing a copy of the order by virtue of which the Empress granted me the village of Krugloe and the surrounding land, inhabited by 2,500 peasants. The estate had belonged in the past to the Hetman Oginski and covered a very considerable area, extending over both banks of the Drutsa. At the first partition of Poland the river Drutsa marked the boundary of the old provinces of Great Russia. Most of Oginski's domain, therefore, his forests, several villages and hamlets, had remained in Poland, for they were on the bank of the river, but it was not considered fitting to say all this to Her Majesty. She remained convinced that the whole of the Krugloe district was my property and that she had presented me with a gift in no way inferior to those she had already made to her Ministers and several nobles.

I made the journey to town to thank the Empress, and I have often since, now that I know Krugloe, recalled her words on that occasion, when she said she was very pleased to have given me such a large estate which the ungrateful Oginski had not deserved to own. (Oginski had been a declared enemy of Russia, had even undertaken hostile action against her, and although under great obligation to the Empress, had refused to

swear the oath of allegiance as a Russian subject in so far as his lands in
Belorussia were concerned.)

I was truly amazed the following year when I visited Krugloe and saw
the peasants, scarcely human to look at, filthy, idle, poor, and yet completely addicted to drink. There was not even enough wood for fuel, and
in order to obtain some for the little distillery, there was nothing for it but
to have recourse to the neighboring landowner. There was no waterway
to transport such goods as there might be, only one cow for about ten
persons of both sexes, and one horse for every five peasants. Besides, the
population, including newly born infants, was 167 short of the estimated
2,500, which proves the negligence of Crown property supervisors who
allow every kind of abuse for money and think only of taking what they
can. This is why the most wretched of all peasants are those that belong
to the Sovereign.

I had the right, without involving the Empress in any trouble, to apply
to the Senate to make good the number of peasants specified in the decree
by which Her Majesty had made her gift to me. But I did nothing, I kept
silent, and for two years I invested what, for me, was considerable capital,
to improve the property.[1]

The Marshal of the Court signified to me Her Majesty's pleasure that
I should attend the concerts which were given in her private apartments
and to which no one, not even her ladies-in-waiting, had access save by
special permission. I mention this to show that everything that could give
rise to envy and was of no real value was lavished on me at the time.
This sort of thing always makes many enemies for one at Court, yet my
fortune was always less than modest.

I went to one of these concerts the following day and as soon as the
Empress caught sight of me she came up to me and said: "Why, you have
come all by yourself!" I did not grasp the meaning of that remark until
she said: "Your children are not with you, and I do not want you to be
bored here." Words which failed me at first because I did not understand

[1] This is not quite true. Princess Dashkova did not keep silent either about her "missing"
peasants or about Krugloe's unfavorable situation. She wrote to Potemkin suggesting that
he should take Krugloe for himself, and obtain for her the grant of another property
(Averchino) in central Russia, where she would have even more peasants than stipulated
in the original deed of gift. She was, she said, ready to pay in cash for any labor force
received over and above her due.—K. F.

the Empress's remark came back to me and I thanked her with a sincerity of emotion which did not escape her.

I did not have a house in Petersburg, and, in order to economize on my own expenditure and be able to give my son all the money he needed, I spent as much time as possible in the country and thus avoided paying rent. One day, Her Majesty asked me if I was living in my country place. On my replying to her in the affirmative, she said it was dangerous for my health to stay in late autumn in a house which she knew to have already been damaged by the widespread floods that had occurred before my return to Russia. And she added that if she could say so without offense, my land was a marsh which would aggravate my rheumatism, and if it had not been for her decision to let me make my own choice she would have bought for me the house of the Duchess of Courland. "Pray go and see if it suits you," she said then, "and let the price of it be charged to me."

I told Her Majesty how grateful I was and promised to have a look at a few houses in the course of the week, without revealing my intention of buying one for fear of an increase in the price. I saw the Duchess's house and that of Madame Neledinskaia. The first was the bigger of the two and situated in a better street, all the apartments were richly and elaborately furnished and its price was 58,000 roubles. The second was on the Moika, it was more simply furnished and cost only 40,000 roubles. I decided on that one and requested Madame Neledinskaia to give me a week in which to tell her definitely whether I was buying or not, and asked her to make an inventory of the furniture, none of which I hoped she would afterward remove. She promised this to me.

At the end of the stipulated period, I came back to find to my amazement that Madame Neledinskaia had already moved and that almost all the furniture had disappeared. I asked a servant—the only human being left in the house—for the inventory of the furniture, but he replied that none had been made. I was indignant at this behavior of which I should never have suspected Madame Neledinskaia, and having learned from Prince Golitsyn that he had seen her from his windows all that week busily transporting her furniture into the house she had rented, I resolved to bear the unpleasant consequences of my own good faith without noising it abroad or letting the public into my confidence with regard to my simplicity and the deceitful conduct of that lady. I merely sent her word that as she had broken the terms of our agreement, I no longer considered myself under an obligation to buy her house, but as she had left it and had rented another, I should take hers for a year at a rent of 4,000 roubles, which she would never have received from anyone else.

In any case, I intended availing myself of Prince Potemkin's services to petition Her Majesty that instead of presenting me with a house, she should grant me a favor which I had more at heart: the appointment of my sister Polianskaia's daughter as maid-of-honor. My sister ardently desired this, particularly since a certain person who had promised it to her had instead employed all his influence to obtain this distinction for one of his sisters-in-law.

When I saw the Empress again she asked me if I had made the choice of a house. "I have rented one," I answered. "And why not buy it, then?" retorted the Empress. "Because," I said laughing, "the purchase of a house is as serious a matter as the choice of a husband; one must think it over not once but many times."

The whole thing gave me a lot of private satisfaction and I thought I had the right to be pleased with myself, even though I was plied with ceaseless questions: how was I duped by Madame Neledinskaia? Why did I not buy a house?—for it was common knowledge by then that any house I should want to buy would be paid for out of the Empress's privy purse. Someone I do not want to name said to me in the course of a very sincere conversation:

"If you hesitate to accept the offer of a house you will perhaps be duped by the Court as you have been by Madame Neledinskaia; few people know your motives, fewer still will be able to understand them."

In reply I quoted a certain stupid German baron who insisted on speaking French though he knew it very badly; when told that he was unintelligible in that language, his answer was always the same: "What do I care! *I am perfectly intelligible to myself.*"

"This," I said, "will invariably be my answer to any such comment," and it was a comment that annoyed me all the more in that some people wanted to lend it a point of irony.

CHAPTER XXII

⁕

The time was approaching when I would settle in town, and I soon found on closer inspection that I had lost nothing in not buying the house.

Life was proceeding calmly and I had no worries. Prince Potemkin promised that my wishes with regard to my niece, Miss Polianskaia, would be granted, and urged me to buy a house without delay as Her Majesty might conclude that I was not intending to stay in Petersburg. I therefore went to see the house of the Court banker Fredericks, lately deceased, and settled for it with the widow at the price of 30,000 roubles.

When I asked the Empress for permission to buy it, she replied that she had long ago given orders to pay the price of any house I might buy out of her privy purse. To do her justice, she wished my choice had been more magnificent, and so she asked me why I preferred my new house to that of the Duchess of Courland which she had offered to me.

Fearing that my scruples of conscience might be taken for misplaced affection, I told the Empress that Frederick's house was situated on the English Quay where I was born, and that as Her Majesty had made my life worthwhile, I had chosen that quarter of the town to live in.

On that occasion I was indeed dupe of my own conscientious scruples; for the house I bought had no furniture at all, and though I saved Her Majesty's privy purse half the expense the Empress would have incurred on my behalf if I had bought the house she had offered, I did not want to utter a word about the furniture that had to be bought. The furniture I chose was of the simplest kind though clean, and consisted only of the most indispensable pieces, but even so I added 3,000 roubles to my debts. However, as it was neither the first time nor the last that I was dupe of my own disinterestedness, I made up my mind to say nothing about it.

Soon after, Prince Potemkin, as friendly and considerate as ever, told me that Her Majesty had heard of my debts and not only wanted to pay them, but fearing that I should incur some again, intended to have my house in Moscow rebuilt and furnished at her own expense.

I earnestly entreated the Prince to dissuade the Empress from doing this, but rather to remind her of the wish I had most at heart and one I had taken the liberty of confiding to her, regarding my niece, Miss Polianskaia. I saw my sister every day, I told him; she was greatly depressed, and no amount of favors from Her Majesty could efface my feelings of being at least partly responsible for her downfall in 1762.

The affair dragged on. At last, on 24 November—the Empress's name-day and mine—after a grand ball given in the Palace, I did not go to the Empress's private apartments to finish off the evening, but instead, on seeing one of Prince Potemkin's A.D.C.s, begged him go and tell the Prince that I should not move from where I was without a present from him first, in the shape of a copy of the decree I had been waiting for for so long, making my niece maid-of-honor. I think that those who still remained in the ballroom were very surprised to see me there after the Court had retired, and had they known the reason for it (or the consequence) they would once again have dubbed me "dupe." For this is what resulted of the compromise I offered in exchange for the fulfilment of my sister's wish: my house in Moscow was not built at Her Majesty's expense, neither were my debts paid, and when I wanted to leave Petersburg I sold my Petersburg house to pay my debt to the bank. However, I never felt sorry for what I had done for my sister.

A long hour passed. At last I saw the A.D.C. holding a paper in his hand, and I could hardly contain myself when I read that my niece had at last been made maid-of-honor. I went off like a streak of lightning to rejoin my sister who, I knew, was having supper with a Vorontsov cousin of ours, and had the pleasure of seeing her in a perfect ecstasy of delight at the good news I brought her. I was also most happy at having accomplished what she wanted more than anything in the world.

The following month a ball was given at the Court, I forget on what occasion. After making her usual round of ladies-in-waiting and foreign Ministers, in the course of which she had a word for each one of them, the Empress came back to me and said:

"I should like to speak to you."

"I am always ready to listen to Your Majesty with the greatest respect."

"I cannot do so now," she said, to which I replied:

"At any time and wherever you may desire it, Ma'am."

She left me, to speak once more to some of the foreign Ministers who were standing at the other end of the room, and then, as she stopped in the middle of a small circle between the two rows of guests, she caught my eye and made a sign for me to come up. I had the impression of falling from the clouds when Her Majesty said she had the intention of suggesting I should accept the appointment of Director of the Academy of Sciences. I was struck dumb with astonishment, and the Empress had time to tell me several very flattering things which she thought would induce me to accept her proposal.

"No, Ma'am," I said, "I cannot accept any office which is beyond my capacities. If Your Majesty were not making fun of me, I should tell you that my affection for you, among many other reasons, does not allow me to risk making myself ridiculous and bringing discredit on you for making such a choice."

To conquer my scruples, the Empress even affected to see in my unwillingness to conform to her wishes a lack of attachment to her person.

All those who have had the honor of approaching Her Majesty know that she had all the eloquence, grace, and tact necessary to convince people or win them over. There was no need for her to exercise any of these qualities for my sake, because my attachment to her, as firm as it was disinterested, impelled me to obey her in everything that did not go against my principles.

Anyway, she had no success that time. "Put me at the head of your washerwomen," I said to her, "and you will see with what zeal I shall serve you."

"Now it is you making fun of *me,* suggesting an occupation so unworthy of you!"

"Your Majesty thinks she knows me, and yet you are not aware that I have enough pride in me to imagine that any employment you might grant me would gain in dignity by my acceptance of it. As soon as I am at the head of your washerwomen this will become a great Court office which everyone will envy me. I have no idea how to do the laundry, but the mistakes that I shall make as a result of my ignorance will be of no consequence, while the faults committed by the Director of the Academy of Sciences will all be serious and will bring discredit on the Sovereign who has selected him."

Her Majesty again waved aside my objection and bade me remember those who had filled that office; their abilities, she said, were far below mine.

"All the worse for those," I replied, "who had so little respect for themselves that they could assume duties they were incapable of performing."

"Well, then," she said, "let us leave it at that—everyone is looking at us. As to your refusal, it has only confirmed my opinion that I could not have made a better choice."

This conversation threw me into a fever, and my face must have betrayed the utmost agitation, for the expression of the ladies among whom I resumed my place could not conceal the satisfaction they felt at witnessing what they thought had been a disagreeable scene for me. Countess Matiushkina, who was forever asking questions, wanted to know the significance of my long private conversation with Her Majesty.

"You see me, Madam, in a state of great agitation," I replied, "but it is the Empress's kindness and her excessively high opinion of me that are the cause of it."

I ardently longed for the ball to be over in order to be able to write to Her Majesty that same evening and suggest to her even stronger reasons for my refusal. As soon as I was back at home I wrote a letter which might have angered any other Sovereign, for in it I took the liberty of saying that the private life of monarchs sometimes escaped the attention of history, but never their bad or harmful nominations for public office; that God himself, by creating me a woman, had exempted me from accepting the employment of a Director of an Academy of Sciences; that I was aware of my own ignorance, and that I had never desired to be a member of a learned Society, not even of the Arcadian Academy in Rome, though I could have bought the honor for a few ducats.

When I finished my letter it was nearly midnight and too late to send it to Her Majesty. But being eager to get rid of the whole business and to prevail upon the Empress to abandon a project which seemed to me quite literally absurd, I went to see Prince Potemkin, the threshold of whose house I had never crossed before.

I sent in my name, and a message to say that I wanted to see him even if he were in bed, to speak to him of something which was very important to me.

As a matter of fact, Prince Potemkin really had gone to bed. I told him of what had just passed between the Empress and me, to which he replied that he had heard about it already from Her Majesty, who had set her heart on entrusting me with the administration of the Academy of Sciences.

"But," I exclaimed, "I do not want to accept this office, and should fail to do justice to myself if I did accept it. Here is the letter I wrote to her—read it, Prince; I shall then seal it and leave it with you so that you can let the Empress have it in the morning as soon as she is awake."

Prince Potemkin read the letter and . . . tore it to pieces: "How dare you, Sir," I cried in utter amazement and rage." How dare you tear up my letter to the Empress?"

"Listen to what I have to say, Princess, before you lose your temper," he replied. "You are very attached to Her Majesty; no one doubts that. Why then do you want to offend and distress her?—for I have already told you she has been thinking of nothing else these last two days. However, if you really persist in your refusal—here is a pen; all you have to do, Princess, is to give yourself the not very serious trouble of writing another letter. I am speaking to you as a man who has your interests at heart and I must tell you, too, that the Empress considers this appointment as the best means of securing your companionship and keeping you in Petersburg. She is bored by the fools who surround her."

I was no longer angry with the Prince, for it is not a feeling that lasts any length of time with me. I told him I would write a more restrained letter which I would give to my footman to deliver to one of Her Majesty's palace servants so that she could see it in the morning. But I begged him to second me in my attempts to prevail on the Empress to dismiss this nonsensical idea from her mind. As I took leave of him I repeated once again to the Prince that I hoped he would continue to give me his support.

My agitation was such that I did not even bother to change when I reached home, but began immediately to write, and remained in my Court dress till the morning, writing and turning over in my mind the events of the previous day.

At seven o'clock I sent my servant and received in reply a note from the Empress in which she said that I was a very early riser and added many kind and flattering things, but affected not to see a refusal in what I had written to her.

Late in the afternoon I received a letter from Count Bezborodko, enclosing the copy of a Decree which had already been sent up to the Senate and by virtue of which I was appointed Director of the Academy of Sciences. At the same time the Decree dissolved the Commission set

up some time previously to administer the Academy on the requisition of
the professors and other members of it, after the complaints made against
Mr. Domashnev.

I felt nothing but consternation and confusion at the receipt of this
document. I gave orders not to let anyone into the house, and, as I
paced up and down my drawing room, I ruminated on all the embarrassment that the appointment would cause me and the degree to which
is would tax my strength. Worse—I foresaw that it would continually
create misunderstandings between me and the Empress.

Count Bezborodko's letter also contained the following words:

"Her Majesty has commanded me to tell you, Madam, that you may
always discuss with her any business relating to the Departments placed
under your direction, and that she will always be ready to remove all
difficulties you may encounter."

Here I was, then, harnessed to the plough which, broken-down as it
was, became my responsibility, without even the assistance of the Commission I have just mentioned. I took it upon myself to send the Chancellery of the Academy a copy of the Decree, together with a behest that the
Commission should remain in force for two days more and that I should
be furnished with information on the various branches of the establishment and on the functioning of the printing office and works, and so on,
as well as with the names of the custodians of the different collections,
library superintendents, and so on, and that the heads of some of these
branches should the very next day submit a report to me on the nature of
their duties and on their respective branches. At the same time I begged
the Commission to let me have all available details concerning the duties
of a Director so that I should be perfectly familiar with mine before I
began to act even in the merest details; and finally I begged these gentlemen to believe, and to assure their colleagues, that one of the duties I had
prescribed to myself was to have for them every consideration that their
knowledge and their talents deserved.

I flattered myself that I should thereby avoid making initial blunders.

The following morning I attended the Empress's toilet, during which
her secretaries and the chiefs of various Departments were assembled in
order to receive Her Majesty's orders. I was surprised to find Mr. Domashnev among them. He accosted me to tell me, among other things, that he
was ready to enlighten me on the nature of my duties. Amazed at his presumption, I told him as politely as I could that I had made it my rule for
the future to watch over the interests and the well-being of the Academy,

that I should treat its members with perfect impartiality, showing them esteem and consideration in accordance with their talents, and that for the rest my ignorance was so complete that I should have recourse to the wisdom of Her Majesty, who had promised to give me the benefit of her guidance.

Just as he was beginning to answer something or other, the Empress half-opened the door, but on seeing us, quickly shut it again and rang her bell. A footman ran in and came back to tell me that Her Majesty commanded my presence in her room.

"It gives me great pleasure to see you, Madam," said the Empress to me. "Tell me, pray, what could that brute Domashnev have been saying to you?"

"He was instructing me, Ma'am," I replied, "in the way I should behave in an office I am assuming in which, though I may take greater care than he that my integrity be not questioned, yet I shall no doubt be more ignorant than he is. I do not know," I continued, "whether I should thank Your Majesty for this apparent proof of your high opinion of me or whether I should condole with you on the extraordinary step you have just taken in making me Monsieur le Directeur of an Academy of Sciences."

Her Majesty assured me that she was not only pleased, but proud, to have made that choice.

"This is very flattering, Ma'am," I said, "but you will soon tire of leading the blind, for indeed I shall be an ignoramus at the head of Science."

"Enough," said Her Majesty. "Do not mock me any more. And I hope this is the last time you have spoken to me like this."

As I came out of the Empress's room I met the Marshal of the Court, who told me that he had last night been commanded by Her Majesty—in case I came that morning—to invite me to dinner at her private table and to inform me that thenceforth I could dine at her table whenever I wanted; I should, however, always consult my own convenience, but it would give her great pleasure whenever I came.

I received many compliments on the proof Her Majesty had just shown me of her high favor and consideration by placing me at the head of so important a Department; others, on seeing me look rather sad, were sufficiently discreet not to embarrass me with their congratulations. But all generally felt jealous, all the more so as my somewhat awkward behavior at Court made them regard me as a very minor figure.

Early next morning, which was a Sunday, I received the visit of all the professors, officers, and servants of the Academy. I told them that I should

visit the Academy the following day, and if they had any business to discuss with me I begged them to come to my room at any hour convenient
to them without waiting to be announced.

I spent the evening reading the reports which had been presented to
me and trying to make myself familiar with the labyrinth into which I
was about to venture, for I was entirely convinced that my slightest mistake would become known and criticized. I tried, too, not to forget the
names of the most important inspectors and officers of the Academy, and
the following day, before going there, I paid a visit to the great Euler. I
say "great" because he was, without any doubt, the greatest geometrician
and mathematician of his age, besides being familiar with every branch of
science; his industry was such that even after he had lost his sight he continued his researches and made discoveries, dictating his work to Mr. Fuss,
who was married to his granddaughter. He left behind him a great deal
of material that went to enrich the publications of the Academy for many
years after his death. Disgusted, like everyone else, with Domashnev's
behavior, he no longer attended the Academy and took no interest in its
proceedings, apart from signing an occasional protest in common with
the other members and even writing directly to Her Majesty whenever
the great Domashnev took it into his head to launch into some ruinous
undertaking.

I begged him to accompany me to the Academy at least this once,
adding that I did not claim he should bother to attend it in future, but
that as this would be my first appearance at a sitting of a scientific body,
I wanted to be introduced by him. He seemed flattered by my great consideration for him. We had known each other for a long time, and I may
venture to say that he had considerable regard for me ever since I was a
very young girl, some fifteen years before I assumed the Directorship of
the Academy.

He came with me in my carriage, to which I also invited his son,
Permanent Secretary of the Academic Sittings, as well as his grandson,
Mr. Fuss, who, since the great man was blind, had the task of guiding his
steps.

As I entered the Conference Hall, I said to the professors and other
members there assembled that though I was an ignorant person myself, I
wanted to mark my respect for science and could find no more solemn
and impressive a way of doing it than by being introduced by Mr. Euler. I
spoke these few words before sitting down and noticed that the Professor
of Allegory, Mr. Stählin, had taken his place next to the Director's chair.

Mr. Stählin had received that appellation—God knows why—in the reign of Peter III, together with the rank of State Councillor, equivalent to a major-general, and claimed for that reason to be second in importance only to myself. In fact, his rank was as allegorical as his science and, indeed, the whole of his personality. I therefore turned to Mr. Euler and told him to sit down wherever he thought fit, for any place he occupied would always be the first. His son and grandson were not alone in showing appreciation and pleasure at my remark, for the eyes of the professors, who all had the highest respect for the venerable old man, were filled with tears.

From the Academicians I passed to the Chancellery, which dealt with all administrative and financial matters and where the various officials were assembled. I told them the idea was current among the general public that peculation had been rife under the former Director and that the Academy not only lacked funds but was heavily in debt; that henceforth the common duty of us all would be to redress these abuses, the shortest and most efficient method of achieving this being to squander nothing and stop all misappropriations; that I, for one, was determined not to enrich myself at the Academy's expense, and should therefore not allow my subordinates to do so; that it would thus be best for each of us to resolve to do nothing for the sake of personal gain, and that if we held fast to that principle I should be in the position to reward the zeal and raise the salary of those who deserved it.

The Bulletins, which had formerly been published in two quarto-sized volumes every year, were then reduced to one volume, till finally their publication was suspended altogether for want of type; the printing works was in utter confusion and lacked everything. Very soon I put it into shape again, acquired fine type and had two volumes of the Bulletins published containing for the most part articles supplied by Mr. Euler.

Prince Viazemskii, as Minister of Justice, asked Her Majesty whether he should have me sworn in, as was customary when taking employment under the Crown.

"Unquestionably," replied the Empress, "for I have never made a secret of Princess Dashkova's appointment to the Directorship of the Academy; true enough, I have no need for fresh assurances of her loyalty to me and the country, but the ceremony would give me pleasure because her appointment would thereby gain in sanction and publicity."

Prince Viazemskii, therefore, sent a message to me by his first secretary that he would expect me the following day in the Senate where I had to be sworn in. I felt embarrassed but could not avoid doing what had to be done by everyone—from the highest to the lowest employee in the service of the Crown.

The next day I went to the Senate at the appointed time, and having to pass, on my way to the Chapel, through the Chamber where the Senators had their sittings, I saw them all assembled there. They rose from their seats, and some whom I knew better than the rest came up to me.

"You are," I said to them, "surely as surprised as I am myself at seeing me come here to swear an oath of loyalty to Her Majesty whose very name has for long been engraved on my heart. But one must obey, and not believe oneself exempt from a duty prescribed for all. To this is due this unusual event—the appearance of a woman in your august sanctuary."

As soon as the ceremony was over (during which my shyness, as always on special occasions, did not fail to make me feel embarrassed to the point of spasms and cold sweat), I hastened to beg the Minister of Justice to furnish me with all the documents which the Chancellery of the Academy had lodged with the Senate relative to the general feeling of dissatisfaction with the former Director and certain of his activities, as well as with the explanations and justifications offered by him. He promised to send them to me the same day, and it was by reading them that I was able to form an idea, however partial, of the task I should have to fulfill.

The Academy had two funds which had to be shown separately in the account books—one known as the Administrative Fund and another called the State Fund. Both were more or less empty, and I had great difficulty in keeping the two separate. There were debts to booksellers in Russia, Paris, and Holland, and as I did not want to ask Her Majesty for money, I reduced the price of books printed at the Academy by thirty percent and thus in a short time established a brisk trade in them. I used the money obtained in this way to pay off the Academy's debts and was soon able to make good the arrears of the State Fund which was in the hands of the State Treasurer, the above-mentioned Prince Viazemskii. The Administrative Fund was wholly the responsibility of the Director, being, so to speak, his own creation used in special circumstances, for example for the payment of bonuses and the making of purchases not provided for by the original charter of the Academy. Besides, the money of the Administrative Fund served to cover the deficit of the State Fund, itself the natural result of the rise of prices over the years.

I found only seventeen pupils in the school, and twenty-one young artisans who were being educated and trained at the Academy's expense.

I raised the number of the former to fifty, and of the latter to forty. I had the satisfaction of retaining Mr. Fuss, who had wanted to leave the Academy, and I doubled his salary as well as that of Mr. Georgi.

The following year I raised the stipends of all the professors and I established three courses of lectures—on Mathematics, Geometry, and Natural History—which had to be given free of charge and in Russian by native professors. These were paid 200 roubles out of the Administrative Fund at the end of each course. I often attended these lectures myself and had the satisfaction of seeing children of impoverished Russian gentry and young subalterns in the Guards derive benefit from them.

CHAPTER XXIII

W inter was almost over when Prince Potemkin left for the Army. My son, whom the Prince both liked and esteemed, accompanied him and even traveled in the same coach. When passing through Belorussia the Prince deviated from his route in order to see for himself and form his own opinion of Krugloe, which some considered would make my fortune, while others set rather a low value on it. From there he wrote to me an encouraging letter, assuring me that the estate could with time be made to yield more than it did. He had given, he said, instructions to Brigadier Bauer, who was administering some lands of his adjoining mine, to introduce better order in Krugloe than there had been under the overseers of the Crown and to do all he could to increase the revenues of the property, both on his own initiative and on written instructions from me.

"Besides," wrote the Prince, "there is a large village there bearing your name (Dashkovo), which you could have in compensation for the deficiency in the number of peasants stipulated in the deed of gift."

In fact, it would have been easy to obtain that piece of property for me as the King of Poland, from a sense of obligation to my late husband, could without any difficulties have come to an arrangement with his sister who was its present owner and the nobleman who was heir to it, both of them being completely indifferent about it. But Prince Potemkin would never agree to my writing to the King or to Count Stackelberg, our Ambassador in Poland, as he wished to arrange it all himself. However, I never obtained Dashkovo nor anything else to compensate me for my losses at Krugloe.

The separation from my son was, of course, a source of great grief to me. I could not become accustomed to his absence, but my life had been spent in constant sacrifice of my own wishes and pleasures for the sake of my children, and I agreed to his departure for the Army because this was useful for his career and because the military profession which he had chosen for himself made it essential. He wrote frequent letters to me, and was shown particular favor by Prince Potemkin, to the great astonishment of all who knew the casual attitude which that spoiled child of fortune usually had to people. I was, therefore, fairly free from worry, though tired and annoyed by various details of Academic administration and particularly by my endeavors to find some means to stop the wasteful expenditure which had been tolerated in the Academy for many years past.

The following summer Their Imperial Highnesses the Grand Duke Pavel and his wife returned from abroad. I rarely visited them, on the pretext that my time was absorbed by a work well above my powers and that the distance between Gatchina and the Palace of Strelna, where the Empress allowed me to live during the summer, was so great as to make it quite a journey.

Their Imperial Highnesses invited everyone of any importance. Guests stayed for several days, sometimes longer, were kindly and politely treated, and made—so I was assured—to feel at their ease.

The Grand Duke pressed me to come, but I declined the invitation. I let it be known that no one would appreciate more than I the pleasures of a delightful life in Gatchina and the advantages of paying my court to Their Imperial Highnesses, but I was sure that all that happened in Gatchina was reported to Tsarskoe Selo and all that happened in Tsarskoe Selo was reported to Gatchina, and hence I wished to deprive Her Majesty of the right to question me, and the Grand Duke of the right to consider me a tale-bearer. I added that millions would not tempt me to interfere between mother and son, and that I was convinced a moment's reflection on my behavior would earn for me the esteem of His Imperial Highness.

For ten years afterward I faithfully followed this line of conduct, and never visited Their Imperial Highnesses except on State occasions when they were attended by the whole Court. The Empress never asked me anything on the subject of Gatchina, knowing that I did not frequent it. And if ever in moments of irritation with her son she told me what it was that made her angry, I invariably expressed surprise that Her Majesty should want to make a third person party to the dispute, when all she had to do to be certain of her son's obedience was to make her wishes known to him.

As will be seen later, this firm and honest line of conduct did not even result in my being so much as left in peace by Pavel I, or save me from being harassed and persecuted by him in common with those whom he claimed to have offended him or harmed his interests.

At about this time Count Andrei Shuvalov came back from Paris, and soon succeeded in inciting the favorite, Lanskoi, against both my son and me. One day, when speaking with the Empress of the ease with which excellent copies of well-known masterpieces could be obtained in Italy, I expressed regret that I could not find here a bust of Her Majesty, such as I wanted to have. The Empress ordered a footman to bring one, made by the famous Russian artist Mr. Shubin, and gave it to me as a present.

"But this bust is mine," exclaimed Lanskoi in protest. "It belongs to me."

The Empress told him he was mistaken, at which he threw a furious glance at me, and I answered back with one expressing nothing but contempt. Ever since then Her Majesty would always interrupt him to put a stop to his wrangling.

The Minister of Justice, Prince Viazemskii, soon began to create difficulties for me in connection with my work as Director of the Academy. Either he would take no notice of the recommendations I made to the Senate for the promotion of those of my subordinates that deserved it; or else he would fail to supply me with the necessary information for establishing the limits of different provinces, of which I wanted to publish better maps. At last he had the temerity to ask my Treasurer why he did not let him have the monthly account of the Administrative Fund at the same time as he brought him that of the Academy's State Fund. I immediately wrote to the Empress tendering my resignation on the ground that Prince Viazemskii wanted to establish a system of accountancy which had never existed in the history of the Academy—not even under my predecessor who had been suspected of peculation. I reminded Her Majesty that it was at my urgent and pressing request that she let me present to her every month the accounts of the Administrative Fund, which I had done regularly and had had the satisfaction of hearing Her Majesty express her admiration at the successful increase of the Fund. Finally, I added that I could not allow the Minister of Justice to encroach on the powers of the Director in a matter so essential to the welfare of the Academy, and still less could I allow him to doubt my integrity.

Prince Viazemskii received a reprimand, and the Empress begged me to forget his foolish conduct. This Minister, it must be admitted, was a hard-working man and his Department was run smoothly and methodically, but he was ignorant and vindictive. He bore me a grudge because I had given employment to victims of his persecution whom he had deprived of work, and therefore, of their daily bread. Another thing, too, increased his dislike of me. The Academy published a new journal which included a few pages written by the Empress and also by me. Councillor Kozodavlev and several other members of the Academy contributed some passages in prose and verse, including a few satirical pieces which Prince Viazemskii took to be applicable to himself and his wife, especially after he discovered that Mr. Derzhavin, whose poems were admired and avidly read by everyone, was also a contributor to the journal. For he thought that, as in the past he had victimized Mr. Derzhavin and had been the cause of his losing his post of Principal Vice-Governor, the latter was now taking a poet's revenge.

I had a thousand and one difficulties to overcome. Prince Viazemskii continued to oppose as much as he could any good I tried to do, including even such schemes of public benefit as new and more precise maps of the different provinces the limits of which had been changed in the course of the recent territorial reform that had established new administrative areas. That measure, very beneficial to the country in that it brought order and civilization for the first time into the interior, was worthy of the great Catherine. Justice could now be administered locally without the necessity for people to travel to the Capital, thousands of miles away, in search of it. For the Empress did not like the Russian proverb which says: "God is too high and the Tsar is too far—we cannot seek justice from either, so suffering must be our lot." Roads were improved and rendered safe, inland trade was made easier and prospered in consequence, magnificent law courts, cathedrals, and palaces for the Governors of the various provinces were built in the Provincial Capitals at the Empress's expense, and civil police ensured order and security which the great distances made it so difficult to keep.

Far from sending me information on the territorial changes, Prince Viazemskii retained and held back the information sent to me at my request by the Provincial Governors. But as I did not want to worry the Empress continuously with my complaints, I exercised all the patience I could muster.

In the month of July my son returned from the Army as bearer of despatches announcing the capture of the Crimea. My surprise and especially my joy at seeing him sooner than I expected were beyond words, but he stayed for only a few days and went back to the Army with the rank of

Colonel. I was all the more pleased at this act of favor on the Empress's part, as it removed him from the Guards, gave him an opportunity of employing his talents at the head of a regiment, and made it no longer necessary for him to live in Petersburg.

One day, as I was walking with the Empress in her garden at Tsarskoe Selo, we spoke of the richness and beauty of the Russian language. I expressed my surprise to Her Majesty that, though herself a writer and fond of our language, she should not yet have established a Russian Academy. We needed, I said, rules of grammar and a good dictionary to do away with the absurdity of using foreign words and terms while having our own which were far more vivid.

"I do not know why this has not been done," answered the Empress. "I have wanted such an Academy for many years and have even issued the necessary orders."

"That is surprising, Ma'am," I said, "for there is nothing easier. Models already exist, and you have only to make your choice."

"Would you please sketch me out a plan for one?" said Her Majesty.

"But surely," I replied, "this would be better done if you order one of your secretaries to present you with a plan of the French Academy, the Academy of Berlin, and a few others, together with some notes on what should be added or omitted in the case of an Academy of our own."

"I beg you," she said again, "to take the trouble of it on yourself, and I shall then be sure that your zeal will brook no delay in accomplishing an object which I must to my shame admit not having done anything about until now."

"It is not a question of trouble, Ma'am," I replied, "I shall obey you as promptly as possible, but I have none of the books I need here, and I would once again assure Your Majesty that any of the secretaries in your antechamber would accomplish the task better than myself."

However, I was not able to make the Empress change her mind, and I had to submit and obey.

In the evening, when I had retired to my apartments for supper, I drew up, before going to bed, a short sketch of what I considered should constitute an Academy of the Russian Language. My astonishment can, therefore, be well imagined when I received back that same imperfect outline of a plan which I had made in a hurry to please the Empress, confirmed by Her Majesty's signature as if it had been a well-thought-out document officially presented in the appropriate manner. It was accompanied by an Order-in-Council, appointing me President of the new

Academy. A copy of the Order had at the same time been communicated to the Senate in confirmation. The Empress obviously would not hear of a refusal on my part.

Two days later I returned to Tsarskoe Selo in the vain hope of prevailing on Her Majesty to choose another President. As this proved impossible, I told Her Majesty that I already had the necessary funds for the annual maintenance of the Russian Academy, and that all her expenses would be limited to the purchase of a house. She expressed both astonishment and approval when I told her that the 5,000 roubles that she paid out of her Privy Purse for translations of the classics would suffice for my purpose.

"But I should like the translations to continue, all the same," she said.

"So they will, Ma'am," I replied. "Our students and pupils of the Academy of Sciences will do them, subject to correction by the Russian professors, and the 5,000 roubles of which the Directors of the Academy had never rendered any account to anyone, and which, to judge by the few thousand translations that have appeared up till now, have been considered by them as their pocket-money to be spent for their own needs, will be usefully employed. But we need a few casts and one or two medals every year to reward those who have accomplished most. I shall have the honor," I added, "to present you with a statement of receipts and necessary expenditure, and we shall then see whether there will be anything left for the casts and the medals."

In fact, in the estimate which I presented to her I stipulated that there should be two secretaries with a salary of 900 roubles each, two translators with a salary of 450 roubles each, and one treasurer. I also needed four disabled soldiers to heat the stoves and guard the house. The total of all wages and salaries came to 3,300 roubles, and the 1,700 roubles that remained were to be spent on fuel, papers, and the purchase of books. These were to be bought little by little every year, pending the time when I should offer my library for the use of Academicians. But anyhow at the end of ten years the Academy would have quite a considerable library of its own.

The expenses I have listed left nothing for casts and medals, and the Empress therefore provided 1,250 roubles per annum to cover the necessary costs. But she seemed even more astonished than pleased at my estimates. In none of the similar estimates presented to her was the Head or President ever forgotten—a considerable salary was usually fixed for him. I, on the other hand, did not earmark a single penny for myself, and this useful establishment was therefore to be administered at no extra cost to the Crown beyond the 1,250 roubles granted by Her Majesty for casts and medals.

I shall end all I have to say about the Russian Academy by referring the reader (should he be interested) to my last report presented to Her Majesty. Suffice it to say that with three years' arrears of the Empress's grant originally intended for the translation of the classics, but not paid out to Mr. Domashnev—that is to say, with 15,000 roubles in addition to what money I could spare from the Administrative Fund—I built two houses in the courtyard of the one which Her Majesty had given to the Academy, thus adding 1,950 roubles to its annual revenue; I had the house furnished and provided it with a very considerable library; I left 49,000 roubles as a fund, placed in the Foundling Hospital, and I had the dictionary finished and published. All this in a matter of eleven years. (However, the Emperor Pavel took away from the Academy all the three houses, giving it in exchange a piece of land which had nothing on it except a forge.) I say nothing of the Russian Academy building, whose front elevation has been greatly admired, for though it was built under my direction it was at the Empress's expense. Besides, I have already said that nothing interested me as much as architecture, and, therefore, I include it among my pleasures.

Here I must add that I had many difficulties and much unpleasantness at Court. The more enlightened members of the public recognized my merits and admitted that the foundation of a Russian Academy and the amazing speed with which the Russian dictionary—the first we ever had—had been compiled were due to my zeal and public spirit. The courtiers, on the other hand, found the dictionary inconvenient, based as it was on etymological principles. Even Her Majesty asked me several times why we had not listed the words in alphabetical order. I told her that in the second edition, which could be completed in under three years, the words would appear alphabetically, but that the first dictionary of a language had to be etymological in order to show, and even find, the roots of words. I do not know why the Empress, who had a facility for understanding even the most profound things, seemed not to grasp my meaning, but I do know that I was very annoyed, and in spite of my reluctance to declare Her Majesty's opinion regarding our dictionary at a sitting of the Academy, I decided to raise the subject at our first meeting, leaving out, however, a great many questions with which I had been constantly worried. All the Academicians, as I had expected, stated that the first dictionary could not be compiled in any other way, but that the second edition would be more complete and would be arranged alphabetically.[1]

I repeated to the Empress, the next time I saw her, the unanimous opinion of all the Academicians and the reason they gave for it. Her Majesty, however, seemed to cling to her own. She was, at the time, interested in a so-called dictionary edited by Mr. Pallas. It was a sort of glossary in ninety to a hundred languages, some of which were represented by no more than a score of words such as Earth, Sky, Water, Father, Mother, etc. Mr. Pallas was a scholar famous for the publication of his travels in Russia and for his great knowledge of natural history. He lacked all principles and morals, he was vicious, he was out for personal advantage and he dared to run up the expenses of printing the book which, to please the Empress, he referred to as a dictionary, to a sum of over 20,000 roubles, over and above the cost to Her Majesty's Privy Purse of couriers despatched to Siberia, Kamchatka, Spain, Portugal, and so on, to bring back a few meager and useless words in different languages.

However, useless and imperfect as this peculiar work was, it was pronounced to be an admirable dictionary and caused me considerable annoyance.

---

[1] Princess Dashkova remained President of the Russian Academy from its foundation in 1783 to her dismissal by Pavel I in 1796. The Academy continued to exist as an independent body till 1841, when it was merged with the Petersburg Academy of Sciences and became its Department of the Russian Language and Literature. Its original aim was, as its Charter puts it, "to purify and enrich the Russian language and make rules for the use of words in speech and poetry." In practice, its first important undertaking was the Etymological Dictionary of the Russian language, completed in 1789–94 in six volumes containing over 43,000 words. The Russian language in the eighteenth century was in a state of flux as a result of a mass introduction of foreign words (mainly by Peter the Great) as well as of new words and expressions coined by the literary school and followers of Lomonosov. It was the Dictionary's task to put some order into the semantic chaos by establishing a standardized linguistic usage, sanctioning some innovations and weeding out others—mostly those of foreign origin. The Alphabetical Dictionary, mentioned by Princess Dashkova as a remote possibility, was published in 1806–22, also in six volumes, but containing 51,000 words.—K. F.

CHAPTER XXIV

In order to get some rest I went to my house in the country, which I was having built in stone, and renounced all society and visits to town. The two Academies gave me so much work to do that I had no time to waste. I was made responsible for three letters of the alphabet, and had to collect all words beginning with any of these three. Then every Saturday we met to search for the roots of words thus collected by the Academicians. Besides, I spent a few days every week at Tsarskoe Selo. My time was thus entirely taken up.

During this winter, 1783, my son obtained two months' leave to see me, and I made over his father's property to him, by an act confirmed by Her Majesty. I reserved a part for myself, but no longer had the worry of administering his. He received more than his father had left him, his sister, and me—and not a pennyworth of debt, so that I could tell others and, what is more, myself that I had not badly administered the trust which the other guardians had entirely abandoned to me.

The following summer, Mrs. Hamilton came over from Ireland to see me. I would be hard put to it to express the joy I felt at the visit of this highly esteemed and very dear friend. She was presented to Her Majesty by special favor at Tsarskoe Selo, where foreigners were not usually received.

I requested leave of absence from Petersburg for a period of three months and took my friend to Moscow. There she saw all the curious and interesting sights of that ancient capital as well as the fine country around it, after which we went to my favorite estate—to Troitskoe—where I wished to live and die. I was delighted to see how much my friend admired the beauties of that lovely spot, and though an Englishwoman, accustomed to the beautiful gardens of her own country, she approved and admired mine which not only had I entirely planned, but where every tree and every shrub was of my own choice and planted under my own supervision.

I organized a village fête for my friend, which pleased and affected her and the memory of which will remain with me so long as I live. A village had been newly built a few miles away from Troitskoe. I had all the peasants who were going to dwell in it gathered together, all dressed in their best clothes, embroidered by the women, as is the custom with us. The weather was gorgeous, and I made them dance on the grass and sing Russian songs. My friend, who had never seen or heard anything like it, was delighted with it all—the songs, the dances, the women's dresses. Russian dishes and drinks were not forgotten, and the whole formed such a truly national picture and was so novel for Mrs. Hamilton that she enjoyed it more than the most magnificent Court entertainment I could imagine.

At the moment when these good people were about to drink my health I presented my friend to them as the person to whom their respect was due, told them their new village must be called 'Hamilton' after her, and wished them all kinds of prosperity in a place which bore so dear a name. I then presented them with a gift of bread and salt and sent them away so happy and grateful that the memory of that day is still preserved in the little colony. My friend took a lively interest in their happiness, paid them several visits, and had their welfare at heart to the very end of her life.

(I must explain here that the gift of bread and salt is an ancient custom, religiously observed throughout Russia. When a person goes to live in a new house the nearest relatives and friends present him with those things. Among the gentry the gift takes the form of a piece of furniture, jewelry, or anything else that might be wanted. But among peasants it is still what it was in the good old days—a loaf of bread with a little salt, conveying the wish that the new inhabitants should never lack these two necessities of life.)

From Troitskoe we went to Krugloe, my estate in Belorussia, near Mogilev, given to me by the Empress. In this way, my friend was able to see a considerable part of the provinces of Moscow, Kaluga, Smolensk, and Mogilev. We came back to Petersburg very nearly at the end of autumn.

At about that time of the year it was customary for the Academy of Sciences to read the works sent up the previous year by various scholars competing for various prizes. I did not relish figuring at these scientific conferences, particularly when they met in public session. But Mrs. Hamilton was so keen to see me perform my part of Director that I yielded to her insistent entreaties and was forced to overcome my extreme unwillingness to appear in that role. As the newspapers had announced the date on which the prizes would be distributed and had made it known that the sitting would as usual be public, there was a great concourse of people, including foreign Ambassadors and even ladies. I made my speech as short as possible, cutting it down to five or six minutes. All the same, I nearly fainted, and my shyness, which never leaves me on such occasions, was so great that I was covered with sweat and felt feverish, and had to have recourse to a glass of iced water which had been prepared for me.

I was delighted when the session was over, and I have never since presided over one held in public.

About that time we heard of the death of Mr. Shcherbinin's father. A false friend of my daughter's, in the hope of extracting jewels and money from her all the more easily if she were no longer with me, advised her to write to her husband, from whom she had been separated for many years, offering to go back to him. When I heard that she had written to him I did not think it proper to oppose the weight of my maternal authority to her wishes, but I did all that friendship and affection could do to dissuade her from carrying out her intentions, giving many powerful reasons which it is unnecessary to detail here. Tears, entreaties, and bitter sorrow amounting almost to despair affected my health. I foresaw all that in fact happened afterward. Besides, I was well aware of my daughter's extravagance, and the fatal embarrassments into which it would soon lead her were clear to me in advance. She promised not to remain in Petersburg, but to live instead either with her husband's family or on her estates.

I must be spared the recital of certain events which I cannot recall without a shudder. Suffice it to say that I became very ill and suffered spasms and fits of vomiting that resulted in an internal rupture. I soon became so weak that my sister and Mrs. Hamilton entertained fears for my life. I could not recognize the streets through which I was daily driven in my carriage on the way to my country house; my mind was alive only to the grief my daughter caused me and to forebodings of the future.

One day, my sister and my friend prevailed on me to take the road to Annenhof, and we stopped in a wood bordering on my estate. I had had nothing built there yet, and two posts with a beam overhead served as an entrance gate to my grounds. The carriage went slowly on in front, followed by my friend and my sister. I remained slightly behind, and as

I was passing through the gate the heavy cross-beam fell on my head. A scream from my sister and my friend brought back the servants, who were looking for mushrooms in the wood. I sat down on the ground and, begging my companions to keep calm, I took off my night cap and hat which, I believe, had saved my life, and asked them to see if there was a fracture, for the place hit by the beam was giving me pain. There was no external mark, but my friend insisted that we should get into the carriage and return to town as quickly as possible to consult Dr. Rogerson. I thought, on the contrary, that it would be preferable to walk as much as I could, to draw the blood to the legs and procure a more general circulation.

When we reached town, the doctor was immediately called. He looked worried and asked me whether I felt sick, but I smiled saying that though I had felt it, I was sure he would not have to trepan my skull, for there was a genie watching over me who made me live at all costs and in spite of myself.

Indeed, this accident had no consequences; I was not to be destroyed by physical shocks and pains. Would to God I had been as well armed against ills of a moral nature!

My health, though impaired, was gradually improving, but my friend's departure in the summer following, 1785, plunged me back into a melancholy which I could overcome only by constant activity, either by occupying myself with the two Academies or by inspecting the work and buildings on my estate. I even worked with the masons building the walls of my house.

The following winter my son and Prince Potemkin came to St. Petersburg for a short time, and the absurd rumor that my son would be favorite was again revived. One day, Mr. Samoilov, Prince Potemkin's nephew, called at my house to inquire whether Prince Dashkov was at home. He was not, and Samoilov therefore paid me a visit, in the course of which, after a few preliminary remarks, he said that his uncle, Prince Potemkin, wished to see Prince Dashkov early in the afternoon, hinting that that was the 'lover's hour'.

I answered that nothing of what he was saying was any concern of mine, and that perhaps he ought to be saying it to Prince Dashkov. Personally, I told him, I was too fond of the Empress to oppose her in any of her desires, but I had too much self-respect to have any part in dealings of that nature, and if ever my son became favorite I would use his influence but once only—to obtain leave of absence for several years and a passport to go abroad.

Catherine II in 1762
(From an engraving by Chemezov)

When the time came for my son to return to his regiment my sorrow at his departure was lessened by the fact that it put an end to all these conjectures.

The summer following, Her Majesty went to Finland.[1] She put as much charm and friendliness in appealing to me to accompany her as if it were a great sacrifice on my part to do so, whereas I was, in fact, very glad to

---

[1] The reason for the journey was to meet King Gustavus III of Sweden. It was a difficult time for Catherine for purely personal reasons. Grigorii Orlov, her one-time favorite and the only one she ever wanted to marry, had just died. "I beg of you," she wrote to the King before setting out from St. Petersburg, "not to remind me of the losses I have suffered . . . for I do not want to weep when I am with you."—K. F.

Princess Dashkova in old age.

make this excursion in order to see Finland and dissipate a melancholy I was unable to shake off. The King of Sweden was expected to come to Frederikshamn, and I was curious to meet him and compare him to the Duke of Sudermania whom I know well.

This meeting of two enlightened Sovereigns, relatives and neighbors, promised to be very interesting, and I gratefully accepted the Empress's proposal.

On the day fixed for our departure I received a visit from the Chargé d'Affaires of His Swedish Majesty because the Minister, Mr. Nolken, had gone to meet the King. The Chargé d'Affaires told me it was the King's intention to decorate me with the Grand Cross of the Order of Merit, and he was highly gratified to learn that I should be accompanying the Empress, as His Majesty had always ardently desired to know me.

"This latter sentiment, Sir," I replied, "is highly flattering; as to the decoration, I beseech you to dissuade the King from granting it to me, firstly, because I am a country-cousin type of person, embarrassed enough to wear on my shoulder the Order I already possess and secondly, because this distinction has never yet been conferred on any woman and will therefore increase the number of my enemies by giving rise to more jealousy than any pleasure this favor can afford me."

I concluded by begging him to assure His Swedish Majesty that I was deeply aware of his kindness, and that it was the high esteem in which I held his character and intelligence that encouraged me to make this refusal.

We left the Palace that evening and crossed the river by launch. On the other—the so-called Vyborg—side we found our coaches waiting for us and proceeded in them to the town of Vyborg, the former capital of Finland, where we lodged in different streets. I was allotted a very good and, better still, a very clean house. The next day, the judges, certain officers of State, and the nobility as well as the military, were presented to Her Majesty who greeted them with all the grace and goodness that were typical of her and that won every heart.

I have so little taste for detailed descriptions of my journeys that I have failed to describe events in their right sequence. I should have said that we slept on our way at one of the Imperial country residences where there was a Palace which very comfortably lodged us all. I ought also to have mentioned who were the persons accompanying the Empress. I was the only woman. The rest were all men—Mr. Lanskoi (the favorite), Count Ivan Chernyshev, Count Stroganov, Mr. Chertkov, all of them traveling in the Empress's coach, which thus contained six of us altogether. The other members of the suite were the Master of the Horse Mr. Naryshkin; Mr. Bezborodko, Principal Secretary; Mr. Strekalov, the Comptroller of the Imperial Household; and two Chamberlains who were sent in advance to the Swedish frontier to pay their respects to the King and announce the Empress's approach.

The following evening we arrived at Frederikshamn, where we were less well lodged than hitherto; and the next day the King himself came. He was immediately conducted to Her Majesty's apartment. His suite remained in the ante-room and were introduced to me. Here we made acquaintance, and when the two Sovereigns entered, the Empress presented me to the King.

The dinner was gay, and later the Empress and the King had a private conference together. This was a daily habit all the time we remained at Frederikshamn.

I have very little faith indeed in the sincerity of crowned heads when they have to deal with each other; I think, even, that in spite of all the resources which intelligence, wit, and courtesy can afford, they find each other boring after a while, and politics in the end render their daily intercourse both embarrassing and heavy.

The King of Sweden, under the name of the Count of Haga, came on the third day to my door. I sent out to say that I was not at home, and when I came to the Empress's apartment that evening, before the usual circle of friends had yet assembled, I told her that I had refused Count Haga's visit. She was not pleased at this, but I told her that the King's visit to Paris had so frenchified him that he could have found no pleasure in the company of a person as simple and sincere as myself. Her Majesty begged me to receive the King the following day and to make the visit as long as possible.

It was obvious that Her Majesty wanted more time for herself and less time to spend with the King. I therefore obeyed, and received him the following day. We had a very interesting conversation. His Majesty had a great deal of wit and intelligence and was very eloquent, but he also had the prejudices of a king, and, what is worse, of a traveled king— that is to say, he had false notions about everything he had seen abroad. For these illustrious travelers are only shown the most favorable side of things; everything is so arranged that they can see only the deceptive exterior. Another evil attendant on the travels of sovereigns or their heirs is that neither incense nor adulation is spared to gain them over. When they return home, therefore, they expect adoration from their subjects and are not content with anything short of it.

This is why I have always been against these illustrious personages traveling abroad; I would far sooner they traveled about in their own country, without pomp and ceremony, the expense of which is borne by the people and not by the Court, and with the firm resolve to obtain full information regarding each province.

In the course of our conversation, I perceived that His Swedish Majesty had been completely gulled in France, that he had swallowed with immense relish all the flattery lavished on him and that he, therefore, was greatly prejudiced in favor of that country and its people. I took the liberty of not always agreeing with him, basing my opinion on my own experiences in France during the two separate occasions on which I had been there and had journeyed both into the interior and to the frontier provinces, adding that I was too unimportant in comparison with His Majesty for people to bother to mislead me, and I was consequently allowed to see things as they really were. Count Armfelt, famous for the misfortunes and the persecutions he afterward suffered at the hands of the Duke of Sudermania after the King's death, shared many of my views. In a word, I was very pleased when the Royal visit came to an end and the King was conducted to the Empress's apartments, where I followed him soon after.

His Swedish Majesty left the following day, after making presents to the members of the Empress's suite. To me personally he gave, as token of his friendship, a ring with his portrait surrounded by huge diamonds which made it monstrous.

Both parties left Frederikshamn at the same time. We went straight to Tsarskoe Selo, where we arrived the day before the anniversary of Her Majesty's accession to the throne, so that I did not even have the time to go to town. The very first thing I did was to unset the diamonds round the King of Sweden's portrait and give them to my niece, Miss Polianskaia, who, with the other maids-of-honor, was present at the celebrations. (I afterward put in little pearls to replace the diamonds round the King's portrait.)

On our way back to Tsarskoe Selo I was subjected to a ridiculous attack by the favorite, Lanskoi. Prince Bariatinskii, as Grand Marshal of the Court, had orders to send daily to the Academy for insertion in *The Petersburg Gazette* a report on our progress and on all that happened in the different cities through which we passed and places where we stopped, and so on and so forth. The Prince spoke to me about it, and I told him that whatever he signed would be published at once, as I had long ago given orders to that effect. I had also issued instructions that nothing should be published on the subject of our Court unless it had been signed either by him or by Orlov, the Deputy Marshal, and nothing should be changed—not even the spelling.

Lanskoi told me that the *Gazette*'s accounts of Her Majesty's dinners and halts during our recent journey had made no mention of any person apart from Her Majesty except myself.

"You can," I replied, "ask Prince Bariatinskii for the reason. I have neither written nor sent the articles, and he will even be able to tell you that since I have been administering the Academy the *Gazette* has never contained anything concerning the Court which has not been sent in by him and Orlov over their signature."

"But all the same," he insisted, "you alone are mentioned apart from Her Majesty."

"I have told you already," I answered, "you must apply to Prince Bariatinskii if you want to know why there is no mention of your names in the *Gazette*. Personally, I never saw a single word of any of those articles and have never even given them any thought."

The favorite went on repeating the same thing. Tired of listening to him, I said:

"You know, Sir, great as is the honor of dining with my Sovereign— and I fully appreciate it—it does not surprise me, for it is one I have always enjoyed ever since I left my cradle. The late Empress Elizaveta was my godmother, and she came to our house more than once a week. I have often dined sitting on her lap, and later, when I was able to sit on a chair, I dined at table with her. I am not likely, therefore, to publish in a *Gazette* something to which I have always been accustomed and to which my birth entitles me."

I judged our silly conversation to be at an end, but not at all—he insisted on returning to the charge. The drawing room was beginning to fill with people, and I said to him, loud enough to be heard by everyone, that a person whose actions had no other motive but honesty and whose services were devoted entirely to the welfare of his country might not always enjoy a brilliant fortune or wield great influence, but must at least be free from anxiety as he quietly pursued his course, and might sometimes survive those dazzling but fragile meteors that were often seen to burst.

The Empress then appeared and delivered me by her presence from this stupid conversation.

My own words turned out to be prophetic. Lanskoi died the following summer, less than a year later, and he quite literally burst—his belly burst.

CHAPTER XXV

❦

That winter I had many domestic worries, and my health suffered very much in consequence. In the spring I asked for a two months' leave of absence, during which I went to Troitskoe. On my return journey I passed through Krugloe, where I stayed no more than a week, but had the satisfaction of seeing that the property had improved considerably, that my peasants were less wretched and less lazy, that they had twice as many horses and head of cattle as they had had when they were first given to me, and that they esteemed themselves happier now than they had been either under a Polish master or under the administration of the Crown.

The work in connection with the two Academies diverted my mind from sad thoughts which became increasingly frequent.

The war with Sweden soon broke out and enabled the Empress to give proof of that firmness of spirit which can be seen in the history of her reign.[1] A curious episode occurred in the course of the war. I have already mentioned that at the time of my first journey abroad I had made the acquaintance of the Duke of Sudermania, the brother of the King of Sweden. He now sent a flag of truce to Kronstadt with a letter for Admiral Greig, asking him to forward to me a box which he had found in a vessel he had seized, but which was addressed to me. And to it he added a letter which he had written to me himself.

As a foreigner and also one of my intimate friends, Admiral Greig saw himself obliged to act with the utmost discretion on this occasion, and he sent the whole thing to the Council of State at Petersburg. The Empress, who at that time almost always presided over its meetings, commanded

---

[1] The war of 1788–90, ending with the Peace of Värälä.—K. F.

the box and the Duke's letter to be sent to me without opening them. I was then at my country house, and was greatly surprised to learn that a messenger of the State Council wished to see me. The messenger handed me a large packet and the Duke of Sudermania's letter couched in the most flattering terms, in which the Duke wrote that he had found the packet, addressed to me, in one of the ships which had fallen to him as prize during the present war between Russia and Sweden. As he had lost none of the esteem for me with which I had inspired him when we had first met in Aachen and Spa, and did not wish the war, so unnatural, in his opinion, between two Sovereigns so closely related to each other, to interfere with private individuals, he hastened to forward the packet to its rightful destination.

The packet was from the famous Franklin, whose feelings of friendship and esteem for me had prompted him to propose my membership of the highly respected and celebrated Philosophic Society of Philadelphia. I was unanimously elected and received a Member's Diploma, and from that time on the Society never missed an opportunity of sending me works it had published. The packet contained several of these, as well as a letter from the Secretary. It flattered me far more to receive Franklin's letter than the Duke's, for I considered him to be a very superior man who combined profound erudition with simplicity of dress and manner, whose modesty was unaffected, and who had great indulgence for other people. I wrote to Franklin and to the Secretary of the Philosophic Society thanking them most sincerely for the works they had sent me.

But before doing so I dismissed the messenger, telling him that I would at once go to the Palace myself and show the papers to the Empress. I did, in fact, drive immediately to town or rather straight to Court, even though it was half past four in the afternoon—a time at which no one, not even the Ministers, presented himself. On entering the Empress's dressing room I told the footman on duty that if Her Majesty was not busy I should be delighted to speak to her and show her the papers I had received that morning.

The Empress invited me into her bedroom where I found her writing at a small table. I handed to her the Duke of Sudermania's letter, adding: "And these are letters from Franklin and the Secretary of the Philosophic Society of Philadelphia, of which I am an unworthy member."

When the Empress had finished reading the Duke's letter, I asked her what her commands were on the subject. "Please," she said, "let this correspondence drop—don't answer him."

"The correspondence," I replied, "is hardly a close one, since this is the first letter I have received from him in twelve years. The Duke will think me rude and ill-mannered for not answering his letter, but it is a small sacrifice to make—I wish I could make greater ones every day. But let me remind Your Majesty of the faithful portrait I once drew for you of that Prince—perhaps you will find that he has not written this epistle for the love of me, as the saying is, but because he wanted to clutch at an opportunity to negotiate his own interests separately from those of the King his brother."

Her Majesty would not agree to a continuation of this correspondence, but it became obvious a few months later that I had judged the Duke rightly for what he was, and that it would have been possible to detach his interests from those of his brother, and thus paralyze the Swedish fleet.

On leaving the Empress—who had invited, or rather pressed, me to stay the evening and see the play that was to be performed at the Hermitage—I met her equerry, Mr Rähbinder, who was alone in the antechamber, as it was too early yet for the arrival of any of the company. Mr Rähbinder, a man of great merit in the full sense of the word, and always a good friend of mine, came up to pay his respects, saying that he knew why I had been to see the Empress.

"That is very probable," I said, thinking of the flag of truce and the Duke of Sudermania's letter. "But I should like to know all the same how you came to hear of it."

"I received a letter from Kiev," he replied, "which informed me that your son's marriage took place just as he was leaving Kiev with his regiment. The ceremony was performed during a halt."

I nearly fell backward, but had sufficient strength in me to ask him the name of the girl my son had married. He said it was Alferova, and seeing me about to faint, the poor man could not understand why his words had produced such an effect on me.

"A glass of water," I said to him, "for Heaven's sake!"

He ran to get it for me, and when I had recovered a little, I told him my interview with Her Majesty concerned a letter I had received from the Duke of Sudermania, and he was the first to inform me of a marriage which may be reprehensible, since my son had not asked for my approval.

My poor Rähbinder was extremely sorry at finding himself the bearer of such unpleasant news, but I begged him not to mention it again and to try to divert my thoughts by talking about something else; I could then, perhaps, recover my strength and my wits sufficiently to obey Her Majesty's most kind command to spend the evening with her.

But the effort I had to make very nearly proved my undoing. For it was noticed that I looked worried and uncomfortable, and the conclusion might well have been drawn that I was entertaining a criminal correspondence with the enemies of the State, had not Her Majesty spoken to me several times, and, noticing that I was sad and too sunk in my own thoughts to understand anything happening on the stage, made her conversation with me as gay and amusing as only she knew how.

After the play I did not join the others in the Empress's apartments— I went home instead. Overwhelmed by mental anguish and distress, I succumbed to a nervous fever and for days could do nothing but weep. I considered my husband's behavior to his mother when he wanted to marry me, and could not help thinking that all the sacrifices I had made for my children and the constancy with which I had devoted myself solely to my son's education should have entitled me to more confidence and consideration on his part. I had always imagined that I had deserved my children's friendship and respect to a greater degree than my mother-in-law, and that therefore my son would consult me on a matter so important to our mutual happiness as his marriage.

Two months later I received a letter in which he asked my permission to marry the girl, although he was already married to her and it was common knowledge and gossip in Petersburg.

I was aware by then that the girl was pregnant, and I had gathered information about her family; to find myself now treated with derision by being asked to give my consent to something that had already taken place almost drove me out of my mind. The marriage seemed to me both inconceivable and ridiculous, because the young person had neither beauty nor wit nor education. Her father had lately risen from shop-assistant to officer at the Customs, where he had stolen and plundered to increase his fortune, while the mother, though born a Potemkina and therefore of good family, had become a prostitute and had married that man for lack of anyone better to take her.

My son's letter was accompanied by another from Field-Marshal Count Rumiantsev in which the latter spoke of the prejudice of birth and of the instability and insufficiency of riches, and generally gave the impression of offering me advice. In fact, his letter was all the more ridiculous, to put it mildly, in that I had never given him occasion and, still less, *right,* to interfere between my son and me in a matter of such essential moment. I replied, with biting sarcasm disguised as most perfect civility, that among all the follies to which I might be prone, the tendency to attach exaggerated weight to the advantages of birth and to wax enthusiastic about them

had never had a place; that not having His Excellency's gift of eloquence
I should not undertake the task of describing to him the sentiments that
led me to prefer a good education and the type of character it ought to
produce, to the bauble of childish ambition, and so on.

To my son I merely wrote these few words:

"When your father wished to marry Countess Catherine Vorontsova,
he drove post-haste to Moscow to ask his mother's consent. You are married already; I have known it for some time, and I also know that I deserve
no less than did my mother-in-law to expect obedience and friendship
from my son."

I continued to suffer from a fever brought on by the state of my nerves,
lost all appetite and was wasting visibly away. Alone in my house, I fancied
myself alone in the universe, since I had lost the consolation of those from
whom I could have expected it.

In the winter my physical health somewhat improved, and I busied myself with my duties as Director of one Academy and President of the other.
I had assigned to myself the task of assembling all words beginning with
three letters of the alphabet, for the dictionary of the Russian Academy,
the first in our language to list words in their etymological order. I also
accepted the work which had been adjudged me at a general meeting of
all members and which consisted in explaining in precise terms all words
bearing upon morals, politics, and government.

This task—no easy one for me—occupied much of my time, and during some of the day took my mind off the sad thoughts that beset me. I
never went out to see people except once or twice a week to spend the
evening with the Empress in a small and select circle of friends who made
up what was known as Her Majesty's Set.

In the spring I went to live in a country house belonging to my father.
It was further away from town than my own which was not yet finished,
and the few people who came to trouble my solitude did so in vain, for no
visitors were admitted. I spent the summer in a mood so despondent that
but for the grace of God I should not have triumphed over the thoughts
of gloom and despair that had taken possession of my mind. For as soon
as I fancied myself forsaken by my children, life became a burden which I
should have surrendered readily—indeed, gladly—to anyone who came
to destroy it.

But the following year was even worse. I obtained leave of absence for
two months to visit my lands in Belorussia and in Troitskoe. On my return,
my sister, Madame Polianskaia, told me that a dressmaker, Genoutzy by

name, had obtained an injunction against my daughter, forbidding her to leave Petersburg, that the police were therefore keeping a close watch on her, and that she was so ill that Dr. Rogerson considered her life would be endangered if she did not leave immediately for the waters and baths of Aachen.

This was heart-breaking news. I went to see my daughter the very next day and found her up, but very much changed, breathing with difficulty, and with a greenish tinge to her complexion. As soon as she saw me she wanted to throw herself at my feet. I did not let her. Instead, I threw my arms round her and kissed her, and told her she must keep calm and look after her health, and all might yet turn out for the best provided she behaved a little better in future. I cut short my visit, against my own natural inclination, for I thought she would want to rest after the shock my sudden appearance must have caused her. Besides, I needed to be alone and even to go to bed to soothe my nerves.

The following day, I went to see her again, and when I thought she felt a little better I suggested she might come and stay with me at my little country place near Petersburg. I promised to settle with her creditors, obtain Her Majesty's permission to let her go to the baths of Aachen, and arrange for her departure in the summer by standing surety for her and her debts, and furnishing her with all the money she required for the journey. She seemed to recover a little, and when I had arranged everything, she left for Aachen accompanied by an English friend of mine called Miss Bates, while I remained alone in Kirianovo.

We had agreed, my daughter and I, that after she had taken the waters and finished her baths at Aachen, she would come back to me without further waste of time. Instead, as soon as her course of treatment was over she left for Vienna and thence for Warsaw, and after thus uselessly squandering the 14,000 roubles I had given her for her journey she was left with no money, ran into debt and was for a time in great peril as she happened to be in Warsaw when there was a kind of revolution throughout Poland.

The excellent Miss Bates, having received the assurance that Madame Shcherbinina would continue her travels indefinitely, asked for permission to return to me. She bravely crossed Germany in a chaise with no one to accompany her but one German servant who could speak the language. Yet although it was a comfort for me to have Miss Bates, I deplored my daughter's senseless conduct which laid her open to all sorts of unpleasantness and distressed a fond and loving mother who had generously forgiven her all the sorrow she had caused her. It grieved me, too, that my daughter would no longer have Miss Bates by her side—that good and kind person who would have preserved her completely from the deceits and treachery of disloyal companions.

Miss Bates found me much changed. Her surprise and grief were great and unconcealed, but they became even greater when I told her of all the mental anguish through which I had passed. Everything—the past, the future—seemed black to me. I had fallen a prey to dark and horrible thoughts. I shudder now to confess that the idea of suicide came to my perplexed mind, and but for religion—the failing soul's support, the unfortunate's shield and protection against despair—I do not know what excess I might not have committed. Neither the thought that self-immolation was always a coward's way out, nor any other reasoning would have sufficed to save me from myself. I was too unhappy to obey the voice of reason, or ambition, or any other human feeling. I longed ardently for death.

CHAPTER XXVI

That winter, I suffered less from rheumatism, although the dampness of my country house had latterly increased. I drove out in my carriage to take the air, and followed my custom of dining twice a week with the Empress.

At one of those dinners Count Bruce, who happened to be the General A.D.C. on duty that week, speaking of courage, expressed surprise at the dash and valour which he had seen in soldiers scaling the walls of a town from which they were being shot at.

"This," I said to him, "does not surprise me at all, for the most faint-hearted man, the greatest coward in the world, could force himself to assume some sort of momentary courage and leap into the fray, in the belief that it will not last long. Besides, Sir, if you do not mind my saying so, a man who is ready to devote his life to a cause and, if necessary, to endure long drawn-out suffering for the sake of it, requires, in my estimation, a courage very different to soldierly valour in battle. If you were to let your foot or hand be rubbed in one spot with a blunt wooden blade and bore with it patiently for a long time, I should consider you braver and more master of yourself than if I saw you marching against the enemy for two hours at a stretch without showing any inclination to retreat."

The Empress understood me, but the Count began on a train of reasoning which was not very clear and cited suicide as proof of courage. I could not help replying that I had given much thought to that fatal act and after due consideration had finally concluded that, quite apart from failing in one's duty to the Creator and to society, deliberate self-infliction of death is a clear proof of a lack of fortitude, and it is lack of courage and patience that explains why men commit this cowardly act.

Her Majesty never took her eyes off me, and I told her with a smile that I should never do anything to hasten or delay my death, and that in spite of the sophism of J. Jacques Rousseau which had greatly appealed to me in my childhood because I had admired courage even then, I considered that it required a greater strength of mind to bear with suffering without recourse to a final remedy which we have not the right to use.

The Empress asked me what sophism of Rousseau's I was referring to, and in which of his writings I had read it.

"It is, Ma'am," I answered, "in the New Héloïse that he says: 'We are wrong to fear death, for so long as we are, It is not, and when It is, we are no more.' "

"He is a very dangerous author," replied Her Majesty. "His style makes him fascinating reading, and he goes to young people's heads."

"I refused to see him, Ma'am," I continued, "when we were both of us living in Paris. His way of keeping his incognito proves what a charlatan he was in his pretended modesty, and how tormented with the desire to make everyone talk of him and to draw, if possible, the whole world's attention to himself. His writings are certainly dangerous, as Your Majesty has just remarked, for young people will easily mistake his sophistries for syllogisms."

From that day the Empress never let a single opportunity escape for distracting and diverting me; and I was deeply touched by her kindness. One day when we were alone together she asked me to write a play in Russian for her theater at the Hermitage. In vain did I protest that I had not a shadow of a talent for that sort of composition. She returned to the subject again and again, and said that the reason why she was pressing me to do it was that she knew from personal experience how much it amused and occupied the author. In the end I was forced to promise her a play, but on one condition: that she read the first two acts, corrected them, and told me frankly whether they ought to be thrown in the fire. She agreed, and I set to work that same evening.

I finished two acts the following day and took them to the Empress the day after. The name of the play was Mr. This-and-That (Toisiokov), after the principal character, for I did not want people to fancy that I had in mind any particular individual living in Petersburg, and chose the most universal type of all—a man with a weak character—unfortunately so common in our society.

Her Majesty very kindly retired to her bedroom together with me in order to read through my piece of extempore writing which did not, in my estimation, deserve that honor. Some of the scenes made the Empress laugh, and whether out of the goodness of an indulgent heart or out of a certain fondness for me which she sometimes showed, she found those two acts perfect. I told her the plot and the ending which I proposed to have in the third act. There again, Her Majesty forced me to change my intentions by asking me to have five acts in all. However, I think the play lost all the more by being drawn out in that way, because it bored me and I felt that unnecessary padding would make the plot somewhat stiff. In the end, I finished it as best I could, and two days later a fair copy of it was already in Her Majesty's hands. The play was given at The Hermitage and printed immediately afterward.

Early in the following year I begged Her Majesty to grant my son a three months' leave of absence from his regiment to enable him to go to Warsaw, pay his sister's debts, have her released, and bring her back home. Her Majesty gave her consent, and I had to sacrifice all the money I had and borrow some to live on for six months until the income from my property started coming in. My son made the journey and brought back his sister to Kiev, where he was stationed, and whence I received letters from them both confirming their arrival. These were the first I had received from my children for many years, and as no other interest or love had ever taken their place in my heart, it may well be imagined how miserable I had been.

My brother, Count Aleksandr, employed in his Department of Trade and Foreign Commerce a young man named Mr. Radishchev, who had been to Leipzig University and of whom he was very fond. One day in the Russian Academy, I was shown, as proof of the fact that we had many writers who did not know their own language, a pamphlet written and published by that same Radishchev. It was the life and eulogy of a certain Ushakov who had studied with him at Leipzig. I mentioned this to my brother the same evening, and he immediately sent a man off to a bookshop to buy the pamphlet for him. His protégé, I remarked, had the itch to write, though neither his style nor his ideas had been properly digested, and some of his thoughts or expressions were dangerous in the times in which we lived.

A few days later my brother told me I had been too severe on Radishchev's little work; he had read it and found it merely useless, since the man whom it was about, Ushakov, had never said anything remarkable, and that was the end of it.

"I may have been a little severe in my judgment," I agreed, but as he was interested in the author, I thought it my duty to warn him of what I fancied I had seen in that silly little pamphlet. A man who had done nothing in his life but sleep, drink, and eat could only find a panegyrist in someone with a mania for seeing himself in print. That writer's itch, I said, might one day induce his protégé to write something really reprehensible.

And so in fact it turned out. The following summer I was spending my leave of absence in Troitskoe when I received a letter from my brother informing me that to his great distress my prophecy about Radishchev had been fulfilled, for that man had published a work which, he was sorry to admit, could be taken for a tocsin to revolution; he had been denounced and banished to Siberia.[1]

Far from being gratified at the correctness of my conclusions as proved by this catastrophe, I was greatly saddened by the fate of Radishchev, and even more by the distress which it caused my brother and was likely to cause him for a long time. I foresaw, too, that the man of whom Count Aleksandr was so fond, but who was no friend really, would try to involve him in this affair. In fact he did, and under any sovereign other than the great Catherine he would have succeeded in doing him harm, but on her he made no impression. However, my brother was disgusted by his behavior, which, joined to the intrigues of the Minister of Justice, upset him so much that he asked for a year's leave of absence, pleading ill-health which necessitated a period of rest and country air. He was granted his leave and went to live on his estate, while I remained in Petersburg, feeling quite alone among people who seemed to me more odious than ever. I hoped that he would come back before the period he had set himself was over, but he did not wait for the expiration of his leave to put in a request for resignation, which was duly granted. It was in the year 1794 that he finished his career of public service, which had been useful to his country and honorable to himself.[2]

A year and a half after this, the widow of one of our most famous writers of tragedies, Kniazhnin, begged me to publish his last tragedy,

[1] Ushakov's influence on Russian political thought, via Radishchev, was, in fact, greater than realized by Princess Dashkova. Radishchev's main work, for which he suffered exile to Siberia, was in effect an attack on the institution of serfdom, thinly disguised as a diary and entitled *A Journey from Petersburg to Moscow.* For further details see Index under Radishchev, Aleksandr, and Ushakov, Fedor.—K. F.

[2] In fact Aleksandr Vorontsov's retirement was forced upon him and lasted from 1791 to 1802 when he became Chancellor. See Index under Vorontsov, Aleksandr.—K. F.

which was still in manuscript form.[3] All the proceeds were to go to his children. As the man who approached me on Madame Kniazhnina's behalf was Mr. Kozodavlev, a Councillor at the chancellery of the Academy of Sciences, I told him I would issue the necessary instructions as soon as he had read it and reported to me that it contained nothing contrary to law and religion. I would, I said, have all the more pleasure in entrusting him with this work as he had a perfect knowledge of the Russian language, was himself an author, and knew perfectly well what we were allowed to publish and what we were not.

Mr. Kozodavlev said in his report that the play was based on certain historical events that had occurred in Novgorod; he had found nothing in it to which censorship could take exception, and in fact, it all ended with the triumph of the Sovereign and the submission of Novgorod as well as of the rebels. Thereupon, I gave instructions to have the play printed at the least possible cost to the playwright's widow. The consequences that flowed from this, and the circumstances to which they were due, were so absurd as to be hardly credible. Field-Marshal Count Ivan Saltykov, who never read anything, claimed, at I know not whose instigation, to have read the tragedy and informed Prince Zubov, the favorite, that it had very dangerous implications at the present time. I have no idea whether the Empress or Prince Zubov had read it, but I soon had the visit of the Chief of Police[4] who asked very politely for a signed order which would give him admission to the storeroom where the Academy's books were kept, to enable him to take all the copies of the tragedy there were, as the Empress considered the play too dangerous for circulation.

I gave him the signed order he had asked for, adding that I did not think he would find a single copy: but that the tragedy was included in the last volume of The Russian Theatre which the Academy had printed on its own account; he could, if he liked, spoil the volume and tear the play out, which would merely make me laugh as it was less dangerous to sovereigns than many a French tragedy acted at The Hermitage.

In the afternoon it was Mr. Samoilov, the Minister of Justice, who came to reproach me, on the part of the Empress, with having published the play. I do not know whether the object of all this was to intimidate

---

[3] The tragedy was called Vadim of Novgorod. The hero is made spokesman for the Veche (National Assembly) of medieval Novgorod. The publication of the play coincided with the revolutionary events in France, and, in the circumstances, it was interpreted as a subtle attack on monarchical institutions. See Index under Kniazhnin, Iakov.—K. F.

[4] Nikita Ryleev. For further particulars see Index under that name.—K. F.

me or to anger me, but it was not attained, which ever it was. I spoke very firmly and calmly to Count Samoilov and expressed my surprise that Her Majesty could have entertained so much as a moment's suspicion that I should disseminate anything prejudicial to her interests; as to the allusion he said the Empress had made to Radishchev's book (he quoted her as saying that "this tragedy of Kniazhnin's was the second work of a dangerous kind which had been published"), I wished Her Majesty would compare the two, and particularly that she would compare this wretched tragedy, against which she had been so unfavorably influenced, with any of the French tragedies which were being acted in the public theaters as well as in her own. In any case, it had nothing to do with me, as before authorizing the author's widow to have the play printed for her profit, I had submitted it to the censorship of Councillor Kozodavlev; and I did not want to hear any more of it.

The following evening I went, as usual, to Her Majesty's apartments where her so-called "set" always foregathered as of right. I saw the Empress come in looking both embarrassed and displeased. I went up to her and asked how she was.

"In excellent health," she answered, "but what have I done to you that you should publish dangerous maxims directed against me and my authority?"

"I, Ma'am? Surely you do not think that?"

"Do you know," said the Empress, "that I shall have that tragedy burnt by the Public Executioner?"

I could clearly perceive by the expression of her face—or at least I fondly imagined I could—that that last phrase had been dictated to her, and that it was foreign to her heart and mind.

"And what do I care, Ma'am, if it is burnt by the Executioner? Whoever has to blush for it, it will not be me. Only, for God's sake, before you act in a way so little in harmony with all you do and say, read the play, and you will find it has an ending which is all you yourself and anyone attached to the monarchial form of government can desire; and please remember, Ma'am, that I am neither its author nor the person who will make money out of its publication."

I said this with an air which did not admit of a reply. The Empress sat down at her card table and I did the same.

Two days later I went to the Empress to present my report, determined never to do so again and to hand in my resignation without further ado unless she invited me, as she always did, to accompany her to her Jewel

Chamber in which the great and the small diamond crowns were kept, and where we used to sit and talk alone and quite freely while her hair was being combed and dressed.

Mr. Samoilov whispered into my ear as he came out of the Empress's apartments:

"Her Majesty will appear in a moment. She does not seem to harbor any resentment against you, so don't you worry!"

I answered in my ordinary tone of voice, so as to be heard by those who happened to be in the room:

"I have no need to worry, because I have nothing to reproach myself with. I should be sorry for Her Majesty's sake if she entertained unjust thoughts or sentiments toward me, but in any case I am no novice at suffering injustice."

The Empress soon appeared, and after giving her hand to kiss to those who happened to be in the room, said to me:

"Would you like to come with me, Madam?"

I hope that the readers of these Memoirs will believe me when I say that Her Majesty's invitation gave me immense pleasure, not for my own sake, but for hers, for I felt with sorrow that had she not extended it, my resignation and departure from Petersburg would not have redounded to her credit. I hope, too, that this sentiment will not be attributed to presumptuous pride, which has never been one of my foibles.

In any case, I was so pleased that the Empress had not forced me into a complete breach with her that scarcely had I crossed the threshold of her room than, holding out my hand, I asked her to give me hers to kiss and to forget all that had lately passed between us.

"But, indeed, Princess. . . ."

But I did not let her continue, and quoted a common Russian proverb: "*A grey cat has jumped between us and we must not call it back.*"

The Empress had the goodness to adopt the same attitude as I did. She chuckled good-naturedly and changed the subject. I felt gay and cheerful and made Her Majesty laugh heartily at dinner.

CHAPTER XXVII

The war with Sweden was over. Peace was signed in early August 1790 [1] and there was every hope that a highly advantageous treaty would soon be concluded with the Turks. And when it was—shortly afterward [2]— it was such as to justify all the optimism felt in Petersburg and was well in keeping with the valour of our Army and the dauntless patriotism of some of our officers. In such fear of the Russians did the Turks go that none of the subsequent intrigues of the French could prevail upon them to measure themselves once more against us.

I longed to see my brother again and to revisit my favorite estate. I wished, too, to withdraw entirely from public service as well as from the turmoil and tumult of a life at Court, but I did not want to leave Petersburg before settling my daughter's debts. Besides, I owed 32,000 roubles to the bank on my own account, which I had originally borrowed to pay for my son's education and my travels abroad. As I wanted to live in peace and devote myself entirely to rural pursuits, I decided to sell my house in Petersburg and not to leave town before ensuring for myself that complete independence which can only be the fruit of an untroubled mind.

Mr. Shcherbinin had made over a fine piece of country property to his wife and another one to his cousin, Madame B————. His mother and sisters obtained the rest of his property in trust, and administered it in the hope of annulling these deeds of gift. Mr. Shcherbinin, on the other

[1] The Peace of Värälä, which brought no advantages to either side.—K. F.
[2] The Peace of Jassy 1791, by which Russia obtained Bessarabia and Turkish *de jure* recognition of the Russian occupation of the Crimea.—K. F.

hand, could have terminated the trust, for the Russian law governing the administration of property on behalf of persons declared incapable of administering it themselves very obviously favors the latter. All they have to do is to answer a few questions, for the relatives' application to act as trustees to be rejected. Mr. Shcherbinin made no move in that direction, and even let himself be persuaded by his mother and sisters that their administration of his property was all for his own good.

When I took steps to render my daughter free from her creditors by going bail for her debts during her stay in Aachen, I examined all the bills and drafts signed by her and therefore recognized by her as valid. Among them there were bills not only signed by her husband as well as by herself, but obviously incurred on his behalf as shown by the articles detailed in the bills. These I could not accept without letting myself be fooled. I therefore wrote to Mr. Shcherbinin's trustees and it was from them I learned that he had made over to my daughter a very fine piece of property and had signed a perfectly valid legal document to that effect. I told them they should apply to the Senate which alone possessed the right to confirm or annul it and asked them to examine the bills that had been presented to us; they could then decide in all conscience, which bills I should settle personally, which they should accept on Mr. Shcherbinin's behalf, and which we should pay jointly. The thing dragged on while the Senate was deliberating upon it. I did not want to give the impression of keenness that the land should be awarded to my daughter, for in fact I did not want it at all, being convinced that my daughter's share in the dissipation of her husband's wealth had been all too great. I even had the courage to tell the Minister of Justice, who had considerable influence in the matter, that all I wanted was for the Senate to make its decision, so that before leaving for the country I should know whether I had to mortgage or sell my own property to pay my daughter's debts. I had already sold my house and was living in my father's vast mansion, alone with a very few servants or maids to serve me. I had the impression of being an unhappy princess over whom a wicked wizard had cast an age-long spell.

At last, the Senate's decision gave me back my freedom of movement. The decision was favorable to my daughter and was confirmed by Her Majesty. I paid most of my daughter's debts outright and went bail for the rest, promising to settle them soon after my arrival in Moscow. The administration of my daughter's estate was entrusted to me. The dues I imposed on her peasants were so moderate that they considered themselves lucky indeed and those of them that had left their homes came back again. But, as a result, my daughter's revenues which I received, hardly sufficed to cover the interest on the money I had spent on her.

After thus settling her affairs, I wrote to Her Majesty asking her permission to resign from the administration of the two Academies, and to have a two years' leave of absence from my duties as lady-in-waiting in order to restore my failing health and put my affairs in order.

The Empress did not want me to resign from the Academy altogether, and agreed only to my two years' leave of absence. In vain did I argue that the Academy of Sciences especially would suffer by having an absentee head. She desired me to appoint someone who would be answerable to me and would have no power to do anything without first writing to me to obtain my instructions. She also insisted that I should continue to receive my salary as Director of the Academy of Sciences. This, it is true was equivalent to only 3,000 roubles and had not changed since the time of Mr. Domashnev, who was completely idle and did nothing but ruin the Academy.

The Empress expressed to Count Bezborodko her alarm at the thought that I should wish to retire; and for my part, though I greatly desired to live in the country and see more of my brother, Count Aleksandr, the thought that I should not see my Sovereign for a long time or perhaps ever again, filled me with dismay. My love for her was quite disinterested, for I had been passionately fond of her at a time when she was not Sovereign yet, and I was in the position to be of far greater service to her than she was to me. And though in her treatment of me she did not always obey the dictates of her heart and mind, I continued to love her, admired her whenever she gave me occasion to do so, and considered her far superior to any of the most famous Sovereigns that had ever sat on the Russian throne.

I have lately been reading two books published in Russia. One is called *Catherine the Great* and the other, *Anecdotes of the Reign of Catherine II*. They express feelings which all true Russians must entertain and cherish in their hearts toward a sovereign who really was a mother to her subjects. I must, however, point out an error which occurs equally in both books. It is stated that Catherine knew Greek and Latin, and that of all living languages she preferred French as being the pleasantest.

I think I can say definitely that she knew neither Greek nor Latin, and if to foreigners she spoke French rather than German this was because she wanted people to forget that she was born in Germany. And, indeed, she succeeded, for I have often heard peasants in conversation with me refer to her as their countrywoman as well as their mother.

But I remember her saying on several occasions when discussing writers and European languages with me that German was much richer and more virile than French, and that it was a pity it was not softer, for then French would not be so generally spoken. She thought Russian, which blended the strength, richness, and virility of German with the softness of Italian, would one day become the universal language.

Having at last put everything in order before my departure, I went to spend my last evening with the Empress at the Tauris Palace. She showed me so much attention that I scarcely knew how to take leave of her. At the usual hour Her Majesty withdrew and I wanted to ask her permission to take leave of her in her own room. But the way was barred by the Grand Duke Aleksandr and his charming wife.[3] I saw Prince Zubov in conversation with Their Imperial Highnesses and whispered in his ear to let me pass as I wanted to kiss the Empress's hand, perhaps for the last time, as I had everything ready for leaving Petersburg the following day.

"Wait a moment," he said and presently disappeared. I thought he was going to tell Her Majesty that I wanted to take leave of her, but a full half hour elapsed and no messenger came to fetch me. I went into a room next door, and on finding there one of Her Majesty's footmen I asked him to inform her that I wanted to kiss her hand before leaving Petersburg. He came back in another quarter of an hour to tell me that the Empress was expecting me. Imagine my surprise on entering her room, when instead of that serenity of expression which she had had throughout the evening, instead of an affectionate farewell, I was met with a countenance depicting irritation and even anger.

"I wish you, Madam, a happy journey," was all she said to me.

When people who are in the habit of judging themselves strictly have an untroubled conscience, they cannot think that they have given offence. This was precisely my case; I fancied that Her Majesty had received some unpleasant news that had greatly upset her, and as I withdrew I silently prayed for her peace and prosperity.

The following morning I received the visit of Mr. Novosiltsev, a close relative of Maria Islavishna, who was of the Empress's household and

[3] Later Emperor Aleksandr I and Empress Elizaveta.—K. F.

very much in her confidence.[4] He had come to take leave of me, and I asked him whether Her Majesty had received an unpleasant message the previous night because I saw her suddenly change countenance. But he emphatically denied that there had been any message, and added that the Empress appeared in excellent humor that morning. He had just come from the Palace and would have heard from his cousin if there had been anything. He would, in turn, have told me, as he was a friend of mine. As it was, I did not know how to explain the Empress's attitude during my leave-taking.

Soon I received a letter from the Empress's secretary, Mr. Troshchinskii, which explained the riddle to me. Enclosed in the letter was a tailor's bill signed by my daughter and her husband and accompanied by an affecting petition from the tailor himself couched in terms calculated to flatter and interest Her Majesty. Mr. Troshchinskii informed me on Her Majesty's behalf of her surprise that after contracting to pay my daughter's debts I should think of leaving Petersburg without honoring my obligations.

I must admit the letter made me most indignant, and I resolved forth-with never again to return to Petersburg. I replied to Mr. Troshchinskii that I was even more surprised that Her Majesty should suspect me for an instant of such degrading conduct, that I was returning the bill in order to let her see, if she took the trouble of having it examined, that it was a debt owed by Mr. Shcherbinin to a man's tailor for his own uniforms and his servants' liveries; that I was under no obligation to pay the debts of my son-in-law whose fortune was at least equal to mine; that moreover I had referred the tailor to the Trustees of Mr. Shcherbinin's property who, seeing that the bill regarded no one but Mr. Shcherbinin, had in my presence assured him that the debt would be paid in under two months (it was in fact paid a few months later); that the tailor was entirely satisfied when he left me; and that if he had afterward changed his mind or else had written his petition at the dictation of someone eager to injure me, I did not see why in all justice I should suffer for it.

The author of the petition did, in fact, turn out to be a sycophant of Prince Zubov and it was Zubov, as I soon afterward discovered, who had handed it to the Empress just before I was admitted into her presence on the eve of my departure. He thereby did me a grievous wrong, for I never saw the Empress again, and yet this did not prevent me from treating him

[4] See Index under Perekusikhina, Maria.—K. F.

with cordiality in Petersburg after the accession of the Emperor Aleksandr I and particularly in Moscow after His Majesty's coronation when he was, on the whole, unpopular and held in little esteem.

At last I left Petersburg, with a mixture of feelings which would all have been of one kind if only the sentiments I had always cherished for Catherine II had been capable of alteration.

I took a roundabout way to my destination in order to visit my estate in Belorussia and make arrangements to receive the money I had to pay to my daughter's creditors. But I only stayed eight days there, and no more than a week at Troitskoe, so impatient was I to see my brother, Count Aleksandr.

I had to pass through Moscow on my way to his estate, and there, too, I stopped for only a few days, enough to give the necessary orders for arranging the ground floor apartments of my house simply and unpretentiously but so as to make them habitable in the winter.

I now regarded my public life as being at an end. My head had been proof against the intoxication of success, particularly in the administration of the two Academies, and it was hardly surprising, therefore, that I should have held out against the shocks and reverses of fortune to which Fate had made me a butt. For it is my firm belief that whoever knows how to contain ambition and pride within their proper bounds knows, too, how to hold out against misfortunes.

I now wanted to devote myself entirely to a life in the country and to the love which bound me to my brother. And I looked forward to it not merely with calm and assurance, but with a pleasure which was only disturbed when I reflected that the persons whom I had cherished and respected had damaged their own reputation by treating me with unfair and undeserved harshness.

My arrival was a very pleasant surprise for my brother, but I did not feel I could stay long with him as I was afraid that unless my house were fitted up and heated before the frosts set in I should not be able either to receive my guests there or to live in it myself.

I therefore left for Moscow to supervise the work that was being carried out in my house, and my brother rejoined me earlier than usual.

The following year my brother came to stay with me at Troitskoe. He was delighted with my garden and with my various plantations and buildings, and when I visited him in the autumn he gave me full powers to change the layout of his garden, according to my own taste, and to carry on with the work of tracing out the plantations and walks on which I had been engaged for six days during my stay with him in the previous year.

In the summer of 1796 I went to stay on my estate near Mogilev, where I received letters from several persons in Petersburg who were well aware of what was happening and what was being said at Court. They wrote of their pleasure at the thought of seeing me soon again, for Her Majesty had said several times that she was going to write and invite me to Petersburg so that I could conduct the Grand Duchess Aleksandra to Sweden, so certain was it that her marriage to the King of Sweden would take place.[5]

Letters arrived from my relations in Moscow expressing regret that I should soon be leaving them, and speaking of the strong rumor that a courier had already been despatched by the Empress to request my return to Petersburg. Thereupon I went back with all speed to Troitskoe and from there wrote to the Empress, once again asking that either I should be allowed to retire or at least that my leave of absence be prolonged.

Her reply was gracious, but she only prolonged my leave for another year. However, as I was worried that my long absence might be interpreted unfavorably by her, I wrote to some reliable friends asking them to tell me sincerely in what terms the Empress spoke of me, whether she was spiteful about me or whether she was not. They assured me that Her Majesty had several times spoken in a way which showed how pleased she was with the idea of using my services to conduct her granddaughter to Sweden.

"I know," she said, "that Princess Dashkova loves me too much to refuse me something she knows I have set my heart on, and I shall then not have to worry for my young Queen."

[5] The marriage never took place. King Gustavus IV of Sweden, then aged seventeen, arrived in Russia with his uncle, the Duke of Sudermania, in the autumn of 1796, and after some initial difficulties caused chiefly by religious considerations, agreed to sign the marriage contract. On the day fixed for the ceremony, the Empress—grandmother of the prospective bride—waited for the King to make his appearance in the Great Drawing Room of the Palace, attended by all her family and Court, by dignitaries of Church and State, and by the Diplomatic Corps. The King, however, failed to appear. Instead, five hours later, while the Empress was still waiting, he sent a message that he was, after all, unwilling that his wife should remain Greek Orthodox in a Lutheran country and that he would, therefore, return home without signing the contract. The Empress collapsed with a stroke, and though she afterwards recovered, a second stroke less than two months later proved fatal. See Index under Gustavus IV and Aleksandra.—K. F.

CHAPTER XXVIII

❦

On my return from Krugloe to Troitskoe I applied myself to the completion of the buildings I had begun. Four houses were finished and I laid out plantations which, to me, made the garden pure delight. Every tree, every shrub had been planted either by myself or under my supervision in the exact spot where I wanted it. One is so apt to regard with affection the work of one's own hands, that I have no hesitation in saying that I found Troitskoe to be altogether one of the finest country estates I had ever seen either in Russia or abroad.

There was one reason in particular why I preferred staying in Troitskoe more than anywhere else in the world and found consolation in my life there, and that was the prosperity of my peasants. During the forty years of my administration their number increased from 840 to 1,550. The number of women, whom we never reckon in our calculations, had increased even more, since none of them wanted to marry outside my property, while girls of neighboring estates would often marry peasants from Troitskoe.

I had added to my library, which had by now become very considerable. The ground floor apartments were very comfortably furnished to enable me to live in them more pleasantly during the autumn when I usually suffered from attacks of rheumatism, the result of my life in Scotland. That year was no exception and I was ill during the whole of October until the beginning of November, when a blow fell which for Russia represented the greatest possible disaster and which brought me to the very brink of the grave.

The Serpukhov Marshal of Nobility,[1] Mr. Grigoriev, a most estimable

---

[1] An appointment somewhat akin in some of its functions to a Justice of the Peace as well as to a Lord Lieutenant of a County.—K. F.

and loyal man, very attached to me, came to see me one evening. I was struck, the moment he entered the house, by his unhappy expression and, indeed, the consternation which was very obvious in his demeanor.

"What is the matter with you?" I asked.

"Do you not know, Madame, of the misfortune that has befallen us? The Empress is no more!"

My daughter, who happened to be with me, feared that I should fall and wanted to hold me up.

"No," I said, "have no fear for my life. It is my unhappy fate to survive this blow. I am reserved for other misfortunes yet to come, and to see my country as unhappy as it has been glorious and prosperous in the reign of Catherine II."

I shook in every limb and had nervous spasms that reduced me to a pitiful state and lasted for twenty-four hours, during which I had the sad conviction that death would not ensue.

The words I had uttered at the first shock of the news were all too prophetic. Terror and anxiety soon became the constant feelings of every man and woman. Every family had victims to mourn. Husband, father, uncle suspected in his wife, his son, his heir an informer who might send him to perish in a dungeon or in the depths of Siberia.

Soon my nervous spasms and insomnia affected me to such a point that I could only rarely leave my bed and then only for a short time.

However, I was able to go to Moscow at the beginning of December in order to have leeches applied, quite determined to return to Troitskoe at the first opportunity, for I had already received the copy of a Senatorial decree by virtue of which the Emperor[2] dismissed me from all my offices. I requested Mr. Samoilov, who was still Minister of Justice, to present my humble thanks to His Majesty for having relieved me of a burden too heavy for me to bear.

Having written the letter, I awaited with resignation the persecution which was bound to come, but I found myself caught in a dilemma before I had time to leave for Moscow. A letter reached me, signed Donaurov, in which the latter officially informed me of His Majesty's command to deprive me of all my offices. Now it is not possible to write to a Russian, and even less to address a letter to him, without putting not only the man's surname, but his Christian name and that of his father as well (for example, Ivan son of Boris is known as Ivan Borisovich). But as I did not know the name of that man's father I was at my wits' end what to do, for

[2] Pavel I.—K. F.

failure to answer and acknowledge the receipt of the Emperor's mandate
was a crime against the Emperor. On the other hand, failure to address
the person sending the mandate by his proper style and title would have
implied contempt and would have been tantamount to making an enemy
of him. I decided to write to my cousin, Prince Kurakin, who was still
in favor at the time, asking him to inform Mr. Donaurov that I had not
replied to him immediately because I did not know his proper style of
address and did not want to offend him by making a mistake on that
point; as to my dismissal, I regarded it as an act of favor on the part of
His Majesty.

I informed my brother, Count Aleksandr, of what had just happened
to me, and was dumbfounded when he told me that Donaurov's father
had been pantry-boy in my uncle's, the Grand Chancellors', house, and
had been promoted butler, and then head butler after marrying a Kalmyk
girl who was my aunt's favorite maid.

Deportations and arrests became so frequent that news of them reached
me in spite of my friends' attempts to spare me further distress by concealing them from me. Catherine II's death was a profound shock to me,
and I was struck with consternation at the misfortunes of my country and
at the general terror, for there was not a single family among the nobility
that did not have at least one member either exiled in Siberia or confined
in a fortress.

My ill-health and the melancholy thoughts that it engendered made life
difficult for me, and unless I had been willing to bring it to an untimely
end, it was essential for me to go to Moscow, not to consult the doctors
in whom I had no trust, but to apply leeches and thus calm the blood and
give it a more regular and a healthier circulation.

I arrived in Moscow at nine o'clock on the morning of 4 December and
found in my house some of my relations, worried and impatient to see me,
since they were afraid I might succumb to the grief of losing Catherine II.
My brother, Count Aleksandr, also arrived a few moments later. I was
obliged to go to bed, and midday had not yet struck when Mr. Izmailov,
the Governor-General, was ushered into my room. He was apparently in
a hurry to go to the Senate, and had scarcely sat down before he said to
me, almost in a whisper, that it was his duty to inform me by command
of His Majesty the Emperor, that I must immediately go back to my place
in the country and ponder on the events of the year 1762. To this I replied
in a voice loud enough to be heard by my relatives and friends who were
present, that I should always ponder on the year 1762, and that His Maj-

esty's orders would be all the more faithfully carried out as the events to which he was possibly alluding could never for me be a source of either regret or remorse. If only, I added, the Emperor were to analyze them critically himself, he would not treat me in this way. As to my immediate departure for the country, His Excellency could see for himself that I was unable to do that since it was absolutely essential for me to have leeches applied, but I could assure him that I should definitely take my departure either the following evening or, at the latest, the morning after. Thereupon, the Governor got up and bowed himself out.

Everyone in the room was sad and dejected except myself. My brother was dismayed, and it was left for me to try to revive his courage.

I left Moscow on 6 December. My health was reduced to a struggle against death. Every other day I wrote to my brother and other members of my family, who also wrote very regularly to me. Several of them, including my brother, told me that Pavel I's behavior toward me was dictated by what he thought he owed to his father's memory, but that at his coronation he would change our fate. I shall quote my reply to my brother as one of the many prophecies I have made which have come true:

"You tell me, my friend, that after his coronation Pavel will leave me alone. You do not know him then. Once a tyrant begins to strike he continues to strike until the victim is totally destroyed. I am expecting persecution to continue unabated, and I resign myself to it in the full submission of a creature to its Creator. The conviction of my own innocence and lack of any bitterness or indignation at his treatment of me personally will, I trust, serve me in place of courage. Come what may, and provided he is not actively malevolent to you and to those near and dear to me, I shall do or say nothing that will lower me in my own eyes. Goodbye, my friend, my well-beloved brother. All my love."

Confined to my bed or stretched out on a sofa, all the time in acute pain, unable to move or even to read much, I had time to ruminate on what had befallen me, on what I had done and on what remained for me to do.

I had a great desire to go abroad as soon as I could obtain permission, but was held back by my love for my son. His financial situation was precarious, since he never looked after his affairs and his debts might have reduced his income to less than modest proportions, if I had not been there to help him by managing and improving my own property rather than spending all I had.

The past afforded me a certain consolation. The disinterestedness and firmness of my character gave me a peace of mind which in itself may not have been an adequate substitute for all else, but at least it supplied me with pride and courage to sustain me in my adversity.

I learned that it had been the object of some of the late Empress's favorites to goad me to despair and make me commit some indiscretion which would alienate me from the Empress by rousing my naturally quick temper. Count Mamonov was among them, but having more wits about him than his predecessors, he had come to the conclusion that the Empress's natural sympathies could not be alienated to the extent of making her responsible for some act of really grave injustice toward me—unless, of course, my own behavior made such a thing possible. And that could certainly have happened if bitterness against my Sovereign had led to some outburst of temper on my part and consequent resentment on hers. He, therefore, did certain things surreptitiously against my son and me which could have embittered me. But I loved the Empress too much and saw too clearly through the dislike for me of all her favorites, not to distinguish between acts genuinely her own and those due to the influence of creatures whom I refused to idolize and of whose power I pretended to be ignorant.

Apart from the pain and despair which I felt at the thought of the irreparable loss my country had sustained by the Empress's death, the past raised up memories which impelled me to consider my own immediate conduct. For the immediate present was alarming enough.

From the very moment he ascended the throne Pavel gave expression to his hatred and contempt for his mother. He hastened to break, or rather destroy, all she had done, and her wisest measures were superseded by arbitrary or fantastic acts. Appointments and dismissals succeeded each other so rapidly that hardly was a person's appointment announced in the press than he was made to give up his functions. It was impossible to know to whom to apply. Exile and detention left few families without a victim. The general feeling was that of terror producing suspicion and destroying the trust which should have existed among people related by ties of blood. Bewilderment and fear gave rise to apathy and stupor, fatal to the most important of all virtues—the love of one's country. The future seemed to hold nothing for us but misfortune without end.

Ill, sad, and frightened for my friends, my relations, and my country, I lived on in the hope that my life would not last long. Soon enough, my prophecy that Pavel would continue to persecute me came true.

Lieutenant-Colonel Laptev, a distant relation of my grandmother, whose promotion in the service I was fortunate enough to have helped, came to see me. He said he did not want to rejoin his regiment without seeing me as it would be difficult for him to get away again, but that he could not stay for more than that one evening for his father's illness had already made him overstay his leave.

He remained with me till after midnight, when I sent him off to have some rest. At three o'clock he informed me through my personal maid that he had a letter for me and that he had to speak to me. I replied that the following morning would be soon enough and that he must have a rest after his tiring journey. Thereupon he sent word that a special courier from Moscow had brought a letter for me.

Suspecting that I was to be the victim of some new persecution, I requested that Mr. Laptev be allowed to come in. As soon as he did so he handed to me the letter which the courier had brought from Mr. Izmailov, the Governor-General of Moscow. The substance of the letter was that the Emperor ordered me to leave immediately for an estate of my son's, situated between two towns named in the letter and located in the northern part of the Province of Novgorod. Neither the estate nor its village was mentioned by name, but I was to live there till further orders.

I had my daughter woken up, and dictated to her my reply to Mr. Izmailov, in which I said that in spite of my wish to carry out His Majesty's orders without delay and my indifference to the exact spot where I should vegetate or be buried, I was obliged to put off my journey, since I had never been in any of my son's Novgorodian estates, even in the distant past when I was still managing his property, and would not know how to find the way to a village the name of which had not been communicated to me. Therefore, I said, as it seemed to me more prudent to avoid Moscow and as I might be reduced to wandering aimlessly about along the byroads, I had sent a servant back with the courier to ask my son's steward whether a few peasants from these villages were not, by any chance, living in Moscow; one of them could then be despatched to me and serve as a guide.

I had great difficulty in trying to revive my daughter's hopes and courage, while she cried and clung to my knees. Someone awoke Miss Bates to give her the terrible news which had thrown my whole house into consternation. She came into my room shaking like a leaf. I pressed her hand and said that before deciding on a course of action prompted by affection for me she should give some thought to it and remember that she was perfectly free not to follow me in my exile, but stay in Troitskoe or in my house in Moscow for as long as she wished. She replied with great firmness that she was determined not to leave me and that no one in the world could make her change her mind. I took her in my arms and we wept like a couple of children.

After giving my letter to Mr. Izmailov's courier and despatching one of my servants with him, Mr. Laptev came to tell me without a tremor that he had decided to accompany me to the place of my exile. All my expostulations were in vain. I drew a vivid picture of all the misfortunes he would bring upon himself and the grief I should feel at the thought of being their involuntary cause. I reminded him that he had already overspent his leave by several days; that I could not make use of post-horses when traveling through byways whose length I did not know, and therefore should have to make the journey with my own horses and we could not estimate the time it would last; that the Emperor could treat him as a deserter; that His Majesty's certain anger at his keen interest in me and at the boldness of his conduct made me tremble for his sake, that he would, at the very least, be reduced to the ranks, and be obliged to serve as a private soldier.

"Private, colonel, general—they are all the same now," he retorted, "—nothing to boast about. I hope you will not order your servants to throw me out, for if you do not give me a place in one of your carriages I am resolved to stand behind your *kibitka.*" (This is a half-open carriage swung low on runners in the winter; in the summer it has wheels and is more uncomfortable.) "Nothing can make me alter my decision to see for myself the place to which you have been banished. Would you kindly, therefore, protest no more."

Knowing well that young man's proud, indeed stubborn, character I stopped arguing, as I feared he might aggravate his case by going off in my pursuit on his own account. His keen and sincere joy at obtaining what he wanted was proof enough of his attachment.

I did not know then that his concern for me was rendered all the greater by the arrival of an obscure stranger who was haunting the village and was always walking about pen in hand ready to jot down anything he saw or heard. Once, when drunk, this man revealed that he was a spy sent to bribe my servants and discover anything that was happening around me. He immediately made a note of it all (for instance, the names of people staying in my house or coming on a visit, conversations at table, etc.), and he declared that in the course of my journey I should be torn away from my friends, ill-treated, and sent into the depths of Siberia.

I was the only one not to be in the secret. Without knowing it, I was in the power of any and every servant. Any rascal could have destroyed me and made his own fortune by turning informer—a profession which was then esteemed above any other.

At last by sheer luck a peasant from the village of my exile was found in Moscow; he had turned up in town with a load of nails of his own manufacture.

A cousin of mine, Princess Dolgorukaia, arrived at Troitskoe and never left me until my departure. The daughters of two of my cousins were staying with me then—Miss Islenieva and Miss Kochetova. Miss Kochetova was in poor health, and her parents had entrusted her entirely to my care until she should be quite recovered. She was very sorry to leave me and did so most reluctantly, but I wrote to her father in Moscow saying that, however much of a solace his daughter might be to me, I could not in all conscience take her with me into exile, beyond the reach of doctor, surgeon, or help, while the state of her health demanded constant medical attention. I therefore begged him to come at once and take away both her and her cousin. He arrived two days before my departure and left the next day with my two young cousins, who showed the greatest regret at being separated from me. He took Miss Islenieva back to her mother, and put his own daughter in the care of doctors, after promising to keep me constantly informed about her health. I should add that on my return to Troitskoe, following an Imperial order, her parents brought her back to me on their own initiative, for I should never have taken the liberty of immuring her in the country with me when at her age she ought to have wished to go out in Society.

CHAPTER XXIX

Princess Dolgorukaia, whose wit, behavior, and sentiments made her into a very extraordinary woman and a loyal and sincere friend, was infinitely dear to me. She tried to foresee all that could possibly ease my life in a peasant hut deprived of furniture and comforts, and busily put together and packed such things as she thought I might need. She did her best to conceal her grief at my predicament, but her tears flowed freely when she was in any other room but mine. The day before my departure I dragged myself with the help of my maid into her bedroom, and there I found her bathed in tears. I kissed her with great affection and reproached her for making so little use of her superior intelligence. I begged her to hold back her grief for just another forty-eight hours, for unless it was Heaven's will that my life should be prolonged for further suffering and misfortune, I should not, in my then state of health, survive a day, or at the most two, of the journey, but if, on the other hand, my dead body were not brought back within that time, she could be sure that the journey and the fresh air had given me back my strength and I should yet live to enjoy her company again. And so I did: I saw her once more on my return from exile, but scarcely two years later she was cut off in the prime of life, leaving me for ever disconsolate at the loss of a dear and faithful friend.

On 26 December 1796 I went to church—or, rather, was taken there, as I could neither stand nor walk by myself. I had asked my relations and ordered my servants at Troitskoe to refrain from weakening still further whatever powers of resistance I might have, by tender and affecting farewells. On leaving church I therefore went straight into my *kibitka* to start for an unknown destination, as I had heard it rumored in the neighbor-

hood the day before that after traveling a certain distance I should be
made to change my route and be relegated to some distant and lonely
convent.

None of this happened. On the contrary, I daily regained strength and
had an excellent appetite on a diet of cabbage soup frozen into solid chunks
which had to be boiled to turn them into liquid. It was also feared—quite
wrongly—that as I had never travelled in a *kibitka* before, this might do
me harm and especially increase my rheumatic pains. But instead I felt
better than I had for the past six weeks.

At our first halt for the night after Troitskoe, Mr. Laptev saw a man he
had previously noticed going past us in his *kitbitka* talk to the owner of the
hut I was occupying. Mr. Laptev wanted to know who the man was. The
peasant whom he asked for information was a little the worse for drink,
and replied that he could not quite make it out himself, for only a short
time ago the man had claimed to be a member of the Princess's retinue of
friends and servants, "and now," added the peasant, "he is ordering me—
and says he has the authority to do so—to go in the hut and see that the
Princess is really there."

This envoy of Arkharov was scarcely a cunning diplomat, for when
Laptev asked him—as usual rather petulantly—why he wanted to know
the whereabouts of the Princess and how he dared send someone into
her room at that late hour and disturb her rest, his answer showed clearly
enough he was spying on us not on the Emperor's orders, but only on
those of Arkharov. He was, in fact, afraid that I should be informed and
said to Mr. Laptev in a tone of voice which he tried to make menacing
that if he, Laptev, frightened me by telling me of what he had just heard
the responsibility would be entirely his.

Twice in the course of our journey between that halt and the town of
Tver we very nearly perished, and the second time was the worse. A violent snowstorm obliterated all traces of the road, and for *seventeen hours* we
wandered about without knowing where we were. There was no house
in sight, the horses could go no further, and the servants, convinced that
death was inevitable, prayed and wept.

I ordered the coachman to stop, and assured him that the wind would
go down when dawn broke, and that as soon as the horses were a little
rested we should find some inhabited place. Three quarters of an hour
later the coachman thought he could discern a light some distance away. I
noticed it too, and despatched the strongest of the servants in its direction
to see what it was. He came back in half an hour with the information

that it was a tiny hamlet of five cottages. We wended our way there, the horses barely dragging our carriages along, but in the end we as well as those poor beasts were saved from a probably slow and terrible death.

It so happened that that little village was quite out of our way and that in the last nineteen or twenty hours we had gone no more than about four miles from the place where we had slept. On our arrival in Tver we were very agreeably surprised to learn that the Governor, Mr. Polikarpov, had prepared excellent accommodation for me. That worthy man immediately came to see me, and when I expressed my thanks and also my fears that in view of the vindictive character of the Monarch he might get into trouble for his good treatment of an outlaw, he replied:

"I do not know, Madam, what has passed between you and the Emperor in your intimate correspondence. I have seen no decree dealing with your banishment; you must, therefore, let my conduct toward you be dictated by the respect I have always felt for you ever since I can remember."

He sent us a good supper in spite of the Guards that filled the town on their way to Moscow for Pavel's coronation.

The following morning we left after a light breakfast, and as we had to have the same horses for the whole journey we never did more than forty miles a day—often less.

In the town of Krasnyi Kholm we had the good fortune of discovering that the Marshal of Nobility was Mr. Kruse, nephew of the famous doctor, and a man of great honesty and good upbringing. He was very polite and helpful, and supplied us with provisions which we could not have obtained in villages and in peasant huts.

We left again very early in the morning after a few hours' rest for the horses and sleep for ourselves. That day we had incontrovertible proof that the courier who sometimes preceded and sometimes followed us was a spy sent by the younger Arkharov, and that he kept a daily journal of all that happened in our peripatetic colony. Arkharov himself had been vested by the Emperor with the powers and duties of an inquisitor, an employment by no means repugnant to his coarse and brutal nature.

On one occasion, Mr. Laptev happened to enter a hut which the spy had just left, and found a letter which he had written to Mr. Arkharov and forgotten there. It was not sealed, and we were able to read his comments on the fact that I had been very ill and that Laptev was still with me. He also said—apparently to add some interest to his epistle—that my servants had stolen a fur coat from a peasant, whereas in fact this must have been done by his own servant who had a very poor fur coat, while mine had been fitted out with fine new ones the day before we had set out on our journey. After this we always used to raise a sort of trapdoor leading to a cellar below, which floors have in peasants' cottages, to see that Arkharov's commissioner was not hiding there, trying to listen to our conversation.

Soon I had greater cause for alarm, and a fear which never left me until I was back in Troitskoe and in receipt of reassuring letters from my brother and other friends to the effect that my son had not been persecuted by the Emperor.

On my arrival in the town of Vesyegonsk, I received the visit of the acting Marshal of Nobility, who came together with his predecessor. The former was cousin to Mr. Arakcheev, the most faithful instrument of Pavel I's tyranny and persecution. His predecessor, who had been deprived of his appointment—itself dating back to Catherine II's time—so that it could be given to Arakcheev's cousin, was an officer who has seen about forty years' service and had nine wounds to his credit. I had the greatest difficulty in consoling the old soldier and vainly tried to change the subject of conversation from that of his compulsory retirement to something else. He invariably came back to it, till at last I thought of asking both Marshals, the retired and the acting, to take Miss Bates and my daughter to see the fair which was then one of the greatest in the Empire.

No sooner were they gone than an officer came in with a letter for me. It was from my son, who had sent the courier to see me, to give orders to the peasants at Korotovo (my place of exile) to obey me as their true mistress, and then to return with news of me.

A thunderbolt bursting in the room could not have frightened me as much. In my mind's eye I already saw my son sent to Siberia for disobeying the Emperor's order forbidding the employment of officers for carrying despatches. For Pavel was so strict on this point that he had the Princes Suvorov and Repnin severely reprimanded—and the reprimand published in the *Gazette*—for having sent officers with despatches for himself. And my son had not only given and signed orders which he had no right to do, but had rendered himself even more culpable in the Emperor's eyes by showing an interest in his mother who was the object of the Emperor's persecution.

I asked the officer whether he had been seen by anyone in town, and whether he had met the Marshal of Nobility on the way. He assured me that he had not. I implored him to leave at once for Korotovo, which was only twenty-one miles away; I should, I said, speak to him there, but in the meantime he must leave the town immediately and must take a route which would save him going right through it.

As soon as my party returned from the fair, we started on our journey and arrived late at night at the spot indicated by the Emperor as my place of domicile.

My own hut I found to be quite roomy, the one opposite was set aside for the kitchen, and the best in the adjoining street was prepared for my daughter.

The first thing I did was to send away Mr. Schreidemann, the officer despatched to me as courier by my son, but I was inexpressibly frightened and worried when, after his departure, my son's servant told me that not only had Mr. Schreidemann been seen by the Marshal of Nobility, but out of sheer swank and foolhardiness he had introduced himself to the Marshal, who had thereupon demanded to have his passport and had kept it.

Night and day, I had no repose, for even in my dreams I had visions of my son being dragged away to Siberia. I wrote to my brother and to a number of friends urging them to give me news of my son, but I was not completely reassured even when they told me that he had been given the command of a regiment.

Occasionally, Pavel had an acute sense of justice, and there were moments when he gave proof of exceptional wisdom and magnanimity. He heard, through the Marshal of Nobility, of Mr. Schreidemann's journey, and yet evinced no anger at my son's conduct. Later, when I was back at Troitskoe, he read in Mr. Arkharov's reports that several friends and relations of mine had come to see me and spend some time with me, but his comment was merely:

"This is quite natural, for now is the time to show Princess Dashkova the friendship and gratitude which some people may feel toward her."

So far as my own life at Korotovo was concerned, I felt free of worries and very pleased at having a roomy hut, far better than anything I had hoped for. It is true that my three maids shared it with me—in the night, that is, for the day they spent in Miss Bates's hut—but thanks to their consideration, attention, and neatness, I was not in the slightest inconvenienced by this. Besides, someone had had the foresight to hang up a thick green curtain which divided the room in two and separated the mistress from the maids.

Immediately after I arrived in Korotovo a little incident took place which affected me greatly. It should be pointed out that it is the custom

in Russia for the gentry, before setting out on a journey and at the end
of it, to go to church where a Te Deum is sung, after which the priests
usually come to the big house to bless the traveler and to offer him their
best wishes on his return. The priest makes the sign of the cross over him
and the man kisses his hand. Thus, as soon as I had reached my destination, the priest at Korotovo came to my hut and pronounced a solemn
benediction while blessing me with his cross, but instead of letting me
kiss his hand as the custom was, he begged me, with tears in his eyes, to
let him kiss mine.

"It is not your rank, mother," he said, "I respect, but the fame of your
virtues which has penetrated even to this remote corner. I speak in the
name of the whole village: you have brought up your son well and he has
become a good master, which to us is very important, and though we are
sorry for you in the misfortune which has brought you here among us, it
is a great happiness for us to see you, for it is as if we had been allowed
to see an angel."

I was tired and weak, and the unexpected and artless expression of
attachment from these poor peasants whom I did not know at all, in a
place to which I had been sent in order to be unhappy, suddenly overpow-
ered me with such a sharp sensation of happiness that I could not help
interrupting the priest and kissing him as if he had been an old friend.
Everyone present burst into tears at the sight, and Mr. Laptev and others
assured me that never at the height of my prosperity had I inspired them
with as much respect and veneration as at that moment.

CHAPTER XXX

❧❦❧

Being greatly worried on Mr. Laptev's behalf, I sent him back the very next day after our arrival. But Heaven spared me the regrets I should have had, had he fallen victim of his gratitude and attachment. When the Emperor heard he had accompanied me to Korotovo, he said:

"Here is no petticoat stripling; this man wears breeches"—a phrase often used by His Majesty when he wanted to express his admiration for a man of grit and courage.

The battalion of which Laptev had command was one of those lately reduced by Pavel, and he was therefore left without any appointment. The Emperor, however, gave him a regiment and soon afterward made him Commander of the Maltese Order.

During my stay in Tver I wrote to my cousin, Prince Repnin, asking him to find out what crimes His Majesty imputed to me, since he felt justified in treating me in the way he did. I added that as he, Prince Repnin, knew what my sentiments had been during the reign of Peter III, he could prove to the Emperor's satisfaction and to that of all decent people that I had never pursued either my personal interests or the criminal elevation of my own family. I named the village to which I was banished for God knows how long, and indicated several academicians whose integrity of character and sincere attachment to me should be a sufficient pledge that his answer could be safely entrusted to their keeping till such time as I could send a peasant to one of them to collect any letters, including his, that they might hold for me.

As the oath of allegiance, which was sworn to every new sovereign, was required only of the gentry, the Third Estate, the Army, and the Civil Service, the peasants, being the property of the gentry, were exempt from taking it. I do not know by virtue of what whim it was ordered that everyone, including the peasants, should swear the oath of allegiance to Pavel I.

This unprecedented measure caused enormous harm to the country. The peasants imagined that they would no longer belong to their landlords, and a number of villages in different provinces rose up in revolt, refusing either to work for their masters or to pay them their dues. The Emperor was obliged to send troops to put an end to the revolt, which in one estate, belonging to Mr. Apraksin and Princess Golitsyna, whose maiden name was Chernysheva, assumed so stubborn a character that cannon had to be fired, and many people fell victim to the error into which they had been induced by this new measure.[1]

In some provinces, Civil Service clerks—the most pernicious element in all Russia—went round villages belonging to private individuals among the gentry, persuading the poor ignorant peasants that if they should declare themselves willing to belong to the Sovereign they would be freed of all obligation toward their masters. Two such clerks traveled all over the Archangel Province and in the north of Novgorod making these insinuations, and before my arrival they had spoken to my son's peasants suggesting that in return for a little money they should convey their wishes to the Emperor. The peasants angrily refused to have anything to do with these suggestions, and said that they felt themselves more fortunate than the peasants who belonged to the Crown.

The risings forced the Emperor to despatch Prince Repnin to these two Provinces. On his way through a town near the village where I was confined, he sent for the parish priest and besought him to convey a letter to me in absolute secrecy. The priest gave a solemn promise to carry out faithfully the Prince's wishes, and fulfilled his promise, for one day, as I was looking out of the window, I saw a priest whom I did not know coming straight toward my front doorstep. I immediately went out to meet him, but had scarcely time to reach the steps before he thrust my cousin's letter into my hands and disappeared after briefly bidding me have hope in Divine mercy.

Prince Repnin expressed his unhappiness at his inability to be of the

---

[1] The total number of peasants involved in the rising on the Apraksin-Golitsyn estate was about 13,000, but they were joined by peasants from neighboring estates as well. The year 1797 witnessed similar risings throughout European Russia, most of them due mainly to economic causes.—K. F.

slightest assistance and advised me to write to the Empress, begging her to intercede for me with the Emperor. I must admit I was loath to ask for favors of a Princess whom I did not believe to be favorably disposed toward me. I was in no hurry to write the letter, and I should never have asked to be transferred to Troitskoe if I had been alone in suffering the consequences of a life at over sixty degrees latitude north in a peasant hut, surrounded by marshes and vast impenetrable forests, which made it impossible to go out even during the brief and late summers. But my daughter, Miss Bates, my servants—they were all suffering, and perhaps even more than I, since it was all for my sake. I, at least, gathered support from the feeling of my innocence, the purity of my conscience and a certain moral pride which gave me strength and courage, but which I had never previously suspected in myself and which, after giving the matter much thought, I could only attribute to resignation, a sentiment proper to every rational being.

What rendered our situation still more melancholy was the fact that the freezing over of the marshes had opened up a way across them which shortened the road from Petersburg to Siberia by several miles, so that most of the unfortunate exiles were now driven past my very windows. Once, on seeing a *kibitka,* different to the small kind used by peasants, stop in front of a hut, with the horses unharnessed, I sent out a servant to inquire about its owner. The owner, in turn, asked the servant to whom it was *he* belonged. On hearing my name he begged permission to come to see me for a moment, adding that he was connected with me by his uncle's marriage to a relation of mine.

Though under the present circumstances it was hardly proper for me to receive visitors and I had not the least desire to do so, yet the idea that he might require some help and that I might be useful to him made me invite him, and to start a conversation and discover who he was, I asked him how he was related to me. He said that Mr. Razvarin, a cousin of his late mother's, had had, as his first wife, a distant cousin of mine. His speech, I noticed, was not fluent, his face was twitching and he was shaking all over.

"Are you not well?" I asked. "You seem to be in pain."

"No," he replied, "no more than I probably shall be all my life," and he told me his story. A few of his brother subalterns in the Guards had spoken of the Emperor in offensive terms which had been repeated to him; he had found himself implicated in this affair, and had been put to the torture during which all his limbs were dislocated. His companions were sent to Siberia, while he was dismissed from the service and had received the order to proceed to Vologda and live on an estate of an uncle who was made responsible for him.

Seeing that I could not be of any use to him I cut short the visit, for it caused me immense pain, and long afterward the vision of that young man with his dislocated limbs, and his nerves so to speak torn to shreds, haunted my terrified imagination.

Soon after I had the visit of Madame Vorontsova and her daughter. She was the widow of a cousin of mine, a little distant, it is true, but for whom I had great esteem. This woman, really worthy of respect from every point of view, wanted in this way to show me her gratitude for all I had done for her younger son, whom she had entrusted to me at the age of seven. I had made myself responsible for his education and upbringing till he reached the age of sixteen, when he entered the Army with the rank of major. His moral principles, his general conduct, and his affectionate respect for his mother formed the solace of her life.

She lodged in the hut next to mine and stayed with me for a week. We had had the foresight to take from Troitskoe some books, and we employed a few pencils to cover with drawings and sketches of scenery a deal table which was washed every three days to be used again for the same purpose as we had to economize on paper—these, and the funny pranks of a little servant boy, and perfect resignation, all helped to fortify my patience. And on seeing me so calm and composed my companions, too, armed themselves with patience and with courage.

On learning that at the melting of the snow and ice at the end of April the river near the village always swelled and came out of its banks for a distance of about two miles, and that there were no boats or rafts for transport across the river other than the little fishermen's skiffs, and as we had arrived in *kibitkas* on sledges and could not now obtain wheeled carriages, I decided to write to the Empress asking her to intercede with her husband and obtain for me permission to go to Troitskoe. I should certainly not move out of it without orders, I said, but we should be more within reach of medical help and lodged in my house where we should be in far greater comfort than in a peasant's hut.

Within the same cover I enclosed an unsealed letter for the Emperor. The tone in which it was couched was, I must admit, haughty rather than pleading. I began by describing the state of my health which, I said, was such that were it merely the question of my physical condition, it would not be worth His Majesty's while to read my letter or mine to write it, for the time of my death was a matter of indifference to me, but neither humanity nor religion allowed me to see innocent people suffer in sharing a banishment which my conscience told me was undeserved; never, I added, in the lifetime of the Empress his mother had I harbored any ill-feelings toward him, and I ended by asking his permission to return to my estate of Troitskoe in the Province of Kaluga, where my companions and even my servants would have better accommodation and would receive medical attention in case of illness.[2]

I sent this letter by post, and I must admit that we awaited the results not without impatience.

I heard afterward from someone then living in Petersburg and intimately familiar with what passed in Their Majesties' inner apartments that my epistle had very nearly been disastrous for us. But Providence once again intervened in my favor. Pavel I's fairly frequent changes of mind and I know not what delay in the journey of the courier who had been sent to strike perhaps the last blow at a woman scarcely alive and merely defending herself against a cruel fate, reversed the sentence and in place of evil brought us consolation and relief.

When the Empress received my letter and gave the Emperor the one addressed to him he flew into an inconceivable rage, drove her away saying that he did not want to be overthrown like his father, and refused to

---

[2] The letter Princess Dashkova in fact sent to the Emperor made no mention of servants or companions and was not quite as haughty and lackadaisical in tone as she suggests. It was as follows:

'Most merciful Sovereign,

The compassionate heart of Your Imperial Majesty will forgive a subject, oppressed by age, sickness, and, what is worse, by the sorrow of living in the shadow of Your anger, if she appeals to her Monarch's benevolent heart. Be merciful, Sire, grant me the only favor I ask of you, allow me to end my days quietly on my estate in Kaluga, where I shall at least have a roof over my head and be within easier reach of doctors' help. Should unhappiness be reserved for me alone while it is Your Majesty's desire to make the whole Empire happy and while you bestow happiness on so many? In satisfying my request You will bring back life to an unhappy woman who to her dying day will glorify the name of a kind and compassionate Sovereign, and who remains, in steadfast loyalty,

Your Imperial Majesty's
and Most Merciful Sovereign's
most humble, obedient and faithful subject.
Princess C. Dashkova.
Korotovo Village, near Cherepovets, January 1797.

Princess Dashkova took no pride in this letter, and pruned the copy she sent to her brother Aleksandr of all the more obviously insincere expressions of flattery.—K. F.

accept my letter. He immediately despatched a courier with the order to deprive me of pens, ink, and paper, to share my hut with me and to keep a close watch on me so that I should have no communication with the outside world.

The Empress informed Miss Nelidova, the Emperor's favorite, of her lack of success, whereupon Miss Nelidova gave the letter to His Majesty's youngest and favorite son, the Grand Duke Mikhail, and led him into His Majesty's presence.[3] The Emperor took the letter, with a countenance a little less severe than usual, read it, and said as he embraced his son:

"There is no resisting you, ladies, you know how to set about it."

The ladies flattered and cajoled him in a thousand ways, and he wrote me a letter of which the following is the literal translation:

"Princess Catherine Romanovna, since you wish to return to your estate in the Province of Kaluga, you may do so. I remain your well-wisher and very affectionate, Pavel."

He then summoned Mr. Arkharov, the military Governor of Petersburg, and ordered him immediately to despatch a second courier to overtake the first and deliver the message to me.

Whether inadvertently or out of spite, this Mr. Arkharov, who was the elder brother of the Governor of Moscow, chose as second courier one who had just returned from Siberia whither he had been taking an unfortunate Guards officer, who was going into exile. Having just done over 2,500 miles there and back without a rest, there was little chance that he would catch up with a man who had started several hours in advance. But Fate was obviously beginning to tire of persecuting me; the second courier overtook the first and sent him back.

On seeing a *kibitka* at my front-door steps, surrounded by my servants, I went out to have a look and came face to face with the Emperor's courier. Miss Bates had vainly pressed him to tell her what order he had brought with him. He could give no answer other than that he knew nothing and had an Imperial decree for me. When I told him I was Princess Dashkova he handed to me the above-mentioned letter.

Before I had time to break the seal the good Miss Bates fell on her knees in front of me saying, 'Oh, let us take courage, my dear Princess, God is everywhere—even in Siberia," she grew pale and trembled all over. I raised her up and asked her to calm herself and let me read what

[3] The Grand Duke Mikhail was not yet born at the time. The letter was put into the hands of the eight-months-old Grand Duke (later Emperor) Nikolai.—K. F.

the message contained. When I told her we had permission to return to Troitskoe she fell at my feet again, in a fever and delirium, and I made her, though with the greatest difficulty, go to bed.

I then ordered my servants to give a glass of wine and some refreshments to the courier, but he refused either and asked only for a corner in which to sleep, not having done so for the last few days.

My daughter was informed of the happy news which made my servants mad with joy. The following day I dismissed the courier, and after asking him what his annual wages were I gave him nearly double the amount. It was his turn then to become mad with joy, and I should have been the only person there perfectly calm and composed if I had not been worried for Miss Bates's health. She was delirious and recognized no one but me. I never left her side except to write and make arrangements for sending forward some of my companions, as I wanted to travel light, and was quite determined not to leave until Miss Bates could undertake the journey without any risk.

I gave the Emperor's courier an unsealed letter for Mr. Arkharov, asking him to transmit it to Mr. Lepekhin, Permanent Secretary to the Russian Academy and Professor of Natural History at the Academy of Sciences, a great friend of mine, to whom I described all that had happened to me and gave my address at Troitskoe. However, Arkharov was mean enough to keep back that letter. Letters to my friends in England I despatched with a peasant who delivered them to Mr. Glynn, an English merchant living in Petersburg.

During the eight days that Miss Bates's fever lasted, I put everything in readiness for our journey so as to avoid all difficulties and delays. As soon as nothing remained of her fever except a certain weakness, I sent forward my own horses, which I had kept at Korotovo, seventy-five miles in advance, and ten days after the welcome arrival of the courier we started on our journey.

I could not end this part of my narrative without mentioning the extraordinary helpfulness and tact shown me by the peasants every day of my life at Korotovo. Twice a week on returning from the town market, they brought everything they could find that was good and even rare, for my table. A few days before my departure I learnt that the women who came every day with eggs, cakes, and tarts did it only in order to see me, and they had agreed among themselves to take turns at it so that each could have an opportunity of convincing herself personally that I was still alive. Several times I asked the peasants why they were so fond of me even though they had not belonged to me for many years past, and their answer never varied:

"We have become rich under your management, and you have brought your son up to follow your ways; he may have raised our dues a little, but they are still far lower than those our neighbors pay to their landlords."

CHAPTER XXXI

These worthy peasants supplied several relays of horses, so that I was able to cover in one day a distance it had taken me two and a half days to cover on the way out. We left Korotovo at the end of March in full winter, but when after nine days' traveling we reached the Protva, which flows past my garden, and land at Troitskoe, there was practically no snow. The banks of the river were green and the poor horses had to drag our carriages, which were still on runners instead of wheels, over sand, clay, and grass. We, therefore, decided to spend one more night on the way.

At last, on the tenth day, we arrived at Troitskoe. The church where we alighted first, though large, was filled to overflowing with the servants I had left behind, and with the inhabitants of sixteen villages and hamlets which belonged to me.

After the service they all thronged round me and wanted to kiss my hand and tell me how delighted they were at my return, but I could hardly stand up and begged them to spare me till my strength had come back. I was deeply affected by this demonstration of attachment to me and the unfeigned joy that beamed on every countenance, but any further exertion was quite beyond my power, and my exhausted body yearned for bed and rest.

The very next day I sent off a servant to Moscow to let my brother know of my return to Troitskoe. I also wrote to my cousins Princess Dolgorukaia and Princess Mavrocordato, asking them for their news as well as for anything they might have heard about my son and their friends and relations. So far, I could bless Providence, for they had none of them been persecuted by the tyrant.

I was informed that eighty-seven private soldiers and one officer were

quartered in my town house. My steward had had the good sense to seal
the doors leading to the main body of the building, on the pretext that
as I had had to quit in a hurry with no time to seal anything in particular, I had left order to seal all doors. This brilliant idea saved me from
the expense of having quartered on me one of those wretched generals,
invariably referred to as "Gatchina soldiers," who would have spoiled my
furniture and made the whole house filthy.

My summer villa likewise was occupied by ninety soldiers and six warrant officers; apart from other expenses that this occasioned, 3,000 round
logs of timber tied into rafts and floated down the river Moskva from one
of my farms did not suffice as fuel which I had to supply. The result was
that I was obliged to buy some more, and therefore reluctantly decided
to sell the villa; I loved it for its garden which thirty years of care had
rendered perfect, and which I could enjoy even in winter, as several paths
and drives were always swept clean of snow, strewn with sand and kept
scrupulously tidy, so I could use them for my walks. The resultant cost
of upkeep was slight compared to the expense, inconvenience, and petty
wrangling inevitable in connection with such guests.

Besides, I did not know whether I should ever be allowed to live in
Moscow, nor did I want to have my permanent residence there, especially
since I had returned to Troitskoe, where all my relations and genuine
friends came to see me. Moreover, I knew that a system of espionage had
been established in all big towns and particularly in Moscow, all the more
dangerous as denunciations represent the surest means of succeeding with
suspicious and apprehensive tyrants.

In the summer I calmly resumed my occupations—gardening, agriculture, building—and as I did not have a single servant who understood
any of these things, my time was fully taken up. This made me physically
tired, but sound sleep put me right again and was all the more necessary
as I never failed to wake up at the fatal hour at which I had been roused
in order to be informed of my banishment to Korotovo. Rarely was I able
to fall asleep again, and was, therefore, obliged to have about an hour's
rest after dinner.

Rainy days kept me indoors and gave me the opportunity of making
drawings and plans of buildings and plantations which I intended to have
made, or else I browsed in the library. I wanted to have new books from
abroad, and therefore assigned a certain annual sum of money for that
purpose, and wrote an order to that effect. I discovered that the importa-
tion of books was almost completely forbidden, although there was a flood

of pamphlets libelling Catherine II, which my friends did not think they should send me. However, I obtained all that could be found in Moscow, and I shall not finally put down my pen without adding to these Memoirs (which may not deserve to be passed down to posterity, but will perhaps interest my friends and their descendants) some notes that, I hope, will prove the falsehood of assertions dictated by hatred and envy.[1]

In the year 1798 my son was in Petersburg. So fond did the Emperor become of him that he was moody and irritable whenever my son failed to dine at Court. My son spent whole hours alone with His Majesty in his study, and was often admitted to the Empress's presence with no one else but the Emperor and Miss Nelidova, to the exclusion even of Their Imperial Highnesses.

Immediately on his arrival in Petersburg he begged the Grand Duke Aleksandr (the present Emperor) to try and obtain permission for me to live in Moscow and visit my estates. I wrote to my son, as soon as I heard he was going to Petersburg, that he must look to his own safety and not think of me. I repeated this most emphatically several times, saying that I liked so much living in Troitskoe that I preferred it to life anywhere else in Russia, and that my method of treating my peasants did not require my personal supervision for the administration of my other estates and the collection of the modest dues that I had imposed on them. Consequently, I said, I neither desired nor needed a change of residence.

My son, nevertheless, applied to His Imperial Highness, who promised to do what he could, but more than a month passed without any effect. My son mentioned this to Mr. Nicolai, Director of the Academy of Sciences and First Secretary to Her Majesty, who held him in high esteem.

One day, Mr. Nicolai happened to enter the Empress's apartment just as she was speaking with Miss Nelidova about the influence Prince Dashkov had on the Monarch, and was expressing her astonishment that he should not employ it to obtain some freedom for his mother. Mr. Nicolai thereupon explained to Her Majesty that my son had solicited the Grand Duke's patronage in this matter, and was both grieved and worried because His Imperial Highness's promises had not produced any result. He even suggested that it would be generous of them if they both used their influence in the same cause. They made no actual promises, but said they would see what they could do.

---

[1] The notes remained unwritten.—K. F.

Mr. Nicolai reported this conversation to Prince Dashkov. A few days later, Prince Aleksei Kurakin informed him by Imperial command of His Majesty's wish to grant him 5,000 peasants. To this my son replied that he immensely appreciated His Majesty's kindness and would forever be deeply grateful to him for it, but he desired nothing except freedom for his mother.

The following morning on parade Prince Aleksei Kurakin came up to my son and transmitted to him His Majesty's command that I should be set free, adding that he was going to inform me of it immediately. This he did in the following letter:

"Madam and dearest Aunt,

I am happy to be able to inform you of His Majesty's command granting you permission to live on your estates, change your place of abode and even visit the Capital in the absence of the Court. However, should the Court be in residence you can live on such of your estates as is nearest to the Capital."

When the Emperor appeared on parade my son wanted to throw himself on his knees in front of him, but the Emperor would not let him; instead, he embraced him and kissed him, and my son, forgetting how small His Majesty was, lifted him right off the ground as he took him in his arms. He wept and the Emperor wept too; this was the first and last time the Guards were witness to a scene of sensibility.

Pavel I's favor lasted till his departure. He consulted my son on his military plans and in connection with the war he wanted to undertake. Even the operational plans which my son drew up were drawn up in the intimacy of the Emperor's study, as was the disposition of our troops. And he decided—very confidentially—to entrust my son with the command of an Army corps stationed at Kiev. He even gave him several blank orders signed by himself, so that my son could fill them in whenever necessary without loss of time. Our Ministers at Vienna and Constantinople, Count Razumovskii and Mr. Tamara, as well as the Commander-in-Chief, Black Sea Fleet, were instructed to cooperate with Prince Dashkov on all occasions.

My son was sent from Petersburg straight to Kiev where he was to make all the final arrangements and communicate them to the Emperor.

Who would have thought while all this favor lasted, that my son would be dismissed within the year for representing to the Attorney-General, Prince Lopukhin, that one of the prisoners in the Kiev fortress, named Altesti, was in fact innocent of the crime laid to his charge? He had been accused of settling some soldiers as peasants on the land granted to him by the late Empress. This was untrue; there was not a single soldier settled on his land, but he had been a great favorite of Prince Zubov's, and had enjoyed his boundless confidence while acting as his secretary in the preceding reign. This may have been reprehensible and caused some harm, but there was nothing more to it than that. Perhaps, too, Prince Lopukhin had chosen a moment when the Emperor was in a bad mood to speak to him of my son's action, and he had done it, possibly, because he was an insincere man, vindictive and underhand. In any case, the Emperor wrote to Prince Dashkov as follows:

"As you meddle in things which do not concern you, you are hereby dismissed from your command.—Pavel."

My son did not want to entrust the blank orders with the Emperor's signature and other important papers to the courier who had brought him this strange letter. He wrote to His Majesty asking him to have the goodness to send someone he could have confidence in, for the purpose. Pavel took his time in sending for these papers, but when the courier finally reached Kiev, Prince Dashkov returned everything to His Majesty including his letters and, having settled his own affairs, he went straight to his estate in the Province of Tambov.

CHAPTER XXXII

The following summer I visited my Belorussian estate and found that innumerable depredations had been committed there by my Polish steward in the mistaken belief that I should be despatched to Siberia. I took a number of measures on behalf of my peasants, and appointed a Russian to administer the property.

On the way back I went to spend six weeks with my brother. There I planted several trees and shrubs, and removed others that had been planted in ugly and graceless zigzags, and was able to improve his garden.

My brother and I spent hours alone together, and the subject of our conversation was always something which affected us both deeply—the misfortunes of our country and of almost every single individual; for whoever was not personally a victim of Pavel I's despotic tyranny had the fate of a friend, a relation, of someone near and dear to bewail.

For some reason or other the idea had become firmly fixed in my mind that the end would come in the year 1801—that Pavel would cease to live. I told this to my brother who asked me whether I had any reason to think so and on what my hope was based. I could give him no satisfactory explanation for my idea, but it became a settled conviction.

In January of that year my brother reminded me of my prophecy. "Well," he said, "the year has begun."

"Yes," I replied, "but we are only in January yet. Let us wait and see if it comes true before the year is out."

And so it did, for on 12 March Providence allowed the Emperor's existence to be brought to a close, and with it all the public and private disasters, for taxation and persecution were growing and multiplying with every day that passed. Many a time since then I have thanked Providence that I had been excluded from Pavel's Court and thus saved from the wretched duty of making an appearance at it. Nature had not endowed me with the gift of pretence, so essential when dealing with Sovereigns and even more with the people round them. Disgust, contempt, indignation—there they all were, writ large on my countenance whenever I felt them. Misfortunes and worries without number would therefore have been my lot, for it could truly be said of the unfortunate Emperor that not only was he vain and proud of the supernatural preeminence he attached to his rank, but that he gloried, too, in behaving like a Prussian drill-sergeant. He was a coward by nature and subject to bouts of suspicion, living in constant fear of plots which he imagined were being hatched against him. He acted by spasms, his every action dictated by the whim of the moment, all too often, alas, violent and cruel. People approached him, therefore, with a feeling of terror not unmixed with contempt.

How little did the daily life of Pavel's courtiers resemble that of people who had had the happiness of living close to the great Catherine! She was easy of access, but never at the cost of her own dignity, so that the respect with which she was approached was untinged with servility or fear. Indeed, her presence inspired religious veneration and a respect deeply felt and quickened by love and gratitude. Gracious and full of charm and gaiety, she wanted her rank to be forgotten in private life, but had it been possible to lose sight of it for an instant, the generally felt conviction of her natural superiority would still have remained to inspire a pious respect inseparable from her person and every thought of her.

On his return to Moscow my brother mentioned my prophecy to several persons, and I was annoyed by the questions people asked me in that connection, as I was not at all clear in my own mind how and why the idea had occurred to me. He soon received letters from the new Emperor urging him to come to Petersburg and take an active part in public life.

My cousin Tatishchev, Chamberlain, member of the Department of Foreign Affairs, responsible too for our dealings with Asiatic Courts, came to see me in Troitskoe with an invitation from His Majesty. But I could not at my age and in my state of health alter my opinion on the subject of life at Court and be anxious to appear at one. I kept my cousin for only three days in Troitskoe so that he could spend a few more with his mother and family in Moscow, and urged him to return as quickly as possible to his post, to prevent anyone else obtaining it, as sometimes happens at the beginning of a new reign. I charged him with a letter for the Emperor in which I thanked His Majesty for remembering me, expressed my regret at being unable to hasten immediately to Petersburg, my health being too impaired just then to allow me to undertake a journey, and assured him that as soon as I was able to travel I should at once gratify the lively desire I had of paying my respects to him.

At the end of April I left Troitskoe for Moscow in order to see my brother, Count Aleksandr, before his departure for Petersburg. We agreed that he should leave before me while I should remain for another week in Moscow not only to recover my strength a little, but also to avoid inconvenience and delay at the relays, since we both needed a fairly considerable number of post-horses.

It was in May that by short stages I arrived in Petersburg. I had known the Emperor for twelve years, had grown to love him and was pleased to see him again, but I was even more pleased to see that beauty was the least of the qualities that distinguished his consort. Her good sense, her general knowledge, her modesty, all the gracious qualities that charm bestows, tact, and discretion beyond her years, all made me fond of her. She spoke Russian correctly by then and without any foreign accent.

But it pained me to note that Aleksandr was surrounded entirely by young men who ridiculed older people, while the Emperor's own shyness (caused, I think, by his deafness) led him to avoid the elder generation. The four years of the reign of Pavel, who had made nothing but drill-sergeants out of his sons, had been lost for the purpose of application and study. Military reviews and uniforms occupied the center of his attention. I foresaw that the Emperor's goodness of heart and the principles of justice and humanity which had been instilled in him would not prevent him putting all his trust in people immediately surrounding his person and giving free rein to Ministers and office-holders.

At the end of July I left Petersburg for Troitskoe by the roundabout way of my estate in Belorussia. In view of the coronation it was my intention to set myself up in dresses as much as in equipages which, I must admit, I had entirely neglected in the past seven years, and therefore, possessed none of these things.

I borrowed from the bank 44,000 roubles, of which I spent 19,500 roubles to pay a letter of exchange of my son, and 11,000 to cover a debt incurred by my cousin Dmitrii Tatishchev. The rest I assigned for some small improvements to my house, and for making an appearance at the coronation ceremonies, if not with any magnificence at least with a certain decency which my rank required.

Before my departure I obtained the Emperor's promise that at the forthcoming honors my cousin, Miss Kochetova, should be named maid-of-honor, and Prince Urusov, who had just married another cousin of mine, Miss Tatishcheva, gentleman of the chamber.

I arrived in Moscow a fortnight before Their Majesties. Their Majesties' entry into the city was solemn and magnificent. Over fifty carriages of the Court and as many of the nobility took part in the procession. After the carriages of Their Majesties and of the Imperial Family, came the one occupied by the Empress's sister, Princess Amelia, and by me, as the first lady of the Imperial Court. Then followed the other ladies-in-waiting and maids-of-honor, the great dignitaries, and so on. Their Majesties proceeded immediately to the Kremlin Cathedral where we all alighted to hear the Te Deum.

As I like neither ceremonies nor etiquette nor official functions, I shall say no more about them. Besides, all coronations are much the same; suffice it to say that the young Emperor and his charming consort won the hearts of all the inhabitants of Moscow, a world rather than a city, so vast and populous is it and so varied the inhabitants. For there the manners and ways of modern Europeans jostle the patriarchal customs of more ancient days and the usages and habits bequeathed by the Tartars.

During the sojourn of the Court in this ancient residence of our Sovereigns I led a most tiring life. The Sloboda Palace was almost six miles away from my house, and rarely a day passed without my going there. I believed I could be of some use to the Empress Elizaveta in informing her on a number of points which, though trifling in themselves, were not to be spurned if she was to create the favorable impression I desired for her sake. She was kind enough to say to my brother I was her guardian angel, and but for me she would often have been embarrassed in playing her new role on a strange stage. Certain it is that my great fondness for her helped me to bear with the weariness of it all and with the boredom of ceremonies, etiquette, and the other ingredients of Court life with its atmosphere so suffocating to a simple old rustic like myself. Never could I have brought myself to do it merely for motives of personal interest.

After the Court's departure for Petersburg I resumed my normal way of life and left for Troitskoe at the beginning of March as I had always done. The following year I went to my property in Belorussia in order to finish and have consecrated the new church which was being built on my orders in the middle of the principal square of Krugloe; and as my brother, Count Simon, was due that summer to arrive in Petersburg from England where he had been Minister Plenipotentiary during the Empress's reign and where he had remained as a private individual during the reign of Pavel, I set off there in the month of July.

Great was my indignation on learning that for all the disagreement among the people surrounding the Emperor, they were unanimous in disparaging the reign of Catherine II and in instilling in the young monarch the idea that a woman could never govern an Empire. On the other hand, they all extolled Peter I, a brutal and benighted tyrant, who sacrificed excellent established institutions, the laws, rights, and privileges of his subjects to his one ambition which aspired to change all things without distinction, be they good, bad, or useful. Foreign writers, out of ignorance or disregard of truth, have proclaimed him the creator of a great Empire, which in fact had played a more important role before his time than during his reign.

In and out of season I spoke out frankly and perhaps a little too vehemently on the subject of these new-fangled ideas. One day, when almost all the Ministers of this new and incongruous administration, as well as some of the Emperor's intimate friends, were dining at my brother's, Count Aleksandr's, the conversation turned on the reign of Catherine II. All the events of her time were criticized for no valid reason, some abuses Prince Potemkin had allowed in the Army confounded with the acts of the Empress, and no distinction made between the ignorance and untrustworthiness of the Ministers and the purity and wisdom of her own designs always directed toward the welfare and prosperity of her Empire. Several of my relatives, including my brother, joined in, in the same strain. All this excited in me feelings I should not like to, and now perhaps no longer could, describe, but what I did say in refutation of these rather unfair statements I said with all the heat and sincerity I usually have on such occasions. However, the conversation and my own outburst affected me so much that that same evening I fell dangerously ill.

I must mention, as proof of the love and respect that was still felt for Russia's great Sovereign and benefactress, that during the course of my illness my door was besieged by visitors of both sexes wanting to know whether I was out of danger. This general interest in my person was due to the fact that the conversation at my brother's had become the talk of the town, but I should gladly have done without that interest if only a single one of my wishes for my country's happiness, or of the truths I was doing my utmost to spread, had taken root and sprouted.

I found Petersburg much changed in comparison to what it had been under the Empress. It contained now no one but Jacobins or drill-sergeants; I say drill-sergeants, because from private to general every individual was occupied solely with the handling of arms, and as the movements and measures of the drill were frequently altered, constant learning and practice were absolutely essential.

I returned to Moscow when autumn was already pretty far advanced. However, I went on to Troitskoe, as the land there demanded constant care and attention, and I could therefore not absent myself for long, for if it was personal inclination that made me my own architect and my own gardener, it was necessity that made me a farmer.

I shall pass over in silence several years that followed, for they can offer nothing of interest to the reader, and if the sorrows which oppressed my heart were such that I should willingly have concealed them from myself, I could not now reveal them to the general public.

The Emperor was kind enough to take on himself the debt I had incurred at the bank, and at the end of August 1803 I received a far greater and, for me, far more precious consolation in the arrival of Miss M. Wilmot, cousin of my dearest and best friend, Mrs. C. Hamilton, daughter of the Archbishop of Tuam. Miss Wilmot came to Troitskoe to spread around me by her conversation, by our reading together, by her sweetness and charm, those gentle pleasures which friendship and the cultivation of things of the mind are able to yield, and which can be compared to nothing else I know.

I already had the privilege of being acquainted with the father and several relatives of that angel of comfort and solace sent to me by Heaven itself as well as by the worthy Mr. Wilmot and Mrs. Hamilton. These relations of hers had so fashioned her mind and character that she can truly be said to be an object of admiration for all those who know her and are capable of appreciating her.

A heart as loving as mine has a lively sense of pleasure at rendering her this tribute and at expressing gratitude for the great trust which she herself as well as her family had reposed in me, by letting her stay with a person who needed care and attention to soothe the bitter moral sufferings which before her arrival made me long for the close of every day as bringing nearer to its end the painful task that fate had assigned to a sorrowful existence. Never, never will I be able adequately to acknowledge all I owe her. My solitude has become a paradise to me now—or, rather, it would have become if . . . and that does not depend on her.

That which my relations have not been able to obtain from me, I have done for her: I wrote these memoirs because she earnestly desired me to do so. She is their sole owner on one condition only—that they will not be published before my death. I may say now quite definitely that I have written nothing but the truth, to which I have strictly adhered, often even to my own disadvantage; I have omitted only what might have been injurious to others, but this is no loss to the reader. If my life continues for some little time I shall record some anecdotes of the reign of Catherine justly called the Great; I shall recapitulate the beneficent acts of her reign, and I shall draw a paraliel between her and Peter I, whom some have ventured to compare to that illustrious Sovereign who was so much superior to him, and whose rule made Russia a leading Power respected and feared by the whole of Europe.

In conclusion, I may truly say that I have done all the good it has been in my power to do; that I have never done any harm to anybody; that oblivion and contempt have been my only revenge for the injustice, the intrigues, and the slander of which I have been victim; that I have done my duty as well as I have been able to perceive and understand it; that my heart was honest and my intentions pure and I was thus able to bear with bitter sorrows to which, but for the comfort of my own conscience, my excessive sensitivity would have made me succumb; and lastly, that I contemplate the approach of my own dissolution without fear or apprehension.

Troitskoe,
27 October 1805.

AFTERWORD
A. Woronzoff-Dashkoff

O f late there has been a revival of interest in the life and works of
Princess Ekaterina Romanovna Dashkova. Her role in the coup of 1762,
involvement in journalism and letters, directorship of the Academy of
Sciences, as well as her final exile and seclusiveness have been the subject
of a number of publications.[1] A consequence of this renewed attention
has been the appearance in Russia of several recent editions of her autobiography *Mon histoire* (most often translated as *Memoirs* or *Zapiski*).[2] The
various publications of this work have helped illuminate Dashkova's life
and times, while simultaneously, and perhaps unwittingly, resurrecting
a nineteenth-century controversy concerning the reliability and authenticity of the two extant manuscript copies. The roots of this controversy
go back to the history of the *Memoirs*'s composition, translation, and initial
publication—a tale of intrigue, war, arrest, interrogation, and shipwreck.

Dashkova had just returned from exile in the north of Russia imposed
on her by Pavel I, when she was visited by Martha and later Catherine
Wilmot, cousins of her friend Mrs. Hamilton. Fascinated by stories and
anecdotes of life in the court of Catherine II, Martha persuaded a seemingly reluctant Dashkova to record her experiences in autobiographical
form. The work proceeded quickly, and Martha is evidently mistaken
when she writes that it was begun in the autumn of 1804.[3] Actually, on
10 February 1804 Martha notes in her journal that "The Princess has
begun to write her life. Her motive for so doing is friendship to me,
as she says she will give me the manuscript & liberty to publish it. It
will probably be a most interesting work."[4] Thus, the initial draft was
written in approximately twenty-one months, since the last page of the
Memoirs is dated 27 October 1805. Martha confirms the latter timetable

when she states that "I think it [the memoir] was completed in about two years."[5] As Dashkova wrote, Martha copied the manuscript and even undertook an English translation. On 29 March 1804 she explains, "I have begun to translate into English the dear Princess's history as she writes it in French."[6] Yet by her own admission Martha's command of French was uncertain.[7] Indeed, notes she sent to Dashkova, which the latter would correct while referring to herself as "votre maître de langue française," attest to Martha's lack of proficiency.[8] So the task of translation fell to Catherine, Martha's sister, upon her arrival in September 1805. On 29 April 1806 Martha remarks that "I write (I should say I *copy*) the Princess's History every day, Kitty [Catherine] translates it, and that occupies our Mornings . . ." and again on 9 November 1806: "I began yesterday to copy out Kitty's translation of the Princess's History after having finished copying the same thing in French & since that all the Empress Katherine's Letters to Princess Daschkaw."[9]

It is therefore safe to assume that in addition to the two copies of the *Memoirs,* which the sisters had labored over so assiduously, Catherine Wilmot had also drafted an English language translation while still in Russia. Interestingly, many years later in a series of letters to Lord Glenbervie describing the preparation of Dashkova's manuscript for publication, Martha does not mention translating it.[10] In 1807 Catherine left for home taking with her one copy of the *Memoirs* and presumably the English-language version. Afterward, when Martha was also planning to depart, hostilities broke out between Russia and England, and the authorities were informed that she was carrying out some important secret documents. In point of fact, Martha had in her possession the original copy of the *Memoirs,* Dashkova's correspondence with Catherine II, and some miscellaneous papers. Arrested and interrogated for five days, Martha took fright and burned the manuscript. Set free, she was allowed to sail home only to be shipwrecked and cast away on an island before returning to her native Ireland.

With the original destroyed, only two copies of the *Memoirs* remained: Catherine's in Ireland and another in Russia among Dashkova's papers and documents. Though one might guess that the two were identical— they were not. Dashkova's copy was a draft version that in all likelihood was not meant for publication and did not contain some of the later additions and notes. It is clear that Dashkova wanted her story to be told abroad and made several provisions to that effect. For instance, she left a description of her participation in the events of 1762 with her friend Mrs.

Morgan.[11] In a letter dated 1816 Mrs. Morgan communicates to Martha the fact that Dashkova gave her a sketch "of that one brilliant act in her life" with the admonition to publish it after her death. In another letter she adds that when Dashkova "quitted Ireland, about the year 1781, she gave me a manuscript brochure, containing what I think may be properly titled Minutes of the Revolution." [12] Martha also relates how on several occasions Dashkova expressed the desire that her work be published in the West.[13] Even if Martha was determined to comply with her friend's wishes, she delayed publication for some thirty years, mostly due to the strong opposition of Simon Vorontsov, Dashkova's brother. He found his sister's document to be devoid of historical truth and doubted its authenticity. Simon never forgave his sister her support of Catherine II, and therefore cannot be considered an objective reader.

Martha Wilmot's (now Bradford) English-language translation appeared in 1840 and is a highly edited, greatly condensed literary reworking of the original. Martha did not hesitate to exercise broad editorial freedom, dividing the text into chapters and including major omissions, revisions, and transpositions. She did not, all the same, introduce the type of personal recollections and anecdotal material recommended by Lord Glenbervie in his letters of 1812–13.[14] Martha's altered version of the *Memoirs,* often far from the original, served as the basis for succeeding translations into Russian (1859), back into French (1859, 1966), German (1857, 1918), and Czech (1911). Excerpts also appeared in various Russian journals such as *Moskvitianin, Sovremennik,* and *Russkaia starina.*[15] The manuscript itself was inherited by Catherine Brooke, Martha's daughter, who in 1882 appended supplementary documents and donated the archive to the British Museum Library. To date, the fullest, most complete rendering of the *Memoirs* remains Kyril Fitzlyon's 1958 English-language translation from the Brooke copy. In his introduction Fitzlyon writes that "the full version of the Memoirs has never hitherto appeared. This, therefore, constitutes the first attempt to present them in their entirety"(22). But he does not elaborate, nor does he isolate or identify the additional passages. Moreover, notwithstanding a scrupulous adherence to the original text, Fitzlyon admits his own alterations, including chapter divisions and certain other infelicities that will be discussed below.

Meanwhile, after Dashkova's death in Russia, the draft copy existed only in manuscript versions and was well known by, among others, Aleksandr Pushkin.[16] Appearing in print only in 1881 when Petr Bartenev published it in the *Arkhiv kniazia Vorontsova,* its "discovery" produced a certain amount of confusion and bewilderment among commentators.[17] Some had thought that the *Memoirs* were originally written in English; others could not understand the many discrepancies that existed between Martha's translation and the Vorontsov copy.[18] This confusion led to an interesting polemic pursued at cross purposes by M. Shugurov and Prince A. Labanov-Rostovskii on the pages of *Russkii arkhiv*. Never having seen the Brooke copy, Shugurov asserts that Martha had inserted new material based on stories and anecdotes related to her by Dashkova.[19] Unfortunately, Labanov, the Russian Ambassador in London, inspected the Brooke archive without reference to the Vorontsov copy and similarly compared it to Martha's translation.[20] In a memorandum dated December 1880 Martha's two daughters, Catherine Brooke and Blanche Elisabeth Bradford, write that they had lent the manuscript to Labanov who kept it from a week to ten days. It seems that the Vorontsov family had discovered a version of the work among their papers and wanted the Brooke copy evaluated.[21] Still, in his article Labanov claims that it was indeed Shugurov's study that motivated his own investigation.[22] Labanov is correct when he concludes that the Brooke copy represents the final, most complete draft of the work. He also notices that some of the additions are written in Dashkova's hand, and provides a detailed description of the entire archive, including letters, documents, and other materials. But because it was available to him for such a short time, Labanov could identify properly only a small number of the additions, especially since he often confused Martha's changes for the 1840 edition and Dashkova's original revisions.[23]

Thus, despite the many translations of the *Memoirs* both in Russia and the West, a systematic, textual comparison of the Brooke and Vorontsov copies had never been undertaken. Nor, until recently, had any attempt been made to define and describe thoroughly the additions contained in the Brooke copy.[24] Veselaia feels that the Vorontsov version "is, in our opinion, the most authentic while Moiseeva claims, rather unconvincingly, that the original is in St. Petersburg. She explains that it is in Martha's hand only because Dashkova dictated the work.[25] However, it is highly unlikely that Martha could take dictation in French since her command of the language was uncertain. In fact, neither editor has seen the British Museum archive nor do they take into account the additions and notes found there. Also, Eidelman incorrectly asserts that the St. Petersburg version is more complete. He bases his claim on a comparison of the 1859 and 1987 Russian translations rather than the French-language originals.[26]

Discussing the work's genesis, Martha states that Dashkova wrote quickly adding sections to the end of the manuscript and marking them with the word "omission."[27] She goes on to explain that there were no more than six or seven such sections. In reality, there are many more, and it is impossible to distinguish between additions and notes, for no clear system exists. The question of how to incorporate these sections into the body of the work has been handled differently. Moiseeva and Veselaia duplicate Bartenev's decision to reproduce all notes and omissions as footnotes, but, as a result, interrupt the narrative flow with lengthy, distracting, and often unwieldy digressions. Opting for stylistic elegance and readability, Fitzlyon absorbs them into the text by means of transitions that are at times of his own composition.

Ranging in size from several sentences to lengthy passages, there are nineteen additions and notes in the Brooke copy (used by Fitzlyon) that were never transcribed in the Vorontsov copy.[28] These additions and notes represent only the major, most apparent lacunae appearing in recent editions of the *Memoirs*. Other, perhaps less obvious (though no less significant) problems also demand attention. Thus, in the Vorontsov copy, Dashkova characterizes Peter I as "a brilliant and benighted tyrant." Fitzlyon's translation of "a brutal and benighted tyrant" is based on the Brooke copy and corresponds directly to Dashkova's well-known dislike of Peter I. On the other hand, Fitzlyon points to historical inaccuracies in the memoir and contradicts Dashkova on a number of occasions. Yet Dashkova is often correct: For example, Roman Vorontsov, her father, was in fact the Chancellor's younger (Fitzlyon, 23; this edition, 31) not elder (321) brother.[29] Anastasiia, her daughter, was afflicted by "un défaut dans la construction de son corps"—a physical problem (142), not a "sexual inadequacy" 316 (Fitzlyon edition), 143 (this edition).[30] Hence, in addition to the *Memoirs,* further study and research are required before a fuller, more definitive account emerges of Dashkova's life and works.

Notes

1 For instance, Heldt (64–70) discusses the conflict of public versus private selves; Lozinskaia adheres too closely and uncritically to Dashkova's memoirs (see Cross's review). Drawing on Sukhomlinov (1: 20–59 et passim), Nekrasov, Kolominov and Fainshtein focus on Dashkova's role at the Russian Academy. See also Cross's "*By the Banks of the Thames.*" Full references to cited works and authors are found in the bibliography; page numbers to Fitzlyon's edition are noted parenthetically.

2 Moiseeva's 1985 rendering is based on a translation published by Chechulin in 1907

from the French original in vol. 21 of Bartenev, *Arkhiv kniazia Vorontsova*. Moiseeva reproduced her version in *Literaturnye sochineniia* (31–262) and again in *Zapiski i vospominaniia* (67–280). Veselaia proposes an updated translation from the same original, and additionally reproduces the letters from Russia of Dashkova's Anglo-Irish friends, Catherine and Martha Wilmot. The Moiseeva and Veselaia editions have been reviewed by Cross. Also of interest is the 1990 facsimile reprint of the 1859 Herzen edition.

3   Bradford, I: xxii.

4   Wilmot, 79.

5   Bradford, II: 241.

6   Wilmot, 88.

7   Bradford, II: 278.

8   Royal Irish Academy, 12 L 25.

9   Wilmot, 267, 272.

10   Royal Irish Academy, 12 M 18.

11   This is perhaps the account Dashkova subsequently included in a long letter: "Iz pis'ma," 185–91. It provides an interesting comparison to the *Memoirs,* which were written some forty years later.

12   Royal Irish Academy, 12 M 18.

13   Bradford, II: 49; Shugurov, "Miss Vil'mot," 191.

14   Royal Irish Academy, 12 M 18.

15   See the detailed bibliography in Pontremoli, 356–63.

16   Gillel'son, 132–44.

17   The manuscript is now at the St. Petersburg Branch of the Institute of Russian History, Russian Academy of Sciences (f. 36, nos. 750–52).

18   Semenskii, 427; Shugurov, "Miss Vil'mot," 210–14; among others.

19   Shugurov, "Miss Vil'mot," 150–217.

20   Labanov, 366–79.

21   Brooke, 4.

22   Labanov, 366.

23   In a response to Labanov's article, Shugurov, "Zametki," stays with his by now indefensible opinion.

24   Cross, *Study Group,* stresses the need to compare extant manuscripts. Also, see my "Additions and Notes in Princess Dashkova's *Mon histoire.*"

25   Veselaia, 31; Moiseeva, *Literaturnye sochineniia,* 25.

26   N. Ia. Eidel'man in Rudnitskaia, *Spravochnyi tom,* 259.

27   Bradford, II: 240.

28   (1) Dashkova describes how in her early years she rummaged through her uncle's official papers (26–27). (2) Peter III tells Dashkova about his intention to get rid of his wife Catherine II and marry Elizaveta, Dashkova's sister (46). (3) Fitzlyon does not translate this clarification of terms for family relations in English and Russian (Brooke Family Papers, Additional MSS. No. 31, 911. P. 130 (end of Part I). (4) Dashkova explains that in default of male clothes Dashkova could not go out to join Catherine II the first night of the coup (72). (5) She goes on to describe a joyous meeting with Catherine II (73). (6) Catherine the Great's triumphant entry into the

jubilant capital with Dashkova at her side reflecting on the bloodless coup (79). (7) Dashkova recalls anecdotes dealing with the reign of Empress Anna. In order to conflate the texts, Fitzlyon adds the following transition: "However, to go back to the main thread of my story" (87–88). (8) A revision enlarging on Dashkova's joy at seeing her husband (91). (9) Revision of a passage dealing with the Dashkovs' move into the palace and how they would dine with the Empress (91). (10) Dashkova writes that her illusions concerning the friendship of Sovereigns are now nearly dead (91–92). Fitzlyon omits an introductory sentence at the bottom of page 128, Brooke copy. (11) During a storm at sea Dashkova lectures her children on the importance of courage and trust in the Divine Will (121). (12) A letter Dashkova received in Haarlem from Prince Golitsyn: The first version, which appears in the Vorontsov copy, is crossed out and rewritten. The second is also crossed out since Martha omitted it in her translation (152). (13) Seemingly, Martha's note explaining that the two tables Dashkova bought for Catherine II were later presented to Emperor Aleksandr. In order to adapt the note, Fitzlyon changes the third-person narration ("La princesse") to first person (176). (14) Dashkova expands the section concerning the aims of her son's education and the reasons for traveling to England to achieve these aims (188–89). (15) She cites a Russian proverb that Catherine II disliked (216). (16) Dashkova explains that the Russian Academy building was constructed under her direction but at the Empress's expense, and mentions her great love of architecture (219). (17) She describes a village celebration of song and dance organized in honor of Mrs. Hamilton (223). (18) Dashkova states that lately she has been reading two books entitled *Catherine the Great* and *Anecdotes of the Reign of Catherine II*. She goes on to discuss Catherine the Great's attitude toward languages (248–49). (19) In Korotovo, the village to which Dashkova was exiled by Pavel I, the priest expresses his love and admiration for Dashkova and her son (268). For a more detailed description of the omissions see my "Additions and Notes."

29   Alekseev, 22–23.

30   According to Bartenev, 460, she was hunchbacked.

SELECTED BIBLIOGRAPHY

Works

Bartenev, Petr, ed. *Arkhiv kniazia Vorontsova*. 40 vols. and index. Moscow: V. Got'e 1870–1897.

Bradford, M., trans. and ed. *Memoirs of the Princess Daschkaw, Lady of Honour to Catherine II, Empress of All the Russias. Written by Herself: Comprising Letters of the Empress, and Other Correspondence*. 2 vols. London: Henry Colburn, 1840.

Brooke Family Papers, Additional manuscripts. No. 31, 911, British Museum Library.

Chechulin, N. D. *Zapiski kniagini Dashkovoi*. St. Petersburg: A. S. Suvorin, 1907.

Fitzlyon, Kyril, trans. and ed. *The Memoirs of Princess Dashkova*. London: John Calder, 1958.

Herzen (Gertsen), A. I., ed. *Zapiski kniagini E. R. Dashkovoi*. 1859. Moscow: Nauka, 1990.

"Iz pis'ma kniagini E. R. Dashkovoi k grafu Germanu Keizerlingu . . . ," *Russkii arkhiv* 3 (1887): 185–91.

Moiseeva, G. N., ed. *Ekaterina Dashkova. Zapiski 1743–1810*. Leningrad: Nauka, 1985.

————, ed. *Literaturnye sochineniia*. Moscow: Pravda, 1990.

————, ed. *Zapiski i vospominaniia russkikh zhenshchin XVIII—pervoi poloviny XIX veka*. Moscow: Sovremennik, 1990.

Pontremoli, Pascal, ed. *Mémoires de la princess Daschkoff*. Paris: Mercure de France, 1966.

Royal Irish Academy, Unpublished manuscript, 12 L 25, 12 M 18.

Veselaia, G. A., ed. *Zapiski. Pis'ma sester M. i K. Vil'mot iz Rossii*. Moscow: Moskovskii universitet, 1987.

Biographies

Hyde, H. Montgomery. *The Empress Catherine and Princess Dashkov*. London: Chapman and Hall, 1935.

Ilovaiskii, D. I. *E. R. Dashkova*. Moscow: A. L. Vasil'ev, 1884.

Lozinskaia, L. Ia. *Vo glave dvukh akademii*. Moscow: Nauka, 1978.

Ogarkov, V. V. *E. R. Dashkova. Ee zhizn' i obshchestvennaia deiatel'nost'*. St. Petersburg: V. T. Shtein, 1893.

Schlegelberger, Gunther. *Die Fürsten Daschkowa*. Berlin: Junker und Dünnhaubt, 1935.

Suvorin, A. *Kniaginia E. R. Dashkova*. St. Petersburg: A. S. Suvorin, 1888.

Taigny, E. *Catherine II et la princesse Daschkoff*. Paris: Chez G. Paetz, 1860.

References, Criticism, Literary and
Historical Background

Alekseev V. N., ed. *Vorontsovy: Dva veka v istorii Rossii*. Vladimir: RIO, 1992.

Alexander, Meena. *Fault Lines: A Memoir*. New York: Feminist Press at the City University of New York, 1993.

Anderson, Bonnie S., and Judith P. Zinsser, ed. *A History of Their Own: Women in Europe from Prehistory to the Present*. 2 vols. New York: Harper and Row, 1988.

Atkinson, Dorothy. "Society and the Sexes in the Russian Past." *Women in Russia*. Ed. Dorothy Atkinson, Alexander Dallin, and Gail Warshofsky Lapidus. Stanford: Stanford University Press, 1977.

Bartenev, Petr, ed. *Arkhiv kn. F. A. Kurakina*, vol. 7. Saratov, 1898.

Bisha, Robin. "The Promise of Patriarchy: Marriage in Eighteenth-Century Russia." Diss. Indiana University, 1993.

Brodzki, Bella, and Celeste Schenck, ed. *Life/Lines: Theorizing Women's Autobiography*. Ithaca: Cornell University Press, 1988.

Burgin, Diana. "After the Ball Is Over: Sophia Parnok's Creative Relationship with Marina Tsvetaeva." *The Russian Review* 47 (1988): 425–44.

————. "Laid out in Lavender: Perceptions of Lesbian Love in Russian Literature and Criticism of the Silver Age, 1893–1917." *Sexuality and the Body in Russian Culture*. Ed. Jane Costlow, Stephanie Sandler, and Judith Vowles. Stanford: Stanford University Press, 1993: 177–203.

————. "Signs of a Response: Two Possible Parnok Replies to Her 'Podruga'." *Slavic and East European Journal* 35 (Summer 1991): 214–27.

————. *Sophia Parnok: The Life and Work of Russia's Sappho*. New York: New York University Press, 1994.

Castle, Terry. *The Apparitional Lesbian*. New York: Columbia University Press, 1993.

Catherine II. *The Memoirs of Catherine the Great*. Ed. Dominique Maroger. Trans. Moura Budberg. London: Hamish Hamilton, 1955, 1961.

Chukovskaia, Lidiia. *Pamiati detstva*. New York: Chalidze Publications, 1983. English translation: *To the Memory of Childhood*. Trans. Eliza Kellog Klose. Evanston, Ill.: Northwestern University Press, 1988.

————. *Sofia Petrovna. Povesti*. Moscow: Moskovskii rabochii, 1988. English translation: *Sofiia Petrovna*. Translated by Aline Worth (revised and amended by Eliza Kellog Klose). Evanston, IL: Northwestern University Press, 1988.

Costlow, Jane, Stephanie Sandler, and Judith Vowles, ed. *Sexuality and the Body in Russian Culture*. Stanford: Stanford University Press, 1993.

Cross, A. G. *"By the Banks of the Thames": Russians in Eighteenth-Century Britain*. Newtonville, Mass.: Oriental Research Partners, 1980.

————. Reviews of Lozinskaia, Moiseeva and Veselaia in *Study Group on Eighteenth-Century Russia Newsletter* 6, 14, 16 (1978, 1986, 1988): 71–76, 73–74, 38–43.

de Man, Paul. *Allegories of Reading: Figural Language in Rousseau, Nietzsche, Rilke and Proust*. New Haven, Conn.: Yale University Press, 1979.

Dolgorukaia, Natal'ia Borisovna. *The Memoirs of Princess Natal'ja Borisovna Dolgorukaja.* Ed. and trans. Charles E. Townsend. Columbus, Ohio: Slavica, 1977. Bilingual edition.

Dostoevskaia, Anna. *Vospominaniia.* Moscow: Khudozhestvennaia literatura, 1981. An English version of Dostoevskaia's memoirs is: *Dostoevsky: Reminiscences.* Trans. and ed. Beatrice Stillman. New York: Liveright, 1975.

Dudgeon, Ruth. "Women and Higher Education in Russia, 1855–1905." Diss. George Washington University, 1975.

Durova, N. A. *Kavalerist-devitsa: Proisshestvie v Rossii.* 2 parts. St. Petersburg, 1836. *The Cavalry Maiden: Journals of a Russian Officer in the Napoleonic Wars.* Trans., ed., and introduction by Mary F. Zirin. Bloomington: Indiana University Press, 1989.

Dvoichenko-Markoff, Eufrosina. "Benjamin Franklin, the American Philosophical Society and the Russian Academy of Sciences." *Proceedings of the American Philosophical Society* 3 (August 1947): 250–57.

Faderman, Lillian. *Odd Girls and Twilight Lovers.* New York: Penguin, 1991.

———. *Surpassing the Love of Men: Romantic Friendship and Love Between Women from the Renaissance to the Present.* New York: William Morrow, 1981.

Farnsworth, Beatrice, and Lynne Viola, ed. *Russian Peasant Women.* New York: Oxford University Press, 1992.

Folkenflik, Robert, ed. *The Culture of Autobiography: Constructions of Self-Representation.* Stanford: Stanford University Press, 1993.

Forrester, Sibelan. "Wooing the Other Woman." *Engendered Species: Issues in Slavic Literatures.* Indiana University Press, 1996.

Foucault, Michel. *The Archeology of Knowledge and the Discourse of Language.* Trans. A. M. Sheridan Smith. New York: Pantheon Books, 1972.

Fuss, Diana. *Essentially Speaking: Feminism, Nature and Difference.* New York: Routledge, 1989.

Gillel'son, M. I. "Pushkin i *Zapiski* E. R. Dashkovoi." *Molodaia gvardiia* 10 (1974): 132–44.

Ginzburg, Evgeniia. *Krutoi marshrut.* English translation: *Journey into the Whirlwind.* Trans. Paul Stevenson and Max Hayward. San Diego: Harcourt, Brace, Jovanovich, 1967; and *Within the Whirlwind.* Trans. Ian Boland. San Diego: Harcourt, Brace, Jovanovich, 1981.

Glickman, Rose L. *Russian Factory Women.* Berkeley: University of California Press, 1984.

Grant, Judith. *Fundamental Feminism: Contesting the Core Concepts of Feminist Theory.* New York: Routledge, 1993.

Griffiths, David. "Catherine II and the Problem of Female Sovereignty." Paper, AAASS Convention. Honolulu, November 1993.

Gunn, Janet Varner. *Autobiography: Towards a Poetics of Experience.* Philadelphia: University of Pennsylvania Press, 1982.

Harris, Jane Gary. "Diversity of Discourse: Autobiographical Statements in Theory and Praxis." *Autobiographical Statements in Twentieth-Century Russian Literature.* Ed. Jane Gary Harris. Princeton: Princeton University Press, 1990.

Heilbrun, Carolyn. *Hamlet's Mother and Other Essays.* New York: Ballantine Books, 1990.

———. *Writing a Woman's Life.* New York: Ballantine Books, 1988.

Heldt, Barbara. *Terrible Perfection: Women and Russian Literature.* Bloomington: Indiana University Press, 1987.

Helly, Dorothy O., and Susan M. Reverby, ed. *Gendered Domains: Rethinking Public and Private in Women's History.* Ithaca: Cornell University Press, 1992.

Herzen (Gertsen), A. I. "Kniaginia E. R. Dashkova." *Polnoe sobranie sochinenii*. Moscow: Akademia nauk, 1957. 12: 361–422.

————. *My Past and Thoughts: The Memoirs of Alexander Herzen*. Abridged. Trans. Constance Garnett; rev. Humphrey Higgins. Berkeley: University of California Press, 1973.

Hokanson, Katya. "Empire of the Imagination: Orientalism and the Construction of Russian National Identity in Pushkin, Marlinskii, Lermontov, and Tolstoi." Diss. Stanford University, 1994.

————. "Pushkin's Invention of the Caucasus." *Russian Review* (July 1994), 336–52.

Holmgren, Beth. "For the Good of the Cause: Russian Women's Autobiography in the Twentieth Century." *Women Writers in Russian Literature*. Ed. Toby W. Clyman and Diana Greene. Westport, Conn.: Praeger, 1994. 127–48.

————. *Women's Works in Stalin's Time*. Bloomington: Indiana University Press, 1993.

Jelinek, Estelle C., ed. *Women's Autobiography: Essays in Criticism*. Bloomington: Indiana University Press, 1980.

Johanson, Christine. *Women's Struggle for Higher Education in Russia, 1855–1900*. Kingston: McGill-Queen's University Press, 1987.

Kaminsky, Amy. "Issues for an International Literary Criticism." *Signs* 19 (Autumn 1993), 1: 213–27.

Koblitz, Ann Hibner. *A Convergence of Lives. Sofia Kovalevskaia: Scientist, Writer, Revolutionary*. Boston: Birkhaüser, 1983.

Kolominov, V. V., and M. Sh. Fainshtein. *Khram muz slovesnykh (Iz istorii Rossiiskoi Akademii)*. Leningrad: Nauka, 1986.

Kornilovich-Zubasheva, O. "Kniaginia E. R. Dashkova za chteniem Kastera." *Sbornik statei po russkoi istorii posviashchennykh S. F. Platonovu*. 1922. Würzburg: Jal-Reprint, 1978. 355–70.

Kovalevskaia, S. V. *Vospominaniia. Povesti*. Moscow: Nauka 1974. English translation: *A Russian Childhood*. Ed. and trans. Beatrice Stillman. New York: Springer-Verlag, 1978.

Labanov, A. "Eshche o 'Zapiskakh' Kniagini Dashkovoi." *Russkii arkhiv* 1 (1881): 366–79.

Labzina, Anna Evdokimovna. *Vospominaniia Anny Evdokimovny Labzinoi 1758–1828*. 1903. Newtonville, Mass.: Oriental Research Partners, 1974.

Landes, Joan B. *Women and the Public Sphere in the Age of the French Revolution*. Ithaca: Cornell University Press, 1988.

Larina, Anna. *Nezabyvaemoe*. Moscow: APN, 1989. English translation: *This I Cannot Forget*. Trans. Gary Kern. New York: W. W. Norton, 1993.

Likhacheva, E. O. *Materialy dlia istorii zhenskogo obrazovaniia v Rossii 1086–1901*. St. Petersburg: M. M. Stasiulevich 1893–1901.

Liljeström, Marianne, Eila Mäntysaari, and Arja Rosenholm, ed. *Gender Restructuring in Russian Studies*. Helsinki: University of Tampere, 1993.

Lionnet, Françoise, *Autobiographical Voices: Race, Gender, Self-Portraiture*. Ithaca: Cornell University Press, 1989.

Longmire, R. A. "Princess Dashkova and the Intellectual Life of Eighteenth Century Russia," Thesis. University of London, 1955.

de Madariaga, Isabel. *Russia in the Age of Catherine the Great*. New Haven: Yale University Press, 1981.

Mailloux, Luc. "La princesse Daschkoff et la France." *Revue d'histoire diplomatique* 1 (1981): 5–25.

Mandelstam, Nadezhda. *Vospominaniia.* 4th Ed. Paris: YMCA Press, 1982. English translation, *Hope Against Hope.* Trans. Max Hayward. Intro. by Clarence Brown. New York: Atheneum, 1970.

Marcus, Jane. "Invincible Mediocrity: The Private Selves of Public Women." *The Private Self: Theory and Practice of Women's Autobiographical Writings.* Ed. Shari Benstock. Chapel Hill: University of North Carolina Press, 1988. 114–46.

Meehan, Brenda. *Holy Women of Russia.* San Francisco: Harper, 1993.

Meehan-Waters, Brenda. "Catherine the Great and the Problem of Female Rule." *Russian Review* 34 (July 1975): 3:293–307.

Nekrasov, Sergei. *Rossiiskaia Akademiia.* Moscow: Sovremennik, 1984.

Norton, Barbara T. "Historical Assessments of Russia's Eighteenth-Century Female Monarchs." Paper, "New Understandings of the Experience of Women," Moscow, 22–24 May 1994.

Offen, Karen, Ruth Roach, and Jane Rendall, ed. *Writing Women's History: International Perspectives.* Bloomington: Indiana University Press, 1991.

Olney, James, ed. *Autobiography: Essays Theoretical and Critical.* Princeton: Princeton University Press, 1980.

Panaeva, A. Ia. *Semeistvo Tal'nikovykh.* 1848. Leningrad: Academia 1928.

———. *Vospominaniia.* 1889. Moscow: Khudozhestvennaia literatura, 1972.

Peterson, Linda. "Institutionalizing Women's Autobiography: Nineteenth-Century Editors and the Shaping of an Autobiographical Tradition." *The Culture of Autobiography.* Ed. Robert Folkenflik. Stanford: Stanford University Press, 1993. 80–103.

Ratushinskaia, Irina. *Grey is the Colour of Hope.* Trans. Alyona Kojevnikov. London: Hodder and Stoughton, 1988.

Rudnitskaia, E. L. *Spravochnyi tom k zapiskam E. R. Dashkovoi, Ekateriny i I. V. Lopukhina.* Moscow: Nauka, 1992.

Said, Edward W. *Orientalism.* New York: Random House, 1978.

Sedgwick, Eve Kosofsky. *Tendencies.* Durham, N.C.: Duke University Press, 1993.

Semezskii, V. I. "Kniaginia Ekaterina Romanovna Dashkova." *Russkaia starina* 3 (March 1874): 407–64.

Shugurov, M. F. "Miss Vil'mot i kniaginia Dashkova." *Russkii arkhiv* 2 (1880): 1:150–217.

———, "Zametki ob angliiskom perevode 'Zapisok' Kniagini Dashkovoi." *Russkii arhiv* 2 (1881): 132–40.

Shuraawi, Huda. *Harem Years: The Memoirs of an Egyptian Feminist.* New York: Feminist Press at the City University of New York, 1987.

Smith, Sidonie. *A Poetics of Woman's Autobiography: Marginality and the Fictions of Self-Representation.* Bloomington: Indiana University Press, 1987.

Smith, Sidonie, and Julia Watson, ed. *De/Colonizing the Subject: The Politics of Gender in Women's Autobiography.* Minneapolis: University of Minnesota Press, 1992.

Sokhanskaia, N. S. *Avtobiografiia.* Moscow: S. I. Ponomarev, 1896.

Sommer, Doris. " 'Not Just a Personal Story': Women's *Testimonios* and the Plural Self." *Life/Lines: Theorizing Women's Autobiography.* Ed. Bella Brodzki and Celeste Schenck. Ithaca: Cornell University Press, 1988.

Stanton, Domna C., ed. *The Female Autograph.* Vol. 12–13 of *New York Literary Forum,* ed. Jeanine Parisier Plottel. New York: New York Literary Forum, 1984.

Stites, Richard. *The Women's Liberation Movement in Russia.* Princeton: Princeton University Press, 1978, 1991.

Sukhomlinov, M. I. *Istoriia Rossiiskoi Akademii.* 8 vols. St. Petersburg (publisher unavailable) 1874–1887.

Terras, Victor, ed. *Handbook of Russian Literature.* New Haven: Yale University Press, 1985.

Tishkin, G. A. "E. R. Dashkova i uchebnaia deiatel'nost v Peterburgskoi Akademii nauk." *Ocherki po istorii Leningradskogo universiteta.* Leningrad: Leningradskii universitet, 1989.

Todd, Janet. *Women's Friendship in Literature.* New York: Columbia University Press, 1980.

Torres, Lourdes. "The Construction of the Self in U.S. Latina Autobiographies." *Third World Women and the Politics of Feminism.* Ed. Chandra Talpade Mohanty, Ann Russo, and Lourdes Torres. Bloomington: Indiana University Press, 1991.

Tsvetaeva, Marina. *Marina Tsvetaeva, A Captive Spirit: Selected Prose.* Trans. J. Marin King. Ann Arbor: Ardis, 1980.

Tur, Evgeniia. *Semeistvo Shalonskikh. Iz semeinoi khroniki.* St. Petersburg: M. M. Stasiulevich 1880.

Vomperskii, V. P. *U istokov Rossiiskoi filologii: E. R. Dashkova. Slavianskoe iazykoznanie. XI mezhdunarodnyi s'ezd slavistov.* Ed. M. E. Tolstoi. Bratislava, September 1993. Moscow: Nauka, 1993. 339–349.

Vowles, Judith. "Marriage à la Russe." *Sexuality and the Body in Russian Culture.* Ed. Jane Costlow, Stephanie Sandler, and Judith Vowles. Stanford: Stanford University Press, 1993. 53–72.

Wachtel, Andrew. *The Battle for Childhood: Creation of a Russian Myth.* Stanford: Stanford University Press, 1990.

———. *An Obsession with History.* Stanford: Stanford University Press, 1993.

Whittaker, Cynthia H. "Princess E. R. Dashkova's Concept of Enlightened Absolutism." Paper, AAASS Convention, Honolulu, November 1993.

Wilmot, Martha and Catherine. *The Russian Journals of Martha and Catherine Wilmot, 1803–1808.* Ed. The Marchioness of Londonderry and H. Montgomery Hyde. London: MacMillan & Co., 1934, 1935. New York: Arno Press, 1971. References in the introduction are to the 1971 edition; references in the afterword are to the 1935 edition.

Woolf, Virginia. *A Room of One's Own.* New York: Harcourt, Brace and World, 1957.

Woronzoff-Dashkoff, A. "Additions and Notes in Princes Dashkova's *Mon histoire.*" *Study Group on Eighteenth-Century Russia Newsletter* 19 (September 1991): 15–21.

———. "Disguise and Gender in Princess Dashkova's *Memoirs.*" *Canadian Slavonic Papers* 32 (March 1991): 61–74.

———. "E. R. Dashkova's Moscow Library." *Slavonic and East European Review* 72 (January 1994): 60–71.

Woronzoff-Dashkoff, A., Vladimir Somov, and Sergei Iskul, ed. *Mon histoire: Mémoires de la Princesse Daschkova.* "Archives de l'Est," Paris: Editions Universitas, forthcoming.

INDEX AND
BIOGRAPHICAL TABLE
OF REFERENCES

NB: The index was compiled by Kyril Fitzlyon and covers only the text of the memoirs.

merely the truncated form of his father's, in accordance with a common practice for illegitimate children at the time.) In his youth he traveled in Western Europe and was presented in Paris to the Duchess of Anhalt-Zerbst, Catherine II's mother, whose lover he is said to have become; it has even been hinted, probably slanderously, that Catherine was his natural daughter. His position in Russia and at Court after Catherine became Empress was certainly unique: he was officially declared to be responsible for all his actions directly to the Empress and no one else; Catherine at all times treated him with the highest (some said, filial) respect and heaped honors upon him. Far from being the ridiculous dotard of Princess Dashkova's *Memoirs* he was a man of outstanding abilities, particularly in the educational sphere, where he introduced important reforms (including the first Russian schools for girls), and which, together with charitable institutions, formed his main interest. His ideas were those of the French philosophes (particularly Rousseau) and he was convinced that education would eventually create "a new race of men," provided the younger generation were isolated from the older. The solution he proposed was the Arnoldian one of boarding schools which would concentrate on the formation of character rather than book-learning, and would help in creating an educated bourgeoisie—a middle class, itself to be made as numerous and as powerful as possible. Not all his ideas took root, but he did become the founder of the Russian educational system and of many charitable institutions (Foundlings Home, Home for Indigenous Widows, Savings and Mortgage Banks for the poorer classes) and the earliest advocate in Russia of free and universal education for both sexes. As President of the Academy of Arts and head of the Department of Government Buildings, he is responsible for much of the architectural aspect of St. Petersburg, of which the best-known features are the quays along the Neva and the canals, the Neva bridge, and Falconet's monument to Peter the Great.

Bezborodko, Aleksandr, Prince (1747–99): 93, 194, 202, 203, 223, 243

Secretary of Catherine II, responsible, from 1781, for her foreign policy. After Catherine's death, he is said to have given to the new Emperor, Pavel I, the only existing copy of the Empress's will, depriving him of his right of succession in favor of his son Aleksandr. Pavel destroyed the will and rewarded Bezborodko with vast estates, 16,000 serfs, great sums of money, the Chancellorship of the Empire and the title of Prince. However, Bezborodko died a little over two years later.

Biron, Charles-Armand de Gontaut, Duke of (1700–88): 162

French Marshal, Governor of Languedoc.

Biron, Ernest-Johann (1690–1772): 90

Lover of the Empress Anna, elected Duke of Courland at her behest and with the help of Ludolf-August von Bismarck, the Iron Chancellor's disreputable ancestor in the Russian service; real ruler of Russia during Anna's reign and Regent of Russia for three weeks after her death, until arrested by Field-Marshal Münnich (q.v.) on 8 November 1740, with the approval of Princess Anna Leopoldovna, mother of the three-months-old Emperor Ivan VI (q.v.). Thereafter, Princess Anna Leopoldovna was herself declared Regent and Biron banished first to Siberia and then to Yaroslavl. He returned to St. Petersburg as a result of Peter III's general amnesty of 1762. Catherine II reinstated him in his rights as ruling Duke of Courland, and he eventually died peacefully in his capital, Mittau, having three years previously

ceded all powers to his son Peter, who himself reigned till 1795 when the Duchy
was absorbed by Russia. Biron's origins were obscure and certainly very humble.
His real name was Bühren, the German equivalent of the Latvian Birins. After his
rise to power, he changed his name to Biron, and on the strength of it claimed
kinship with the French Dukes of that name whose coat-of-arms he adopted. His
descendants, domiciled for the last century and a half in Germany, are now known
as Princes of Biron-Wartemberg, though the head of the family continues to style
himself Duke of Courland.

Blair, Hugh (1718–1800): 147

Scottish Presbyterian Divine, writer of *Sermons,* famous in his time, professor of
Rhetoric and *Belles-lettres* in the Edinburgh University.

Boerhaave-Kaau, Herman (1705–51): 33

Dutch doctor, came to Russia in 1740 and eventually became Personal Physician to
the Empress Elizaveta. He died in Moscow. Through his mother, he was nephew to
the great teacher of chemistry and medicine, Hermann Boerhaave, whose name he
added to his own.

Boileau-Despreaux, Nicolas (1636–1711): 33

French poet.

Bredikhin, Sergei (1744–81): 61, 74, 75

Member of the group of young officers taking part in the conspiracy that successfully placed Catherine II on the Russian throne. His role in the few days preceding
the Palace revolution is accurately described by Princess Dashkova, who, however,
omits to say that he had been drawn into the conspiratorial group by Grigorii Orlov.
Catherine had known of Bredikhin's activities for many months before the coup
d'état, and after her coronation rewarded him with a gift of money equivalent to
180,000 roubles. In 1770 he took part in the Silistrian campaign, was promoted to
Brigadier and on his return to St. Petersburg made Court Chamberlain.

Breteuil, Louis-Charles-Auguste Le Tonnelier, Baron de (1730–1807): 82, 126

French diplomat and statesman, ambassador successively in Denmark, Sweden, Austria, and Russia. He was a friend of Princess Dashkova and thereby aroused the
jealousy of Count Solms, Frederick the Great's Minister in St. Petersburg, who was
afraid of being outwitted by colleagues with better access to political information.
In a despatch to the King of Prussia Solms stated as a fact that the Princess had
revealed to Breteuil the secret of Catherine's plot to seize the Russian throne and
obtained from him some financial support "for the good of the cause." Catherine,
according to Solms, knew nothing of the transaction at the time, and on hearing
of it, compelled Princess Dashkova to return the money. This, clearly, is the origin
of the rumor mentioned by the Princess, that she made use of foreign money to
finance the coup d'état. There seems, however, to be no truth in it whatever. Breteuil's appointment on 12 July 1789 to the post of Chief Minister of the Government
in France after Necker's dismissal provoked a popular insurrection leading to the
taking of the Bastille two days later.

Browne, George, Count (1698–1792): 185

Irish adventurer, soldier, and statesman in Russian service. Born in Dublin and
educated in Limerick, joined in 1725 the army of the Elector of Pfalz, and in 1730
transferred his allegiance to Russia. Took part as officer of the Russian Army in wars

against Poland, Turkey, Sweden, and Prussia, in the course of which he was eventually promoted to General and given every existing Russian decoration. In 1762 he was made Governor-General of Riga, was responsible for spectacular achievements in the economic, administrative, and educational development of the Baltic provinces and was rewarded with the title of Count. In the course of his extraordinary adventures in the Russian Army he was taken prisoner by the Turks, sold into slavery, and after changing owners several times in the slave market was able to make good his escape and steal very important secret instructions of the Turkish government regarding its future war with Russia.

Bruce, James, Count (1732–91): 234

Russian general, Governor-General first of Moscow and St. Petersburg and then, at his own request, of St. Petersburg only; descendant of a Scotsman, James Bruce, who came to Russia in the time of Cromwell. He was a man of considerable personal courage, but of extreme conservative views, a zealous defender of the Russian Orthodox church against the deist and masonic influences infiltrating into Russia from the West. He was married to Praskovia Rumiantseva, sister of the Field-Marshal, and owed his career to his wife's friendship with Empress Catherine.

Bruce, Praskovia, Countess (1729–86): 53

Sister of Field-Marshal Rumiantsev-Zadunaiskii (q.v.) and wife of General James Bruce. Beautiful and dissolute, she was an intimate friend of Catherine II, until discovered to be carrying on an intrigue with Catherine's lover, Rimskii-Korsakov. She was banished from Court and died seven years later.

Brühl, Henry, Count (1700–1763): 183

Buturlin, Aleksandr, Count (1694–1767): 35, 37

Field-Marshal, Senator, and Governor-General of Moscow. Under the Empress Elizaveta he was made Member of the Council of Ministers and appointed Commander-in-Chief of Russian troops and sent against Frederick the Great in the Seven Years War. Peter III recalled him from his command and reappointed him Governor-General of Moscow. His spectacular rise was, no doubt, at least partly due to his having been one of the Empress Elizaveta's lovers. He was father-in-law to Princess Dashkova's sister, Maria (q.v. under Buturlina, Maria) and husband of Princess Catherine Kurakina (died 1772), whose unsuccessful attempts at curtseying in Western European style are described by Princess Dashkova.

Buturlina, Maria, Countess (1737–17??): 32, 54, 55

Sister of Princess Dashkova. A colorless personality. Wife of Peter, son of Field-Marshal Aleksandr Buturlin (q.v.). Mother of Dmitrii Buturlin, a well-known bibliophile and man of encyclopedic knowledge whose library, one of the greatest in Russia, was entirely destroyed during the 1812 Fire of Moscow. Nothing daunted, he formed a second library which, after his death, was dispersed at an auction sale in Paris.

Byers, James (1733–1817): 172–174, 177

Scottish architect, archaeologist, and antiquary, member and fellow of many learned societies. Lived for forty years (1750–1790) in Rome, collecting ancient sculpture. The most famous of his acquisitions was the Portland Vase (now in the British Museum), which he sold to Sir William Hamilton (q.v.). His erudition and helpfulness were appreciated by the Papal Court no less than by Princess Dashkova, and earned him the nickname of "the Pope's antiquary."

Catherine I, Empress (1684–1727): 34

Empress of Russia 1725–27.

Catherine II, Empress (1729–96): 35, 36, 45–50, 52, 53, 59, 60, 62, 65, 67 (and note), 68, 69, 73, 74, 76–80, 82, 83, 85–87, 91–113, 116–118, 124, 126, 133, 137–143, 153–156, 159–161, 167, 170, 176, 181, 183, 185, 189–207, 210–217, 220, 221, 223–231, 234–240, 242–246, 247 (and note), 249, 250, 252, 259, 266, 272, 274, 276, 278, 279, 281

Empress of Russia 1762–96. Catherine was the daughter of a minor German princeling of the House of Anhalt-Zerbst, and of a princess of Holstein. In 1744 she was invited to Russia by the Empress Elizaveta and affianced to Grand-Duke Peter, heir to the Russian throne. Frederick the Great of Prussia encouraged the marriage for political, and the Empress Elizaveta mainly for sentimental, reasons (in her youth she was betrothed to a prince of Holstein, Catherine's uncle, who died before the wedding ceremony). The marriage was a failure, but Catherine early made the resolution to submit to every indignity in order eventually to seize the crown of Russia. This she was able to do on 28 June 1762, after her husband had been on the throne for six months. The main landmarks of her reign were: educational, financial, and local government reforms, annexation of the Crimea and the northern shores of the Black Sea, partition of Poland, extension of serfdom and the strengthening of the power and wealth of the landowners. As a result of the impetus given by Peter the Great earlier in the century, Russian industry continued to expand during her reign in spite of the strain imposed on the national economy by recurrent peasant revolts. One of them, led by Emelian Pugachev, assumed the proportions of a civil war, during which Pugachev's bands controlled—more or less loosely—vast stretches of territory from Tiumen to Tsaritsyn (now Volgograd) and from near Nizhnii Novgorod to the Urals. Throughout her reign Catherine can be said to have ruled with the help of her lovers—favorites—the first of whom, Sergei Saltykov, was the putative father of the Emperor Pavel. Excluding unofficial liaisons and short-term attachments such as Aleksandr Mordvinov, Catherine had twelve favorites in the course of her life in Russia, two of them before she had seized the throne and ten after. The post of favorite came to be regarded almost as an official appointment, for which candidates were recommended as they would have been for any other post. After the Empress's approval the procedure was always the same: the successful candidate was promoted to General, made personal A.D.C. to Her Majesty, and assigned apartments (usually those vacated by his predecessor) in the Palace; the very first night he invariably found 100,000 roubles waiting for him in a drawer of the writing table. More money, valuables, serfs, lands and sometimes titles followed later in varying degrees of impressive profusion. Allusions by Princess Dashkova to the different favorites are so frequent that it may be convenient to list them in their order of appearance on the scene of Russian history:

Name	Date of birth and death	Years of favor
Sergei Saltykov	1726–17??	1752–55
Count Stanisław-August Poniatowski (later, King of Poland)	1732–98	1755–58
Prince Grigorii Orlov	1734–83	1760–72
Aleksandr Vasilchikov	1744–1803	1772–74
Prince Grigorii Potemkin	1739–91	1774–76

*In 1781 Lanskoi shared his duties for a few weeks with Aleksandr Mordvinov. Mordvinov, however, was never officially recognized as favorite.

Charles XIII (1748–1818): 137, 222–225, 227–229
> King of Sweden 1809–18. Brother of King Gustavus III, during whose reign he was known as Duke of Sudermania (Södermanland). Regent 1782–96 during the minority of his nephew (Gustavus IV), though with no real power. Ascended the throne after the deposition of Gustavus IV. After the Union of Norway and Sweden in 1814 he became the first King of the two countries, though, in fact, after his adoption of Bernadotte as Heir Presumptive in 1810, his rule became nominal only. He was the last Sovereign of the House of Vasa.

Charlotte, Queen: 151

Chernysheva, Avdotia, Countess (1693–1747): 90
> Wife of Grigorii Chernyshev, one of the main collaborators of Peter the Great. She was herself a close friend of Peter's and used her influence over him to protect the interests of members of the Imperial Family and in particular of the Emperor's two nieces. It was to this she owed her special position at Court, when one of the nieces ascended the throne as Empress Anna.

Chernyshev, Ivan, Count (1726–97): 108, 223
> Field-Marshal and Admiral of the Fleet, Minister of the Navy, Ambassador in London (1768–70), youngest son of Avdotia Chernysheva.

Chernyshev, Zakhar, Count (1722–84): 108
> Field-Marshal, Viceroy of Belorussia, son of Avdotia Chernysheva. Took part in the Seven Years War and captured Berlin. He and his brother Ivan were intimate friends of Catherine II at the time when she was Grand Duchess and supported her when she seized the throne. As Viceroy of the newly annexed Belorussia he showed brilliant administrative gifts, which he afterward applied, with remarkable effect, during his tenure of office as Military Governor of Moscow.

Choiseul, Etienne-François, Duke of (1719–85): 128
> Minister of Foreign Affairs and of War, as well as Prime Minister of France in all but name under Louis XV.

Collot, Mademoiselle: 160, 161

Cullen, William (1710–90): 147
> Scottish physician, professor of medicine in Glasgow University and one of the most celebrated teachers of medicine of his day.

Damer, Anne Seymour (1749–1828): 173, 174, 175, 176
> British sculptress, daughter of Field-Marshal Conway. She received a brilliant education and according to Horace Walpole "wrote Latin like Pliny and modelled like

Bernini." However, some of her work was said, perhaps maliciously, to have been "ghosted."

Dashkova, Princess (17??–1785): 37, 40–43, 52, 59, 99, 103, 114, 115, 140–142, 230, 231
Mother-in-law of the writer of the present *Memoirs*.

Dashkova, Aleksandra, Princess: 105

Dashkova, Anastasiia
See Anastasiia Shcherbinina

Dashkova, Anna, Princess (1773–1810): 229, 230
Wife of Pavel Dashkov (*q.v.*). Her mother was a cousin of Potemkin's, but had a doubtful reputation. Her father, Simon Alferov, had the misfortune in Princess Dashkova's eyes of being of merchant stock. Pavel Dashkov was therefore considered to have committed a *mesalliance* and Princess Dashkova was bitterly hostile to the marriage, though she afterward relented and took Anna in to live with her after Pavel's death. The marriage was not a success and the couple separated two years after the wedding. There were no children.

Dashkov, Mikhail-Kondratii (1736–64): 36–44, 48, 50–52, 57–59, 95–99, 102–107, 109, 112–114, 231
Lieutenant-Colonel, husband of Princess Dashkova. A gay and attractive young man with no intellectual pretensions, trapped, according to contemporary scandal, into marrying the Grand Chancellor's niece. The marriage seems to have been a success partly due to its briefness and partly to the frequency and length of occasions during which husband and wife were obliged to live apart by force of circumstance.

Dashkov, Pavel, Prince (1763–1807): 39, 112–114, 116, 117, 119, 122, 123, 140, 141, 143, 144, 146–150, 152, 154, 155, 158, 160, 163, 164, 166, 167, 170, 171, 173, 175, 177, 182–185, 189, 190–193, 207, 211, 212, 217, 220, 221, 229–231, 251, 253, 259–261, 269, 272–274, 277
Lieutenant-General, son of Princess Dashkova. Thanks to his mother's insistence he received a very thorough education (M.A., Edinburgh University), but made little use of it, preferring to enjoy life in ways more orthodox for a rich young guards officer of the period. For a time he was attached as A.D.C. to Grigorii Potemkin (*q.v.*), served in Poland and took part in the war against Turkey. After Catherine II's death he gained the favor of the new Emperor Pavel I, was promoted to lieutenant-general, and became military governor of Kiev, Inspector of Infantry of the Ukrainian Division, Colonel-in-Chief of the Kiev Grenadiers. The Emperor's favor, however, lasted barely two years. Dashkov was implicated in the Altesti affair (*q.v.*) and received a curt note of dismissal. After Pavel's assassination he returned to Moscow where he died six years later. In 1785 he married secretly from his mother a Miss Anna Alferova (*q.v.* under Dashkova, Anna) but had no children from her, and his name and property passed on to his cousin Ivan Vorontsov. His three illegitimate children were brought up by his sister, Anastasiia Shcherbinina (*q.v.*).

Denis, Louise (1712–90): 133
A writer of at least one comedy and several short stories, she is famous merely as "Voltaire's niece" (her mother, Catherine Arouet, was Voltaire's sister). Whether she was also his mistress has been debated, but never proved. (She had the reputation of being attractive and amusing in her youth—though Princess Dashkova found her to be neither in her old age—and was said to entertain her uncle's

numerous guests with "the charms of her bed, while he offered them the grace of his wit."

Denny, Lady Arabella (1708–92): 150

Daughter of Thomas Fitzmaurice, 1st Earl of Kerry and wife of Arthur Denny, Member of the Irish Parliament for Co. Kerry. A celebrated Irish "blue-stocking" famous for her good works; founder of the Magdalen Asylum for Fallen Women and of the Foundling Hospital for Children in Dublin.

Derzhavin, Gavrila Romanovich (1743–1816): 212

Statesman and incomparably the greatest Russian poet of the eighteenth century; helped to develop Russian poetry, particularly lyric poetry, by cleansing it of rhetoric and introducing far more simplicity into its structure and vocabulary than was usual in his time. Provincial governor and Senator under Catherine II, President of the Board of Trade under Pavel I, Minister of Justice under Aleksandr I.

Diderot, Denis (1713–84): 123–127 (and note), 130, 156–158, 160

French philosopher, editor of the *Encyclopédie.*

Dmitriev-Mamonov, Aleksandr, Count (1758–1803): 252

Eleventh in succession (and the one-before-last) of Catherine II's lovers, his years of favor lasting from 1786 to 1789, when he was succeeded by Platon Zubov (*q.v.*). Was originally sent to Catherine by Grigorii Potemkin (*q.v.*) as candidate for the role of official favorite and was immediately approved. However, he eventually committed the solecism of falling in love with one of the maids-of-honor and was abruptly dismissed, just as Catherine was about to appoint him Vice-Chancellor. Nevertheless, Catherine magnanimously gave the bride away herself and richly endowed the newly married couple in recognition of the young husband's past services. See under Catherine II, Empress, for list of favorites.

Dolgorukaia, Elizaveta, Princess (1763–98): 255, 256, 270

Wife of Mikhail Dolgorukii, sister of Pavel Bakunin (*q.v.*) and granddaughter of Princess Dashkova's aunt, Praskovia Vorontsova. She was a cousin of Mikhail Bakunin, the famous Russian anarchist of the nineteenth century.

Dolgorukii, Vladimir, Prince (1720–1803): 119, 138, 183–184

Russian Minister at the Court of Prussia 1762–81.

Domashnev, Sergei (1742 or 1746–96): 136, 203–205, 215, 243

Grigorii Orlov's successor and Princess Dashkova's predecessor as Director of the Academy of Sciences. After graduating from Moscow University, he joined the Army, became a staff officer, took part in the Russo-Turkish war in 1772 and, rather surprisingly, commanded the Albanian Legion. During his directorship of the Academy he made himself ridiculous by his inefficiency, his doubtful financial honesty and his tenth-rate literary productions in the shape of poetry and essays. However, he was the first to advocate the reform of the Russian alphabet by eliminating the letter Ъ; this occasioned a great deal of mirth at the time, but eventually he won the day—150 years later.

Donaurov, Mikhail (177?–1816): 249, 250

Major-General, Senator. His social origins may have been as described rather superciliously by Princess Dashkova, but by the 1780s he had already become Secretary and Librarian to the Grand Duke Pavel, and it is, therefore, somewhat surprising that Princess Dashkova does not seem to have heard of him. On ascending the throne in 1796 Pavel made him Head of H.M. Cabinet (the Emperor's private chancellery). But he was an unpopular man and the intrigues of his numerous enemies at Court finally forced him out of office. Pavel's successor, Aleksandr I, had him recalled and appointed Senator.

Elagin, Ivan (1725–94): 110, 111

Senator, Director of the Court Theater, personal secretary to Catherine II, who prized highly his intelligence, used his help in the writing of her plays, and sometimes signed her letters as "Chancellor to Mr. Elagin." He was one of the earliest Russian freemasons (affiliated to the English lodges) and became the first Grand Master of the Order in Russia.

Elizaveta, Empress (1709–61): 31, 32, 33, 39, 40, 45–48, 50, 51, 54, 70, 71, 82, 90, 94, 185, 226

Empress of Russia 1741–61. Daughter of Peter the Great and his second wife, Catherine. Born out of wedlock, she was legitimized by her parents' subsequent marriage. After the death of her mother, Catherine I, in 1727, lived first at the Court of the boy-Emperor Peter II, and then in semi-retirement during the reign of her cousin Anna and the Regency of Anna Leopoldovna, until she seized the throne on 25 November 1741. Was secretly married to a Ukrainian cossack, Aleksei Razumovskii.

Elizaveta (1779–1826): 277, 278

Russian Empress, wife of Aleksandr I (q.v.), daughter of the Margrave of Baden.

Elmpt, Johann-Martin, von, Count (1725–1802): 164

Native of Russia's Baltic provinces, general in Catherine II's service. In 1769 he occupied Moldavia, then a Turkish province and annexed it to Russia. His son, mentioned in Princess Dashkova's memoirs, died unmarried and the name and title devolved on Elmpt's daughter and her issue.

Eropkin, Peter (1724–1805): 141

Senator, General. During the 1771 outbreak of plague in Moscow he commanded government troops sent to put down the rioting and organized relief works for the alleviation of distress. He was married to Elizaveta Leontieva, aunt (through his mother) of Princess Dashkova's husband.

Euler, Johann-Albrecht (1724–1800): 205

Eldest son of Leonard Euler, Secretary to Academic Conferences at the Academy of Sciences in St. Petersburg. Mathematician, physicist, astronomer.

Euler, Leonhard (1707–83): 205–206

One of the greatest mathematicians of the eighteenth century. A Swiss by birth, he came in 1727 to Russia on the invitation of Catherine I's Government, and became member of the Russian Academy of Sciences. He left Russia in 1741 at the request of Frederick the Great to become member of the Academy of Sciences in Berlin. In 1766 he returned to St. Petersburg and died there seventeen years later. One of his most important contributions was the editing and publication of a Russian atlas. A man of encyclopedic knowledge (he knew the *Aeneid* of Virgil by heart from beginning to end), he incurred the ridicule of the philosophes by his deep religious convictions.

taire exclaim that it could have been written by Plato and Molière in collaboration. He was famous for his striking predictions based, in fact, on a shrewd reading of political and social tendencies and events. One such prediction—that economists will end up by producing a religion—seems particularly striking.

Gardel: 158
It is not certain which of the two brothers Princess Dashkova has in mind: Maximilien (1741–87) or Pierre-Gabriel (1758–1840). Both were famous French ballet dancers and choreographers, successors to Vestris and Noverre.

Geoffrin, Marie-Thérèse (1699–1777): 123, 124, 127
Friend of the philosophes and *encyclopédistes,* who was able to make her house into a meeting place for the intellectual and artistic elite of Paris. Twice a week she gave dinners—for artists on Mondays, for writers on Wednesdays, while members of the aristocracy, distinguished strangers, and certain intimate friends, such as Diderot, d'Alembert, Poniatowski, gathered in her house later in the evening any day of the week.

Georgi, Johann-Gottlieb (1729–1802): 208
Professor of natural history and chemistry at the St. Petersburg Academy of Sciences. Son of a German pastor, he came to Russia in 1770, and remained there for the rest of his life. He undertook scientific expeditions in East European Russia and in Siberia (partly in conjunction with Pallas and Lepekhin (*q.v.*) and composed an ethnographical description of the Russian Empire which is still of considerable interest. He practiced medicine—one of his many activities—and was considered one of the best doctors in St. Petersburg.

Glebov, Aleksandr (1722–90): 71
"General-in-Chief" and "Procurator-General" (equivalent to Minister of Justice). He owed his career less to native shrewdness than to his friendship with Peter Shuvalov (*q.v.*) and to his marriage to Catherine I's niece. Took Catherine II's side at the time of Peter III's overthrow; during his tenure of office was responsible for the abolition of the Secret Police and for the introduction of paper currency for the first time in Russia.

Golitsyn, Dmitrii, Prince (1721–93): 179, 182
Russian Ambassador at Vienna. After many years at that post he was retired at his own request and replaced by Andrei Razumovskii (*q.v.*). He died the following year without returning to Russia.

Golitsyn, Dmitrii, Prince (1734–1803): 126, 151, 152
Russian diplomat and writer, Minister at The Hague. While serving in the Russian Embassy in Paris became an enthusiastic admirer of the philosophes, corresponded with Voltaire and Diderot and published a number of books on such subjects as: "De l'esprit des économistes, ou les économistes justifiés d'avoir posé par leurs principes les bases de la révolution française." In 1768 was appointed Minister to The Hague where he remained till his death. A convinced rationalist and a deist in approved eighteenth-century style, he was amazed at the sudden conversion to Roman Catholicism of his son Dmitrii, who was ordained priest and became a well-known missionary among the Red Indians of the United States.

Golitsyn, Mikhail, Prince (1697–1775): 90
Fool at the Court of the Empress Anna (*q.v.*). Brought up by his grandfather Vasilii

inferred from Princess Dashkova's words, seems to have been due to diphtheria. He was ninth in succession and the youngest of all the favorites, having been appointed to that post at the age of twenty on Potemkin's recommendation (see under Catherine II, Empress), but he apparently had a genuine love for the Empress who was by then almost precisely double his age and who had aroused his jealousy by taking on another lover (Aleksandr Mordvinov) in 1781. Lanskoi showed such despair that Mordvinov was dismissed after a few weeks, without graduating to the full status of official favorite. In spite of this *contretemps,* Catherine seems sincerely to have loved the gentle and unassuming Lanskoi and she was made so distraught by his death that she allowed several months to pass before accepting another favorite from the hands of Potemkin.

An officer in the Izmailovskii Guards and strong supporter of Catherine against Peter III. Refused to accept Panin's "Regency Plan" and helped to proclaim Catherine Empress of Russia in her own right. See also Roslavlev, Nikolai.

General, brother of Princess Dashkova's mother-in-law, the Dowager Princess. He was involved in Bestuzhev-Riumin's political intrigues and in his consequent fall from favor.

Emperor of Austria and Grand Duke of Tuscany, son of the Empress Maria Theresa and brother of Joseph II. Intelligent, unemotional, and efficient, his reign in Tuscany (1765–92) brought great material prosperity to the State and unpopularity to himself. He succeeded his brother Joseph to the throne of the Holy Roman Empire in 1790 and his two years' reign as Emperor was dominated by events in France.

Permanent Secretary of the Russian Academy. Son of a private soldier in the Russian Army, he was sent to Strasbourg university at Government expense, became one of the foremost Russian naturalists of his day, headed a scientific expedition to North and East European Russia, and was the first holder of the gold medal which the Academy awarded annually to the most deserving of its members. This gold medal was first offered to Princess Dashkova, but she declined the honor in favor of Lepekhin. He was the moving spirit behind the Russian Academy and the ablest of Princess Dashkova's collaborators.

A Hanoverian subject, son of a French emigrant, he arrived in Russia in 1713 as personal physician to Peter the Great. During the Regency of Anna Leopoldovna (*q.v.*) he took part in many Court intrigues and helped the Grand Duchess Elizaveta to seize the throne of Russia. Later, he quarrelled with Chancellor Bestuzhev (*q.v.*), whose anti-French and anti-Prussian policy he opposed (in return for a pension of 15,000 livres from Paris and the title of Count of the Holy Roman Empire granted to him at Prussia's request). He was tried, tortured, and banished to Uglich and then to Velikii Ustiug whence he returned under Peter III.

General. Took part in the Russo-Turkish and Russo-Swedish wars; in 1800 was Russian Envoy Extraordinary in Naples.

with young men selected by Elizaveta to be her own lovers. Was finally married off by the Empress at the age of forty to Dmitrii Matiushkin, a man famous for his good looks.

Medici, Cosimo de (1389–1464): 174

Ruler of Florence.

Melgunov, Aleksei (1722–1788): 53, 56, 71

Lieutenant-General under Peter III, whose great favorite he was, he became, after a short eclipse due to Peter's overthrow, Senator under Catherine; held for a time other appointments such as Governor-General of Novorossiisk and Governor of Yaroslavl and Vologda. Intelligent and fairly unscrupulous, he was able to win Catherine II's favor by posing as a philosophe and translating bits out of the *Encyclopédie*. He became a freemason at the time when it was the fashionable thing to be.

Melissino, Ivan (1718–95): 155

Head of the Holy Synod (Department of State responsible, since the abolition of the Patriarchate, for all Church affairs). Tried unsuccessfully to introduce radical reforms into the Church, more in conformity with certain types of Western Protestantism, e.g., marriage of bishops, abolition of the communion of infants and of prayers for the dead, Bible-reading in church instead of traditional prayers, closing of all monasteries. He was Greek by origin, though born in Russia. Married to Princess Praskovia Dolgorukaia.

Mercy-Argentau, Florimond Claude, Comte de (1727–94): 54

Austrian diplomat, minister at St. Petersburg at the time of Catherine's coup d'état of 1762. In 1766 he was transferred to Paris and was instrumental in bringing about the marriage of the Dauphin (later King Louis XVI) and Marie-Antoinette whose close personal friend and adviser he became, thereby gaining immense influence at Court. After the revolution he was appointed Governor-General of the Belgian provinces and ended his career as Ambassador in London.

Meshcherskii, Platon, Prince (1713–99): 71

Governor-General of the Ukraine (1769–75) and later of many other Russian provinces.

Mirovich, Vasilii (1740–64): 109–111

A young officer commanding the guard at Schüsselburg Fortress near St. Petersburg, where the deposed Emperor Ivan VI (*q.v.*) was kept imprisoned. Moved by his prisoner's tragic fate, he decided to free him and proclaim him Emperor. Mirovich was able to persuade the garrison to come over to his side and with its help arrested the Fortress Commandant. Ivan VI, however, was killed by his bodyguard acting on previous instructions, and Mirovich was captured, tried, and executed.

Mocenigo, Demetrio, Count (17??–1801): 166

Member of a famous Venetian family. He rendered great services to the Russian Government during the first Russo-Turkish war by providing the Russian fleet with food supplies, maritime maps, and military information through a network of spies, all at his own expense. Fearing reprisals from the Turks, the Venetian Government imprisoned him and allowed his property to be looted. He was freed at Russian insistence and became Russian chargé d'affaires at the Tuscan Court.

Mulgrave, Lady: 147, 148

attempt to do so was made immediately after Catherine II's coup d' état which he supported, though his own plan favored the Grand-Duke Pavel (to whom he became tutor in 1760), with Catherine as Regent. Though never appointed Chancellor, the conduct of Russian foreign policy from 1762–81 was in effect entirely in his hands. He aimed at creating a Northern Alliance grouping Russia, Prussia, Poland, Sweden, and, perhaps, Great Britain against the Franco-Austrian League; opposed the partition of Poland partly on moral grounds and because he considered Poland as an indispensable member of his alliance. Catherine's rapprochement with Austria against Prussia undermined his position and he retired in 1783. His second attempt at limiting Imperial power involved him in an abortive conspiracy against Catherine. He was a man of remarkably wide education, very liberal views, and scrupulous honesty, a freemason, fond of good living and especially of women. Whether he was Princess Dashkova's lover (or father or both) remains uncertain; there is less doubt concerning his relations with her first cousin, Countess Anna Stroganova (q.v.). For his family connection with Prince Dashkov, see illustration of the Dashkovs, et al.

Panin, Peter, Count (1721–89): 57, 105, 109–13

General, Senator, brother of Nikita; took part in the Seven Years War and in the war against Turkey (1768–74). Captured Bendery in Moldavia from the Turks, but his victory, though complete, was judged by Catherine II to have been too sanguinary and altogether destructive. Incensed at this lack of appreciation of his services, he went into snarling retirement immediately after the war, and was considered by the Empress to be her "foremost enemy." However, in 1774, he was recalled to command Government troops against the great peasant revolt led by Pugachev. After Pugachev's capture he was appointed Governor of the provinces devastated by what in effect was a civil war and very rapidly and efficiently restored order and comparative prosperity.

His last direct descendant, Sofiia Panina, was the first woman in Europe ever to become Minister. She was put in charge of the Department of Social Welfare in Kerenskii's last pre-Bolshevik Government. She died as a refugee in the United States in 1956. For his family connection with Prince Dashkov, see illustration of the Dashkovs, et al.

Passek, Peter (1736–1804): 61, 67, 68, 74, 75, 81

Head of one of the four sections into which the conspirators, plotting to raise Catherine to the throne, were grouped. His arrest on 27 June 1762 precipitated events which led to Catherine's coup d' état the following day. The Empress personally freed him on her way to the thanksgiving service in the Kazan Cathedral, and his career was henceforth assured. He was given money, land, serfs, and promoted to the rank of Governor-General of two Belorussian Provinces and finally Senator. In spite of a very limited intellect he was invariably successful in everything he undertook, including such dubious ventures as the appropriation of Princess Radziwiłł's jewels and his nephew's property.

Pavel I (1754–1801): 33, 44 (note), 46, 56, 65, 68, 78, 84, 93, 96, 101, 102, 106, 141, 177, 210, 211, 215, 216 (note), 249–253, 258-260, 262–265, 266 (and note), 267, 272–277, 283

Emperor of Russia 1796–1801. Son of Catherine II and—officially—Peter III. There is, however, some evidence that his real father may have been Sergei Saltykov. His

Sister of Princess Dashkova and mistress of Peter III. Described by various authorities as quite exceptionally dull-witted, small, squat, fat, and startlingly ugly, with a dark, sallow complexion, a puffy, pockmarked face, a very noticeable squint, and an irritating habit of spitting, using obscene language, and starting brawls especially when drunk. Was nevertheless deeply loved by Peter, who apparently had the intention of marrying her and proclaiming her Empress after divorcing Catherine. Catherine, in turn, bore her no ill-will and after establishing herself on the throne bought a house for her in Moscow, was godmother to her children, and made one of them her maid-of-honor. Three years after Peter's assassination she married a Court Chamberlain, Colonel Aleksandr Polianskii, by whom she had a son, Aleksandr, and a daughter, Anna. Anna, mentioned by Princess Dashkova, was made maid-of-honor to Catherine and later married Baron d'Hoggier, the Dutch Ambassador to the Russian Court.

Poniatowski, Stanisław, Prince (1755–1833): 145

Nephew of the last King of Poland (q.v. under Poniatowski, Stanisław-August). The King tried unsuccessfully to persuade Catherine II to recognize him as heir to the Polish throne. After the fall of Poland he went to live in Rome and Florence where he formed a magnificent collection of modern and ancient statuary. His present-day descendants are French citizens and bear the name of Poniatowski di Monte Rotondo, with the title of Prince.

Poniatowski, Stanisław-August (1732–98): 108, 112, 127, 144, 145, 209

Last King of Poland, reigned 1764–95. In his youth (1755–58) he was a lover (her second) of the Grand-Duchess (later Empress) Catherine, who raised him to the throne with the backing of the Czartoryski family and "the Russian Party." During his disastrous reign Poland was dismembered twice. He abdicated four years before his death and finished his days in St. Petersburg where Pavel I made him a gift of the Marble Palace, erstwhile property of Grigorii Orlov (q.v.), who had many years previously succeeded him in Catherine's favors. The story is told (though its authenticity is doubtful) that while still King he sent the actual throne of Poland to Catherine, in gratitude for her part in placing him on it; she had it adapted as a lavatory seat, and fell off it after an apopletic fit from which she died in a few hours.

Potemkin, Grigorii, Prince (c. 1739–1791): 140, 144, 154, 156, 161, 170, 189, 191, 193, 195 (note), 197–199, 201, 202, 209, 210, 220, 279

Probably the most outstanding personality among Catherine's lovers (of whom he was fifth in succession), surpassing them all in the vastness of the fortune he was able to build up and the power he was able to wield (though in that last respect he was rivalled by Platon Zubov, q.v.). He remained favorite for only three years (1774–76; see under Catherine II, Empress) and retired from the post of his own accord. However, he continued to exercise great influence over the Empress, most of whose subsequent favorites were appointed on his recommendation. His main and lasting title to fame was his administration of South-Eastern European Russia, particularly the Crimea, for which he received the title of Prince of Tauris. Most of the towns he had helped to found in that part of the country have very successfully taken root and now represent large and thriving communities.

Potemkin, Pavel, Count (1743–96): 189, 190

Cousin of Grigorii Potemkin, writer, soldier, and statesman. In 1783 was able to

Scottish historian, famous in his day, but now neglected. His main work was the *History of the Reign of the Emperor Charles V.* He was for a time Principal of Edinburgh University.

Scottish doctor, spent fifty years in Russia (1766–1816) as Court Physician to Catherine II, Pavel I, and Aleksandr I. He had a vast circle of friends among all conditions of men including most Russian statesmen and courtiers of his time. This, and his propensity to dabble in politics, made him into a source of useful information for Catherine whose devoted confidant he was and at whose death he was present. In the course of his medical career he acquired a considerable fortune, bought some land in Dumfriesshire, built himself a house there and lived in it in some state after his retirement in 1816 till his death seven years later.

Lieutenant-General. While still a major in the Izmailovskii Guards, he took part in the conspiracy to overthrow Peter III (1762), and rendered signal service to the Empress Catherine by refusing to accept Panin's "Regency Plan" (Catherine to rule as Regent till the majority of her son Pavel, who should thereafter be vested with full powers modified by a Constitution). When on the day of the coup d' état Roslavlev and his friend Lasunskii were informed that the Empress had agreed to Panin's proposal, they refused it their support, declared Catherine to be Sovereign Empress in her own right, and made their regiment acclaim her as such, thus turning the day in her favor. Dissatisfied with the reward he duly obtained after Catherine's coronation, Roslavlev joined the opposition (led by Khitrovo) to the growing influence of the Orlov brothers and to the Empress's supposed intention of marrying Grigorii Orlov. This, and especially his frequent references to a document Catherine had allegedly signed agreeing to Panin's Regency Plan, led to his incarceration. He was freed two years later, and compulsorily retired with the rank of Lieutenant-General.

Russian General and statesman. He owed his career and his title to the favor of Emperor Pavel I who made him his adviser on foreign affairs and member of the Emperor's Council. He was Governor-General of Moscow during the Napoleonic Invasion and was (or was held to be) responsible for the decision to set fire to it; the pamphlets he wrote and distributed did much to encourage the population in its resistance to the French invaders. His daughter, Sofiia, married a Count Eugène de Ségur and became the authoress of perhaps the most popular of all French children's books published in an edition known as the *Bibliothèque Rose.*

French poet and historian. He was secretary of the French Embassy under the Baron de Breteuil (*q.v.*) in St. Petersburg during 1762 and wrote a brilliant though not very reliable account of Catherine's coup d' état. He also wrote a history of the first partition of Poland, but agreed, at Catherine's urgent request, not to have any of his work published till after her death. However, he read numerous and lengthy excerpts from it at social gatherings, and on the strength of these was elected Member of the French Academy to the great surprise of the general public who knew nothing of him except his rather second-rate verses.

He was a great admirer of Princess Dashkova and attributed to her the honor of being the chief organizer of Catherine's successful insurrection. His view prevailed in France and elsewhere, and explains the enormous curiosity with which her appearance was everywhere greeted.

Rumiantsev-Zadunaiskii. Peter, Count (1725–96): 142, 189, 191, 230

Field-Marshal, won his first public recognition as a result of brilliant victories in the Seven Years War. Appointed Governor-General of the Ukraine by Catherine II; commanded the Russian Army in the 1768–74 Russo-Turkish war which ended in a complete defeat for Turkey, a highly advantageous peace for Russia, and the rank of Field-Marshal as well as many other honors and distinctions for himself. He also commanded for a time one of the Russian Armies in the Russo-Turkish war of 1787–91.

Ryder, John (1607?–1775): 121, 122, 130, 131, 283

Protestant Archbishop of Tuam. He was born in Warwickshire, son of a Nuneaton haberdasher, but was consecrated Bishop in Ireland and appointed in 1742 to the See of Killaloe. Ten years later he was promoted to Archbishop of Tuam and Bishop of Ardagh. He was a man of evangelical views, kindly and courteous. The last few years of his life were spent in Nice, where he died after falling from his horse.

Ryleev, Nikita (174?–1808): 238

Chief of Police, later Governor, of St. Petersburg. His duties included the censorship of books and periodicals and he was thus technically responsible for allowing the publication of Radishchev's *Journey from Petersburg to Moscow* (see Radishchev, Aleksandr). However, the fact that censors rarely bothered to read the books submitted to them and exercised their functions with great laxity was sufficiently well recognized for Ryleev to escape all punishment or even reprimand. He had the reputation of being a pleasant and easy-going man of extreme stupidity and was the butt of a host of probably apocryphal stories such as ordering all landlords to notify the police in case of fire, *three days in advance.*

Rzewuski, Wacław (1706–79): 112

Polish diplomat and statesman.

Saldern, Caspar (1711–88): 56

A German by birth, he headed the Government of the Duchy of Holstein when the reigning Duke (afterward Russian Emperor Peter III) was also heir to the Russian throne. Later, under Catherine II, he became a Russian diplomat and was appointed Ambassador in Warsaw. The first partition of Poland took place while he was still occupying that post, but it was effected over his head, which moved him to ask for his own recall. Princess Dashkova probably refers to an incident which occurred some time after when he tried to establish the Grand-Duke Pavel as co-sovereign with Catherine II. Catherine, infuriated at these rather clumsy attempts at limiting her power, at first wanted him to be brought to her in chains, but afterward relented and merely dismissed him from all his posts. He died in Holstein.

Samoilov, Aleksandr, Count (1744–1814): 156, 162, 220, 238–40, 242, 249

Senator, Minister of Justice, Chancellor of the Exchequer.

Shcherbinina, Anastasiia (1761–1830): 39, 83, 85, 112–114, 117, 119, 123, 140, 141, 143–145, 147, 148, 149, 152, 158, 170, 177, 183, 189, 191, 217, 219, 232, 233, 236, 241–243, 245, 246, 249, 253, 259, 260, 268

men of his time in Russia, Acting (and highly active) President of the Academy of Sciences while Kirill Razumovskii was nominal Head. When Razumovskii was appointed Hetman (in effect, Viceroy) of the Ukraine, Teplov followed him and became the actual ruler of the country in his stead (1750–62), though when the office of Hetman was later abolished, it was abolished to a great extent on his recommendation. He was a useful and highly prized member of the conspiracy that put Catherine II on the throne and (inevitably) was present at and probably helped in, the murder of Peter III. He was very influential in the educational reforms of Catherine's reign, and actively cooperated with Betskoi (q.v.), of some of whose plans he was the probable real author.

Tisdal, Philip (1707–77): 121–122

Irish politician, Solicitor-General (1751) and Attorney-General (1760) of Ireland; he would have been appointed Lord Chancellor of Ireland but for his Irish nationality. His immensely rich wife was the chief patroness in Dublin of Angelica Kauffmann.

Troshchinskii, Dmitrii (1754–1829): 245

Russian statesman, secretary of State, Senator.

Ungern-Sternberg, Karl, Baron (1730–99): 53

General-A.D.C., to Peter III, later served under Rumiantsev-Zadunaiskii (q.v.).

Ushakov, Fedor (1748–70): 236, 237 (and note)

One of twelve young men sent by the Russian Government to Leipzig University, author of a few, not very original, tracts on such diverse subjects as "Capital Punishment," "Love," "Reason"; one-time assistant to Teplov (q.v.). The basis of Ushakov's strongly anti-Rousseauist philosophy was that "man is born neither good nor bad," but is shaped by external circumstances, which generally cause him to protest against despotism, slavery, and arbitrary forms of Government. His importance lies mainly in the lasting influence he was able to exert on Radishchev (q.v.) and through him, on Russian intellectualist thought.

Veselovskii, Avraam (16??–17??): 134

Russian "Resident" (ambassador) in Vienna 1715–19. Was ordered to leave Vienna after the conclusion of an alliance between England, Austria, and Poland directed against Russia. In Berlin, on his way home, he heard of the execution by Peter the Great of the Tsarevich Aleksei and members of his party, accused of opposition to Peter's reforms. Being himself involved in political intrigues on the side of the Tsarevich, he wisely preferred to remain abroad for the rest of his life. His brother Fedor, Russian "Resident" in London (1717–20), was responsible for protracted but abortive negotiations aiming at the union of the Anglican and the Eastern Orthodox Churches.

Volkonskii, Mikhail, Prince (1713–86): 68, 87, 88, 109

General. Became famous in the Seven Years War. In 1764 commanded the Russian Army corps which imposed on Poland the election as King of Stanisław-August Poniatowski (q.v.).

Volkov, Dmitrii (1718–85): 55 (and note)

Statesman. He started his professional career as clerk in the Department of Foreign Affairs; in 1756 he was appointed Secretary (in effect—Head) of a special Government Committee dealing with military and other matters. In 1762, during the few months of Peter III's reign, he was appointed Secretary of a Council of State for

[Note: This is the original text of the index compiled by Kyril Fitzlyon. It is given here in its entirety, although I do not always agree with Fitzlyon's interpretations.—J.G.]

Kyril Fitzlyon (Kyril Zinovieff) has translated and edited a number of works from Russian and French including F. M. Dostoevsky's *Winter Notes on Summer Impressions* and L. N. Tolstoy's *A Landowner's Morning*.

Jehanne M Gheith is Assistant Professor in the Department of Slavic Languages and Literatures at Duke University.

Alexander Woronzoff-Dashkoff is Associate Professor in the Department of Russian at Smith College.

Library of Congress Cataloging-in-Publication Data
Dashkova, E. R. (Ekaterina Romanovna), kniaginia, 1743–1810.
[Mémoires de la princesse Daschkoff. English] The memoirs of Princess Dashkova / translated and edited by Kyril Fitzlyon ; introduction by Jehanne M Gheith ; afterword by A. Woronzoff-Dashkoff.
Includes bibliographical references. ISBN 0-8223-1621-8 (paperback)
  1. Dashkova, E. R. (Ekaterina Romanovna), kniaginia, 1743–1810.
  2. Princesses—Russia—Biography. 3. Russia—Court and courtiers—Biography. 4. Scholars—Russia—Biography. 5. Authors, Russian—18th century—Biography. 6. Rossiĭskaia akademiia nauk.
  I. Fitzlyon, Kyril. II. Gheith, Jehanne M. III. Woronzoff-Dashkoff, A. (Alexander) IV. Title.
DK169.D3A3   1995
947'.06'092—dc20[B]   94-39804 CIP